The Disarmament of Hatred

The Disarmament of Hatred

Marc Sangnier, French Catholicism and the Legacy of the First World War, 1914–45

Gearóid Barry

Lecturer, National University of Ireland, Galway, Republic of Ireland

palgrave
macmillan

First published 2012 by
PALGRAVE MACMILLAN

Palgrave Macmillan in the UK is an imprint of Macmillan Publishers Limited, registered in England, company number 785998, of Houndmills, Basingstoke, Hampshire RG21 6XS.

Palgrave Macmillan in the US is a division of St Martin's Press LLC, 175 Fifth Avenue, New York, NY 10010.

Palgrave Macmillan is the global academic imprint of the above companies and has companies and representatives throughout the world.

Palgrave® and Macmillan® are registered trademarks in the United States, the United Kingdom, Europe and other countries.

ISBN 978–0–230–21825–3

This book is printed on paper suitable for recycling and made from fully managed and sustained forest sources. Logging, pulping and manufacturing processes are expected to conform to the environmental regulations of the country of origin.

A catalogue record for this book is available from the British Library.

Library of Congress Cataloging-in-Publication Data
Barry, Gearóid, 1977–
The disarmament of hatred : Marc Sangnier, French Catholicism and the legacy of the First World War, 1914–45 / Gearóid Barry.
p. cm.
Includes bibliographical references and index.
ISBN 978–0–230–21825–3 (alk. paper)
1. Sangnier, Marc, 1873–1950. 2. Sangnier, Marc, 1873–1950—Political and social views. 3. Politicians—France—Biography. 4. Catholics—France—Biography. 5. Pacifists—France—Biography. 6. World War, 1914–1918—Influence. 7. World War, 1914–1918—Peace. 8. Catholic Church—France—History—20th century. 9. Christian democracy—France—History—20th century. 10. France—Politics and government—1914–1940. I. Title.
DC342.8.S25B36 2012
944.081′5092—dc23
[B] 2011052950

10 9 8 7 6 5 4 3 2 1
21 20 19 18 17 16 15 14 13 12

Printed and bound in Great Britain by
CPI Antony Rowe, Chippenham and Eastbourne

To my parents and my brothers

Contents

Figures

Acknowledgements

Writing this book has been a journey on which many people have kept me company. I am delighted to thank those, both named and unnamed, who offered help and wise words at important points. In the first instance, I thank my former doctoral supervisor, John Horne, at Trinity College Dublin (Republic of Ireland), for his unstinting intellectual and personal generosity. I am grateful to my PhD examiners, Annette Becker and Alan Kramer, for encouraging me to begin the road here. Barbara Wright of the TCD French Department helped me as I made my first research trips to France. She has remained encouraging ever since. Seminars at the L'Ecole des Hautes Etudes en Sciences Sociales (Paris), moderated by Christophe Prochasson and Stéphane Audoin-Rouzeau, and at the Institut d'Histoire du Temps Présent, then at Ecole Normale Supérieure de Cachan, challenged me positively.

I am very grateful to the Irish Research Council for the Humanities and the Social Sciences which funded my doctoral research with the award of a Government of Ireland Research Scholarship. I thank the Fondation Irlandaise at the Irish College, Paris, which also assisted me. I am greatly indebted to National University of Ireland, Galway, and to its Millennium Fund, administered by the Vice-President for Research, Professor Terry Smith, and his successors, which facilitated new research that broadened the book's scope. I have the good fortune to work at NUI Galway's History Department, with colleagues who are both good scholars and good people. The heads of discipline in my time here – namely, current head Steven Eillis and former head Dáibhí Ó Cróinín – have worked to uphold the best traditions of the department. They helped me find the time and space to finish this project. Gearóid Ó Tuathaigh commented on an early draft. I also acknowledge the vibrant research culture within NUI's School of Humanities, the College of Arts and at our dedicated humanities research centre, the Moore Institute, where I had the honour of presenting a research paper representing part of this work in March 2010. Philip Dine, Morwena Denis and Mairéad Ní Bhriain (French Department) helped with the trickier translations, though I am responsible for the final inclusions! I thank our history administrators Phil Faherty and Maura Walsh as well as staff at NUI Galway's James Hardiman Library, especially Bríd Walsh, Geraldine

Curtin and Maura O'Malley in the Inter-Library Loans section. I thank my students for stimulating questions (and answers).

Further afield, I thank the directors and staff of the various archives and libraries I consulted for their practical assistance to me, including the superb Bibliothèque de Documentation Internationale Contemporaine (BDIC), the Bibliothèque Nationale de France, the Archives de la Préfecture de Police (Paris) and the Archives Nationales de France, where Françoise Aujogue was especially helpful. I encountered similar goodwill at the Vatican Secret Archives and the Istituto Luigi Sturzo (Rome). In London, the Library of the Religious Society of Friends was very considerate. I thank all of these, and Dominique Laxague, for permission to quote material here. Permission to reproduce the illustrations has been kindly granted by the Insitut Marc Sangnier (IMS, Paris) and by Frédérique Joannic-Seta on behalf of the BDIC. For the permissions to use the Jean Carlu poster on the cover of the book, I thank the following most sincerely: the Carlu estate, artists' rights bodies ADAGP (Paris) and DACS (London) and the Musées des Arts Décoratifs (Paris). The help of Elizabeth Walley and Richard Etienne at DACS and of Rachel Brishoual at Les Arts Décoratifs was greatly appreciated. The IMS archives have been vital to this book. For this repeat visitor, its archivists, including current archivist Anne-Valérie Etenard, have always been helpful beyond the call of duty. The Sangnier family, in the person of Marc Sangnier's grand daughter Annicette Sangnier, is a generous but unobtrusive presence for scholars working there. In July 2011 news came of the death of Annicette's father, M. Jean Sangnier, in his 100th year. Honoured for his own early role in the French Resistance, this son of a public figure was a person of substance in his own right. The interviews he gave me in 2003 made tangible, through 'time regained', the hopes and fears of the era he grew up in. His unaffected nature was the mark of his own personal dignity and generosity of spirit.

In matters of book production, many have helped at various stages. Ultan McDonagh's help was indispensable in IT and photographic matters. I am happy to acknowledge that some of the themes of this book were anticipated, albeit in different formats, in journal articles which I enumerate here: 'Marc Sangnier and "the Other Germany": The Freiburg International Democratic Peace Congress and the Ruhr Invasion, 1923', *European History Quarterly*, 41 (2011), pp. 25–49 and 'Rehabilitating a Radical Catholic: Pope Benedict XV and Marc Sangnier, 1914–1922', *Journal of Ecclesiastical History*, 60 (2009), pp. 514–33. I remain very grateful to editors Lucy Riall and Francis King at *European History Quarterly* and to editor Diarmaid MacCulloch at the *Journal of Ecclesiastical History* and to their anonymous readers, for their help and encouragement. The International Society of First World War Studies permitted contact with many researchers, especially of my own generation. Previous presentations of mine at its biennial conferences have appeared in Brill's *History of Warfare* series. My paper at Oxford (2003) has appeared as 'Marc Sangnier's War, 1914–1919: Portrait of a Soldier, Catholic and Social Activist' in Pierre Purseigle (ed.), *Warfare and Belligerence: Perspectives in First World War Studies* (2005), pp. 163–88. That in Washington, DC (2007) has appeared under the title ' "The Crusade of Youth": Pacifism and the Militarization of Youth Culture in Marc Sangnier's Peace Congresses, 1923–32', in Jennifer D. Keene and Michael S. Neiberg (eds), *Finding Common Ground: New Directions in First World War Studies* (2011), pp. 239–66. I am indebted again to these editors and to those who acted as official and unofficial commentators on my work at these conferences, namely Robert Gildea, Jay Winter, Tammy Proctor, Martha Hanna, Pierre Purseigle, Andrew Donson, Leonard V. Smith, Dennis Showalter and Heather Jones.

At other conferences, other colleagues offered further insightful comments. Peter Farrugia and Oscar Arnal showed characteristic goodwill in sharing their considerable knowledge about French Catholicism and pacifism, and it was a great honour to share a panel with them on ' "Progressive" Social Catholicism in the Third and the Fourth French Republics' at the Joint Meeting of the American Catholic Historical Association and the Canadian Catholic Historical Association at St Michael's College University, Toronto (Canada), in 2011. I would particularly like to thank the Toronto organizers, Terence Fay S.J., Edward Jackman O.P. and Peter Meehan, as well as our panel chair, Peter Bernardi S.J., for their interest and welcome. When I spoke on 'French Catholics and Catholic Transnationalism in Europe after the First World War' at the Society for the Study of French History's annual conference held at Trinity College Dublin in 2009, Julian Wright was kind enough to provide valuable pointers on Foreign Minister Aristide Briand that I have integrated here. I would also like to thank Eamon Duffy, Richard Rex and John Pollard for their interest in my work on 'Marc Sangnier and the Modernist Crisis', as presented at the History of Christianity Seminar at the Faculty of Divinity, Cambridge, in March 2010. In France, historian Olivier Prat and Stegan Gigacz, moderator of the website 'Sillon.net', were encouraging too. Finally, on direct manuscript preparation itself, I am grateful to all staff I have dealt with at Palgrave Macmillan; Jenny McCall, Ruth Ireland, Clare Mence and their former colleague Michael Strang deserve my sincere thanks for their professionalism and their patience, as do the anonymous readers of the manuscript. My particular thanks go to Matthew Taylor for his very scrupulous copy-editing and to Cherline Daniel and Kate Boothby at Integra. The assistance of friends closer to home in rereading final proofs came at a vital stage and I am greatly in debt to Anthony Daly and Clare Walsh for their cheerful and valuable help.

I have climbed the steepest slopes of this mountain since 2009. I tally some of those closest in that time, though no such list is ever complete. In France, I recall Marie-Louise Gaultier-Voituriez, Odile Force, Cécile Vigour, Etienne and Laure Godin, Annette Ossedat and her late husband, Lucien. 'Les amis de Cachan', now dotted across France, were there for me too. At work, co-teaching or working the 'evening shift' fostered kinship with Mary Harris and Kim LoPrete. Enrico dal Lago helped me keep on track and tease out themes in the manuscript. I thank him most warmly as a colleague and as a friend. Many friends helped directly and indirectly, and actively supported this project in some way. They included Colm Brennan and Janis Morrissey, Ultan and Michelle McDonagh, Daithí Ó Corráin, Bryan McCabe, Joe O'Neill and family, Anthony Daly, Cormac Ó Corcoráin, Mícheál Ó Fathartaigh, Meredith Lulling, Tora O'Dowd, Mairéad Corless, Kathleen Payne, Fiona Killeen, Jim Carr and family, Ellen O'Flaherty, Valerie Hickey, Patrick Burke, Brian Mac Cuarta S.J., Fr. Patrick Hickey, Noel O'Sullivan, Pearse Walsh, Michael Manning, Tomás and Joan Ó Cofaigh, Eugene and Louise Barry, M.H., Nikolai and Karien Limburg and Raymond O'Donnell, Director of Music at Galway Cathedral, and my friends in its cathedral choir. Galway religious communities – La Retraite sisters and the Poor Clares – showed supportive interest throughout. Many in Barryroe and in Cork (including my extended family) were good friends too. My greatest debt of all is to my family: to my brothers Séamus and Shane and to my parents Seán and Ann. Even Sherlock Holmes had to get his curiosity from somewhere; our parents made us aware early on of the living history around us. Totally unselfish, their support gave me the belief to endure and to prevail. This book is dedicated to my brothers and to them. As is said in Irish, *go raibh fada buan sibh!*

Gearóid Barry
NUI Galway

Abbreviations

Abbreviations in the text

French organizations

APD	Association pour 'la Paix par le Droit'
CFTC	Confédération Française des Travailleurs Chrétiens
CGT	Confédération Générale du Travail
CLAJ	Centre Laïque des Auberges de Jeunesse
FRD	Fédération des Républicains-Démocrates
JOC	Jeunesse Ouvrière Chrétienne
LFAJ	Ligue Française des Auberges de Jeunesse
MRP	Mouvement Républicain Populaire
PCF	Parti Communiste Français
PDP	Parti Démocrate Populaire
SFIO	Section Française de l'Internationale Ouvrière
UFM	Union Fédérale des Mutilés

German organizations

BNV	Bund Neues Vaterland
DFG	Deutsche Friedensgesellschaft
DVP	Deutsche Volkspartei
FDK	Friedensbund Deutscher Katholiken
SPD	Sozialedemokratische Partei Deutschlands

British organizations

UDC	Union of Democratic Control

International organizations

CIAMAC	Conférence Internationale des Associations de Mutilés et Anciens Combattants
FOR	[International] Fellowship of Reconciliation
IKA	Internacio Katolika
ILO	International Labour Organization (League of Nations, Geneva)
LICP	Ligue Internationale des Combattants de la Paix

LICRA	Ligue Internationale Contre le Racisme et l'Anti-sémitisme
RUP	Rassemblement Universel pour la Paix
SIPDIC	Sécrétariat International des Partis Démocratiques d'Inspiration Chrétienne
WILPF	Women's International League for Peace and Freedom

Abbreviations for archival references

ADVP	Archives départementales et communales de la Ville de Paris
AHAP	Archives Historiques de l'Archévêché de Paris
AN	Archives Nationales de France
APP	Archives de la Préfecture de Police de Paris
ASV	Archivio Segreto Vaticano
BDIC	Bibliothèque de Documentation Internationale Contemporaine (Nanterre)
ILS	Istituto Luigi Sturzo (Rome)
IMS	Institut Marc Sangnier (Paris)
LSF	Library of the Religious Society of Friends in Britain (London)
MAE	Ministère des Affaires Etrangères (Quai d'Orsay)
n. d.	no date

Introduction

In the history of France, 25 August 1944 was a day of days, to be hallowed for ever as the moment of deliverance when Paris was liberated after four long winters of German occupation. On the evening of that fateful day, when distant peals of gunfire had mingled with the first shouts of carnival and celebration, a Jeep crossed the capital at breakneck speed. There were two passengers on board, dashing across town to one of the city's sports stadiums, where they were billed to speak at a victory rally. The older of the pair was Marc Sangnier, then 72 years old, who, more than 40 years earlier, had been the founder of the Christian Democratic movement called Le Sillon, meaning 'The Furrow'. His driver was Maurice Schumann. On Armistice Day 1930, at the age of 19, and at the pinnacle of Sangnier's charismatic activism for reconciliation between France and Germany, the young Schumann had had his political views marked for life by an encounter with Sangnier. Jewish by birth, Schumann converted to Catholicism in 1942, while he was the voice of Free France at the BBC in London with the signature announcement 'Honneur et patrie'. Whereas Schumann had served France from abroad, Sangnier had lived out the trials of the 'dark years' in France itself. As he was whisked through a city beginning to breathe again after the German surrender, Sangnier must surely have recalled an even more hair-raising journey along the same streets six months earlier. On 18 February 1944 the Gestapo had taken him from his offices on boulevard Raspail at the start of a month's imprisonment for subversion, which he served at the city's Fresnes prison. The fate of three helpers arrested on that terrible day was as yet unclear to the elder statesman of the Christian Democrat resisters. This new (happier) car journey over, Sangnier and Schumann arrived at the Vélodrome d'hiver – site of the shameful detentions and deportations of Jews in 1942 – where the founder of the Sillon now addressed a rally welcoming the new birth of liberty. The sentiments expressed that August evening were similar to those he articulated throughout the Liberation period, sentiments which he recapitulated at the founding congress of a new political movement, the Mouvement Républicain Populaire (MRP), the following November. There, Marc Sangnier boldly declared again his sense of an imminent democratic transformation in 'a true and profound revolution': 'Today, the obstacles have fallen. If we will it, we can. [...] We are not going "to the people." No! We are the people.'[1]

With the Liberation of France in the summer of 1944, Resistance movements emerged into the bright light of day. At the same moment, the nationwide youth hostels movement, one of whose early promoters Sangnier had been in the 1930s, re-emerged from the shadows of illegality cast by a German ban at the height of the Occupation. The end of the war also saw the birth of a new generation of Catholic lay leaders, veterans of the Resistance, who had greater political credibility than many of their bishops.[2] During the Paris uprising, leaflets appeared from a group called the Mouvement Populaire de Libération calling for political liberty, the defence of the family and economic justice – ending 'the reign of King Money'. On 25–6 November 1944 this movement became the Mouvement Républicain Populaire (MRP), which melded together the progressive spirit of post-Liberation France with long-held Social Catholic beliefs. Taking as its creed the agreed programme of the Resistance, formulated as the Charter of the Conseil National de la Résistance in 1944, the MRP brought together Catholic resisters and interwar Christian Democratic figures, such as Francisque Gay, Maurice Schumann and Georges Bidault. Sangnier's speech at this founding congress captured well the sense of a new beginning in a Fourth Republic, upon which they waited with impatience and high expectations. The MRP achieved remarkable electoral successes in 1945–6 and anchored successive tripartite governments of Socialists, Communists and Christian Democrats between 1944 and 1947. In the elections to the Constituent Assembly of October 1945, Sangnier, who had been made honorary president of the MRP, was returned to parliament along with 143 other MRP deputies.[3]

In the final years of his life, Sangnier's ideas of Franco-German reconciliation were reflected in the European policy of the MRP, even if the vision of a Franco-German motor was not immediately uppermost in French Christian Democrat minds. Indeed, in the country's tripartite government composed of Socialists, Communists and Christian Democrats between 1945 and 1947, Foreign Minister Georges Bidault, a leading light in the MRP and former chair of the Conseil National de la Résistance, pursued an official policy of breaking up Germany, as had been mooted in 1919. When, with the exclusion of the Communists from power in 1947, another MRP politician, Robert Schuman, became Prime Minister in 1947–8, the emphasis of policy shifted. There was more to differentiate Schuman from his near-namesake Maurice Schumann than just the slightly different spelling of their surnames. The 'voice of Free France' had come to this new political camp with a proud republican and Jewish lineage. The more reserved Robert Schuman was, by contrast, an older and more conservative Christian Democrat. He continued to serve as Foreign Minister from July 1948 to January 1953, after his brief premiership, providing continuity in France's German policy. Crucially, this Schuman was a native of Lorraine and a fluent German-speaker, who, at the age of 30, had switched nationality along with the population of his region in 1919. His concurrent terms of office from 1947 to 1953 coincided with the onset of the Cold War, which brought into sharp focus the challenge of defending Western Europe and the need to reconcile German recovery with French security. In the face of American pressure and the formation of the NATO military alliance in 1949, French obstructionism on Germany's long-term fate had run into the ground. Obliged to acquiesce in the establishment of a Federal Republic in West Germany in 1949, the French government saw itself 'forced into a process of rethinking out of which would emerge the "Schuman Plan", the spectacular project for a unification of the European coal and steel industry'. This innovative supranational initiative, drafted by Schuman's adviser Jean Monnet, broke with the example of French occupation of the Ruhr in 1923 and proposed a shared economic authority over what had been Germany's workshop for war. Furthermore, it was rooted in and furthered by the intense debate in the civic sphere on European integration that caught fire between 1948 and 1950. Though the contributors to this nascent European movement ranged from the left to the moderate right, Catholics were key players in this new 'transnational moment' of the 1940s. Wolfram Kaiser's comparative study of political Catholicism in twentieth-century Europe has reconceptualized our understanding of European integration by putting it in the long-term perspective as, in some significant measure, the work of transnational Christian Democrat contacts. Pivotally, this co-ordination built on the foundation of 'left-Catholic cooperation' laid during the interwar years. Sangnier's Peace Congresses were but one crucial example of such 'Europeism', a 1920s' forerunner of Schuman's co-operation with the Christian Democrat

Konrad Adenauer in reincorporating Germany into the family of nations from 1949.[4]

With the exclusion of Communists and Gaullists from power after 1947, the Fourth Republic soon became associated with political inertia. As good pragmatists, the leadership of the MRP became party to the rehabilitation of the centre right around 1950. Such a rightward drift pained elders such as Francisque Gay and Sangnier, but, as party president, Sangnier gracefully accepted a quiet role between 1946 and 1950. He remarked wryly to a visitor on his being like the holy statue that the party brought out for the annual procession before putting him back safely in his niche. However, the evening of his life also saw a dramatic consolation for his life's work. On 9 May 1950 Robert Schuman unveiled his plan which led directly to the creation of a six-member European Coal and Steel Community the following year. Within weeks of this historic announcement, on 28 May 1950, Pentecost Sunday, Marc Sangnier died in Paris. On 1 June the nation honoured him with a state funeral at Notre-Dame. In front of the cathedral, the Christian Democrat Prime Minister, Georges Bidault, gave the funeral oration, as old comrades from the Sillon, from the International Democratic Peace Congresses of the interwar years and the wartime Resistance listened in the pouring rain. Youthful representatives of the youth hostels and scouting movements also stood to attention. No longer young, Georges Lanfry, a veteran of Sangnier's Bierville Peace Congress of 1926 who had planned the Jeune-République disarmament publicity campaigns in the 1930s, now stepped forward to complete the circle, bearing a symbolic bough: it was the Sillon's emblem of a sheaf of wheat bound together by a blood-red ribbon. This book tells the story of the generation-long endeavour of those civic peace activists, both young and old, who joined Sangnier in pursuit of a political and spiritual project for Europe based upon peace, Christian Democracy and friendship between France and Germany.

The question of how societies exit from war's end is an important preoccupation of historians. Even with the legal and military precision of an armistice or a peace treaty, a 'war culture' often persists in popular perceptions, in people's mentalities, affecting and infecting attitudes to the 'former' enemy well into the post-war era. These questions have arisen with particular insistence in relation to the First World War. Historians have recently used the concept of 'war culture' to explain how societies engaged with that war. Only a deep ideological commitment to victory could explain French tenacity in the national cause in 1914–18 at a cost of 1.4 million lives. The French population consented to the sacrifices required of it not merely out of fear of state coercion but also because the war was cast as an existential struggle for France's survival and for civilization itself. With such high stakes, therefore, nothing less than a 'war culture' manifested itself in 1914–18, encompassing, in Audoin-Rouzeau and Becker's words, 'a corpus of representations of the conflict, crystallised into a veritable system that gave the war its deep meaning'.[5] This massive imaginative investment in the common cause required a process of 'cultural mobilization', extending to hatred of the barbaric enemy.[6] In the French case this approach might imply a 'sacred union' version of history, where the war melds together antagonistic factions. However, the degree of popular acquiescence in the war is the topic of lively debate amongst French historians. Intended as a tool of interpretation and not an iron rule, the centripetal narrative of cultural mobilization suggesting generalized, if varying, support for the war works very well in the case of Sangnier; he and his followers (often themselves bourgeois or skilled workers) generally had a stake in the defence of this society. What of those French workers who believed the war was but a cover for further exploitation? A salutary foil to the patriotic Sangnier's material comfort and later centrist pacifism is found in the person of socialist writer César Fauxbras, subject of a recent study by Matt Perry. A pacifist veteran like Sangnier, Fauxbras too had a lifelong relationship with the memory of the First World War but interpreted it differently. Instead of national ecumenism, Fauxbras recalled with bitterness the coercion, the execution of mutineers and the manipulation of the workers by the ruling classes.[7]

Sangnier, in contrast, was part of that broad section of opinion which adopted the 'war culture' aggressively. The problem for securing the peace after the war was that, for many in Europe, this bellicose mentality did not end neatly with the signature of the armistice in 1918. The French Catholic journalist Georges Hoog recognized that such a cognitive gap would hinder the achievement of real peace. Writing in the summer of 1926, at the height of the period of good relations between France and Germany that became known as the 'Locarno honeymoon', Hoog contrasted the official détente between the two nations with the stubborn persistence of the war and antagonism in people's minds in the midst of peace. Looking ahead to a planned gathering of French and German youths at Bierville, in the countryside outside Paris, that would be held the following week, at the height of the annual August holidays, Hoog invested the holiday camp's preparations with an urgent mission:

> Nearly eight years after the cessation of hostilities we must, unfortunately, face facts: neither is the war truly over nor peace really made

> … There is a moral aspect to the problem of peace; we must disarm hatred and dissipate prejudice … we must accomplish the pacific education of international public opinion.[8]

Georges Hoog spoke with authority of the First World War's psychological effects. From a family with strong kinship ties to the 'lost province' of Alsace, he had written anti-German propaganda with gusto during the conflict. As Hoog intimated, French society made uneasy progress towards dismantling wartime mindsets in the 1920s. To describe this uneven process, John Horne proposes the term 'cultural demobilization'.[9] As part of this, the dehumanized enemy would have to be rehabilitated. The historical argument for such a shift in mood from about 1924 is developed by Laurence van Ypersele, who argues that the new diplomacy of German and French Foreign Ministers Gustav Stresemann and Aristide Briand 'sought to reconstruct the retrospective memory of the war by reversing the terms of the war cultures and redirecting the moral capital of sacrifice into peacemaking'. A zealous convert to the pacifist cause, Georges Hoog himself was one of history's eternal footmen, an enabler and a factotum who spent the best part of his life obscuring his own particular role in events for the sake of a greater cause. Hoog had to diminish so that his master could increase. The man whose cause he served as long-time secretary and assistant was Marc Sangnier (1873–1950), patron of the same Bierville estate that hosted the peace camp alluded to above. A politician, journalist and Christian Democratic activist, Sangnier was a pioneer in this process of cultural demobilization in the France and Europe of the 1920s and 1930s, coining the phrase the 'disarmament of hatred' in a speech he gave in Paris in January 1921. In an act of prophetic daring on a public rostrum in Paris in December 1921, and before a crowd of around three thousand, Sangnier hosted the first public appearance in the city by German speakers since the war as part of his first Peace Congress. These International Democratic Peace Congresses hoped to foster an international consciousness. Through the uniformed and serried ranks of youths in torch-lit processions, they reflected the timbre of the times and the general militarization of politics, even pacifist politics.[10]

Sangnier had enormous faith in the power of rhetoric and symbolism. He believed peace could be built only by premeditated and symbolic acts of reconciliation and a liturgy of peace. The purpose of this study is to show how Sangnier, in tune with a broader movement for moral disarmament, was awakened to Christian pacifism by his experience in the First World War before going on to place himself at the centre of a transnational network called the Democratic International. Organizing no fewer than 12 International Democratic Peace Congresses across a host of European venues, including Germany and Austria, in the years between 1921 and 1932, Sangnier's peace movement was a coalition of peace activists, Catholics and others, united in an ecumenical community of reconciliation, especially between France and Germany.

No study such as this emerges from a scholarly void. This study examines a French-led civic peace movement – Marc Sangnier's Democratic International for Peace and its successor groups from 1921 to 1945. Though the French national context was key to its development, this was also a transnational movement *par excellence*. It both reflected and shaped the broader European peace movement. Moreover, Catholicism, the presiding ideology in Marc Sangnier's political life and of his peace activism, forms one of the most vibrant strands of the new transnational scholarship in nineteenth- and twentieth-century European history. This particular peace movement, dominated by the charismatic leadership of Sangnier, which straddled precariously both Catholic and non-Catholic elements of the world peace constituency, had adherents across Europe and sometimes further afield still. As such a tangled entity, the Peace Congresses organized by the Democratic International between 1921 and 1932 should be studied using a subtle conceptual framework which reflects the movement's diversity and its contradictions. This study of the Sangnier movement, therefore, is inscribed in the first instance into the new history of transnational European movements of the first half of the twentieth century. However, it cannot be situated in that highly specialized historiographical category alone. Sangnier the man and his movements must also be related to the broader category of transnational Catholic history, as well as longer-established genres of French national history, including political biography and the histories of French Catholicism and pacifism. These categories of history-writing, operating within the conceptual framework of the nation-state, have often served scholarship well. However, subjects such as Catholicism and the peace movement immediately recall the fuzzy demarcation line that exists between national and transnational history. Though French, Catholics and pacifists in France necessarily acted in an internationalized context as self-confessed followers of transnational creeds, making even more desirable a historical inquiry that crosses those borders.

Drawing on a transnational array of primary sources, in France, Britain, Italy and the Vatican, this study explores a European peace movement that had Franco-German understanding at its heart. The

Democratic International's implantation on both sides of the Rhine is considered, using not just published and manuscript sources but also the extensive secondary literature which exists on German pacifism and Catholicism. This study traces the process of cultural transfer between France and Germany in these years and the creation (or indeed revival) of a European civic space in the 1920s. The 12 political congresses organized by Sangnier between 1921 and 1932 were the pivot of his enterprise. The French writer, Catholic and socialist Charles Péguy, who died fighting for France in 1914, memorably defined congresses as 'ceremonial demonstrations of deep-seated and durable movements'. An innovation of the second half of the nineteenth century, and a response to the growth of the press, representative democracy and mass politics, these were meetings for intellectual exchange, debate and propaganda for the cause – whatever it was. Thus congresses, in Christophe Prochasson's words, 'inscribed into the public space debate on ideas and invited a collective affirmation'.[11] Catholics were no exception to this urge to congregate in what Wolfram Kaiser calls 'forums for transnational communication'.[12] Sangnier's Peace Congresses fit into this schema, as do larger manifestations of this trend such as the Katholikentage in Germany and the Semaines Sociales in France that had come to the fore at the end of the nineteenth century.

The love-hate relationship of the Franco-German 'couple', in war and peace, provides the backing track to this narrative of transnational peace activism. However, while relating Marc Sangnier's peace activism to its German counterparts, this book is not conceived as a sustained comparative study of Sangnier and an approximate movement or figure in Germany. The study is more akin to a choral arrangement of ebbing and flowing parts than to a composition played on two organs simultaneously. Strong influences from Italy and Britain are also charted. The study draws on insights from the fields of comparative history and transnational history. The decade-long experiment in a European civic community that Sangnier and his colleagues christened as their Democratic International has its history told here as an essay in 'cross-national history'. According to Deborah Cohen and Maura O'Connor, 'cross-national histories follow topics beyond national boundaries. They seek to understand reciprocal influences.' Rather than strict binary comparison, 'scholars who work cross-nationally are often more interested in crossings – whether real or imaginary – than they are in the specific national settings ... the subjects of their studies can be as influenced by events abroad as they are by those at home.'[13] Marc Sangnier, as an ultramontane Catholic awakened to the peace movement by the First World

War, was subject to multiple cross-currents – from German Catholicism, from the papacy, from the broad peace movement – all of which got wrapped up with the secular message of salvation discerned by Sangnier and others in the international League of Nations movement.

Within the cross-national approach, historians have attempted to go beyond the national context by means of two approaches: transfer history, as advocated by Michel Espagne in his study of Franco-German cultural transfers, and *histoire croisée* or 'entangled history', pioneered by Bénédicte Zimmermann. Transfer history looks at the interrelationships between two entities, such as France and Germany, and the role of cultural media, broadly defined and including events like congresses, in the transfer of ideas and influences. *Histoire croisée*, meanwhile, has the term 'entanglement' as its 'magic word, not only as a general condition but as an historical process'.[14] This 'connected' or 'shared history' prioritizes transnational crossings and 'orients itself around problems, particularly the "entangled" historical relationships between Germany and France in the nineteenth and twentieth centuries'.[15] The crucible of the First World War and its *longue durée* in Franco-German relations have provided the key reference points in several recent cross-national studies. In 2008, on the ninetieth anniversary of the 1918 armistice, two of the leading historians of the war from national perspectives, the German historian Gerd Krumeich and his French colleague Jean-Jacques Becker, co-authored an integrated Franco-German history of the First World War. Their comparative history synthesized traditional approaches with the transnational application of the 'war cultures' concept; this is an approach that Becker, Krumeich and their colleagues associated with the Historial de la Grande Guerre museum (located at Péronne near the Somme) are particularly identified with. Ilde Gorguet, meanwhile, melds together the medley of secular and religious movements promoting Franco-German reconciliation in the 1920s, including Sangnier's Democratic International, in a transnational study treating in equal depth the peace movements, broadly defined, on either side of the Rhine. More recently, the French and German historians Carine Germond and Henning Türk have come together to edit a collection of transnational essays tracing the cycle of mutual attraction and repulsion in Franco-German relations since the Napoleonic wars and the evolution of the Franco-German duo from 'hereditary enmity' to European partnership. Comparative perspectives inform various studies of 'transfer' in the Franco-German relationship, from histories of pacifism to micro-studies of charitable and humanitarian activity and town twinning.[16]

It is possible to say that political Catholicism forms the near-perfect transnational topic. The associated transnational literature is both extensive and vibrant. Historians such as Wolfram Kaiser, Michael Gehler and Jean-Dominique Durand, to name but three, have contributed much to our understanding of the evolution of Christian Democracy towards eventual integration into democratic politics. Equally, Emiel Lamberts, Vincent Viaene and Martin Conway have added new perspectives in this area.[17] This study of Sangnier's Democratic International is intended to form part of that mosaic. Kaiser's recent study of Christian Democracy and the origins of European union takes as its alpha point the monumental pontificate of Pope Pius IX (1846–78). Kaiser shows how the ultramontane movement for a more centralized, papal and doctrinally uniform Catholic Church contributed to the 'transnationalisation of Catholicism in the nineteenth century'. Kaiser adds that the sustained attack on Catholicism from anti-clericalism in late nineteenth-century 'culture wars' fostered a common experience for European Catholics and 'produced the foundation for incipient transnational party cooperation after the First World War, not least by creating a set of common ideas and facilitating networking across borders on an initially informal level'.[18] In this struggle of the 'two Europes' Catholics mobilized themselves, nationally and transnationally, in modern political forms of political organization and campaigning, even if their political message was often anti-modern.

Pope Pius IX's *Syllabus of Errors* (1864) had confirmed a general tone of suspicion and hostility to 'progress, liberalism and modern civilization' from an embattled church; his successor Pope Leo XIII (1878–1903) was equally guarded about the modern world and zealous in his defence of the papacy's traditional prerogatives. These included the pope's right to act as temporal ruler of the Papal States in central Italy acquired by various means over the centuries. These same territories had been seized during the unification of Italy in the 1860s. Refusing to parley with the new Kingdom of Italy, the papacy maintained its claim to combine secular and spiritual power, an apparent anachronism which infuriated even those liberals who argued for 'a free church in a free state', not to mention the more radical anticlerical constituency. However unyielding he was with the Italian state, though, Pope Leo XIII was also a diplomat with a keen interest in history and the sciences who reckoned the hand of friendship was sometimes a more astute gesture than the clenched fist. Thus, the pope showed a canny ability to outflank liberalism by loudly renewing Catholic commitment to social justice for the poor. Moved by a real concern for the victims of Europe's runaway industrialization, and the imperative of not losing the faithful to socialism, the pope issued the encyclical *Rerum Novarum* in 1891. Though presaged by broader intellectual developments in Catholicism and by the strike mediation undertaken by some bishops, this passionate document electrified Catholic thinking on the social question, so unexpected was its pastoral realism on a pressing issue of the day. Pope Leo's direct prose combined political caution with a striking challenge to the economic *status quo*, even countenancing a place for trade unions, once they were sound on religion. The pope declared:

> Some opportune remedy must be found quickly for the misery and wretchedness pressing so unjustly on the majority of the working class: for the ancient workingmen's guilds were abolished in the last century, and no other protective organization took their place. Public institutions and the laws set aside the ancient religion. Hence, by degrees it has come to pass that working men have been surrendered, isolated and helpless, to the hardheartedness of employers and the greed of unchecked competition.

As Diarmaid MacCulloch points out, in spite of its nostalgia for a simpler pre-industrial past, the document would provide a 'convenient shield' for later Catholics who found common cause with socialism.[19]

Rerum Novarum gave a further impetus to Catholic transnationalism in 1891, since its emphasis on the social question 'had an obvious international dimension in a rapidly growing world economy'. The universalist claims made by the papacy on behalf of the downtrodden even prompted, in the Social Catholic movement in the Netherlands, a striking parody of socialist internationalism with the slogan 'Catholic workers of the world unite: Rerum Novarum!'[20] Kaiser argues though that any tangible internationalizing impact of the encyclical was imperceptible at first. Catholic politics remained 'quite nationally introspective until the First World War', he argues, for fear of appearing to non-Catholic compatriots as remote-controlled from Rome and unpatriotic, at a time when nationalists reproached socialists for their internationalism. The First World War proved beyond doubt the national reliability of French and German Catholics in their own lands and paved the way, in compensation for the bloodshed, for an intensification of transnational Catholic political activity. New 'structural conditions' after the war encouraged Catholic parties in their 'growing interest in transnational networks', which they hoped could provide for 'the easier transfer of ideas and policies across borders'. After the domestic truces of wartime, 'culture war' issues receded in France, Germany and Italy, encouraging worker-oriented Catholic political movements such as the Italian Popular Party to compete directly with the socialist movement for votes. Allied to this, and beginning with the political activist priest Don Luigi Sturzo and his Italian Popular Party, founded in 1919, the Vatican gave its tacit blessing to Catholic participation in democratic politics through parties 'of Christian inspiration'. This pragmatic position was open to revision, as the evolution of Italian Catholic politics from 1922 would show, but in the short term the Vatican's 'changed priorities' in the early 1920s, 'including its strong support for Franco-German reconciliation, gave Catholic parties a much freer hand in developing a less defensive and introspective vision of national and European politics'.[21]

The long-term impact of the Christian trade union movement and of the Vatican's brief season of grace for Christian Democrats was the emergence of what might be called a left-Catholic sensibility in Catholic politics which used the rhetoric of social reform to challenge socialism at the ballot box. In Italy this was associated with 'popularism', the distributivist political programme formulated by Don Sturzo's intellectual circle. In Germany its main advocates were the Christian trade unions and the left wing of the German Centre Party, especially figures such as Joseph Wirth and Joseph Joos. While it is important not to underestimate the nationalist concerns and conservative wings that persisted within the Italian and German parties, both had developed a greater programmatic orientation on general policy issues in the early 1920s, marking them out from their pre-1914 predecessors, which had thought less programatically and more defensively, making of Catholic parties citadels where the faithful banded together to resist the snares and wiles of their church's mortal enemies. It is equally true that leftist elements in each party had a growing interest in transnational networks that would provide for 'the easier transfer of ideas and policies across borders'.[22] However, it would be a gross simplification to cast Sangnier and his Jeune-République party neatly as the French interlocutors in this transnational policy network. Differing conceptions of politics underpinned the polite stand-off between Sangnier and other Christian Democrat politicians such as Sturzo, Joos and Wirth, who sought out 'politically meaningful party cooperation'. As Kaiser puts it:

> Sangnier conceived of his organisation more as a non-partisan democratic European youth movement working for a non-Marxist, anti-capitalist transformation of European industrial society and for some kind of new world order. As such … the Internationale

> Démocratique [Democratic International] transformed itself more and more into a movement of radical pacifists.[23]

The transnational history of pacifism operates clearly, then, as another front in this study. An ambitious agenda in this regard was sketched out by Holger Nehring in an entry in the *Palgrave Dictionary of Transnational History*. David Cortright's book *Peace: A History of Movements and Ideas* is a valuable study with a global focus. Its merits are to give a thematic treatment of the topic over a long duration supported by historical snapshots. However, this means that at the present time a single transnational synthesis of the peace movement in Europe between the wars is still lacking, unlike the history of women in the First World War and its aftermath, where Susan Grayzel's exemplary global history is available, which also gives sustained coverage to the European experience. In terms of transnational approach, Sandi E. Cooper comes closest with her study of patriotic pacifism, but her focus is the period before 1914, not the interwar years. Elsewhere she has broadened her focus by conceptualizing the peace movement across two centuries as part of a more generalized global movement for human rights. In their *Challenge to Mars*, Thomas P. Socknat and the noted peace historian Peter Brock together edited a transnational compendium of new essays on the subject from 1918 to 1945, but the focus of most of its contributors was particular national movements.[24] There have been some isolated attempts to reconfigure the European twentieth century around ideas of peace and harmony, the so-called 'lights that failed', whether successful or not. Jay Winter's recent book on modern utopias is a case in point. However, as asserted above, Europe's peace movement awaits a fully integrated treatment. Brigitte Hamann's study of the 'life for peace' of Austrian countess Bertha von Suttner, recipient of the 1905 Nobel Peace Prize, illuminates both the history of women and pacifism. Von Suttner was an exemplary model for Sangnier and his friends to imitate, but her death (while in despair at war in 1914) separated her from the next generation.[25] The literature on this European peace milieu pales, though, in terms of depth and breadth, in comparison with the huge literature on Franco-German and European interwar diplomacy, another crucial body of history-writing underpinning this book.[26]

Thomas R. Davies's book on the worldwide popular disarmament campaign between 1925 and 1932 is a case study of transnational activism. Davies cites this campaign as evidence for the existence of a 'global civil society' in which interlocking international institutions co-exist with citizens' networks that exercised influence over them.

As we shall see, Sangnier returned again and again to the theme of the 'true' League of Peoples. Bertram Pickard was a British Quaker peace activist who was involved in bringing Sangnier's fourth Peace Congress to London in 1924. Independent of that connection, Davies cites his revealing phrase about just such unofficial international organizations, which Pickard referred to as 'the Greater League of Nations'.[27] Thus, 'voluntary internationalism', as Martin Geyer and Johannes Paulmann point out, 'was driven beyond national boundaries [...] to build strategic alliances with other groups abroad in order to invigorate their domestic position'.[28] The most prominent example of this in Europe before 1914 was the Second Socialist International, founded in 1889. Catholic internationalism intersected with the global political strategy of the Holy See, and, to borrow the phrase of Abigail Green on religious internationalism generally, this was a type of Catholic internationalism that turned 'a body of believers' into a 'body of opinion'. Moreover, Catholic internationalism is a historical paradigm that is currently giving new life to the old category of ecclesiastical history. As a practitioner of this scholarship, Vincent Viaene, observes: 'religious internationalism was an integral part of the "genus" internationalism. It also needs to be considered in its relationship to other forms of non-governmental internationalism – and *vice versa*. Religious internationalism overlapped with, and in part informed, some apparently secular phenomena such as the peace movement or the women's movement.'[29]

The national context, and the tradition of nineteenth-century French Social Catholicism, were what moulded Sangnier in the first instance. Sangnier's rise to European prominence in the Catholic world was facilitated precisely by the renown of those French pioneers he had revered. Only when Sangnier's activities on the pacifist front are integrated with those in the cause of Social Catholicism have we seen his career examined in a more transnational manner. Often, though, such valuable insights seem incidental to the authors' tracing of the transfer of his ideas. Paul Misner has provided a model transnational history of the Social Catholic movement whose coverage of Sangnier and his Sillon movement from 1900 to 1910 shows explicitly that the Sillon was in active dialogue with other ill-fated radical Catholic movements, especially in Italy.[30] In considering the existing treatments of Sangnier's pre-war diaspora of ideas and supporters in Germany, it is worth recalling Winfried Becker's work on the German Catholic intelligentsia and the Sillon, especially its reception in the influential Munich-based journal *Hochland*, edited by Hermann Platz.[31] There were even some young German Social Catholic activists, such as Joseph Probst from the Rhineland, who were drawn to Paris before 1910 by Sangnier's magnetic reputation. Such figures, when they survived the First World War, went on to occupy privileged positions in the Democratic International of the 1920s as honoured precursors.

Though this study is not primarily biographical, it does have a biographical subtext: making sense of the man helps us to understand better his movements. Marc Sangnier grew up in the shadow of two wars. First, there was the memory of France's humiliation at the hands of Germany in 1871, which bred a preoccupation with national regeneration; and second, there was the struggle between Catholics and secularists in France and Europe. He was also an atypical representative of the French left for reasons of his social privilege and unabashed Catholicism. After all, Sangnier first came to national prominence around 1900, as the charismatic leader of the Sillon movement, a Catholic youth movement of democratic hue. Born to lead, if not rule, Sangnier came from a Paris-based bourgeois family of lawyers and scholars with a proud history and an extensive network of country links: he loved the large house at Treignac, in the Corrèze, ancestral home of his maternal family, the Lachauds. France's Belle Epoque was full of men like him whose inherited wealth from property freed them for a charmed existence dedicated to art or social action. His boyhood home in Paris's chic sixth *arrondissement* had something of the freedom of the country because of 'my old garden', a secluded child's world of miniature lanes and imagined kingdoms. As a teenager, Sangnier came to the garden less to cultivate than to study and reflect. At the age of 16 he read the work of Blaise Pascal. For his 'revelation' of faith lived in the real world, Sangnier literally installed the French seventeenth-century Catholic philosopher in the garden in the form of a statue, to which he doffed his cap: 'I always had on me a copy of the *Pensées*: I never passed before the statue of my illustrious and tender friend without uncovering my head.'[32]

His 15 years as a day-boy at the adjacent Collège Stanislas, from 1879 to 1894, were a joy. The sometime dreamer was also fiercely driven: the elite Catholic *lycée* put Sangnier into a special class streaming the school's brightest dozen boys, but he was also remembered as a leader on the games field. At 18 he came first in the national Concours Général in philosophy while dabbling in literature. At home he imbibed the profound religiosity of his mother, Thérèse Lachaud. The priesthood was a possible calling, but he never went beyond contemplating this vocation.

Marc's humanist father, Félix Sangnier, gently taught him there was a world beyond the sacristy. Together father and son undertook a grand tour of Europe and the Mediterranean world in 13 instalments between 1881 and 1891, visiting a dozen countries. Love of the classics etched in the memory their tour of the Greek Acropolis. Significantly, they visited Germany twice, taking in the 1890 performance of the Oberammergau Passion Play on the second occasion. Sangnier's diary of his time in the Maghreb in 1891 shows a young man with a critical mind, remarkably open (for instance, to the noble witness of Islamic daily prayer on board their cruise ship), if occasionally censorious of exotic cultures. The history of the Collège Stanislas also marked Sangnier: it points beyond our received view of unremitting enmity between counter-revolutionary Catholics and the republic in the French nineteenth century. An earlier principal, Fr Alphonse Gratry, had been sympathetic to the liberal Catholics of the 1830s, led by the priest Félicité de Lamennais. When the pope condemned Lamennais's ideas of 'God and Liberty' in 1832, Lamennais was lost to the church. Gratry and Catholic liberal supporters of the Second Republic of 1848 (such as lay academic Frédéric Ozanam, founder of the Society of Saint Vincent de Paul) remained firmly in the church, though. In life, Sangnier would always follow their example of forbearance in the faith over rebellion.[33] In this Catholic republican ambience, Sangnier helped to enliven a schoolboy debating club called La Crypte from 1893 to 1894. Sympathetic to the initiative was staff member and Catholic philosopher Maurice Blondel. The school authorities stood over their toasting the republic and invitations to working-class speakers. Sangnier endured rather than enjoyed his two years at the Ecole Polytechnique, the top military engineering academy, from 1895 to 1897. From 1898 he was free to reconnect with what he and others had begun with La Crypte. He set about establishing cross-class study-circles taking the name of his previous school journal, *Le Sillon*.

Sangnier and his cohort were inspired to trace their new furrow not only by Pope Leo XIII's encyclical *Rerum Novarum* (1891) but also by nineteenth-century French Social Catholics. These men, such as Frédéric Le Play and the pious factory-owner Léon Harmel, were critics of economic liberalism. Sangnier penned a biography of the royalist count Albert de Mun in 1932, so much did he revere De Mun as the founder of the original study-circles of the 1880s. While following the older examples of class collaboration, in terms of ideas the Sillon would be distinctly less paternalistic and would adopt a more interventionist economic analysis than that first generation.[34] Though not its founder, Sangnier rapidly became the Sillon's charismatic leader and great orator. The movement espoused a daring mixture of Catholicism, republicanism and social justice. The Sillon aimed to produce an elite 'that would lead the rest of France's working class in becoming the responsible citizenry of a new republic'.[35] Democracy Sangnier esteemed as the most moral politics, as it was, he argued, 'the social organization which tended to maximise the conscience and responsibility of each'. To exalt men (and at this point, he meant only men) to this high ideal, Sangnier said the Sillon was dedicated to the formation of 'a common soul' – *une âme commune* – a formulation recalling his beloved Pascal.[36] Christianity gave democracy a soul.

In practice, Sangnier conceived of his own leadership as that of a chief rather than a chairman: the journalist Jean Guiraud wrote in 1903 that young fans surrounded him with a 'ridiculous idolatry'.[37] Disenchanted, François Mauriac painted a severe caricature of Jérôme Servet, a fictionalized character based on Sangnier, in his early novel *L'Enfant chargé de chaînes*. Triumphant Sillon pilgrimages to Rome in 1903 and 1904 followed but, thereafter, ecclesiastical politics began to turn against Sangnier, and his experiment was ended by the papacy in 1910.[38] Coupling Sangnier's Christian rationale for reformed democracy with the ongoing 'Modernist crisis' in theology and Catholic intellectual life, Pope Pius X (1903–14), having praised Sangnier's devotion to the papacy, decided that his brand of Christian Democracy went too far and constituted a dangerous and unfiltered engagement with modernity. The Sillon was not the object of a full doctrinal condemnation by the Holy Office but did receive an official warning from the pope. Be that as it may, Pius was certain 'that the breath of the [French] Revolution has passed this way, and we may conclude that if the social doctrines of the Sillon are erroneous, its spirit is dangerous and its education disastrous'.[39] Unlike Lamennais in 1832, Sangnier submitted to the papacy with a dignified reply stating his wish to remain 'Catholic before all' (see Figure 1).

Biographies of the man have, like the curate's egg, been good in parts.[40] Within the recent history-writing of modern France, Sangnier has been more alluded to than studied. Jeanne Caron's in-depth study of the Sillon published in 1967 has stood the test of time for its mastery of political philosophy. Caron brought off the delicate task of being both engaged supporter and careful historian. Around 2005, the centenary of the Separation Law between church and state, Sangnier's roles as defender of Catholic interests and the Sillon as pioneer of workers' co-operatives and internationalism made modest comebacks

Figure 1 Photograph of Marc Sangnier, ca. 1910 (Courtesy of the Institut Marc Sangnier, Paris)

in the historical literature. Sparer by far, though, has been coverage of Sangnier's peace activism, though the important articles of Olivier Prat and Peter Farrugia and the general survey of Catholics and Franco-German rapprochement by Jean-Claude Delbreil should be acknowledged here, as should Delbreil's more recent publications on his intellectual and generational legacy. Surprisingly, given his role as instigator and leader of youth congresses and youth hostels, Sangnier is absent from the broader canvas of youth mobilization in interwar France in the recent study by Susan B. Whitney. Happily, however, a special edition of the journal *Histoire@politique* in 2010 placed Sangnier's later career and his peace scouts at the heart of the elaboration, between the wars, of a 'young Europe' for and by the 'youth of Europe'. Sangnier's career could equally be used to construct a scholarly alternative history of the French Third Republic based on 'political ecumenism', a centripetal counter-narrative to that of the Dreyfus Affair and its enduring culture wars, which scarred France well into the twentieth century. Sangnier's career from 1905 was intertwined with that of French politician Aristide Briand. Recent studies by Julian Wright and Christophe Bellon have hinted at Briand's role as an emblem of such a hidden tradition of tolerance in Third Republic France, linked to reform at home and peace abroad. On all these counts, Sangnier's career deserves to be retrieved from the footnotes and given its place in a broader narrative.[41]

Finally, though, Sangnier's Democratic International cannot be understood without reference to the pre-1914 tradition of Catholic peace societies which nourished it. Here studies are thin on the ground. Roger Chickering alludes to the Catholic peace society founded in 1907 by Alfred Vanderpol, leader of a pacifist sect within the Sillon. Vanderpol can be credited with keeping alive in the Sillon the irenical or pacifist heritage of Alphonse Gratry, that same clerical Renaissance man whose memory Sangnier venerated at the Collège Stanislas.[42] Having put a Catholic gloss on ambient ideas of liberal internationalism in the 1860s, Gratry's imprint on Sangnier in this regard was delayed. Only later – in the 1920s – did Gratry become a posthumous inspiration for Sangnier's pacifism. Before 1914 these pacifist currents were tolerated by Sangnier, but they did not set the overall tone of the Sillon, which became wrapped up in the jingoism of the times. Sangnier's fiery speech, on Bastille Day 1908, at the historic site of the battle of Valmy in September 1792, shows he was as fiercely attached to the republic and the defence of the sacred fatherland as he was to the tradition of the revolutionary *levée en masse*.[43] The Sillon as a whole took a very critical stance on Prime Minister Joseph Caillaux's conciliatory policy towards Germany at the time of the Agadir crisis in 1911. The issue of the amputated territories of Alsace-Lorraine also resonated with the good patriots in the Sillon, as shown by the rapturous reception given to Hansi and Zislin, the Alsatian authors of anti-German caricatures and myth-makers for the 'lost provinces'.[44] The war clouds that finally broke in August 1914 brought together Sangnier's relationship to Catholic activism, the nation and the republic. His was a double incorporation into the war effort, fighting for the nation and for Catholicism. It was also a cultural mobilization against Germany and all he took it to represent.

The unifying thread of the study that follows is cultural demobilization: how, after the war, Sangnier, as a Catholic politician and leader of a transnational movement, moved from that alpha mentality to the omega point of rehumanizing the enemy and the impassioned advocacy of friendship with a new Germany.

1
Marc Sangnier's War, 1914–19

Marc Sangnier spent the years 1910–14 recovering from the trauma of 25 August 1910. On that day the Sillon, the Social Catholic youth movement he had led since 1900, was condemned by Pope Pius X. Accused of pushing too far the identification of democracy with Christianity, Sangnier was thanked for his sincere, if misdirected, enthusiasm and given the chance to make a public repentance. This he did by immediately accepting the disbandment of his movement. Reconstituted in a new form, the Sillon Catholique, this tamed movement was to be under the strict control of the bishops, unlike the lay-driven Sillon where Sangnier had dominated. Sangnier played no role in the Sillon Catholique, nor was he wanted in it by the bishops. Ex-comrades from the Sillon tried to maintain a discreet Sillon network. Discretion was important, as they feared Catholics on the right, especially those aligned to the nationalist Action Française, would accuse them of not abiding by the terms of the pope's letter. Since 1910, Sangnier himself had been far from idle. To avoid the error that had drawn official ire – mixing God and democracy – in 1912 Sangnier founded a new political party, Jeune République, that claimed no religious mandate.

Sangnier remained active on France's political scene. Party to the major church-state conflicts and intra-church divisions of the previous decade, Sangnier found himself caught up in the 'nationalist revival' in French politics that was a response to escalating Franco-German tensions in a series of high-profile crises from 1905.[1] In this context the Catholic peace league known as the Société Gratry (founded in 1907), whose membership overlapped with that of the Sillon, also went into hibernation after 1910. Even in the heyday of the Sillon, between 1907 and 1910, the Société Gratry drew only a minority of Sillon members. Associated with Alfred Vanderpol, this political sect combined contemporary liberal ideas on peaceful international organization and arbitration with elements of Catholic social teaching and papal encyclicals. Sangnier tolerated the Société Gratry without fully endorsing it. Sangnier, as a patriotic French Catholic, was keen that the war declared in 1914 should serve as a moment of reintegration for the church and the nation. Accordingly, in 1916 he became privy to the state's desire to communicate with the pope and the pope's wish to conciliate France while sticking steadfastly to a moral position of impartiality in the hopes of halting this 'suicide of Europe'.

In autumn 1914, at the age of 41, with France subject to German invasion, Marc Sangnier was called back to uniform. The marginal nature of opposition to the war and the large measure of consent to mobilization in 1914 attested to by Jean-Jacques Becker were linked to a broader civic consensus for national defence. Catholics like Sangnier took their place in this alongside other groups with whom they had been lately engaged in bitter ideological conflict. As Alfred Baudrillart, a senior cleric and rector of the Institut Catholique de Paris, wrote on 5 August 1914, 'at the first call, we Catholics fall in behind our worst adversaries'.[2] General to all belligerent nations, this type of patriotic consensus took different names in different places. In Germany it was the 'Burgfrieden' or 'domestic truce'. In France it was called the 'union sacrée', or 'sacred union', in a slogan coined by the president in a message to parliament on 4 August 1914. James F. McMillan described this pact as 'the agreement to bury longstanding political and ideological animosities in response to President Poincaré's appeal to put national unity first'.[3] As intimated in the introduction, however, while this national coalition was broad-based (and generally included Catholics), we should not minimize the importance of those who dissented from it or were outside its clammy embrace.[4] Sangnier did not belong to these marginalized categories, making the 'war culture' paradigm the most applicable for him: his own periods in conventional military service during the war, as well as the political, religious and diplomatic missions he accepted from 1916, display well the seamless links between Catholicism, patriotism and the broader tapestry of the 'sacred union'. Crucially, however, in addition to his experience of high politics (be it in France's wartime government or at the Vatican), Sangnier served long enough at or near the front line to know what he was talking about when it came to the reality of life in the trenches, either under fire or in the fray.

Seeing as the Sillon had been tarred with the brush of socialism by its conservative critics, Sangnier's Jeune République party was accused, from its foundation in 1912, of being anti-militarist. This was unfair on it, though many similar socialist-leaning movements had campaigned against the army and military service before 1914. Leader of the conservative Catholic intelligentsia Alfred Baudrillart wrote in May 1915 that 'it would appear as if Marc Sangnier has conducted himself admirably as a soldier. He has led his men in particularly perilous circumstances and has been named captain. It's an improvement on his pacifist bleating of yesteryear.'[5] The pro-military stance of Sangnier in 1913 on the matter of lengthening military service should have left no doubt, but conservative Catholics were ever eager to believe the worst of the Sillon, including that it had been a nest of bad Catholics and dirty socialists. Governments across Europe had feared mass socialist dissension from any major European war, in keeping with the declarations of international socialist solidarity that had issued from the Socialist International and its congresses; in November 1912, at a moment when regional war in the Balkans had threatened to activate Europe's armed alliances for a continental war, its international meeting held in Basle committed socialists to 'the salvation of peace and civilization'. French socialists also opposed (without success) the Three Year Law, proposed in 1913 but passed into law in early 1914. In August 1914, though, in most belligerent nations, socialists were won over to the defence of the nation, leaving unrealized long-touted plans for a general strike to prevent mobilization. The moral leader of the French Socialist Party, the Section Française de l'Internationale Ouvrière (SFIO), from its foundation in 1905, was Jean Jaurès, who was assassinated on the very eve of war in July 1914. However, well before the crisis, Jaurès, as a reconciler of 'pacifism within patriotism', had distanced himself from the strident anti-militarist wing of his party under the leadership of the firebrand Gustave Hervé. Calling for a democratized national army, Jaurès's seminal work on the theory of patriotism *L'Armée nouvelle* (1911) allied opposition to capitalist war to a steely determination to defend the republic in arms if it was attacked. The July Crisis of 1914 allowed all participants to claim, speciously or not, that they were responding to aggression or an imminent threat. To the dismay of an initially small band of dissenting activists, Germany's SPD voted war credits just as French socialists rallied to the tricolour. The issue of atrocities and the acts of vengeance wrought on civilian populations, not just by the German army in Belgium and France but also by the Russian and Austrian armies on the eastern fronts, served to seal the national covenants of a 'just war'.

Traditionally, historians have interpreted the 'failure' of Europe's socialists to stop war in 1914 as a measure of how shallow the roots of internationalism were in the Second International. French socialists and even committed anti-militarists underwent, in many cases, striking changes of heart which now legitimated defensive war. For the French socialist anti-militarists, though, Paul B. Miller argues that, precisely because French socialist anti-militarism linked the issue of peace to the rhetoric of social progress, 'we can begin to make sense of the process by which these anti-militarist citizens came to identify their cause with that of the often vilified *patrie*; a process that was consummated, not commenced, when the war broke out in 1914.' In his own time Sangnier did not share such an analysis. Taking pains at a political meeting after the war in 1919 to point out he had been for the extension of military service to three years' duration in 1914 – unlike his socialist opponents – Sangnier noted how 'the war had opened the eyes' of socialists like Marcel Sembat to the army's necessity. (Sembat, Jules Guesde and Albert Thomas were three high-ranking Socialists who accepted places in a national unity government on 26 August 1914.) Sangnier even quoted a sergeant in his army unit who had been blacklisted as an anarchist in 1914 but who, while still calling himself revolutionary, was now in the trenches with Sangnier 'to fight like a true Frenchman against Prussian militarism'.[6] He could equally have added the case of Gustave Hervé, an example of the most spectacular conversion from 'social war' to army fever between 1910 and 1914.

As well as the eclipse of socialist anti-militarism, the reintegration of the Catholic Church into the heart of national life in 1914 was another crucial aspect of the 'sacred union' and a critical context for Sangnier's own war experience.[7] The Separation Law had been passed in 1905. The unexpected détente of 1914 between church and state came in the wake of a decade of protracted and bitter struggles between religious, laity and the republic over property and the very presence of religion in the public sphere. Catholics and socialists were now back in the heart of the nation by means of a 'war culture' and cultural mobilization. This could mean papering over the cracks because, as Horne puts it, national mobilization was 'naturally conditioned by the development of political and cultural life in pre-war society'.[8]

Official French Catholic propaganda of these years was but one part of a much broader 'mobilization of intellect', to borrow Martha Hanna's apt phrase, into which the greater part of the French intelligentsia was co-opted. The Comité catholique de propagande française à l'étranger was created by the government in 1915. Chaired by Alfred Baudrillart, this body recruited willing Catholic intellectuals from right to tepid left, constituting a type of Catholic miniature 'sacred union'.

Co-ordinating the writings of Catholic intellectuals and academics, it published propaganda tracts and sponsored world speaking tours to influence uncommitted Catholic opinion, especially American. Tailoring stock French propaganda tropes of 1914, the Catholic Committee produced bespoke Catholic propaganda that echoed the attack on the foe's brutality. It seized on German atrocities and tried to dispel for foreign Catholics the idea that France was a heathen land of priest-bashing libertines.[9] A close collaborator of Marc Sangnier's, Georges Hoog, worked assiduously for Baudrillart's Committee, including writing a pamphlet outlining to neutral Catholics why Alsace-Lorraine should be returned to France.[10] Sangnier, on account of the events of 1910, was too divisive and distrusted and found himself cold-shouldered by the Catholic Committee. Baudrillart, conscious of the Silloniste sympathies of his most gifted propagandists, Hoog and Francisque Gay, fretted that the mere 'accusation of Sillonisme' could be used to discredit the Committee's work in the eyes of conservative Catholics.[11] Even in the trenches Sangnier, to his great hurt, encountered the suspicion of anti-republican Catholics: 'some priests treat us as if we were outside the Church: I have met some on the front who thought I was excommunicated.'[12] Clearly there were internal limits to the Catholic 'sacred union'.

Sangnier's own military service is important for the credibility it gave him subsequently as a 'moral witness' to the war, as a leader and a spiritual mentor on the fighting front. In keeping with his military engineer's training at the Ecole Polytechnique, Marc Sangnier served in the 8th Territorial Battalion of the 1st Regiment of Engineers from 1914 to June 1916, attached to the Company 4/53T, serving an early portion of that time constructing trench defences near Langres, in the department of the Haute-Marne. Under the pressure of an extended war, the idea that the 'territorials' would serve mainly in support roles broke down, allowing men like Sangnier to be active participants, witnessing industrialized warfare at close quarters. The system of rotation developed in the French army was a response to a long war whereby troop use was adapted to increasingly mechanized warfare. Known as *le brassage*, this system led to stop-go tours of duty for units and men that were aimed at maintaining morale and rationing exposure to the most dangerous zones of combat. After Sangnier was promoted to captain in March 1915, his colonel superior wrote of him as 'a valuable officer since the beginning of the campaign. Very devoted, much loved by his men over whom he has a lot of ascendancy'. For his competence and courage he was decorated with the Croix de Guerre-Etoile de Bronze in June 1916. This came as no surprise to his young followers from the Sillon, who were now scattered to the four corners of the French army. Hubert Aubert, serving in the 156th Infantry Division, wrote to him in April 1915: 'you must be a model company commandant, a real leader and a very affectionate father to the men. I am certain they must be happy to serve under your orders.'[13]

Though Sangnier was never too far removed from high politics, here in the trenches he was also close to the lowly prayers of scared men, believer and unbeliever alike. At the front, Sangnier took it upon himself to organize Masses sung by the men, thus informally assuming the additional role of an auxiliary lay chaplain. Religious sentiment in the armies of the First World War is currently a matter of sustained interest amongst scholars. In the French case, much of the debate centres not just on to whom and how men in the trenches prayed but also on quantifying the 'religious revival' within the French army and French society generally during the war. Jacques Fontana and Annette Becker are agreed that 1914 saw a surge of religious observance, the so-called 'return to the altars', amongst lukewarm Catholics.[14] However, contemporary Catholic commentators made exaggerated claims of national conversion. Becker argues that, after this preliminary zeal for traditional practice tapered off, what remained for the duration of the war was a revived religious sensibility, a 'new mysticism' that expressed itself most particularly in the unorthodox spirituality of the trenches.[15] Sangnier himself was under no illusions that all those who readily accepted religious medals or other paraphernalia had been won over to conventional Catholicism. In the Vatican in January 1920, Sangnier reported that, from his observations, only about 30 out of every 1000 men in the French army were dutiful Mass-goers.[16] This unpalatable statistic mirrored the frontline chaplains' reports on Easter communions.[17]

Annette Becker has argued that religion allowed individual combatants to turn their story into 'part of a collective destiny through their faith and fatherland. Such a double investment lay at the heart of the process of total cultural mobilization for the war and the complexity of the war cultures.' In the face of mass death, the mystique of sacrifice epitomized by the literary works of Ernest Psichari and Charles Péguy permeated this war religion. Dolorist Catholicism conditioned its practitioners to welcome suffering as a 'sign of election', a privileged sharing in the Christ's Passion often mediated through saintly female intercessors such as the Virgin Mary and Joan of Arc. Sangnier personally shared the growing devotion to the figure of Thérèse of Lisieux. The French Carmelite nun, who had died in 1897 after a short life of physical and spiritual suffering, was the focus of a huge cult during the First World War. Thérèse's name became known way beyond the Catholic constituency, to make of her the favourite saint of the *poilus,* as the French conscripts were colloquially known. The other crucial point, though, as Sangnier's trench Masses showed, was that many previously indifferent men gained exposure to Catholic liturgy at the front. Jacques Fontana writes of the palpable piety of ceremonies held under imminent danger on improvised altars, with men crying at the singing of the Stabat Mater. This communal prayer was the continuation of the 'shoulder to shoulder' camaraderie of trenches and camps.[18]

The practical ecumenism necessary when men of various traditions were obliged to share a cramped space led to a generalized acceptance that the French clergy, who, unlike in other countries, benefited from no national service exemption, had stepped up to the mark for the nation. Hardcore anticlericalists continued in wartime to cast aspersions on the patriotism of the *curé sac au dos* or on the members of banned congregations who had returned to France specifically to fight under the colours. In this, though, the secular zealots were actually going against the consensus of the 'sacred union'. After the war, Sangnier would make regular references to this shared experience between priest and secularist in the trenches so as to reconfigure a 'sacred union' for peace. In his exploration of wartime personal reconciliation, Joseph F. Byrnes has explored how 'the two groups who represented [...] religious loyalty and secular ideology, the priests and the schoolteachers (long trained to be an ideological and moral counterweight to the clergy), achieved a multiform armistice, limited though it was, in the old religion-secularism wars.'[19] Like these priests, the survivors of Sangnier's Sillon experienced the war as necessary martyrdom and self-immolation for the fatherland.[20]

Clearly, then, as well as his lay apostolate in the trenches, Sangnier remained a father figure for his Silloniste comrades throughout the army. His extensive correspondence with them tied him into a broader 'epistolary tradition' within the army, explored extensively by Martha Hanna and Martyn Lyons.[21] On the level of more public communications among men in the army, though, Stéphane Audoin-Rouzeau has shown how improvised trench newspapers mediated the conflict for participants and also provided some light relief for French soldiers. Old Sillon comrades did not set up the direct equivalent of these rudimentary trench newspapers but did produce a series of impromptu newsletters: *Lettres à un Soldat* (1915–19), *Notre Etoile* (1916–17), and, thirdly, *Nos Annales de Guerre* (1918–19). Produced on a shoestring well behind the lines and overcoming shortages of ink and paper, these journals were then distributed by mail to *anciens militants* in the trenches as a means of preserving the 'âme commune', or 'common soul', that the Sillon had boasted of. As editor and contributor, Georges Hoog was central to the frenetic activity in this segment of the flea press between 1915 and 1919. Produced privately at the home of Emmanuel Rivière in Blois, the paper *Notre Etoile* styled itself the 'republican democrat' newsletter and represented different strands of Social Catholicism, not just the leftist orientation of the Sillon.[22] One Social Catholic activist, Robert Cornilleau, later recalled the joy with which it was received 'in the mud of the trenches' as a reminder of the enduring Christian Democratic cause.[23] However, the paper's linking of Catholicism and the republic rendered it suspect in the eyes of conservative Catholics. Mgr Henry Chapon, the bishop of Nice, one of the few members of the episcopate who had spoken up for the Sillon in 1909–10, sent a friendly warning to Sangnier that his friends in the paper should not overdo 'their very legitimate and necessary defence of Republican and Democratic France' so as not to give the ecclesiastical censors something to use against them.[24] Suppressed by Sangnier himself on this account, the paper continued under a new masthead, *L'Ame Française,* which ran from 1917 to 1924.[25] The other journals for activists who had been 'orphaned' by the ending of the Sillon in 1910 were *Nos Annales de Guerre* and *Lettres à un Soldat.* Both were produced at the Paris-based Catholic publishers Bloud & Gay and offered a warlike mix of Christian redemption theology and republican mystique. *Nos Annales de Guerre* carried a rolling series of obituaries for Sillon activists recently killed 'for the life of *la patrie*'.[26] Both it and *Lettres à un Soldat* recalled the Sillon's long-standing solidarity with their compatriots in Alsace-Lorraine and the justice of France's cause as a 'war of liberation, yes, and not of conquest'. Much like the trench priests whose published jottings endowed the battle with the sacramental, Georges Hoog's Easter message for 1915 wrote of the 'Christian Passover, festival of the resurrection of the Christ who loves the Franks! Patriotic Passover, festival of French resurrection!'[27]

From June 1916 to January 1917 Marc Sangnier was spirited out of the war and sent on a top-level political mission at the request of the French government to visit Pope Benedict XV in the Vatican. Sangnier's departure for Rome represented an extraordinary hiatus in his military service. Sangnier, therefore, did not go through Verdun, though he would return to army duties in France in 1917. Sangnier's son Jean has written of how his father 'was sent on an official mission to the Italian Red Cross. In fact, this mission concerned contacts which the

Minister for Foreign Affairs, Aristide Briand, wished to make with the Vatican.'[28] (Briand was in fact Prime Minister as well as Foreign Minister at that time.) As part of the 'sacred union', Briand and the Republic wanted to achieve internal unity and the good opinion of neutral Catholics by holding out the hope of a healing of the diplomatic rift which had existed between France and the Vatican since 1904. This was delicate because anticlerical slanders (which became known as the *rumeurs infâmes*) propagated the belief that a reactionary clergy was conniving at the republic's defeat as God's punishment.[29] The Red Cross mission was an elaborate ruse, including a meeting with the King of Italy at the Quirinal. After a speech in Padua, Sangnier proceeded to visit field-medical installations at the mountainous Italian front in the north, even if many observers discerned the trip's main aim.[30] 'No one believes he will only be talking about the Red Cross', wrote papal courtier Mgr Jules Tiberghien to Rome of Sangnier's unusual release from regular combatant duties.[31] Baudrillart mocked what he saw as an odd waste of manpower, predicting that 'his visit [...] will raise eyebrows'.[32]

The war, and a new papacy, was about to supersede the condemnation of 1910 and change utterly the relationship of Sangnier and the church hierarchy, especially the papacy itself. This visit to Rome in 1916 was not the first meeting of Marc Sangnier and of Giacomo della Chiesa, the man who had been elected bishop of Rome as the first battle of the Marne raged in September 1914. Much later, in 1920, Pope Benedict XV moved Sangnier by recalling the vivid impression the French layman had made on him, a decade earlier, in an address on the social Gospel in Rome in 1904, when Sangnier's ultramontane popular Catholicism was still the apple of Pope Pius X's eye. In the decade since then, though, both Della Chiesa and Sangnier had seen their careers blighted by the Modernist crisis. Della Chiesa was no Modernist. That was hardly likely from a man that had been appointed Papal Under-Secretary of State, or 'Sostituto', in 1901, in the last days of Leo XIII's long pontificate, making him second in command in the Roman Curia. However, from that important post he was aghast at the excesses of the purge against intellectual and political novelty that took hold from the middle of the first decade of the new century. Its tone offended his cautious temperament and his penchant for fair play.

The election of Pius X in 1903 had indeed altered the politics of the Curia, to Della Chiesa's disadvantage. The new Secretary of State, Cardinal Merry del Val, marginalized him in favour of *intégristes* such as Mgr Umberto Benigni. Benigni was the head of a shadowy anti-Modernist thought police, the secretive Sodalitium Pianum, with agents and informants throughout Catholic Europe who were ever ready to 'delate' (or inform on) suspected Modernists to Rome. Mgr Pietro Gasparri, Secretary of Extraordinary Ecclesiastical Affairs, head of the Vatican 'Foreign Office' and an ally of Della Chiesa's, wrote privately of La Sapinière, as the Sodalitium Pianum was known in French, as 'an occult, espionage organization [...] a kind of Freemasonry unheard of in the history of the Church'.[33] In this fevered atmosphere Della Chiesa's 'promotion' as archbishop of Bologna in 1907 provided 'a convenient exile for an uncomfortable subordinate'.[34] Always loyal, Della Chiesa nonetheless wielded the anti-Modernist axe sparingly in his new diocese. Small wonder he was denied the cardinal's red hat until the summer of 1914. The very fact of his election to the papacy in September 1914 was a blow to the anti-Modernist zealots. Within months Gasparri had become Secretary of State, a post he would retain until 1929. Most significant of all was Benedict's first encyclical, *Ad Beatissimi*, published on 1 November 1914, which did not just deplore the European war as 'a useless slaughter' but also called for concord within the Church. The condemnation of Modernism – understood as unfiltered syncretism of Catholicism with modern ideas – remained, but the unfettered hounding of alleged heretics should end. With the self-styled 'integral' Catholics in view, he decreed that the practice of 'using distinctive names by which Catholics are marked off from Catholics should cease'.[35] All of this made Benedict open both to meeting Sangnier and to exploring with him new avenues for lay apostolate and new beginnings in the political relationship between the Vatican and France.

Marc Sangnier's private account of his audience with Pope Benedict XV on 19 August 1916 is highly revealing.[36] Firstly, Sangnier, the devout Catholic, was eager to prove his obedience to the Holy See, defend himself against detractors and gain approval for his renewed role as a lay Catholic activist. Secondly, in the context of the 'sacred union', Sangnier acted as Briand's emissary, discussing the prospects for better church–state relations in France. Finally, Sangnier pleaded his country's moral case before the 'Holy Father', thereby attempting to influence Vatican policy. He was but one of many supplicants from both sides. The example of the German Catholic politician Matthias Erzberger springs to mind. During his own audience Sangnier exhibited an almost Jansenist scrupulosity about the manner and wholeheartedness of his submission to the papacy. Sangnier weighed every word the pontiff said on his personal situation and carefully reproduced their conversation verbatim. In Sangnier's account, Benedict was emphatic about Sangnier's correctness in his submission to the pope: 'Your attitude was absolutely perfect

[. . .] Yes! Absolutely perfect!' Then, 'we spoke about the condemnation of the Sillon.' Benedict responded reassuringly: 'Everyone makes mistakes. Even Saint Augustine did.'[37] The pope affirmed 'vigorously' the compatibility of republicanism and Catholicism. Ever the diplomat, he would pursue the fight against internal heresy more sensitively than his sainted predecessor.[38] Sangnier left the audience with a renewed mandate for religious activism. As the prelate Tiberghien had written to the Vatican that July: 'He is not alone a fine soul but a veritable force and it is to my mind of great utility not to lose him.'[39] Benedict acknowledged the 'edifying' nature of Sangnier's abstinence but felt it was time for it to end and that Sangnier should involve himself in 'Catholic action', even organizing retreats and religious meetings, reassuring the Frenchman not to fear his critics in this regard.[40] Sangnier thanked the pope and contended that a public papal reprimand of the Catholic anti-republican right would secure the 'sacred union' and conciliate the state.[41]

Sangnier reminded Benedict at the very outset, however, that he was also there on behalf of Briand, who felt that contact with the Holy See could be 'useful' for France. Sangnier, the exemplar of Catholic 'cultural mobilization', had come to plead France's moral case before the pope. With equal tenacity, though, Benedict XV desired to remain the common father of warring Catholics and was not going to let himself be used in a propaganda war by either Cain or Abel. As France and her allies saw it, there was an overriding moral imperative to take sides in the clash of civilizations. The papacy had to condemn 'German barbarism' unequivocally. The use of such Manichean terms had crystallized, in 1914–15, around the issue of the German violation of Belgian neutrality and German military conduct in 1914. From 1914 the papacy adopted a policy of *imparzialità* towards the war in general and the atrocities issue in particular. This effectively meant that the Vatican saw no moral distinction between either set of belligerents.[42] Unsurprisingly, such an apparently relativist position was 'at loggerheads with the cultural mobilisation of each side' but protests (and there were many) were to little or no avail. The papacy was only willing either to engage in charitable relief of human distress in wartime or to make a series of initially discreet attempts to bring about a negotiated peace. The first of these, in 1915, was a precursor to the more celebrated Papal Peace Note of August 1917, which would be greeted with a tone of respectful defiance by the French ecclesiastical establishment.[43] The discussion between Benedict and Marc Sangnier of the moral issues at stake in the war fits perfectly into this schema. Belgium's patriotic hero Cardinal Mercier was engaged in similar efforts. The German bishops responded in kind. Sangnier also lobbied the Curia's rising star and future Pope Pius XII, Eugenio Pacelli (on 14 August), and Secretary of State Gasparri (on 15 August).[44] At the audience with Benedict on 16 August, Sangnier insisted that France was fighting a defensive war, forcing Benedict onto the defensive over the Belgian issue:

> The Pope [*sic*] affirmed that he loved France and had affirmed the injustice of the violation of Belgium. I remarked to him that [...] as long as the occupation of Belgium continued, they [the Germans] persevered in injustice. The Pope replied that I, as a philosopher, ought to understand that the Pope was obliged to treat with the Germans, even in Belgium, where there existed a de facto power.[45]

To Sangnier this papal pronouncement must have been disconcerting. It seemed to acquiesce in the notion that might was right. He could not agree with the pontiff's wish that 'one began to envisage a peace without fighting *jusqu'au bout* [to the finish]' – in other words, a negotiated peace, as suggested by the papacy in 1915 and again in 1917. As so often during the First World War, the 'Eldest Daughter' had to agree to disagree with her 'Holy Father' just as French and German governments, for their own reasons, spurned such proposals for a compromise peace, mediated by the pope or any such neutral entity. On other aspects of relations between the Vatican and France, though, Sangnier's visit was highly satisfactory. The pope made conciliatory noises about relations with the French. He recalled the reported private remark of Briand to Belgium's Cardinal Mercier that it would be impossible for the French state to expel once more members of French religious orders who had served with such distinction on the front. If Alsace-Lorraine returned to France, the pope announced he would be 'extremely conciliatory' and that he hoped for an understanding on the question of the continued application of the Napoleonic Concordat, abolished in France in 1905 but which had never been rescinded in German-ruled Alsace.[46]

Sangnier's visit to the Vatican did not go unnoticed at home. Baudrillart exemplified the suspicion of many when he noted crisply in his diary: 'The pope has received Marc Sangnier [...] But the pope shall not go back on what Pius X did.'[47] As an old ally, Bishop Chapon of Nice was well placed to remind Sangnier how the Roman welcome given to him would 'reawaken the malevolence' of his enemies. Chapon informed Sangnier of at least one written protest from a bishop to Cardinal Gasparri.[48] Bishop Tissier of Châlons had written to Rome for clarification of the audience's import, fearing an 'impertinent' exaggeration of the pope's receptivity to Sangnier's democratic Social Catholicism. 'Sacred union' or not, Tissier was still using the language of the Modernist crisis when he stated forebodingly that 'the Sillon is a subtle doctrine which insinuates itself by the least of open doors.'[49] In this case, Rome was not about to bolt the door. Pacelli, as head of Extraordinary Ecclesiastical Affairs, refused to entertain such complaints in his response. 'The August Pontiff wished to encourage him in popular and social action, for the especial benefit of the working class' and to be in all particulars faithful to the Holy See and the bishops, 'which M. Marc Sangnier accepted perfectly'.[50] In December 1916 the pope also told Cardinal Amette, the archbishop of Paris, of his 'benevolent' attitude towards Sangnier. The pope went on to reassure the archbishop, though, that Pius X's censure of the Sillon still stood. Instead of revisiting old wounds, the pope said he merely wanted 'Sangnier and his friends' not to have 'their hands tied' in the matter of social action that might benefit the church.[51]

Chapon told Sangnier he prayed God to 'deliver you back soon, victorious and in peace, to the great work He destines for you [...] in the regeneration of our Christian France'.[52] But despite Sangnier's visit *ad limina apostolorum* in 1916, the pope's private endorsement of his renewed public role failed to quieten conservative critics. However, as we shall see for the period 1919–20, Sangnier's shuttle diplomacy between Paris and Rome pointed ahead to the new 'ralliement' after the war and the consecration of the wartime reintegration of Catholics into the political centre in the 1919 elections. Also, by giving credence to Sangnier and none to the monarchist right, the pope seemed to be guiding French Catholics towards accepting the republic once and for all, after the failed first 'ralliement' of the early 1890s. Police reported in 1917 that the papal audience gave democrats in the Catholic youth movements hope for the 'resurrection of the Sillon'; it was furthermore regarded as one in the eye for the far-right Action Française, whose chief demagogue and democrat-baiter, Léon Daudet, had stayed at home, shirking, while Sangnier had actually gone 'au feu' and into battle in defence of the fatherland.[53] Chapon wrote to Rome in 1919 to express gratitude for this sensible Vatican strategy of cautious endorsement of Christian democrats, remarking that the alternative, of purging those whose democratic beliefs made them suspected of Modernism, was a political dead-end that injured the innocent and despaired many faithful. The war, the bishop continued, had opened up a 'new world' to lay apostles like Sangnier; 'France does not leave the war converted but riper for conversion [...] We are tolerated and welcomed where, a few years ago, we were forbidden.'[54] The experience of the war and of lay and clerical witness in blood and toil opened new windows of possibility that the church would do well not to close through a retreat into puritan intransigence, advice that we shall see weighed much on Pope Benedict when he formulated the papacy's geo-strategy at the time of the Versailles treaty.

In the spring and early summer of 1917, meanwhile, Sangnier was back in the direct service of the army but not at the front. Instead he served a period as instructor to over 600 late adolescent conscripts of the class of 1918, formed into the Company 22/28, at the depot of the 1er Génie at Versailles. This was another experience as social engineer, one which prompted him to publish his findings on their level of knowledge.[55] Sangnier wrote of his experience with this diverse group (which included a minority of complete illiterates) with the tone of a paternalistic schoolmaster. Referring to them as 'my poor little *poilus*', he saw lurking behind their youthful elixir the same anxiety he had experienced at the same Versailles barracks at which he had arrived as a callow youth 20 years earlier: 'from the first day, upon first contact, we understood and loved one another.'[56] Sangnier's curriculum with these young adult males was rather like that followed by patriotic schoolteachers of wartime France who were in charge of young children and who felt tasked to 'raise their hearts to the fatherland'. Like the schoolteachers described in Mona Siegel's study, Sangnier the master taught a curriculum covering French, history, geography and mental arithmetic. As in schools, even exercises in dictation had a didactic purpose: 'France fights now not alone for her independence; she fights also for the liberty of the world.'[57]

Sangnier had the sense of humour essential to any teacher's survival, seeing the funny side when it came to historical misinformation. The assignment set on great French historical figures since Charlemagne produced some 'comic' results. Revisionism was the vogue: 'Louis XIV, king of France, and Gambetta his minister.'[58] As often happens in exam scripts, exotic minutiae from history captivated students to the detriment of their grasp of the bigger picture. Needless to say, all remembered Léon Gambetta's escape from Paris in a balloon during the Franco-Prussian War of 1870–1, an escapade that 'took on, under the pens of the class of '18, gigantic proportions'![59] Geography allowed for less levity, though, with 'even the most ignorant knowing exactly the invaded departments [...] there is knowledge that the German injury has engraved in the most uncultivated minds.'[60] In French compositions the high rhetoric of liberty and democracy co-existed with more earthy insights: a good soldier 'lets others sleep, doesn't waste food and doesn't get drunk.'[61] Sangnier as popular educator was once again engaged in civic formation, as he had been in the Sillon and as he would be again in the peace movement. By publishing his findings in wartime, Sangnier was certainly pointing out educational deficiencies that post-war France should address, but, more immediately, he was relaying to the public a clean bill of health as to the decency and solid moral fibre of the class of 1918. This was at a time when many feared that defeatism and anti-patriotism had infiltrated the ranks on account of the army 'mutinies' and indiscipline of spring 1917.

Reintegrated, at last, into the regular army, in May 1917 Sangnier was posted to the Seventh Regiment of Engineers as 'capitaine commandant' of Company 15/3T, attached to an infantry division stationed at Montdidier, about 45 miles south of the front on the Somme in part of the 'arrière du front', the vast semi-industrialized zone that sprang up on both sides along the western front. In 1917 there was also a new propaganda drive within the army after the mutinies of the first part of the year. Conceived of by Marshal Foch as an antidote to war-weariness, the marshal wished the lectures to inculcate hatred of the 'Boche', the racialized term of abuse in French for the Germans. They were run in parallel with the home-front campaign of the Union des Grandes Associations contre la Propagande Ennemie (UGAPE), often animated by primary teachers armed with films and other aids. Sangnier actively sought recruitment as an army propaganda lecturer when this new effort was launched. John Horne interprets these twin national propaganda efforts, in the army and on the home front, as part of a more general national re-mobilization for war in 1917, in favour of the absolute necessity of total military victory. The appointment of Georges Clemenceau as Prime Minister in November 1917 closed a period of acute political uncertainty in France that had severely tested the 'sacred union'. No quarter would be given any longer to talk of a negotiated peace, such as had been suggested in mid-1917 by parties as diverse as the pope, some scandal-prone pacifist Radical politicians such as Joseph Caillaux and Louis Malvy and the minority anti-war Socialists. These Socialists subscribed to the spirit of the dramatic Zimmerwald Declaration, made at the Swiss town of the same name in 1915, by anti-war Socialists from ten countries in favour of peace without annexations. In 1917, the French government very publicly denied passports to French Socialists anxious to travel to a similar congress in Stockholm.[62]

Sangnier assumed a new official relationship to the process of wartime mobilization, therefore, when in February 1918 he became an army propaganda lecturer charged with instilling in French citizen-soldiers a deeper understanding of the purpose of the war and their role in it. Sangnier had made concerted use of well-placed contacts in the War Ministry to lobby for such a post, which would, in the words of Captain Deuil, one such sympathizer, relieve him of his current 'thankless role' as a trench engineer.[63] Sangnier gave lectures in the departments of the Meuse and the Marne, and, from May 1918, the Aisne and the Oise as well.[64] Jean Sangnier recalls his father's mission as 'a psychological action as one would call it nowadays, in order to maintain the troops' morale. Lectures, slideshows, cinema. His brief allowed him to circulate along the whole of the front, bringing with him his propagandist material.'[65] Large meetings were supplemented by 'causeries intimes', or small group sessions, suited to Sangnier's personal charm. In seven speaking tours between March 1918 and April 1919 Sangnier gave some 106 lectures in all.[66] In method, Sangnier's propaganda effort was a continuation of that of the Sillon. His diary noted with satisfaction in March 1918: 'Improvised lecture – the best of all – Veritable study circle.'[67] Jean Sangnier adds that for his father 'it was more passionate moral action than rallying the morale of the troops. Already, new vocations were awakened around him.'[68]

Jay Winter has written that 'the Great War spawned the most spectacular advertising campaign to date. Its product was the justification of war.' Based on a mixture of moral outrage, selective reporting and misleading or untrue assertions, propaganda was like 'a lawyer's brief, pleading the cause of the nation before its population and that of the world'. However, while often state-led, propaganda gained its real power from the synergy of public and private campaigns aimed at forming public opinion from above and below. The new propaganda effort in which Sangnier was implicated in 1917 was a direct response to the foreign and domestic shocks of 1917, especially the two Russian revolutions, on account of which 'war aims became central to propaganda. What kind of peace, indeed what kind of post-war world, were questions at the heart of the appeal to public opinion in the last two years of the war.' Catholics, such as Sangnier, took their place in a suddenly crowded market of ideas on the new world as various ideological wares were offered to Europeans ranging from socialist projects to the bourgeois internationalism of US President Woodrow Wilson, who brought his country into the war on France's side in April 1917.[69]

The battle for meaning had begun already in 1914. Contemporaries – especially the Entente powers of Britain, France and Russia – accused the Germans, in a global propaganda war, of having broken 'civilized boundaries' of warfare. In this war, they claimed, Teutonic fury had thumbed its nose at rules of behaviour based on nineteenth-century liberalism that had been painstakingly codified into the international conventions of Geneva (1864) and The Hague (1900 and 1907) on the conduct of war. Of course, as John Horne and Alan Kramer's meticulous reconstruction shows, these charges were more than just propagandist invention: there were at least 130 incidents in Belgium and northern France involving the deaths of ten or more civilians at the hands of German troops, largely in a frantic two-week period in late August and early September. Many historians have debated whether this explosion of violence against civilians and their burning of cities to a crisp demarcated a specifically 'German way of war'. Was the German army's corporate culture itself informed by a will to extreme violence? Reviewing the debate in the context of 'Hitler's first war', Thomas Weber concludes convincingly that this last general charge is unproven: a heavy-handed counter-insurgency strategy was curtailed by the German army too late, but well before the brutal logic of 'absolute destruction' was fulfilled.[70] Neverthless, the German army's irrefutable atrocities fed a rabid essentialism in its opponents' minds: the essentially malign German character soon meant that any ill could be blamed on that race.

Where merited, Sangnier was very anti-German, but he did not dip his toe in the pond of outright racism in which polite society now swam. Invoking the spirit of the Hague Conventions, Sangnier asked what had become of all that legal progress 'under the odious effort of German brutality? The world has been brusquely brought back to the times when, wolf like, man preyed upon man.' Sangnier went on to catalogue German transgressions of the moral code of civilization: 'Have I any need to recall the bombardment of open cities, the torpedoing of commercial shipping, even when neutral [...] the arbitrary condemnations, the massacres of civilians?'[71] Sangnier, moreover, delivered his first round of lectures in the first half of 1918, at precisely the moment when the German Spring Offensive suddenly brought the fighting front deeper into the homeland and threatened the security of the capital once more. The associated German bombardments of Paris forced the issue of German 'barbarity' to the forefront of French life with an intensity not experienced since the first months of the war.

The use of the Big Bertha guns against Paris in the spring of 1918 had devastating effects and unleashed a new wave of 'hate the Hun' rhetoric. The deaths of tens of women and children in the Parisian church of Saint Gervais on Good Friday 1918, during the liturgy of the Passion, enraged France. It also revived memories of the destruction of

Reims Cathedral four years before.[72] The event had, in Sangnier's speech of righteous fury on behalf of its victims, 'a sort of sacrilegious irony at the very moment when Christ was shedding his blood so that men might learn to love one another'. Equally appalling, to Sangnier's mind, was the shelling of the maternity ward of the city's Hôpital Cochin, the spilling of blood on 'white and innocent cradles'.[73] Such references gave these lectures a striking contemporary impact. Another article of faith in the creed of the 'war culture' to which Sangnier wholeheartedly subscribed was the defensive war. France was merely defending herself (and, consequently, civilization) in this conflict. Any Allied reprisals were consequently relativized. Even if the exigencies of war led to military reprisals, was it not still the instigator of this odious system who remained primarily culpable? After the second battle of the Marne in July 1918 the startling German advance of the spring was repulsed by the Allied forces, under Marshal Foch's supreme command. Though the tide appeared to be turning, the dénouement of an armistice in November was by no means preordained, and the necessity of fighting the war 'to the bitter end' retained its motivational power because it was felt necessary to win in order to shape the peace to come. It would indeed be a mistake to assume that the retreat of the Germans in the face of repeated body-blows on all fronts – military and political – in the last months of the conflict did much to cool the anti-German sentiment of the French troops. As Georges-Henri Soutou points out, the 'political military' armistice of 11 November was no real end point of conflict, just a new setting for continuing tensions and ambiguities that would inform the later peace negotiations.[74]

The opportunistic embrace of Wilson's 14 Points by the German High Command in its request for terms in October 1918, abetted by the German civilian politicians, showed a canny appreciation of the rhetorical purchase of ideas of peace without vengeance in 1918, even if both sides often used this rhetoric as a cover for self-interest. Sangnier's lectures put him in the camp of those French who, out of some mixture of socialist, Catholic or liberal internationalism, left open the prospect that a defeated Germany could be purged of the Prussian militarist poison and redeem herself through democratization. Germany might yet make herself safe for peaceful co-existence in Europe. Thus Sangnier's diary of his propaganda tours records a recurring theme, that of the necessity of 'two victories: military victory over the enemy and a moral victory, maintaining after military victory the love of peace, justice and the fraternity of all'.[75] Unlike the French nationalists, Sangnier said Germany was not intrinsically bad but just the victim of a militarist virus whose 'germs' were present in countries other than the Reich. He left open the possibility that Germany was not uniquely to blame for 1914, a view of war responsibility far different from the moral statement made in the peace treaties about Germany and her associated powers.

The internationalist impulse represented within the pre-war Sillon by Alfred Vanderpol and his Société Gratry had been the preserve of a committed minority. However, taking the nineteenth-century priest Alphonse Gratry and his writings on international arbitration as their inspiration, the Société Gratry had kept the pacifist ideal alive in the Sangnier movement. In the context of continued bloodshed and the direct appeal of the pope for his help in working out a Catholic peace diplomacy, Sangnier began to look again at the Société Gratry inheritance around 1917, the year of the pope's famous Peace Note. German-speaking Catholic pioneers such as Fr Jocham Metzger were already spreading Catholic peace propaganda in Germany and Austria. Figures like Metzger would become close collaborators with Sangnier after the end of the war. Papal peace initiatives disposed Sangnier to embrace the Wilsonian vision of the abolition of war and the peaceful arbitration of disputes. The League of Nations, from 1918, provided Sangnier with his new millennium. Walter Lippmann, an important contemporary figure in the US war effort, explained the religious fervour that the League idea produced across the world when he characterized the Wilsonian ideology as 'a crusading doctrine' that made of all wars 'crusades which can be concluded when all the peoples have submitted themselves to the only true political religion. There will be peace only when all the peoples hold and observe the same self-evident principles.'[76]

From the start, Sangnier told the troops at his propaganda lectures of his admiration for Woodrow Wilson.[77] However, this enthusiasm, coupled with his rejection of the idea of a punitive peace, meant some officers were cool towards him. For instance, his diary records a dinner with a General Gourand where they disagreed over the appropriateness of employing Wilson's warnings against 'the feeble language of hatred and vengeance'.[78] After all, the general felt, 'it's necessary to develop hatred of the Germans amongst the *poilus*.'[79] Sangnier made even bolder statements than his hero in the White House, putting the morality of the Allied powers under the lens with some embarrassing results. Just before the armistice, he declared that self-satisfaction and a sense of moral superiority represented real 'moral dangers' for France and her allies. He went on: 'I say we must sort out injustices which can be found on the Allied side before we have the right to demand the resolution of those that are found on the side of our enemies.'[80] In this context he made repeated references to Ireland and Britain's on-off application of martial law there since Easter 1916. In the mould of Jaurès, Sangnier argued that France, the bearer of universal values, was honour-bound to uphold the cause of justice in the world.

For Sangnier, therefore, the conclusion of the war had to be marked in France by moral renewal, a perpetuation of the 'sacred union' at home through 'endurance, discipline, fraternity – [the] profound reform of society'.[81] The sense of urgency about the need to secure and win the peace is seen nowhere better than in the speech he gave at Epernay in January 1919. Epernay, located about 30 kilometres south of Reims, was in the heart of the pivotal Marne département, which had experienced fully the trauma of German invasion in the autumn of 1914.[82] In spite of the heightened sensitivities of the local audience, Sangnier was prepared to suggest the possibility of future reconciliation with Germany rather than just cry for revenge. The speech came merely two months after the armistice, when Germany was still technically the enemy, with hostilities merely suspended. The sudden German Revolution in November 1918 produced a German republic led by a government composed of moderate socialists and liberals that by early 1919 was presiding over paramilitarized chaos. In a fateful move the new state sub-contracted to right-wing militias such as the Freikorps the task of snuffing out socialist revolutions-in-the-making across the land. Nonetheless, on this new precarious German republic, Sangnier was willing to place some future hope in the early weeks of 1919. He played on the emotions of his audience of local schoolchildren and their parents at Epernay with pleas for a Wilsonian settlement that would spare the next generation the horrors that would for ever haunt their fathers. The *Réveil de la Marne* reported how Commandant Sangnier evoked 'the horror of war [...] and of this one in particular', an experience from which he had drawn this moral:

> Victory should give us a new world statute which will prevent a return to war [...And he] affirmed that if more than a million and a half men had offered the sacrifice of their lives, they knew themselves to be not just fighting a war like any other but rather to be making war on war.[83]

Sangnier had survived the war, but his experience marked him as it did his generation and turned him into a 'moral witness' to the tragedy, giving him a sacred duty to bear witness that would weigh heavily on him for the next 20 years. Alongside suffering and loss, though, the war had changed his relationship to the church authorities in a way that would have a significant bearing on his future activism. The papal audience of August 1916 had acted as catharsis for the disorientation caused by the condemnation of 1910. Pope Benedict XV was willing to endorse a new beginning in Sangnier's Social Catholic activism. Winning the peace was now the overriding moral imperative of Sangnier's mission. As an individual, in 1919, Sangnier joined a process of collective mourning for the fallen, but, for all the loss, the war had opened up new horizons of activism, especially peace activism, as he now returned to the life of the civilian and the lay Catholic activist, and stepped forward to begin binding up the wounds left weeping by the war.

2
Demobilization and Politics, 1919–21

In April 1919 Marc Sangnier was demobilized from the army, as part of a huge and intricate process of national military demobilization. This long-drawn-out procedure, which lasted well into 1920, was often frustrating for the 5 million men concerned. In the first instance, there were mixed emotions in the army at the outbreak of peace. The French experienced what Bruno Cabanes calls a 'mournful victory', where the dead were really present on the day of victory. Annette Becker and Gerd Krumeich refer to the veritable dead weight of the fallen on the whole of French society in 1919, in addition to the vast social and fiscal losses incurred. Added to this for men in uniform was the uncertainty as to when they could go home. Some younger men with pressing family commitments leapfrogged over the criteria of seniority and equality that were supposed to mean that the oldest classes of men demobilized first. The tedium of camp routine and discipline did nothing to improve the humour of the long-suffering conscript. Peace treaty negotiations stalled the process on occasion, as men were kept in the field in order for France to hold over Germany the threat of ending the armistice and resuming hostilities. Even after these irritants were overcome, the process of re-entry into civilian society did not always go smoothly. Just as jobs were a pressing concern, so also were ex-combatants confronted with questions of grief, anxiety and memory of the war in their transition from war to peace, all topics that have been of great interest to recent historians. The process of return involved 'unplugging' men from the violence of the war, which was but the start of a long process whose omega point might be reconciliation with the enemy, though not necessarily. In the immediate post-war period, most French soldiers remained staunchly hostile to the Germans in their correspondence; the men projected barely veiled sentiments of revenge onto the imminent French occupation of the Rhineland.[1]

French 'anciens combattants' occupied, from the first, a distinct social role as active citizens whom society expected to complete the regeneration of France begun on the battlefield. These men banded themselves together in a self-conscious moral elite whose claim on society had been earned in the trenches. As Antoine Prost's work on French veterans has shown, their organizations often operated as social welfare networks oriented to an anti-war message. Indeed, Jay Winter, whose scholarship has helped define the field of cultural memory of the First World War, refers to these veterans as 'moral witnesses'. These men, moreover, were burdened not just with moralistic expectations of themselves and of society but also with varying degrees of alienation from the home front, often accompanied by a loss of bearings tinged with guilt towards fallen comrades. Stéphane Audoin-Rouzeau has argued for a micro-historical approach to analyse such 'narratives of mourning', by means of which the historian can piece together a narrative from 'unrepresentative' fragments that provide part of a broader mosaic of loss. Fragmentary evidence of Sangnier's own journey of grief shows that he exemplified this difficult transition to civilian life. In addition, like many others who had held positions of moral or corporate leadership in the pre-war world, his mourning was both personal and corporate, combining personal loss and the loss of comrades and young followers of the Sillon. Part of the process of demobilization was picking up the threads of the old life and attempting the restoration of pre-war social networks shattered by the war. Even beginning this, though, confronted leaders like Sangnier with absent colleagues and the broken circle. Thus, from factories to political movements, a universally felt duty of memory towards the dead of the recent war was mediated through a vast array of civil and private memorials, from public squares to workplaces, schools and churches.[2] Tracing micro-histories of grief, Sangnier's included, we can be guided by the material culture of commemoration. Reflecting on this broad public and private memorialization of the war, Annette Becker has written of how the living used memorials to attempt to resurrect the departed in bronze and stone. The war memorial erected at Sangnier's newspaper headquarters of *La Démocratie* on boulevard Raspail was part of this generalized creation of 'sites of memory'.

Underneath the co-operative restaurant and printing presses on the site, a crypt had existed before the war which was used as a chapel by Sangnier, his family, his employees and supporters. The term 'crypt', as against 'oratory', was not accidental, as followers initiated into the history and rubrics of the Sillon well knew. In its very earliest incarnation the Sillon had begun as a schoolboys' discussion club La Crypte at the nearby boys' secondary school, the Collège Stanislas, that Sangnier had attended in the early 1890s. In 1919 a redecoration of Sangnier's crypt at *La Démocratie* occurred, during which the names of the war dead were literally engraved into the fabric of the site. Commemorative plaques were added, dedicated to the fallen, especially Henry du Roure, lost in battle in 1914, and all Sillonistes who had died 'for the defence of the fatherland, the emancipation of peoples and the liberation of the world'. The material mourning had begun even during the war itself. The recusant Sillon newspaper *Lettres à un Soldat* produced a prayer card in 1918 that bore a photograph of Sangnier in the uniform of the army captain officiating like a lay minister and leading a burial service for unnamed soldiers. Alongside this image was a picture of Henry du Roure accompanied by last words from a final letter written in 1914 that had looked ahead to the restoration of peace when 'we will take up again the noble struggle for integral and divine truth'.[3]

Sangnier's mourning was both private and public therefore. In his spiritual testament *Autrefois* (1933), Sangnier wrote of how 'the war took from me, one after another' many of those he loved best, including his mother, 'victim of her devotion to the wounded'. Mme Thérèse Lachaud-Sangnier had mobilized the family's Parisian apartment as a sick bay for convalescent soldiers. In the course of her ministrations, she contracted a viral illness that killed her. With an odd mixture of the humble and the messianic, Sangnier discerned, with the benefit of 15 years' hindsight, that providence had an ordained purpose for his personal survival: 'God didn't want me [...] I was not yet ready to leave even to go there.' Ranging back over the experience of war, he remarked ruefully on 'the battlefields, the muddy trenches [...and] the dreary boredom of interminable months of foot-dragging in the army zone'. This grimness, though, was offset by the 'precious encounter' with many young soldiers open to the communion of souls he desired. Back in the world of the living, Sangnier visited and remained in contact with the sister of one such soldier, 'Paul'. She, Sr Saint-Marc, was in a convent near the Sangnier family retreat in Treignac. Her brother Paul had been crushed to death in his shelter during a bombardment. The small wooden crucifix Paul had given him as a gift acted as a talisman for Sangnier, who wrote of how he had kissed it at dramatic moments in his own front-line duties when he felt death might be close. The omnipresence of death at the front produced the stoic (and strange) rhetorical question from Sangnier whether there was 'a more marvellous occasion to die than war?' Out there, on the front, the individual loneliness of death fell away as 'great waves [...] transported men, in a crowd, to the other side: the exception, nearly, was to survive'. Sangnier's statement implies strong faith in a communion of souls in the hereafter, even if, as Guillaume Cuchet argues, the realities of war occasioned a 'crisis of Christian death' which unbalanced the established Catholic patterns of a good death, comforted by the sacraments. While the war unsettled the traditional cycle of expiation for the sins of the deceased, whether it hastened the 'end of purgatory' as a cultural reference point is open to debate. Sangnier, for his part, seemed to be almost envious of the departed and wrote as if it were he who was one of the forgotten souls left to sojourn a while in a living purgatory. Sangnier engaged in a five-day 'pilgrimage' in August 1920 to the places where he had served as officer and propagandist between 1914 and 1919. Accompanied by his secretary Paul Châtelat, he laid flowers on the grave of René Pons, a young Silloniste, at Mosières. Such acts of pietas were undertaken by many families, from near and afar, in the 1920s, part of a burgeoning battlefield tourism that encompassed both individual family visits and larger gatherings of veterans' groups. Such acts would be a feature of several of the Peace Congresses that Sangnier was moved to organize from 1921.[4] Though it was hard, it was for the sake of these fallen that Sangnier believed he had to continue the good fight – for France, for Christian Democracy and, ultimately, for peace itself.

Beyond personal feelings of loss, the social and political world was no less daunting for returning soldiers. In France, as elsewhere, the period 1919–20 saw acute social tensions and strikes which reflected the influence of the war and the Russian Revolution. In this fraught atmosphere, how did Sangnier's attitude to Germany relate to broader French attitudes to the peace settlement? How did he react to the domestic upheavals behind which many French saw the long hands of Moscow and Berlin? As Benjamin Martin points out, the Treaty of Versailles concluded in June 1919 was based on Prime Minister Georges Clemenceau's conception of security for France, rather than that of Marshal Ferdinand Foch, supreme Allied commander and France's top general. In the absence of permanent territorial guarantees, the French would have to depend on Anglo-American pledges and German reparations. With the drafting of the peace settlement the world turned to Versailles, and the resultant weight of expectation on President Woodrow Wilson was enormous. Even before entering the war, Wilson had made a speech in January 1917 calling for 'Peace without Victory'. The president claimed the United States pursued a lasting peace based on government by consent, equality between nations and international co-operation. In January 1918 these principles were reformulated as war aims in a message to Congress that traversed the globe as Wilson's 14 Points. Writing on this 'Wilsonian moment', Erez Manela remarks that, at the war's end, a transnational constituency of 'progressives' 'entertained for a while near-millennial expectations for a more peaceful world order based on Wilsonian principles'.[5] Pierre Miquel refers to the halo surrounding the 'Wilson myth' on the French left when he arrived in France in December 1918, the lustre of the prophet which could only be tarnished by diplomatic realities.[6]

Sangnier was not immune to the mixture of hope and anxiety that was in the *Zeitgeist*. When the treaty was signed in June 1919, Sangnier was immersed in reviving his pre-war party, the Jeune République, and his newspaper publications. Sangnier was disposed to support the settlement at this stage, unlike the official view taken by the French socialists, as he viewed it as a just peace that gave France her just deserts in compensation from Germany while holding out the prospect of a new world order through the Covenant of the League of Nations, which was inscribed as the first article of the Versailles treaty. As Jean-Michel Guieu points out, Sangnier and fellow Catholic internationalists were *ad idem* with the civic peace movement represented by the Association pour 'La Paix par le Droit' (APD), for whom France's triumph was that of justice itself. Sangnier's monthly *La Démocratie* reappeared in June 1919, and his first leader article reflected this sense of a momentous occasion. Having invoked the rhetoric of the American president and the memory of the dead, Sangnier stressed the millenarian task facing society:

> Will we accept the reconstruction of society according to the old ways as if the war of nations was only a monstrous episode in a story that returns always to the same way? [...] If we wish the triumph of the Allies to truly mark the destruction of tyrannical autocracy, militarism, secret diplomacy, of war itself, this is the providential hour [...] To let slip this moment would be to risk never again retrieving it. Cruel apathy, fatal lack of faith that would rob the world of the victory prize! Who would dare accept the criminal responsibility for such a miscarriage![7]

Sangnier's first political meetings in the autumn of 1919 reflected the fact that sentiments of internationalism and Germanophobia could co-exist in the one person at this time. The road to reconciliation began with small incremental steps rather than with dramatic bounds of conversion. Trenchantly distancing himself from socialist anti-militarism, he declared himself pleased that most socialists had answered the call of the fatherland in 1914, in contrast to their pre-war internationalist campaigns against capitalist war. Sangnier told a meeting of the Jeune République party in September 1919 of his unwillingness to sacrifice conscription until such time as the League of Nations demonstrated its credentials as guarantor of real collective security. This self-declared 'fervent apostle of Wilson' opined, barely three months after the Hall of Mirrors, that the League was 'aborted at inception'. Sangnier based his peremptory judgement on the League's inaction the week before, when Italian nationalists led by the poet Gabriele d'Annunzio had taken over the town of Fiume from under the noses of Allied troops and League administrators. In August 1919 the Italian government had reached a provisional deal with Yugoslavia on Fiume's neutral status, only to see some of its own troops stage a local coup. Moreover, Sangnier reflected a generalized national angst at France's troubled victory which bred existential anxiety about the gaping demographic gap with Germany the war had served to widen. In October 1919 Sangnier advised the making of love not war: 'we must repopulate [...] because Germany has 90 million citizens and is already thinking of her revenge. If you want to avoid war, have children.'[8]

Sangnier was caught up in the social dislocation caused by the ruination of the *rentier* class he belonged to. This leisured class of *belle époque* bourgeois writers and politicians had inherited private means that permitted them to lead an anti-necessarian lifestyle. Police noted of Sangnier in 1920 that 'part of his fortune, which is very large, and whose value is estimated at several millions [francs], has been dedicated to the requirements of the propaganda effort he animates.' Men like Sangnier could afford to stand for parliament, fail and not fear personal ruin. For many *rentiers*, though, the war exploded their world, with runaway inflation and the dishonouring of Russian investment bonds by Lenin's regime. Even if personally spared this fate, Sangnier shared his class's antipathy to the Russian Revolution. With the Treaty of Versailles ratified in September 1919, Clemenceau set elections for mid-November. Yves Santamaria discerns fear for tomorrow in virtually all of the manifestos of the 1919 election. Conservatives invoked the Bolshevik bogeyman of the 'man with the knife between his teeth'. Sangnier's stance during the election hinged on the logic of 'sacred union' and the ambient anti-Communism. The Bloc National, which won three-fifth of the seats in November, was a coalition of the centre and the right, to the exclusion of the monarchists. Brokered by the centrist Adolphe Carnot and erstwhile left-wingers Aristide Briand and Alexandre Millerand, the pact was presented to the voters as a continuation of the Clemenceau programme in a new 'sacred union' that excommunicated French Bolsheviks.[9] Such an alliance was able to take advantage of a new electoral system which instituted a form of proportional representation that privileged the formation of large blocs and gave such blocs a large winner's bonus in new multi-seat constituencies. The Socialists, internally divided and tainted with Bolshevism, were marginalized, despite increasing their share of the popular vote since 1914.

The proof of Catholic patriotism through the 'sacred union' meant republicans and Catholics were no longer at loggerheads and Catholics formed an important reservoir of Bloc voters. There was even an olive branch from the notorious anticlericalist Clemenceau, while Alexandre Millerand evoked restored ties with the Vatican and a welcome home for banned religious congregations. Bloc manifestos included a judicious line on the secular nature of the state, a compromise privately approved by the archbishop of Paris, Cardinal Amette himself, which stated that 'the fact of the laïcité of the State should be reconciled with the rights and liberties of all citizens.' Fear was another glue for Catholics and the Bloc. As Bishop Henri Chapon of Nice wrote to Rome: 'if we had done as [the Catholic newspaper] *La Croix* would have had us do, forming an exclusively Catholic party, with certain premature demands, we would have been crushed and would have given France over to the most terrible social revolution.'[10]

Sangnier and his party the Jeune République were tempted by the inclusivity of the Bloc and sobered by the certainty of no representation outside the coalition under the new electoral law. For a month Sangnier hesitated, though, in part due to sibling rivalry between leftist Christian Democrats in the Jeune République and the more centrist Christian Democrats of the Fédération des Républicains-Démocrates (FRD). The FRD had joined the putative Bloc National as early as September, whereas Sangnier was initially dismissive of the Bloc's 'reactionary programme'. The Jeune République joined in the Bloc coalition at the last possible moment, on 21 October 1919, when former Silloniste Ernest Pezet brokered a deal that convinced Sangnier's party its leftist identity would be respected. Sangnier had dashed across Paris in a taxicab to a Bloc meeting at the Salle Wagram with the party's decision, but in his hesitancy were sown the seeds of Sangnier's future alienation from the governing bloc and his later separation from Pezet and other Christian Democrats. In this French version of a 'khaki election', though, Sangnier was right on message, condemning *en bloc* French Bolsheviks as the party of the foreigner: 'In the face of an armed Germany, we cannot disarm France because the Germans have begun their revenge by introducing Bolshevism here.'[11] Raw energy coursed through the campaign as Sangnier's supporters drowned out the singing of the Internationale with a rousing rendition of 'La Marseillaise'! Sangnier 'excoriated the traitor Sadoul'. A candidate in the second sector of Paris for the Section Française de l'Internationale Ouvrière (SFIO) – the official Socialist Party did not split between Socialists and Communists until the Congress of Tours in December 1920 – Jacques Sadoul was a French Socialist convert to the Russian Revolution. Absent from his assigned posting in the French army but engaged instead in the Red Army, he was debarred from the French election by the Conseil de Guerre, which condemned him to death for desertion. Many French, including Clemenceau, were livid at Sadoul's 'treacherous' *Notes sur la révolution bolchévique*, published in 1919.[12] Anything, it seemed, would be better than Communism's 'bloody disorder'.

On the day of electoral victory in November 1919, though, the dead remained present, just as they had on the day of military victory a year before. Sangnier had already fought three unsuccessful, but serious, campaigns in the Paris region before the war. In 1919 Sangnier won comfortably, with 79,659 votes, elected alongside two sitting Radical deputies who were running mates for the third sector of Paris, which included the Latin Quarter. Having just been elected to the so-called Blue Horizon Chamber, where military uniforms were ubiquitous, the moment of triumph was bitter-sweet for Sangnier. He wrote later of the moment in strikingly military terms, almost conflating battle and the elections: 'The breach is made, the rostrum of the Palais-Bourbon is taken in high struggle. I am a deputy for Paris.' Another sorrowful victory, though, as through moist eyes he saw not those pressing round to congratulate him but the faces of the lost generation 'who had laboured, suffered and prayed so much to see this moment shine forth'.[13]

In parliament, Sangnier kept faith with the dead, helping to shape the official commemoration of the war. The institutionalization of 11 November as an annual ritual makes it easy to overlook the fact that, in the French case, it was not until 1922 that the eleventh day of the eleventh month became a public holiday. Meanwhile, other dates were mooted in the immediate post-war period, such as Sangnier's proposal in 1920 for an annual Fête des Morts to coincide with the Catholic feast of All Souls on 2 November. Though unacceptable, his proposal underscored the generally felt need to honour 'redemptive sacrifice', as manifested in the grandiose interment of the Unknown Soldier at the Arc de Triomphe on 11 November 1920. Sangnier supported this neutral choice of burial site, away from the politicized Panthéon, so that the anonymous hero could rest undisturbed by 'painful polemics' and the culture wars of the Third Republic.[14]

The newly elected government was less anticlerical than any government in memory, prompting the historians Gérard Cholvy and Yves-Marie Hilaire to dub this period 'the Second Ralliement', with Catholics integrated into the victorious Republic a generation after Leo XIII first counselled pragmatic acceptance in 1890. Anticlericalism had not evaporated, but the glacier was in retreat. The canonization of Joan of Arc in Rome in 1920 helped the thaw. It was crucial for Sangnier to take advantage of the new conciliatory spirit to get a public clarification of his good standing with the church hierarchy and similarly important for the Vatican to buttress the credentials of a key supporter of its foreign policy. Interviewed in the aftermath of his election, Sangnier put 'religious pacification' as his immediate priority.[15] As in 1916, he played an important intermediary role between Paris and the Vatican. Following two years of negotiation, full diplomatic relations between Paris and the Vatican resumed on 16 May 1921, facilitating a final deal on outstanding issues of property and the regulation of worship that had been bitter bones of contention since the Separation Law of 1905. In parliament, Sangnier backed the government on all the key votes pertaining to church-state issues.

This Second Ralliement had as its corollary a new openness on the Vatican's part to the type of Catholic republican activism Sangnier represented. Pope Benedict XV, by his milder enforcement of orthodoxy, was, in Eamon Duffy's words, 'as conciliatory as his predecessor had been confrontational'. Anxious to legitimize Sangnier's activism, but without discrediting his predecessor's letter of 1910, the pope's first attempt at rehabilitating Sangnier in 1916 has already been discussed here. This had been primarily a pastoral and theological exercise, but one with a definite political dimension in preserving channels of communication with the French government. Within the church, though, conservative suspicion of Sangnier remained, and Mgr Chapon of Nice wrote to the pope in May 1919 to complain that the good of the Sangnier's 1916 audience had been undone by bishops' protests, so that Sangnier was 'no longer the apostle [which] is a big loss'.[16]

Benedict received the newly elected Deputy Sangnier and his assistant Georges Hoog in the Vatican on 8 January 1920. To the pope and to Secretary of State Gasparri, Sangnier gave an upbeat assessment of the prospects of restoring diplomatic relations. The Sangnier audience was bound up with the broader contours of the papacy's geopolitical strategy after the First World War. Excluded at Italian insistence from any post-war peace conference in light of the unresolved Roman question, the fact that the Vatican was not a signatory to the eventual Treaty of Versailles turned out to be a blessing in disguise. As John F. Pollard rightly states: 'Much of the Vatican's post-war diplomatic prestige was based on its distance from the peace settlement.' Anxious that Germany's humiliation could undermine future reconciliation, the Vatican objected to the idea of war guilt and the size of reparations. At the 1920 audience the pope counselled cautious collaboration in the politics of peace in an endorsement of 'engaged' faith, 'understanding that the civilising action of the Christianity should correspond to an effort to reform human institutions'.[17]

It would have been too much to expect direct papal endorsement of the League of Nations, which came into formal operation in 1920. The papacy modestly arrogated to itself the task of defining the precise nature of that Christian charity essential to the reign of peace on earth. Benedict XV, like Pius XI after him, failed to overcome his own suspicion of the 'Anglo-Protestant' League of Nations – and its pretentions to the role of global moral arbiter. The encyclical *Pacem* of May 1920 would call on nations to put aside 'mutual suspicion' and join a league or 'a sort of family of peoples [...] to safeguard the order of human society'. The papacy thus spoke the language of international arbitration but remained cool about the Geneva-based League and resented Wilson's mantle as the world's conscience. Harry Kessler, the German diplomat (and Sangnier-admirer), visited the Vatican in June 1921 where he found the Secretary of State Cardinal Gasparri 'scornful' of the Geneva victors' club; Kessler sensed some little Roman jealousy of 'the invention of the Devil in the shape of that Calvinist pastor and president Wilson'. Remarkably, though, the pope used the rhetoric of the new diplomacy to tell Sangnier and Hoog that the right to make war should be removed from heads of state. Even if parliament agreed, this tactic would buy time and, perhaps, peace. With a long-suffering air, he spoke about disarmament and his pain at having his humanitarian work for Central Europe misunderstood, 'the spectacle of Christians [...] as stubborn in their hatred as to refuse succour to hungry children'. Benedict gave very strong support to the Save the Children Fund, set up in 1919. However, back in Paris, Simone de Beauvoir recalled her Catholic mother's apoplexy at his collections for famished Austria at the door of the church of Saint-Sulpice![18]

The audience left no doubt as to the pope's approval of Sangnier's fitness to act as a Catholic representative. The Italian context was also encouraging for Sangnier. In 1919 the Vatican tolerated and even gave guarded encouragement to the new Partito Popolare Italiano (Italian Popular Party), a reformist Catholic political party led by the democratic priest Don Luigi Sturzo. Partially to help combat Bolshevism, the Vatican suspended hostilities with Italy's political institutions and withdrew the Non Expedit rule that had barred Catholics from electoral participation since the unification of Italy. Such endorsement of lay activism contributed significantly to this new Christian Democratic party winning 100 seats in the November 1919 elections. In France, meanwhile, the optics of the Sangnier audience of January 1920 alarmed intransigent bishops as the pope seemed to be endorsing the advocates of compromise with the republic in the ongoing negotiations about the Vatican embassy. Clearly, the pope's moderate 'foreign policy' needed friends, especially in France. In that context the time was right, in early 1920, for Sangnier's incipient internationalist activism to get church approval. In February 1920 Sangnier was the headline speaker at the re-inauguration of the Catholic youth movement in the diocese of Nice. The papacy's blessing of this apostolic work was a deliberate public endorsement of him as a lay Catholic activist, with special reference to peace. The local bishop, Mgr Chapon, wrote to Rome that 'seeing Marc Sangnier rehabilitated' was nothing less than an 'an act of justice'. Gasparri wrote in response to certain bishops' protests that the church welcomed Sangnier back as 'a repentant son [...] putting to work the great influence he exerts on French youth'.[19] This renewed mandate helped pave the way for his lay peace activism, which Sangnier was at last free to resume without taint of disobedience or fear of ecclesiastical sanction.

Armed with papal endorsement for his Catholic activism and sensitized by his papal audience to the global Catholic perspective, Sangnier began his protracted drift away from the conservatism and nationalism of the Bloc National. The first chinks in Sangnier's loyalty to government policy came on linked issues of social reform and the repression of strikes in 1920–1 before developing into an open breach on policy towards the peace movement and Germany. Benjamin Martin writes that, for the right, 'with the war of nations over, the war of classes resumed'. The previous legislature had conceded one of labour's long-term demands in April 1919 by enacting the eight-hour day. The Bloc National government was not interested in any more class conciliation and industrial democracy, though. With the Congress of Tours in December 1920, and the split in French socialism that gave birth to the French Communist Party, the 'red scare' intensified. On 1 March 1921 the state began the trial of ten trade union leaders accused of subversion for their part in the attempted general strike of May 1920. Appalled at the political nature of the charges, Sangnier (with the pacifist teacher Hélène Brion) spoke at the trial in defence of free speech, just as he later defended the disgraced 'defeatist' and former Prime Minister Joseph Caillaux's right to speak publicly. No friend of Communism, Sangnier advocated ideas of worker participation in a democratic workplace that were close to those of Albert Thomas, the reformist Socialist who had been French Minister of Munitions during the war and who, from 1919, was head of the International Labour Organization in Geneva. Such ideas also prefigured the theme of 'autogestion' or 'self-management' that would be echoed much later in the rhetoric of another non-Marxist Catholic, Charles de Gaulle (even if, by 1968, his version seemed quaint). In the context of the 1920s, though, Sangnier was once again betraying his own class.[20]

Sangnier told the Chamber in March 1920 that, if victory meant just 'replastering' the old world, then it was not worth it, that 'a million and a half of our comrades died not alone to push back the enemy [...] but to kill war and militarism'. However, in that same month, the United States Congress refused to ratify the Treaty of Versailles, voiding the British assurance of military assistance to France in the event of attack, undermining France's fragile sense of security *vis-à-vis* Germany. The French search for a 'security substitute' was a recurring theme of the post-war decade. The French attempted to circumscribe German power through the continued military occupations of parts of the Rhineland and the Saar and military pacts with Germany's eastern neighbours in Poland and Czechoslovakia. Reparations became the great running sore of the 1920s, with constant friction between France and Germany over what amount Germany should pay, how she should pay and whether she was in fact paying France back. France felt she had a clear moral case for a German contribution towards the massive bill for reconstruction after a war in which the ten invaded departments' population had halved since 1914. With the French state indemnifying all civilian losses, it turned to Germany, which was considered responsible for the war and therefore liable for the compensation of damages. The report of the Reparations Commission fixing Germany's total liability in 1921 was only the beginning of a new round of disputes concerning German payments. A whole series of summits met to discuss the issue between 1919 and 1924. As early as August 1920, after the Spa conference, where France secured 52 per cent of the anticipated final settlement, Sangnier, who was wholly behind the principle of reparations, identified the paradox of French wrangling with Germany, which meant that 'without one ever daring to say it, a gradual and progressive revision of the inviolable treaty is under way'.[21] Sangnier's key intuition at this point, which was to propel him down a radically new foreign policy, was that economic reconstruction in Europe could only come through transnational solutions brokered by the League of Nations.

Setting aside early criticism of the League, Sangnier, like others among its supporters, felt the young League was still plastic enough to be moulded into an entity worth campaigning for. Thus was coined Sangnier's mantra about its democratization, from a 'society of nations' to a 'society of peoples', a phrase that he constantly repeated for the next ten years. In 1921 Sangnier put down a private member's bill providing for the designation of France's three delegates to the League assembly by parliament rather than government. Eventually Sangnier envisaged direct election by the people, the better to create a 'general interest of humanity', superior to the nation-state, which would turn the League of Nations from a federation of governments into a league of the peoples themselves. Sangnier showed similar supranational enthusiasm as a member of the Foreign Affairs Commission. In June 1921 he acted as rapporteur for the aspects concerning the protection of national minorities in the bill ratifying the treaties of Saint-Germain and Paris. Giving legal sanction to League of Nations guarantees for ethnic and religious minorities in Czechoslovakia, Romania and Yugoslavia, the treaties also qualified the principle of national sovereignty and implied a right of intervention on the part of the League in the affairs of an errant state, a 'progress' towards the global rule of law that Sangnier defended against nationalist objections.[22] Finally, Sangnier and the French League of Nations movement advocated strengthening the League by giving it an armed force that could enforce decisions of the League Council. Within the peace movement, this was a 'realist' departure from the faith of Anglophone pacifists in the moral authority of world opinion alone to enforce compliance. Fearful of European entanglements for the United States, Wilson had ruled out a League army in 1919. In spite of such clever politics and a coast-to-coast campaign for the Versailles treaty (which incidentally broke his health), the president failed the test of domestic politics. Wilson was rebuffed by the US Senate, which refused to ratify the Treaty of Versailles in March 1920. To assuage Congress, plans for US membership of the League of Nations were withdrawn and the US signed a separate peace with Germany. Sangnier, though disappointed at American isolationism, still believed a credible League could be built out of those left in the ring. Acutely aware of France's weakness, he considered her security rested on a strong (preferably armed) League but also on mutual understanding between nations.

Having conferred with the pope, the head of a global church, Sangnier's foundation of a 'Democratic International' in 1921 as a transnational organization was bound to have been influenced by analogous initiatives amongst the Italian Christian Democrats and German Catholic peace activists he rapidly came into contact with. Like socialists, Catholics were trying to restore pre-war transnational networks in 1920. After the war, though, the Bolshevik revolution had made the restoration of socialist internationalism all the more difficult. It was precisely over the issue of joining Lenin's Third International that the French socialist movement split in December 1920 between Socialists and Communists. As Kaiser reminds us: 'Before World War I, party "internationalism" was widely denounced as a specifically socialist and "unpatriotic" phenomenon. Now it increasingly appeared natural for democratic parties to establish transnational links.' In this context, therefore, Catholic internationalism was not just a response to the war and the pope's peace policy but also a response to the 'red scare' in Europe in 1920 when transnational Catholic bodies were actively mobilized as a defence mechanism against Communist internationalism. German-speaking Catholics were particularly susceptible to this ultramontane reflex. Their peace leagues married Wilsonian internationalism with a Catholic and neo-corporatist tradition of the transnational church. Such a vision had been implicit in the social prescriptions of Pope Leo XIII in his landmark encyclical *Rerum Novarum* (1891). In 1920 such internationalism was counter-cultural, as the example of the Catholic trade union movement demonstrates. Between 1918 and 1920 two parallel Christian trade union internationals existed. French Catholic trade unionists refused to sit in the same room as German Catholic trade unionists. Only Dutch mediation brokered a solution. In marked contrast, the Catholic peace movement led in France by Sangnier and its equivalent among German Catholics were more radically internationalist. Indeed, the German Catholic peace movement described its members in 1928 as 'the shock troops at the service of the papal message'.[23]

Oddly enough, the new German Catholic peace movement was really begun in Austria by a German priest, who then returned to Germany in a sort of pacifist Anschluss-in-reverse. This pioneering figure was Max Josef Metzger. Born in the Baden region of Germany in 1887 and ordained in 1911, Metzger was deeply marked by his time as a military chaplain with a German field division in France in 1914. Invalided out in 1915, he was sent by his bishop to Austria to organize the alcohol abstinence movement there. It was in Graz in Austria in 1917 that Metzger founded the Weltfriedenswerk vom Weissen Kreuz (or World Peace League of the White Cross), which fundraised vigorously in neutral states such as Switzerland and the Netherlands. The White Cross was the earliest tangible mobilization of Catholics in support of Pope Benedict XV's peace policy during the First World War. In 1920, at the World Esperanto Congress at The Hague, Metzger launched a new ginger group of Catholic pacifists committed to the revision of the Treaty of Versailles. Styling itself the Catholic Peace International, but better known by its Esperanto acronym IKA, this Catholic International was composed of 19 nations, including Germany. Metzger's movement was filled with particular zeal for the Esperanto language, in which its paper *Katholika Mondo* was produced. A syncretistic language devised in Poland by Ludwik Zamenhof in the 1870s to ease ethnic tensions in multi-lingual regions, Esperanto had been taught in some POW camps during the war. Metzger saw its promotion as key to breaking down national barriers and part of a broader agenda for an imagined future in a post-nationalist world. Letters to the Vatican from Fr Metzger's Catholic International emphasized Catholic reconciliation, including collections from German Catholics to rebuild ruined churches (in France) and international monthly reparation through the Eucharist.[24]

Though Metzger was on the prophetic margins, where he led, other German priests followed. In 1917 Fr Magnus Jocham published a tract called *Wir Christen und das päplisches Friedensprogramm* with the financial assistance of the influential Catholic politician Matthias Erzberger. With the advent of the German Republic in 1919, pacifists come out into the open. The German Catholic journal *Hochland* made an emotional plea to French Catholics to restore internationalism, as feminists, intellectuals and socialists were doing: 'we are all of the same blood, the blood of Christ, so let us stretch out our hands.' In Munich, in 1919, from the bosom of Metzger's White Cross emerged the influential Friedensbund Deutscher Katholiken (FDK), or German Catholic Peace League, founded by Magnus Jocham and the Dominican theologian Franziskus Stratmann, again subsidized by Erzberger, this time to the tune of some 30,000 gold marks. These three priests – the radical Metzger, followed by the more cautious Jocham and Stratmann – were to be key collaborators with Marc Sangnier in an imminent Franco-German Catholic reconciliation project.

They provided a receptive audience when, in 1920, Sangnier wanted to test international support for a Catholic and democratic International recently proposed to him by Italian comrades. As in all such initiatives, Catholic political activists had to move with delicacy lest they seem to be undermining the clerical structure of their church by setting up a parallel lay hierarchy. Nonetheless, buoyed by the success of the Italian Popular Party in the 1919 elections, the Italian Christian Democrats began to moot the idea of a new International. On 25 August 1920 Sangnier's newspaper, *La Démocratie,* edited by his lieutenant Georges Hoog, published a letter from an Italian correspondent, Don Ernesto Vercesi. This priest was an editor of a Catholic paper, *Osservatore Cattolico,* based in Milan. A friend of Sangnier's since 1903, Vercesi had guided the Frenchman on matters relating to Italy and the Vatican.[25] Impressed by the recent foundation of the Christian Trade Unions International, he called for an analogous international Christian body, which would consider social affairs only and deliberately avoid the divisive politics of the Treaty of Versailles.

Marc Sangnier was moved by Vercesi's letter to launch an 'enquiry' in the pages of *La Démocratie* on 25 August 1920 on the desirability of a 'Democratic International'. What followed, between November 1920 and May 1921, was an extensive transnational correspondence published in the paper testing the proposal. In October 1920 the French police noted that Marc Sangnier was trying to 'organize a Democratic Christian International which would stand up against the Bolshevik International'. Hoog wrote that this effort was opportune 'as minds are still haunted by the horror of the battlefields'. From this virtual congress by correspondence the Democratic International would emerge. Don Luigi Sturzo, founder of the Italian Popular Party, wrote in support, as did Fr Metzger from Austria. However, it was the German replies that tugged most at the heart-strings. Fr Magnus Jocham, secretary of the FDK, the German Catholic Peace League, invoked Gospel forgiveness, writing of how the Germans in his group 'waited upon the redeeming words of French Catholics'. The renewal of pre-war friendships that had been put in cold storage during the war was, as John Horne points out, a key element of 'cultural demobilization' in the interwar years. The letter from Joseph Probst to Sangnier that appeared in *La Démocratie,* significantly on Christmas Day 1920, was a classic example of such a renewal of pre-1914 links. Probst was a Francophile Social Catholic from Bruchsal, in the Baden region, who had come to France in 1909 and helped in some of Sangnier's election campaigns. Beloved as an absent brother by Sangnier, Probst publicly wrung out his heart in favour of

> an International at the same time deeply Christian and boldly democratic. How could it not be the ideal of all men seized with the

sentiments of justice, fraternity and love for which we have given, for years, the best part of our hearts and souls and which alone gives sense to our lives?[26]

Even among the peace lobby, though, politics problematized internationalism. Probst's letter also called for the revision of Versailles, 'a pact that flies so much in the face of justice' as to be unworthy of a Christian International. Nor was the Belgian Mgr Simon Deploige in a mood for forgiveness. As rector of the Faculty of Theology at the University of Louvain, he had been a witness to the burning of that city and its library in 1914. Deploige sent a negative response to the enquiry, excluding Germans from the category of 'honest' interlocutors. The intensive 'red scare' made it inevitable that some chauvinistic voices would be raised. Giulio di Rossi, press secretary of Italian Popular Party, stressed the urgency of an alternative International to fight against the 'Green and Red Internationals', referring to the twin ills of anarchism and communism. Though accompanied in print by the editor's disapproval, the enquiry also published a sinister call from Charles de Woelf, of the Hungarian Christian League, for the International to endorse a common anti-Jewish, anti-Masonic agenda.[27] This was an extreme view, though, and there emerged from the correspondence an overall consensus in favour of an International that addressed political issues and was a forum for Catholics, but not just for them alone.

Even before the enquiry drew to a close in May 1921 with Georges Hoog's summation that it had demonstrated a transnational constituency for a Democratic International, it had already had a determining effect on Sangnier's own attitude to the Franco-German issue. In a crucial speech delivered at the Salle Wagram on 17 January 1921, Sangnier invited his party to cast a cold eye on the present state of the League of Nations, the ideal that had sustained fighting men like him 'during the long waiting in the trenches, rekindling [...] our courage by lighting in our hearts the glow of this new world'. Though 'one cannot vote the end of tears', their sacrifice need not have been in vain. A new type of security was required. He asked his listeners to imagine France getting all the financial and military guarantees she wanted from Germany. With a flourish, he spun around from the hypothetical to the interrogative: 'but, in truth, is that sufficient?' No, it was not enough: 'one disarms hatred also.' For even if France disarmed and chained Germany, he asked how France could 'have any security for as long as a people of 60 million men, at our very doors [...] has an aversion to the name of France and a mind for bloody vengeance'. Here Sangnier's determination for national security married the faith-based option of moral disarmament that had gestated in Sangnier's speeches since his wartime propaganda lectures. In a leader in *Jeune République* in early February 1921 Sangnier elaborated on this epiphany by questioning the political wisdom of making Germans pay well into their children's lifetime. Did anyone seriously believe, he asked, that 'for 42 years, a people of 60 million inhabitants, whose force it is said remains intact, that will revive and grow in power through the development of its economic life [...] will accept remaining the dependent of other nations'. A true society of peoples needed the educative zeal of an elite, though, to inculcate the required international spirit. Fully in tune with his leader, Georges Hoog brought down the curtain on the enquiry in *La Démocratie* in May 1921, promising just such action. Hoog announced the imminent convocation of a Democratic International that would engage in 'the formation of this international conscience without which there shall never be a true League of Nations'.[28]

In January 1921, at the moment when Sangnier coined that pivotal phrase 'the disarmament of hatred', the diplomatic omens in Europe were indifferent at best. In France, Aristide Briand had just formed his seventh cabinet, promising quick results on getting German reparations. Reflecting impatience over German application of Versailles, including the promised trial of alleged German war criminals, Briand was prepared to take a tough line with Berlin. Procrastination on disarmament and reparations provided the pretext for Briand, acting in tandem with the British, to occupy three German towns – Duisburg, Ruhrort and Düsseldorf – on 8 March 1921. However, France's weakness meant Briand engaged in nationalistic bluster to belie real concessions. Sangnier would later observe, with irony and personal relief, that it was only in parliamentary debates that Briand had fulfilled his promise to lay 'a firm hand on the scruff of Germany's neck'. In fact, in May 1921 Briand accepted the new London Schedule from the Reparations Commission, wherein France made very considerable financial concessions. This schedule reduced German debt to 50 billion gold marks over 36 years. Presented to the Germans with the menace of sanctions, Briand mobilized the conscript class of 1919, a bluff which served only to heighten France's sense of insecurity without really intimidating the Germans.[29]

Between May 1921 and the summer of 1922 German governments led by Joseph Wirth pursued a policy of 'fulfilment within reason'. Perceived as a willingness to pay, it was in fact, according to Zara S. Steiner, designed not so much to pay reparations as to bring about their further reduction. If that was the intention, it seemed to work. In October

1921, under British pressure, Briand conceded some more through the Wiesbaden agreement which instituted payment-in-kind of Germany's reparations. Now, though, the pragmatic Briand cleverly married the language of moral disarmament to that of national security. The prime minister told the Chamber of Deputies in October 1921: 'Germany is a nation of 70 million with enormous industrial capabilities. The cannons we destroy today can be replaced tomorrow.' Sangnier wanted to put his faith in German goodwill and supported Briand's policy, speaking up in the Chamber on 25 October in defence of the prime minister's distinction between 'militarist' Germany and 'democratic' Germany. Like Sangnier, Briand sensed the need for France not to go it alone without the Allies in a showdown with Germany over reparations. Briand told the International Conference on Naval Limitation in Washington in November 1921 that 'we [French] cannot bargain away our security [...] The true condition for disarmament is for Germany to know that France is not alone.'[30]

There were immediate setbacks for the new policy of understanding, such as the assassination by a German nationalist in September 1921 of the Centre Party party politician Matthias Erzberger, sponsor of the moderate FDK. The League of Nations announcement on the fate of Upper Silesia in October 1921, whose division between Poland and Germany was received in Germany as an insult to the German nation, put strains on Franco-German diplomacy also, especially when French occupation troops were the object of incidents involving pro-German elements.[31] On balance, though, Briand's new policy of giving Germany a chance to prove its good faith gave rise to a mini-thaw in bilateral relations, during which Sangnier felt the Briand government was building up increments of trust with the Weimar Republic, laying – without any fanfare – the groundwork for rapprochement that Sangnier fully supported. This gave heart to Sangnier to proceed to the next step in his own civic peace initiatives taking shape in the new Democratic International. Though former president Raymond Poincaré's ousting of Prime Minister Briand in January 1922 would be a setback for Sangnier's campaign, in December 1921 the barometer of Franco-German relations indicated a relatively calm sea into which Sangnier would launch the craft of reconciliation. Sangnier needed the active co-operation of like-minded French and Germans if his putative movement was to endure as a united force the great challenges that lay ahead in the struggle for peace.

3
'The Traitor in Berlin': Paris, Germany and Austria, 1921–2

Marc Sangnier's zeal for internationalism was driven by the memory of the late war. The international enquiry in the pages of *La Démocratie* in 1920–1 pointed the way to meeting the former enemy face-to-face. The First International Democratic Congress, hosted by Sangnier in Paris in December 1921, was an act of daring in the cause of moral disarmament. Sangnier's transnational networking during a mini-European tour in April–May 1922, visiting Italy, Austria and Germany, knitted him into a web of formal and informal diplomacy and propaganda and put him at the heart of the contested politics of reparations. Sangnier pioneered reciprocal goodwill visits to Germany by the French left in 1922. As a French deputy who was opposed to Poincaré's punitive policy from 1922, Sangnier and his Jeune République party argued passionately that the Weimar Republic risked destruction through the disregard of the French and the hatred of the Pan-Germans. For this, he risked the ire of the French right in parliament and the violence of the far right on French streets.

On Sunday 4 December 1921 a remarkable event took place in Paris at 38 boulevard Raspail, in the well-heeled seventh *arrondissement*. At the Maison de La Démocratie, headquarters of Sangnier's newspapers, occurred the first publicized gathering in the French capital since 1914 where Germans were guests of honour. Georges Hoog wrote of the occasion that its presiding idea was that 'before even disarming soldiers, it's necessary to disarm hatred'. This self-styled International Democratic Congress was the founding act of the Democratic International whose origins lay in the correspondence in Sangnier's periodical *La Démocratie* in 1920. The fact that the word 'peace' was absent from the title of this First International Democratic Congress reminds us that Sangnier's movement was very much a work in progress in 1921. Peace, however, was its overarching theme: hosted in Paris by Sangnier from 4 to 11 December, the event had Franco-German reconciliation at its heart. Its designation as a first congress gave notice that others would follow: after the second congress in Vienna in 1922, the words 'pour la Paix' were added to the gathering's title, effectively making the Paris congress of December 1921 the first of 12 annual International Democratic Peace Congresses. This first congress brought to Paris the German priest and peace activist Max Josef Metzger, who was but one of a remarkable and eclectic cast of speakers. The event soldered together Metzger's own Catholic International movement and Sangnier's Democratic International, which was acting host. This transnational Catholic activism was a moral response to the First World War. Fr Metzger cast this moral imperative in typically ultramontane terms when he told the French and Germans in Paris in 1921 that 'if only the world's three hundred million Catholic consciences were committed to the pope's vision of social justice and peace, Catholics, in alliance with other pacifists, would form an invincible phalanx for peace.'[1]

As well as being an educative congress dedicated to the formation of a moral elite, the event was also a propaganda coup. The French police anticipated it as an event of 'exceptional importance given the number of foreign delegates and the questions discussed', trailing in particular the attendance of Fr Magnus Jocham, president of the Friedensbund Deutscher Katholiken (FDK), the German Catholic Peace League, who had already played a pivotal role in forming the Democratic International in 1920–1. They further noted the respectability of the French interlocutors. Though Catholics were at the heart of this new departure, the congress drew on ecumenical support from the broader League of Nations movement in France. Liberal pacifists such as Léon Bourgeois, Jules Prudhommeaux and Théodore Ruyssen (all of the Association pour 'la Paix par le Droit') and Ferdinand Buisson of the League of the Rights of Man, all men active in the League of Nations movements, were to be in attendance. The congress functioned in the conventional manner of such political gatherings, with a series of themed commissions engaged in detailed discussion before reporting to larger plenary sessions where the major set-piece orations, which set the tone of the event, took place. Prat estimates the figure for committed participants at the congress's working sessions at between 150 and 200, though the plenary sessions attracted some larger crowds.[2] The number of official foreign delegates recorded was 47, representing 21 nations, both European and North American.

The nine German and three Austrian delegates were internationalism made tangible for the Paris audience. The nine German pioneers were a mixture of Catholic and liberal politicians and intellectuals. There were two priests, including Jocham, founder of the FDK, and also the Dominican priest and theologian Franziskus Stratmann. Hermann Platz, professor of French literature at Bonn University, was joined by Carl Muth, director of the influential Catholic periodical *Hochland*. There were also representatives from the German liberal peace movement, including two Reichstag deputies, Carl Schirner and Walther Schüking. Two Centre Party politicians completed the official delegation; Hugo Baur, a Reichstag deputy, was also president of the Centre Party in the state of Baden, the same state from which came Klara Siebert, a member of the Baden Landtag and the sole female German delegate to this Paris congress. Again in keeping with established conventions at such events, the last plenary of the congress, on Saturday 10 December, adopted a set of agreed motions based on the week's discussions. More than practical prescriptions, Sangnier's congress wished to activate popular 'peace energies' inspired by the Gospel and to evangelize on behalf of two fundamental political principles: that there existed a correlation between peace and democracy and that there was no international peace without social justice.[3]

Notwithstanding the high ideals in whose name they had been invited to Paris, the German delegation felt a lingering self-consciousness when they arrived in the City of Light. The ice was broken at the punch welcoming the Germans and Austrians on Sunday 4 December at *La Démocratie*. Anticipating the approaching Christmas, conviviality quickly displaced the guests' awkwardness. Sangnier told them that 'our present task is to make it so that the war was not fought in vain. True peace in the world will exist only when the relations between men and peoples are more normal and fraternal.' Adamant that they represented a new Germany, one that France could profitably treat with, German delegates were at pains to separate themselves from Imperial Germany. During his flying visit, Count Harry Kessler, the German minister in Warsaw, recognized Germany's duty to 'make reparations not alone materially but morally [. . .] creating a new, democratic and resolutely pacific Germany'. The warmth of the French response impressed Kessler: 'we Germans were treated with the utmost politeness and friendliness, not cold-shouldered at all.'[4]

Magnus Jocham, as a priest, let liturgical action speak louder than words, supplementing the Mass he celebrated on the margins of the congress with an act of contrition:

> We have entered France for the first time since the war, our hearts full of an unspeakable sorrow for all the bitterness inflicted on you

> for four years because of Germany. Only one thought can console us [...] that it is not so much the German people as the German government that is responsible. We would never have dared turn up here if we did not know that men [...] such as Marc Sangnier and his friends have recognised that there always were, and still are, two Germanies.[5]

The congress's working commissions between 5 and 10 December immersed participants in the challenges faced by peace activists across Europe. As such, it also provided a platform for the airing of national grievances, not least those of the defeated powers. While Fr Jocham stressed the strength of the German peace movement, he also deplored the League of Nations decision on Upper Silesia in October 1921. This decision had sanctioned the loss of much of this industrial centre to Poland, a League decision that angered Germans and which prompted the Reichstag to be draped in black in protest. Joseph Probst, Sangnier's German adoptive confrère from before 1914, told the Paris audience how this adjudication had unleashed 'suspicion and persecution' of German Catholic peace activists at home.[6] Voices were raised about the economic hardships of the German and Austrian populations, which were in part blamed on Allied bloody-mindedness in the implementation of the peace treaties.

Franco-German tensions came to the fore at the political section on 9 and 10 December and put the congress's discussions squarely in the thick of the ongoing international war of words over war responsibility. Not only did the issue bolster nationalists in each land, but it bitterly divided the peace movement. The French delegate Morane put the matter bluntly: 'Did the Germans present recognize German culpability for the war?' As Hoog later wrote: 'put in this absolute form, the question took on the characteristics of an ultimatum. There was a painful, anxious silence for a few seconds.' Professor Dietrich von Hildebrand of Munich rose to say that Christian conscience came before national loyalty and to accept that the violation of Belgium had been an 'atrocious crime'. Sangnier defused the tension by attempting to make the question one for historians rather than for the delegates, whose task it was 'to create a new, pacific spirit in the world, not to deliver an affirmative evaluation on certain facts belonging to history'. While he would not personally deny the 'responsibility of the Prussianized Germany of 1914', that was part of 'the old, militarized pagan world'. The relieved applause of the delegates showed that Sangnier's desire to draw a veil of amnesia over contested recent events was almost universally shared at the congress. The question of German admission to the League caused blood to boil again the following day. Geoffre de Lapradelle, lecturer in the Paris Law Faculty, claimed that Germany had yet to satisfy the conditions stipulated in Article 1 of the League covenant, which committed all members to have met its international obligations 'prescribed by the League in regard to its military, naval and air forces and armaments'. Under these circumstances then, 'admitting Germany to Geneva [...] without further guarantees would be like "introducing the wolf into the sheepfold".'[7]

In his desire to relegate the blame game to the realm of history, Sangnier was attempting to resolve one of the major conundrums of 'cultural demobilization' identified by John Horne, namely to reconcile the moral judgements made in wartime with the exigencies of post-war reconciliation. Nineteen twenty-one was also the year when German nationalist agitation helped abort war crimes trials held by a German court in Leipzig relating to the late war. Sangnier's first congress represented a broad church of pacifists who from the first pulled in different directions, some advancing nationalist grievances and others arguing that war itself was an intrinsic atrocity to be resisted. Accommodating both moderates and radicals, the first congress adopted concluding resolutions that were cautious, repudiating unilateral disarmament in the absence of a League armed with its own international police force. Endorsement of German inclusion in the League was balanced with a declaration of the just nature of the reparations France and Belgium expected to receive. France's part in the Allied intervention in the ongoing Russian civil war was also censured.[8] Instead of seeking instant diplomatic prescriptions, the congress laid an emphasis on moral disarmament as the week's overriding theme.

Soon the same strategy of sidelining controversies about war guilt and atrocities improvised by Sangnier suggested itself to other parts of the peace movement that had been given added impetus by Sangnier's successful congress. It was Sangnier who facilitated the first contacts between France's secular League of the Rights of Man and its younger German equivalent, the Bund Neues Vaterland (BNV). Sangnier brokered a meeting between leading French Freemason Ferdinand Buisson and the German delegation to his first International Democratic Congress, in Paris in 1921. This private meeting, which took place on 12 December 1921 at the home of Mme Ménard-Dorian, created a rapport between Buisson and German liberals such as Kessler. As a direct result of Sangnier's initiative, the League of the Rights of Man received the first official BNV delegation discreetly at its Paris seat just three weeks later, on 3 January 1922. The BNV president, Hellmut von Gerlach, who led this delegation, would return to France in the final months of 1922 on a more highly publicized speaking tour to make the case for democratic Germany. An immediate fruit of these contacts, though, was the 'Appeal to the Two Democracies' of France and Germany, jointly issued by the French League of the Rights of Man and the BNV. Published in January 1922, just a month after Sangnier's congress, it was the direct product of contacts between the two secularist movements established in December during the Sangnier congress. This new manifesto specifically called for the full opening of all national archives to disinterested research on the underlying causes of the outbreak of war.[9]

In the context of European politics in 1921–2, however, Sangnier and his Paris congress took one particularly outré political stance, and that was on Ireland. Invoking Wilsonian principles, Sangnier did not hesitate to embarrass one of France's wartime allies, Britain, over her relationship with Ireland. Sangnier was influenced in part by an older, nineteenth-century French Catholic tradition of rhetorical fellowship with oppressed Catholic peoples in Ireland and Poland, particularly associated with political thinker Fr Alphonse Gratry, whose intellectual influence on Sangnier we have acknowledged. At the opening punch on 4 December participants reserved a standing ovation not for Sangnier, nor for the returning German prodigals, but for the diminutive figure of Seán T. Ó Ceallaigh, representing the 'Irish Republic' and 'saluting in him the sufferings and heroism of a martyred people'.[10] After winning the 1918 election, the Sinn Féin movement had established Dáil Éireann in January 1919 as a separate Irish parliament. Ó Ceallaigh and his fellow Irish republican George Gavan Duffy represented Sinn Féin's underground government alternately in Paris during the Irish revolutionary era. The ongoing war in Ireland provided a gripping narrative, as seen in the protracted hunger strike and death in 1920 of Cork's Lord Mayor, Terence McSwiney, a major world news story. Sangnier's ten-year-old daughter Madeleine took Holy Communion in solidarity with the martyred mayor.

Nourished by a long-standing interest in Ireland, recalled in his propaganda speeches in 1918, Sangnier publicly thumbed his nose at Britain, which viewed Sinn Féin as seditious. As early as June 1920, in an impassioned public speech 'Pour l'Irlande libre', Sangnier declared that no amount of English coal could buy his silence about the state of Ireland. Effectively, Sangnier was endorsing the recourse to arms in Ireland since 1916 in order to break free of the British Empire. An Irish delegation headed by Eamon de Valera, president of the Sinn Féin government since 1919, was warmly received by Sangnier at *La Démocratie* within weeks of the Paris congress in January 1922. 'Ireland's struggle', Sangnier told De Valera, was like that of Alsace-Lorraine. Invoking the language of Jacobin internationalism, he made Irish freedom part of a universal cause, that of 'all men who love liberty'.[11] Their meeting came, however, at the most inauspicious moment for Sinn Féin, just as the movement was splitting into warring camps over the Anglo-Irish Treaty signed in London on 6 December 1921, during Sangnier's Paris congress. While a bitter civil war lay in store for Ireland in 1922–3, Sangnier had used the earlier seeming window of optimism to advance Irish national self-determination not just out of sentiment but as part of the broader 'Wilsonian moment', even if neither Wilson nor the British would recognize Ireland's cause.

Notwithstanding the Irish digression, the main political minefield negotiated at the Paris congress of December 1921 was the Franco-German encounter. Its happy occurrence was little short of a minor miracle. Sangnier's most public triumph was the concluding meeting of his congress, held on Sunday 11 December before an estimated 3000 people at the Manège du Panthéon, a rented arena on rue Lhomond in the Latin Quarter. It was on this public stage that Fr Metzger, a German national, spoke on behalf of the German and Austrian delegations, marking the first public speech in German in Paris since 1914. Metzger was a suitable choice for such a delicate task: it was this German priest who had begun in Austria the 'Catholic International' known as the IKA, whose ambitious programme of peace and promotion of the Esperanto language soon gained a hearing from German Catholics too. Sangnier introduced Metzger to the Paris audience with an electrifying speech that was an amalgam of mystical internationalism and the French national interest that played brilliantly on the emotions of his audience. 'After the war', he declared, 'the combatants believed it would be the last.'[12] Though the congress was open to all people of goodwill, Sangnier's rhetoric explicitly invoked Catholic reconciliation by acknowledging the Mass said by Fr Jocham the previous Friday in *La Démocratie*'s commemorative crypt dedicated to the war dead. There:

> We received Holy Communion, our God Himself, from the consecrated hands of a German priest. Yes, that was true human fraternity, superior to all, that not even the necessities of national defence are capable of breaking. For even though our evil and ill-built world can betimes oppose brothers on the battlefield, they remain brothers

> because they remain part of the same human community redeemed by the blood of the same Christ.[13]

Sangnier went beyond religious mysticism, though, to address topical concerns. On general disarmament he accepted that France's army, at 800,000 men, was too large, but he also warned that disarming France in a Europe 'still armed to the teeth' would be a crime against both France and peace itself. Sangnier asserted France's right to 'necessary reparations' while arguing that it was 'infinitely dangerous' to keep 70 million Germans outside the League of Nations: 'the more you say to me that Germany still has within her the germs of militarism, the more I will insist on the necessity of Germany entering the League.' Echoing his seminal speech at the Salle Wagram in Paris the previous January on 'the disarmament of hatred', he concluded his address even more boldly, saying: 'No, no, the French jingoists are wrong. When they say: "We shall only have security when there is not a gun or cannon left in Germany", I say: "We shall only have security when there is no more hatred in either France or Germany".' After Sangnier's address, a *frisson* of excitement was palpable as Fr Metzger took the podium on behalf of the Germans and Austrians. At this final rally, speaking directly to the people of Paris themselves, the first German speaker to do so in seven years, Metzger inveighed against the ills of capitalism and nationalism and distanced his fellow German and Austrian Catholics from the old diplomacy of distrust that had 'betrayed peoples to war'. Attacking the 'disastrous machiavelism' and 'sacred egotism' of the diplomats that had brought forth 'brutal and barbarous war', Metzger argued that only a Christian commonweal could provide 'convinced democrats' with the true moral basis for the League of Nations.[14]

Sangnier and Metzger were simultaneously sponsoring a transnational Catholic peace network activated as a response to the pope's peace policy. The Vatican was cognizant of these efforts and sent a telegram of papal blessing to the Paris congress. Georges Hoog later wrote how Benedict 'was happy, we are sure, that France was first to welcome, on her soil, Christians and democrats of all countries without exception [...] serving together the great cause of peace'. During the congress, in a gesture showing how highly respected Sangnier now was at the Vatican, he led a number of Catholic and Protestant delegates to a reception at the residence of the newly arrived apostolic nuncio to France, Mgr Bonaventura Cerretti. The nuncio returned the compliment the following month, in January 1922, when he visited Sangnier's offices at *La Démocratie* and stated the pope's explicit approval of Sangnier's Christian pacifism. 'The war is over', Cerretti declared, '[and] hatred ought to disappear to make way for reconciliation of peoples and love.' Within a week of this most public papal endorsement of Sangnier, Benedict XV took ill and died unexpectedly in late January 1922. Sangnier mourned him as a humanitarian but also as a man of 'audacious' pacifism.[15] He felt he had lost a friend who had 'supported, comforted and defended' him. As sponsor of the international Catholic peace movement who had carefully renewed Sangnier's religious mandate, the dead pontiff had left no doubt as to Sangnier's qualifications as a lay Catholic luminary at a crucial moment in his new mission.

In January 1922, therefore, Sangnier was a French politician who was making a highly publicized *démarche* in Franco-German relations that put his Democratic International on numerous political maps, such as those of the German civic peace movement, the Vatican diplomats and the French government. Sangnier's movement was both observer and actor on these national and international stages. Through his travels in 1922, Sangnier put his movement at the centre of the broader European diplomatic canvas wherein the implementation of the Versailles settlement was the pre-eminent concern between 1919 and 1924. Without ever neglecting its transnational vocation, Sangnier's Democratic International took up the cudgels at home in France in the bitter struggles over policy towards Germany in these years. The Cannes economic conference of December 1921–January 1922 had damaged Prime Minister Aristide Briand's claim to be making Germany pay her dues when his British counterpart, Lloyd George, engineered a hearing for German demands for a moratorium in repayments. Simultaneously undermined in the corridors of parliament back in Paris, Briand left the Cannes conference to announce his resignation to the Chamber of Deputies after a robust defence of his policy. 'Others will do better!' he declared sarcastically as he left the rostrum. Briand's replacement, former president Raymond Poincaré, represented the revenge of the *rentier* class for whom Poincaré embodied the hope 'that if only the treaty were strictly enforced their lives and their fortunes could be restored'. With Poincaré, the bourgeoisie were for budget austerity, sceptical about the League of Nations and doubtful of international arbitration.[16]

The change of premiership depressed Sangnier, who worried at Poincaré's 'isolation policy'. Rapidly Sangnier was drawn into the public dilemma of French leaders in the early 1920s over security and reparations. As seen in the variations in Briand's policy in 1921, French policy vacillated between extracting compensation from the Germans or pursuing collective security through the League as a means to national security. Some French stated (more privately than publicly) the need for lasting territorial guarantees (especially in the Rhineland). As Georges-Henri Soutou reminds us, the Versailles treaty had a 'dynamic and evolutionary side' in the area of occupation and reparations. It had an in-built flexibility to reflect German 'behaviour' and, in the name of executing the treaty, this allowed the French to pursue hard and soft diplomacy alternately as they saw fit. French reparations policy was the other side of the Versailles coin from territorial guarantees. The reparations policy is appreciated variously by historians either as legally and morally correct or as mean and vindictive, in what Alan Sharp describes as 'the cartoon caricature of a large Frenchman demanding money with menaces from a destitute German child'. Soutou demonstrates, in his study of French economic war aims, that the French harboured a project of permanent commercial discrimination against Germany from 1915. France, he argues, used the Versailles treaty as an 'economic arm' to establish French predominance, especially through the inter-Allied control of German raw materials and metallurgy. In contrast to this emphasis on French expansionism, Zara Steiner's general study of interwar European diplomacy makes much play of German foot-dragging on the issue of reparations to give the cumulative impression of 'a country which, though defeated, did not fully accept the consequences of its defeat'.[17] However, in truth, German politicians were often willing to pay but were frustrated with French leaders, who moved the goalposts and who seemed willing to use reparations as a surrogate for additional occupied territories.

When Poincaré returned to office in January 1922, Gustav Stresemann, leader of Germany's centre-right Deutsche Volkspartei [DVP] (German People's Party), warned fellow Germans that Poincaré would defend 'every comma of the Versailles Treaty with fervour becoming a knight of the Holy Grail'. The new French government marked a new bullishness in policy towards Germany. Sangnier was in a clear minority in parliament in querying its methods if not its ends, for he strenuously denied that he was really looking for Germany not to pay anything at all to France. On 29 January 1922 Sangnier pointedly reminded Poincaré in the Chamber that the Treaty of Versailles was kept alive only by Allied co-operation. Sangnier kept his promise to tell Poincaré of the 'other Germany'. Welcoming the forthcoming Genoa Conference, set for April–May 1922, on the economic reconstruction of Europe, Sangnier delighted the left but was derided by the right for calling for Germany's prompt admission to the League of Nations. Poincaré did not share Sangnier's enthusiasm for Genoa. As John F. V. Keiger points out, the Prime Minister kept the reparations issue firmly off the agenda and generally did his best to undermine the conference, declining even to attend but despatching his Justice Minister, Louis Barthou, with a mandate to stall proceedings.[18]

Sangnier's tour of Europe strengthened the Democratic International as a pan-European network. In Rome he met the newly elected Pope Pius XI, who in these same weeks issued a pointed letter to the archbishop of Genoa, aimed at the various European politicians gathering there, reminding them that national security depended more on mutual understanding and Christian love than on 'a forest of bayonets'. On the fringes of the Genoa economic conference itself, Sangnier met the German Chancellor, Joseph Wirth, and Don Sturzo of the Italian Popular Party. The troika's meeting represented a minor triumph for Christian Democratic transnationalism. Wirth spoke publicly of a policy of fulfilment of debts, and Sangnier praised Wirth's reasonableness in his own newspaper upon returning home. Sangnier also met the Soviet Commissar for Foreign Affairs, Grigori Chicherin, and Poincaré's representative, Louis Barthou. Meeting with a Soviet representative was daring, given that many French had been soured by the surprise signature of the Rapallo treaty between Germany and Russia on 16 April 1922, on the margins of this same Genoa conference. For Sangnier such an alliance of outcasts was the undesirable result of French hard-line policy, which had driven the Germans to look east. In Genoa, one week on from the shock of Rapallo, Sangnier met Harry Kessler, one of his most prestigious German guests of the previous December. In private, Sangnier described the 'hysteria' that had greeted news of the Russo-German treaty in Paris, where 'young men got ready to march to the Front'. Sangnier confided to Kessler that he too wished to see reparations paid – 'the mass of Frenchmen wants money, not laurels' – but what he termed Poincaré's obduracy stood in the way.[19]

Undaunted, Sangnier proceeded on to Berlin in May 1922. From the success of the First International Democratic Congress came the creation of a German Committee of the Democratic International, which Sangnier inaugurated with his visit to the Reichstag. At a tea party at the German parliament he met Centre Party politicians and Eduard Bernstein of the German Socialist Party, the SPD. The host, Walther Schücking, assured Sangnier that there was little or no hatred of France at popular level, just political resistance to rapprochement that had to be overcome. Sangnier also took lunch with Wilhelm Marx, leader of the Zentrum party (who would later serve as chancellor). Travelling on to Austria, he went to Vienna, where he shared a box at the opera with the president, Michael Hainisch, and took lunch with Chancellor Johann Schober. The Democratic International, therefore, was not just a transnational talking shop but a real network of aid and solidarity with the young German and Austrian democracies. Continuing the links established in Paris in January 1922, in the aftermath of the first congress, Sangnier called on the prominent liberal Von Gerlach at the headquarters of the new German League of the Rights of Man in Berlin, as part of the same tour. This new German human rights association, modelled on the French League of the Rights of Man, had grown directly out of the BNV. When a high-powered delegation from the elder French League, led by Ferdinand Buisson, toured Germany between 9 and 17 June 1922, even holding a meeting in the Reichstag chamber in Berlin, it was but following the example of Sangnier, who had visited the German parliament a month before.[20]

Though, as a Christian, he predicated it differently, Sangnier's faith in German democracy was part of a more prevalent discourse on the French left about the 'other Germany'. French Socialists and Communists criticized Poincaré's policies as inimical to the democratic goodwill in Germany that would truly guarantee France's peace and her borders. In the League of Nations movement, liberals, including Sangnier, wanted reparations through co-operation rather than confrontation, pinning hopes on the 'good Germany' of the democrats and republicans who represented, in Theodore Ruyssen's words, 'a minority, no doubt, but a minority that we should encourage, support and help'.[21] German pacifism itself was changed by the war with its 'centre of gravity' moving from left-wing liberalism to social democracy. The liberals of the Deutsche Friedensgesellschaft (DFG), or German Peace Society (founded in Berlin in 1892), furnished Sangnier with many important German interlocutors, such as his Berlin hosts Wilhelm Heile and Walther Schücking. Direct contact between Sangnier and Ludwig Quidde, the moral guardian of German liberal pacifism, did not come until later, in 1923. For a brief period, at the foundation of the Weimar Republic, German pacifists were relatively influential. Their credibility as loyal members of the national community was increased by the fact that most of them attacked the Versailles treaty vigorously. A very few pacifists, most notably philosopher Friedrich Wilhelm Foerster, whom Sangnier also met in 1922, dissented and conceded the thesis of German war guilt and war crimes. By contrast, Walther Schücking sat on the German parliamentary committee investigating the events of 1914 and determined to clear Germany's name. At the committee, which sat until 1930, Schücking persistently argued that the imperial government's hostility to the German peace movement was a cause of the war, an assertion that infuriated the right. As Professor of International Law at Marburg University, his pioneering scholarship in the field of international law brought Schücking academic and social ostracism instigated by nationalist circles. In 1928 he became a judge of the International Court at The Hague.[22] In spite of being inside a German liberal consensus, the peace movement was still often beleaguered and endured vitriol and violence.

However, it was Sangnier's first-order contacts with German democratic Catholic circles that had allowed the Democratic International to sprout its first tender shoots. In 1922 Fr Jocham and Joseph Probst of the FDK published a pamphlet in German presenting Sangnier's 'Words of Peace': they declared that 'what Marc Sangnier wants is nothing other than the logical application of the Christian commandment of love.' However, were these not just atypical liberal Catholics whose good faith obscured for Sangnier the essential illiberalism and imperialism of German Catholics as a whole? Marie-Emmanuelle Reytier has shown the often fraught relationship of Metzger and Jocham's democratic movements with mainstream conservative Catholicism. Already, by 1922, the FDK was anxious to avoid the taunt of anti-patriotism and the censure of cautious bishops. Nonetheless, in time Sangnier's message gained an ear in substantial parts of Catholic Germany, while the Fulda Pastoral of the German bishops of 1923, warmly received in France in the *Jeune République* newspaper, showed a new official openness to the Catholic peace movement. The confessional Centre Party itself mirrored the divergent strands in German Catholicism at this time. Richard J. Evans argues that the party remained essentially authoritarian in the 1920s, citing the conservative leadership of Ludwig Kaas from 1928.[23] However, as early as 1917, Centre Party's Matthias Erzberger was associated with peace moves and the push for constitutional reform. Democrats such as Erzberger, Wirth, Marx and Joseph Joos bound the Centre Party to the 'Weimar coalition' of Socialists, Democrats and moderate Catholics that sustained the German republic until it fell over the precipice of the Depression. Wirth, the Reich Chancellor whom Sangnier met twice at Genoa in May 1922, drew on the liberal Catholic tradition of his native Baden to position the Centre Party as a republican and centre-left party, making it a key supporter of Weimar's social welfare reforms. Notwithstanding conservative strands, notably in Bavaria, Centre Party-led coalitions supported Gustav Stresemann's moderate foreign policy from 1924. This part of Sangnier's 'other Germany' was far from chimerical.

The violence wielded against the German peace movement in general wed French fellow travellers all the more to the besieged movement. Soon after the failure of the Genoa conference, Walther Rathenau, the German Foreign Minister, was assassinated as he drove to his office in Berlin on 24 June 1922. Sangnier's trusted colleague, Georges Hoog, linked this murder and the earlier one of Matthias Erzberger (in August 1921) to those of 'three hundred and fifty German pacifists felled by pan-Germanist revolvers'. This was naïve. Erzberger, head of German wartime propaganda, and Rathenau, former head of electrical corporation AEG and erstwhile planner of the German war economy, were in fact pragmatic 'fulfilment' politicians, anxious to observe the terms of Versailles the better to preserve the prestige and integrity of the Reich. Neither Erzberger nor Rathenau had signed the Versailles treaty, but as Erzberger had indeed signed the armistice and they both attempted to work with France they formed part of the gang of 'November criminals', loathed by the radical right as traitors. Rathenau's Jewishness simply added to the odium heaped on him. As Joseph Probst was to tell the Second International Democratic Congress at Vienna in September 1922: 'it is not too much to accuse certain papers of homicide!'[24]

Having immersed himself in European diplomacy and German politics, Sangnier had returned to Paris in May 1922 more convinced than ever that French foreign policy was undermining the moderate constituency in Germany and was a 'danger' to France's long-term interests. Armed with this personal contact, Sangnier used the Chamber of Deputies to cross-examine Poincaré on the disappointing outcome of the Genoa conference in a stormy parliamentary session on 24 May 1922. He told the Prime Minister that all French governments since the war had hesitated between coercion and making concessions to Germany so as to give France the worst of both worlds, seeming both impotent and imperialist. Sangnier defended the idea of 'the two Germanies'. Germany was no chauvinistic monolith, but rather 'France's victory should also be that of those Germans who were subject to, and reduced to slavery by, militarist Prussia.' Sangnier, firmly in support of the principle of reparations, cited the contrasting example of the people of Paris, who had publicly proffered the hand of friendship to the German delegates at his congress four months earlier and the recent goodwill of his German hosts. Poincaré replied directly that Sangnier had been duped on his travels. Sangnier was careful to couch his criticism of the premier in polite terms, and to distance his critique of Poincaré from the ongoing vilification of the wartime leader as 'Poincaré-la-guerre' by the French Communists. Where Sangnier was deferential, Communist deputies such as Paul Vaillant-Couturier and Marcel Cachin violently assailed Poincaré in the Chamber as the 'baleful' nationalist who had unleashed war in 1914 and who would do so again in 1922. Outside parliament, the Communists circulated a distorted photograph purporting to show Poincaré smiling in a war cemetery, a trick so transparently unfair that the overwhelming majority of deputies, including Socialists such as Léon Blum, disavowed it in a special session of parliament in early July 1922. On 24 May, however, the right was enraged with Sangnier; there were cries of 'Bolshevik Christian!' Undeterred, Sangnier invoked the authority of both Benedict XV and Pius XI to support his recurring theme – 'the disarmament of hatred'. Though right-wing deputy Henri Rillart de Verneuil told him to 'go make your speech at Chemin des Dames or Verdun', Sangnier was convinced he was fulfilling his moral and patriotic duty in telling the truth. His supplication of Prime Minister Poincaré at the end of the session serves only to highlight this: '*Monsieur le président du Conseil*, I implore you, you who represent France [. . .] I implore you to give her back her true face.'[25]

The speech was national news. Even if violently criticized by the right, Sangnier received highly significant private support from Albert Thomas, Secretary-General of the International Labour Organization (ILO). From Geneva, Thomas wrote 'a few lines to congratulate you with all my heart':'[the speech] you made the other day was an act of reason, an act of courage.' However, Sangnier's interpellations of Poincaré in May and June 1922 completed the rupture between him and the other Christian Democrat deputies in parliament. Since 1920 Sangnier has singularly failed to unite and give coherence to the Ligue Nationale de la Démocratie, a grouping of 30 Christian Democrats in parliament ranging from centre-right to left. Conceived of by some as the embryo of a broad Christian Democratic party uniting rival cliques, the Ligue began to organize nationally. Suspicious of the conservative tendencies of the mainstream Social Catholic movement, Sangnier preferred to maintain the Jeune République's ideological purity and refused leadership of any such alliance. Neither the 'Republican Democrats' in parliament, such as Robert Cornilleau and Raymond Laurent, nor their associated newspaper, *Ouest-Eclair,* shared Sanngier's faith in democratic Germany in 1922. Cornilleau concluded that Sangnier 'was not made for party action. He's a pioneer, a soldier of the avant-garde, made for commanding an infantry battalion and not an army, still less a group of armies.' With the Jeune République's formal withdrawal in June 1922, both strands of French Christian Democracy continued their evolution, the Jeune République to the left, others towards the centrist Parti Démocrate Populaire [PDP] formed in 1924 that modelled itself on the 'popularism' of Sturzo's – Italian Popular Party.[26] Only much later, from 1925, did the PDP begin Franco-German contacts under the auspices of the Sécrétariat International des Partis Démocratiques d'Inspiration Chrétienne (SIPDIC) which it established as a transnational network of Christian Democratic parties in the mid-1920s.

Unwilling to wait that long for formal contact with Germany, and losing faith in the politicians, Sangnier turned to the people, calling a public meeting at the Manège du Panthéon for Saturday 17 June 1922 to promote the 'other Germany'. However, it was outside parliament in the ranks of the Action Française movement and in the pages of its newspaper of the same name that the most violent opposition to Sangnier's message came, not least in the form of street brawls staged by its henchmen. Its cartoonist depicted Sangnier as a figure of fun, a marionette in a German cuckoo clock. A crude commentary wondered if 'the apostle' had 'made the Boches sick' or produced 'his customary laxative effect'. Actual street violence would follow close on rhetorical violence. At the Panthéon meeting of 17 June about a hundred *camelots du roi*, the paramilitary wing of Action Française, infiltrated the meeting, producing batons and walking-sticks during Sangnier's opening remarks. In the ensuing fracas a score of male listeners sustained head wounds. Sangnier defied police pleas and determined to resume the meeting, having spirited away women and children: 'liberty is well worth shedding blood for; whatever else, I don't want to give into [. . .] a bunch of fanatics.' The meeting went ahead and was trumpeted by Sangnier's supporters as a moral triumph. Action Française placarded Paris with 3000 posters claiming the pacifists had shamed themselves by fleeing from a fight and mocked Sangnier for his preciousness over the shemozzle, in which he had merely lost his watch! This was the man who had gone to Berlin 'to embrace his [German] brothers that [had] killed our own [. . .] To Berlin with the traitor! To Berlin!' Police accounts suggest little popular antagonism to the same meeting, yet the Action Française poster crowed that the pacifist leader had been 'vomited up by the people of Paris'.[27]

Clearly, rhetoric and real violence were siblings for the royalists. The attack showed the robustness of French street politics in the 1920s, with regular strikes and clashes. The *camelots*, or 'hawkers of the King', were ostensibly newspaper vendors for Charles Maurras's nationalist movement. Originating in 1898, at the height of the Dreyfus Affair, the Action Française movement represented, according to Christopher Forth, a new culture of force in France in the early 1900s. Social Catholics like Sangnier had been stock targets since the days of the Sillon. For Maurras, street violence was a means of revitalizing the nation and a potential prelude to the collapse of the Third Republic. For final good measure, the *camelots'* manifesto thundered against this 'false friend of the people, French traitor, chief coward, darling of the communists, ever the hypocrite and liar: that's Tartuffe-Sangnier'. The last epithet was a disparaging reference to the duplicitous do-gooder character Tartuffe in Molière's play *Le Bourgeois Gentilhomme* and recalls the Action Française's literary pretensions, seeing as, from its inception, the movement used savage satirical writing and dyspeptic stage revues to attack favourite targets such as Sangnier and Aristide Briand.[28]

Blooded in the struggle to 'disarm hatred', the Democratic International turned its attention to a Second International Democratic Congress, which was held in Vienna between 26 September and 1 October 1922. Building on the civic thaw begun at Paris in December 1921, Sangnier's spring tour of Germany and Austria helped prepare the way for a second congress, which was to be held in the capital of one of the defeated powers, Austria. The congress's discussions and resolutions reflected both ongoing Franco-German disputes over reparations and the parlous state of the Austrian republic. The country was beset by a major economic crisis, which many Austrians blamed in part on the Treaty of Saint-Germain. Pan-German nationalist campaigns stoked up resentment of the Versailles treaty's express ban on Austria opting for political union with Germany. Austria's new Chancellor, Ignaz Seipel, was not in town to meet the delegates. Seipel was in fact in Geneva, desperately negotiating a League protocol with the major powers, concluded on 4 October, that would allow Austria to raise loans and enable the state to function normally. As a cleric and leader of the conservative Christian Social party, Seipel served two terms as chancellor in the 1920s, during which time he elaborated an authoritarian and corporatist government which hankered after a German connection. The choice of Vienna as venue for this second congress was most likely influenced by Sangnier's closeness to Fr Metzger's IKA, based in Austria, even if Metzger himself was absent in September. However, a very close collaborator of Metzger's, Mgr Sandór Giesswein, leader of the Hungarian Catholic peace movement, lent weight to the occasion in the old imperial capital. Reflecting the pro-peace tenor of their joint efforts, participants and organizers of the congresses began referring to them as International Democratic Peace Congresses, which they numbered retrospectively from the first congress in Paris the previous year. In terms of the pressing political disputes of the day, most of the Vienna congress's resolutions were generalized calls to virtue on the part of religious groups, educators, responsible journalists and women. Apart from calling for international agreements to restructure reparations payments, the most pointed political resolution was that of Médard Brogly, a French deputy, who called on his own country to accept payment-in-kind from Germany in materials (as agreed in principle under the Wiesbaden accord of 1921) but also for France to go further and to accept payment in the form of German skilled labour, linking practical reconstruction and moral reparation.[29]

The most striking element of the Vienna congress, though, was the platform it gave to women's political rights and to their role in the disarmament of hatred. Bringing to the fore an active cell of women activists who would hold positions of authority and influence within the Democratic International in the coming decade, these women's visible leadership role related to broader trends of increasing women's participation in the peace movement and in political activism. This was a particularly valuable avenue for French women participants, as they, unlike their German and British counterparts, continued to be denied the right to vote in the interwar period. Much of the scholarship on women and the peace movement after the First World War has focused on female socialists and the Women's International League for Peace and Freedom (WILPF). Founded in Zurich in 1919, the WILPF's origins went back to the socialist women's conference in The Hague in 1915, which had shown the way to anti-war members of the divided European socialist family, amplifying the pacifist message of exiled French writer Romain Rolland. By the early 1920s, the WILPF's international congresses were marked by radical pacifist calls for the revision of the Versailles treaty. More broadly, Erika Kuhlman has explored women's moral response to the war in the form of humanitarian activism and work for reconciliation. Mona Siegel has shown how women teachers and peace activists shaped the memory of the war: the 'staggering strength of maternal grief' had to be 'converted into a powerful force for peace'. For the peace movement as a whole in the 1920s, therefore, women occupied a privileged position in its rhetoric. Repeatedly at the Democratic International's annual congresses, Sangnier and other male speakers referred to the common suffering of mothers in war. Reflecting both his own Catholic culture and more general cultural references, Sangnier, at one such congress in London in 1924, referred to the figure of the 'sorrowing mother' who 'whether in Germany or France or England had shed the same tears'. This was an appeal to the powerful Christian trope of Mary, the Mother of Sorrows, in the 'Stabat Mater'.

Winter documents the importance of the Pietà – the grieving Mother cradling the lifeless Christ – as an aesthetic template for post-war memorials, not least that commissioned by the German Catholic Women's League and placed in the Frauenfriedenskirche in Frankfurt in memory of lost sons, husbands and brothers.[30] In Sangnier's peace movement, politics and salvation were enmeshed.

Most of the women that gravitated to Sangnier's movement in the 1920s were moderate feminists who would not have recognized themselves in the figure of French anti-militarist schoolteacher Hélène Brion, tried for 'defeatism' in 1917. However, like their more radical sisters, these women shared a sense that, though they were 'denied the right to act politically as citizens because they were women', they should continue to demand such rights specifically as women.[31] The key personality in putting women's stamp on the congresses was Germaine Malaterre-Sellier, the French suffragist and member of the Jeune République party, who was instrumental in having a session at Vienna dedicated to a women's 'peace crusade' and to having corresponding resolutions endorsed by the congress as a whole. As vice-president of the suffragist Union Française pour le Suffrage des Femmes, Germaine Malaterre-Sellier's rise to prominence in the Jeune République (becoming its vice-president in 1929) was symptomatic of that party's conversion to 'reformist' feminism.[32] This 'first wave' feminism confronted the dilemma of squaring women's political rights with the culturally conditioned expectations which cast women as mothers or caregivers. Instead of rejecting outright these essentialized gender roles, the suffragists present in Sangnier's movement embraced them and turned them into an argument in favour of expanded civil rights for women. Who better, they argued, than the mothers and the caregivers to speak and vote for an end to war? In this way, the peace movement offered women peace activists a 'back door' into political activity.[33] Malaterre-Sellier wrote in *Jeune République* in 1921 calling for women's full citizenship 'precisely because she is a mother, an educator and the principal guardian of that inestimable social value – the home'. At Vienna in 1922 she again linked peace and motherhood:

> Women have the right to tell the world their desire that the sons of their flesh be destined no more for slaughter. Let the idea of peace be our obsession! French widows or German widows, mothers of orphans in all nations, raise your children not in hatred of other peoples but in hatred of war, the only hatred allowed, the only legitimate one.[34]

As with the male veterans, the authority of direct experience was crucial amongst these women. Malaterre-Sellier, a bourgeois Catholic who married an army general in 1917, had been awakened to pacifism by her wartime experience as a front-line nurse. Similarly, the British Quaker duo of Ruth Fry and Edith Pye, who came to prominence in the Democratic International from 1923, had also been front-line nurses, whose humanitarian works continued long after the war. The Weimar Republic had granted female suffrage without the restrictions that initially applied in Britain. Already in December 1921 Sangnier had received a German female politician, Klara Seibert, as part of the official German delegation. Active in the Catholic mothers' guild in her native Baden, Seibert had lost a son in the war while she engaged in the care of the sick and injured. She was elected to the Baden Landtag for the Centre Party, where she served between 1919 to 1933, serving also as a member of the Reichstag in the final two years. The Democratic International became itself a beacon of relative equality by electing a female vice-president in Ruth Fry in 1927. French governments were even willing to appoint women as official delegates to the League of Nations assembly and to permanent commissions on children and the family. In 1932 Malaterre-Sellier became the third such French delegate, four years before the first female ministers were appointed to the Popular Front government. In 1922, in the context of the ongoing campaign for women's votes in France, Sangnier made a clear link between the disarmament of hatred and women's suffrage. He bitterly criticized the French Senate for blocking this reform in November 1922. Invoking the moral legitimacy of bereaved women, he declared that women perfectly understood 'the crime that is war. Men shed their blood [...] but you shed tears that still flow. That is why we need you in the fight against war.'[35]

The rhetoric of Sangnier and of Sandór Giesswein, the Hungarian priest and peace activist, at the closing meeting of the congress at Vienna's old Rathaus on Sunday 1 October, jointly encapsulated the meeting's mixture of practical politics and religious revivalism. Sangnier used the language of salvation to announce:

> We are – I am not afraid to use the words – militant pacifists, that is to say we wish to keep all that was generous, valiant and intrepid in the warrior spirit of other times; to gather it and turn it not towards war and hatred but against them, to save all our brethren.

On Friday 29 September, in a guided tour of the Vienna Arsenal, delegates saw the former armaments plant converted to producing agricultural machinery, literally making 'instruments of peace [... from the] engines of war'.[36] This event was filmed for posterity. Giesswein's closing speech echoed Sangnier's biblical certainty in drawing lessons from the amazing sight. Recalling his previous visit to the Vienna Arsenal as a student aged 17, at which time he had been shocked at its 'machines' and 'engines' of death, Giesswein declared that the congress participants should go home determined to hasten 'the day when not alone the Vienna Arsenal but also the workshops of Skoda and Schneider will have done the same', turning swords into ploughshares. Though his own rhetoric could be florid, Sangnier was careful to police the outer edges of the congresses to avoid extremist embarrassment when heady words were in the air. The Vienna congress was the only one of the 12 such congresses where the ultra-pacifist French priest Léon Demulier spoke. His support for papal peace policy extended to his taking an effectively pro-German stance on the peace settlement, rejecting the moral basis of Versailles, which Sangnier still defended. Demulier's publication *La Correspondance catholique franco-allemande* was initially supported by the Vatican until his open collaboration with extreme left anti-militarists caused him to be put under episcopal ban in 1925. Though he spoke at the German Katholikentage of 1930 to denounce his own country, Demulier could not embarrass Sangnier, who had effectively cut him adrift after the 1922 congress.[37]

By contrast, Giesswein, Metzger and Sangnier were at the heart of Catholic transnational peace efforts and had already acted as direct emissaries of the Vatican's policy of European pacification under Benedict XV. As at Paris in 1921, and in what would become an established pattern, Sangnier requested a papal blessing on the work of the Catholic delegates present at the Vienna congress. His request recalled the papacy's stance in favour of the 'disarmament of hatred and the establishment of a stable peace' through material and moral disarmament. The requested blessing arrived in time to be read out at the congress's close. The new pope, Pius XI, looked favourably on Sangnier's Democratic International, awarding its general secretary Georges Hoog a papal honour, the knighthood of Saint Gregory the Great, in November 1922. At Christmas 1922 Pope Pius published a major encyclical outlining the key themes of his papacy. Entitled *Ubi Arcano Dei Consilio*, it set out a programme for the restoration of human society through the 'reign of Christ'. The pope regretted how since the war 'public life is so enveloped, even at the present hour, by the dense fog of mutual hatreds and grievances that it is almost impossible for the common people so much as freely to breathe therein.' In language similar to that of Sangnier, he argued that the post-war peace 'was only written into treaties. It was not received into the hearts of men, who still cherish the desire to fight one another.' Patriotism, the pope warned, could degenerate into a hateful nationalism. [38] Such words acted as implicit endorsement from Pius XI of the transnational Catholic activism of Sangnier, Metzger and Giesswein over the 'exaggerated' nationalism of their opponents.

Endorsed by two popes, Sangnier's place in the European Catholic political elite was secure. However, in 1921–2 Sangnier had reached out not only across the Rhine but also within France to the secular peace movement, even facilitating the vital first links between French and German secularists in the League of the Rights of Man and the BNV. Offering a Catholic variant on the broader discourse of the 'other Germany' on the French left, Sangnier had taken political risks by bringing the Germans to Paris and taking his second congress to Vienna. Giving space to the untapped activism of women was an astute move that energized the Democratic International. Though going against the prevailing winds of diplomacy, these meetings gave sufficient courage to insiders to be worth the inevitable opprobrium from outsiders. This same courage would be severely tested in 1923, with the radical deterioration of France and Germany's relationship on account of the Ruhr occupation. The Democratic International's acts of reconciliation would become even more daring – and the opposition to them even more violent – in response.

4
From Pragmatist to Dove: Freiburg-im-Breisgau, 1923

In 1922 the activism of the Democratic International was put on a European footing after its foundation in Paris in December 1921. These civic contacts between Catholics, democrats and pacifists developed against the strained background of the reparations disputes between the victorious powers and Germany and Austria. This troubled political context and atmosphere of latent conflict was a continuation of wartime enmity. Such political and cultural obstacles were clear to Sangnier from his visit to Germany in May 1922 and his two visits to impecunious and hungry Austria in 1922, especially his second visit, in September, for the Second International Democratic Congress, which had convened in Vienna for a week. That had also been the juncture at which the annual gatherings were formally rebranded as the International Democratic Peace Congresses, merely making official the focus on peace that had been present from the moment of their inception. More generally, the issue of whether Germany could and should pay France war-related compensation, and in what way it should be paid, was a divisive question, akin to a fetid wound on European diplomacy in 1922–3; it infected both countries with anxiety, recrimination and fear for the future. In 1923 strain gave way to full frontal confrontation between France and Germany over the Ruhr invasion begun by France in January 1923. By narrating the incremental stages of the Franco-German confrontation, and then taking a bird's-eye view of the long and ongoing historical controversy over German and French policies, we can then see in their proper contexts Sangnier's political campaigns in France in 1923, and how those campaigns propelled the Democratic International to vertiginous heights of daring by taking the Third International Democratic Peace Congress to Freiburg-im-Breisgau, in Germany itself, in August 1923.

The background to the French-led occupation of Germany's Ruhr district in 1923 is as simple or as complicated as the observer makes the interpretation of bare facts. In 1922 the security concerns of the French government (led by Prime Minister Raymond Poincaré) were bound up with both reparations payments and territorial guarantees. The stakes were as much psychological as pecuniary when it came to reparations for, as Conan Fischer maintains, they had become 'the litmus test of German intentions and the viability of a compromised peace treaty'.[1] The German government of Chancellor Joseph Wirth (1921–2), the Centre Party politician who had so impressed Sangnier in their personal meetings at Genoa in May 1922, claimed to be pursuing a policy of 'compliance' with peace settlement stipulations and to be normalizing relations with France. Poincaré remained sceptical about this 'goodwill'. When, on 12 July 1922, the German government sought a moratorium on cash payments until 1924, Poincaré refused and ordered the review of contingency plans, including those for a military occupation that would seize productive guarantees in the German economy in lieu of reparations duly remitted. Cautious on the extent of German 'compliance' under the Wirth government, Poincaré had no faith in the ability or even the true willingness of the next government, of Chancellor Wilhelm Cuno (appointed in November 1922), to give France satisfaction. When Germany defaulted on resource transfers in December 1922, French plans for invasion were made operative.

In a move characterized by Fischer as 'predatory and explicitly revisionist', Poincaré sent troops into Germany's industrial heartland – the Ruhr – on 11 January 1923, in fulfilment of a long-term threat to take by force the coal and mineral deposits that were France's by right. There was indeed the cover of a Belgian and Italian presence in the force, but Poincaré was acting against the wishes of the British. The week after the troops went into the Ruhr, in January 1923, Sangnier's editorial in *Jeune République* lamented that 'nationalism and pan-Germanism are making up daily the ground they had lost during the Wirth ministry.' Did one really believe that such an operation would inculcate in Germany 'the goodwill to pay?' he asked.

Faced with an occupying force of some 70,000 to 100,000 Allied soldiers, Germany's government and people defied the invader through an official policy of passive resistance aimed against the 'illegal' occupation rather than reparations themselves. 'Active' (i.e., violent) resistance operated with a 'murky, semi-legal status'. Historians have debated long and hard the policies and strategy of the two main protagonists in the Ruhr dispute, with the issue of French 'imperialism' and German bona fides providing twin peaks of neuralgia. Was Poincaré's occupation in 1923 just a matter of sending in the bailiff to collect due debts, or was it in fact an old-fashioned annexationist power grab? Were such incursions inherent in a treaty that heedlessly humiliated Germany? Since the 1990s Zara Steiner's work has maintained that the major problem with the peace settlement was not any intrinsic harshness but the lack of sufficient will to enforce it properly. In an historical debate open to constant revision, the arguments have continued to evolve. More recently, Alan Sharp and Conan Fischer have reminded us just how problematic such treaty compliance was, in practice, in the Europe of its time.[2]

Incontestably, by the start of 1923 Poincaré believed the 'policy of compliance' elaborated in 1921–2 by the Wirth coalition in Germany was not delivering France's needs and rights. However, as well as being a police operation, the seizure of German plant and materials also related to long-term French aims for economic hegemony over Germany, as demonstrated by Georges-Henri Soutou. More fundamentally still, the question arises of whether the French were attempting to undermine the very territorial and political unity of Germany. Such a geopolitical coup had been ruled out by the Versailles treaty itself after the peacemakers rejected the creation of an independent Rhineland buffer-state as advocated by Marshal Foch in 1919. Sharp and Fischer are unequivocal on French designs for the Rhine: 'the French were seeking, not merely to enforce, but to revise the settlement.' No doubt there was a noisy 'Rhineland lobby' in France (led by the nationalist writer Maurice Barrès) who saw in the west bank of the Rhine a springboard for French penetration and influence within the Reich or even as an autonomous polity detached from it. Historians such as Fischer and Stanislas Jeannesson see in Poincaré's occupation of the Ruhr in 1923 proof of France's 'imperialism', Jeannesson referring to it as part of a 'deliberate French policy to separate the Rhineland from the rest of the country and treat it as an autonomous entity.'[3] Jeannesson points to the massive eviction of Prussian civil servants, the seizure of the railways and the creation of a real economic boundary with the rest of Germany to support his thesis.

On German good faith in the matter of meeting reparations payments, the historical jury is similarly deadlocked, with some, such as Sally Marks and Stephen Schuker, maintaining the Germans deliberately used hyperinflation as a means of evasion, while Gerald Feldman argues that in 'the real world of Weimar Germany', social and political circumstances made fulfilment impossible.[4] Moreover, if the Germans were incorrigible laggards, how can one explain their willing return to the negotiating table in 1924, once the tactics of the schoolyard bully employed by France rebounded on them and the French were shamed into a less punitive policy? The Germans' lack of co-operation with France in 1922–3 is best understood as a response to the threat or use of military occupation by France, rather than a refusal of reparations *per se*. Indeed, payments-in-kind to France had in fact continued until January 1923, while the Germans were more than willing to negotiate a new reparations deal once the joint Franco-Belgian force left the region. In 1924, there emerged a revised reparations settlement based on the report of a leading American banker Charles G. Dawes. The German government's hearty embrace of international mediation in the form of the Dawes Plan in 1924 is frankly at odds with Zara Steiner's portrait of a miscreant Germany.

Neither should this make of Poincaré a pantomime ogre, bent on expansion at all costs. In contrast, Sally Marks portrays Poincaré as more of a blunderer, the great procrastinator who had no grand plan: 'the strong man emerges as timid, irresolute [...] and indecisive', consistently failing to grasp opportunities to maximize French power. The recent study by Anna-Monika Lauter reminds us that Poincaré's policy cannot be evaluated in isolation from French domestic opinion on Germany, which she characterizes as sceptical of military adventurism to the point that Poincaré was obliged to dissimulate his more far-reaching objectives behind the cloak of a simple police operation. Indeed, we have seen for 1922 how sensitive Poincaré was to the French Communist caricature of him as 'Poincaré-la-guerre', a successful rhetorical ploy of the PCF, by then two years in existence. In the case of the reliably non-Communist Sangnier, however, his immediate rejection of the Poincaré policy in January 1923 was at total odds with the French mainstream, at the outset in any case. Announcing the invasion to the Chamber of Deputies on 11 January, Poincaré called for 'sacred union' in this supreme hour of war by other means. Deputies obliged; they supported government policy by a margin of 478 to 86, a vote repeated even more emphatically at the end of the year, on 23 November 1923, when the occupation seemed to be yielding some financial dividend. In sum, Poincaré had the support of the moderate right and of some of the Radical Party. This party, founded in the wake of the Dreyfus Affair with the name Parti Républicain Radical et Radical-Socialiste, was the pivotal party of government in France between 1901 and 1940; its programme combined anticlerical republicanism and rhetorical radicalism with the solid defence of the petty bourgeoisie. In 1924, Poincaré's domestic policy and the drastic deterioration in French finances connected with the military outlay for the Ruhr unsettled the Radicals and brought his majority under strain.[5] Already in 1923, a year out from the projected elections of 1924, the peeling away of left-leaning Radicals from the Bloc National helped incubate an alternative left-wing coalition with a different emphasis in foreign policy.

Sangnier's public disagreement with Poincaré nestled in the broader ambit of the French left's critique of national policy, even if parts of the left were cautious of wading in too far in Germany's defence. For instance, some of the liberals close to Sangnier in the moderate League of Nations movement showed ambivalence about condemning specific French actions in the Ruhr, as we shall see at the Freiburg congress that they collaborated in. While well capable of nationalist reflexes when French policy was under attack by outsiders at international gatherings, within France old-style liberal pacifists such as Théodore Ruyssen still spoke the Briand-style language of collective security, arguing that by bringing Germany into the League of Nations, France could 'truss [her] in the bonds of law and solidarity, so that she could never sunder them with a brutal or isolated effort'.[6] On the whole, therefore, in the camp of the opposition to Poincaré, the French League of the Rights of Man voiced objections to French policy and continued fraternal contact with German counterparts, led by Von Gerlach, even sending a prominent member, Paul Langevin, to speak in Berlin in July. As for the political parties of the parliamentary opposition, their German policies accentuated the sour aftertaste of the split suffered by the Socialist movement three years before. At the Congress of Tours (1920) a majority of delegates voted for adherence to the Third International and formed the Parti Communiste Français (PCF). Loudly proclaiming their opposition to capitalist war and militarism, which they viewed as an instrument of the bourgeoisie, the French Communists scandalized many by their apparent anti-patriotism. The Section Française de l'Internationale Ouvrière (SFIO), the Socialist minority who nevertheless retained more parliamentary representation than the PCF, were led by Léon Blum. Themselves also critical of the Versailles treaty and of Poincaré's policy, the Socialists accepted reparations as legitimate but were resolutely opposed to any attempt to undermine German unity.

Socialists in France placed their faith in international negotiations and in the strength and resolve of the SPD, Germany's mass Socialist party, to tame the dogs of war. However, in terms of Franco-German worker solidarity, French Socialists were upstaged and embarrassed by the daring of the French Communists, who aligned themselves with German nationalists against French imperialism. German Communist speakers such as Rosi Wolfstein visited France, while French Communist deputy Marcel

Cachin spoke in support of German working-class resistance to the French policy at a meeting in Essen on 6 January 1923. Politically convenient for the Bloc National, the twinning of the Bolshevik and German threats permitted government repression of French Communism when parliament waived the parliamentary immunity of Cachin and a score of Communist deputies whom they imprisoned. The initiative passed to the Jeunesses Communistes, who shocked public opinion with posters advocating fraternization between French soldiers and German workers in the Ruhr. Though no Communist, Sangnier voted against the lifting of Cachin's immunity, as he felt it was politically motivated manipulation of the law.[7]

Troubled by France's isolation – Poincaré was acting with Belgian support, but without Britain – and echoing the views of the broad left outline above, Sangnier and his Jeune République went on a war footing across France to dissuade public opinion from such perilous adventurism. The party took their critique of Poincaré's policy to the people in a series of public meetings in the first half of 1923. The embedding of their campaign in the rhetoric of the secular left brought Sangnier's Catholics together in a scandalous 'sacred union' with the church's historic enemies, such as Ferdinand Buisson of the League of the Rights of Man, a pact from which Sangnier did not flinch: 'When we were defending France's existence during the war, well were the priest and the Freemason together in the same trenches.'[8] Georges Hoog accentuated the campaign's popular impact across France to his Franco-German audience in Freiburg in August:

> In Rennes, capital of Brittany [...] as in Saint-Etienne, the great working-class town, in Bordeaux as in Lyon, in Paris like at Lille, capital of the devastated regions, everywhere, our ideas received serious, thought-out and ultimately enthusiastic welcome from populations who have suffered too cruelly from war not to passionately desire peace.[9]

Police reports on this campaign show it had a reasonable popular resonance and that the predictable disruptions staged by the Action Française gave it added publicity and showed the tour was too significant for its opponents to ignore. In his stump speeches, Sangnier displayed pragmatic liberalism, pointing out that only co-operation with Britain and the US could make Germany pay her dues. In Nantes, in front of an estimated crowd of 450, he marked out Poincaré as an annexationist, attacking what he called a 'myopic policy' aimed at reversing

German unity. Poincaré had succeeded in blackening France's name internationally, even with the Vatican. Means, rather than the ends, of getting reparations were what divided him from Poincaré. Similarly, in Lyon on 19 March, Sangnier declared his certainty that a prolonged occupation would ruin both countries. This declaration was followed by a 20-minute tumult from the Action Française, who threw rotten eggs and stink bombs. In Lille in May (where the Action Française publicly burned copies of the *Jeune République* paper) he pointed out to a critic in the crowd that the position of that whole swathe of Catholic and socialist opinion in Germany, once favourable to France, had been terribly compromised by the Ruhr. If the government's distrust of Germany was that profound, 'would it not be more logical for [them] to demand the annexation of the Ruhr?'[10] Communist encouragement of French soldiers to fraternize with fellow German workers in the Ruhr was anathema to the French public, but the fair hearing Sangnier's campaign received in the country further supports Anna-Monika Lauter's assertion that mainstream French public opinion was at best ambivalent towards the new 'war' France was taking to Germany.

While Sangnier's campaign in the country was having a slow-burning effect on public opinion, at the end of May 1923 his opponents suddenly catapulted him centre-stage in a manner that could only reflect publicity onto his speeches on the Ruhr occupation. As we have already seen, the *camelots du roi*, the paramilitary wing of Action Française, had long been intimidating their opponents with physical and rhetorical violence. The year 1923 was a particularly busy one for 'the King's hooligans', as Sangnier memorably called them.[11] In the context of the Ruhr crisis, the Poincaré government portrayed the Communists as the 'enemies within'. In this fevered environment an anarchist called Germaine Berton assassinated the head of the *camelots*, Marius Plateau, on 22 January. The extreme right responded by wreaking vengeance on the moderate left. On 10 May a band of 40 *camelots* attacked the former prime minister and convicted defeatist Joseph Caillaux on the street in Toulouse. The left, in turn, felt the government was giving immunity to the supporters of Maurras not given to the French Communists; for the French left it was eerily reminiscent of the Blackshirt mobilization of 1922 in Italy which had helped Mussolini bully his way to prime ministerial office.

Finally, the Action Française pushed its street theatre too far. At 8.20 p.m. on the evening of 31 May 1923 Sangnier, accompanied by Paul Chatelat, his secretary and future son-in-law, was on his way to a rally against the Fascist threat in France hosted by the League of the

Rights of Man. Suddenly he was hauled from a cab on boulevard Raspail, tarred and nearly forced to 'swallow the contents of a flask of castor oil'. Ten minutes' walk away, in the quartier Notre-Dame-des-Champs, a royalist medical student threw the contents of a bottle of ink at Maurice Violette and his wife, soiling the former Radical minister's face. Thirdly, Marius Moutet, Socialist deputy for the Rhône, sustained a head injury in a simultaneous assault.[12] All three had been going to the same meeting. Rescued by two policemen, one of them off-duty, Sangnier, in new clothes, arrived undeterred at the Salle des Sociétés Savantes to a delirious welcome. When the whole of parliament united (apart from the extreme right) to condemn the attacks the following day, Sangnier spoke powerfully from the rostrum, saying he would not be cowed:

> They can do as they wish; I shall always remain above these shameful methods. They can tar me. They can, better than last night, force me to drink Fascist castor oil. They can injure me [...] They can even kill me; but what they will not do is make me hate. That, never.[13]

The incident was clearly a continuation of the earlier attacks on Sangnier's Ruhr speeches and the blows that had rained on Sangnier's Panthéon meeting in June 1922. It also has broader reverberations for our understanding of the nature of French politics in 1920s. George Mosse argues that the war itself engendered a new strain of rhetorical and physical violence in domestic politics in interwar Europe. Such brutalization represents, for Audoin-Rouzeau and Becker, a banalization of violence in domestic politics. Even more apt, perhaps, is Michael Geyer's concept of the creeping 'habitualization of war' in Europe's civil sphere. Geyer describes how both Fascists and militant leftists pursued the 'mobilization of society for war as social therapy, or [...] aimed at the violent creation of new societies [...] defined by war or by the threat of it'. *Camelot* attacks on Sangnier in 1922–3 fitted into a broader pattern of violence from both extremes matched by the violent rhetoric of government against its 'internal enemies', the Communists. These events oblige us to nuance Antoine Prost's argument that French politics was not 'brutalized' by the First World War. French politics was not as violent as Germany's, but political disputes spilled over into the street, undermining Prost's contention that 'this conception of politics as the continuation of war was peculiar to Germany'. By the same token, however, the attack on deputies produced a democratic reflex that counted as a real countervailing republican resilience in France. In terms of more mundane day-to-day politics, the physical attack on the deputies catalysed a shift in Radical Party allegiances in the Chamber in which the issue of the Ruhr was relevant but not central.[14] The decision of 48 Radicals to refuse to vote confidence in the Interior Minister in light of the attack on the deputies marked a cooling of the Radicals towards Poincaré's administration. The broad republican coalition from centre to centre-right elected in 1919 was beginning to break down, with the Radicals tacking to the left. The eternal swing votes in the parliament of the Third Republic, the Radicals were equivocating between centre-left and centre-right again. After public agonizing, conscience and political self-interest miraculously coincided and the Radicals changed horses. The attack on Sangnier was one of the events that sowed the seeds for the victorious 'Cartel des Gauches' coalition of Radicals and Socialists of 1924.

Meanwhile, passive resistance was crippling Germany. The humanitarian situation in Germany pricked consciences in France. The French government set up soup kitchens for the very hungry in occupied areas: the human cost of the pursuit of reparations through occupation was real, especially, as Conan Fischer reminds us, for some 300,000 evacuated children. Humanitarian concern from abroad was not lacking. Communist-leaning French women teachers raised money for children of the Ruhr in 1923, as did French women in the Women's International League for Peace and Freedom (WILPF). Cardinal Schulte, the archbishop of Cologne, made forceful protests. Against this troubled background, Sangnier marked out his distance from those many French Catholics who supported Poincaré. Sincerely appreciative of Poincaré's policy of religious tolerance and non-sectarianism, Sangnier was still unsparing towards ultra-nationalist French Catholics who had found the pope's recent critique of nationalist idolatry distasteful. In parliament, in July 1923, Sangnier burnished once more his credentials as a loyal son of the papacy by being the only Catholic deputy to defend the indirect intervention by Pope Pius XI on the Ruhr crisis. This had taken the form of a published letter to his Secretary of State, Cardinal Gasparri, in which Pius was implicitly critical of French policy as punitive and unjust. Sangnier, in turn, married his own pragmatism on the reparations question to his ultramontane idealism. 'If there should be reparations – and there should, if we need guarantees – as we do – it matters that our concern to procure them does not make us forget the exigencies of divine charity', the deputy declared.[15] Sangnier's next major initiative in defence of the 'other Germany' was also bound to raise eyebrows: going to Germany on a peace mission to the German people while French troops occupied part of their country. The poor backdrop merely made such a daring symbolic act of reconciliation between France and Germany all the more imperative in his eyes.

In spite of practical and political road-blocks, Sangnier and his German interlocutors pressed on. Why go to Freiburg-im-Breisgau, in the state of Baden, though? Though geographically removed from the epicentre of confrontation in the Ruhr, Baden, indeed anywhere in the Reich, was an audacious choice of venue for the forthcoming congress. Symbolically located on the Rhine, a crossroads of German, Swiss and French influences, it was near the new border of the post-1919 Reich, Alsace having reverted to France. Freiburg was a centre of Catholic theology and had a liberal political tradition. In the nineteenth century it had been home to the Freiburg Union, which had pioneered Social Catholic thought even before *Rerum Novarum* (1891). The city was the nodal point in the 1920s of several Catholic internationalist bodies, such as the Union Catholique d'Etudes Internationales and the student-oriented Pax Romana. Joseph Wirth was the local Reichstag deputy. After Hoog's preparatory visit in June, Joseph Probst liaised between Paris and a local committee.[16] The auxiliary bishop of Cologne, Mgr Stoffels, was supportive. But if the local climate was suitable, the German national outlook was dire.

The congress coincided with the dying days of the Cuno government. On 14 August a new coalition of moderates and Socialists took office under Chancellor Gustav Stresemann. By late September the process of stabilization had begun, with Stresemann abandoning passive resistance. However, during the week of the congress itself, between 4 and 10 August, rumours of social and political revolution abounded. In these same August days, Médard Broglie, a French deputy from Alsace who had travelled with Sangnier to Vienna a year before, now pleaded with Sangnier and the French delegates, on the platform of Mulhouse railway station, to turn back for their own safety. In Freiburg itself, Adam Remmele, the Socialist premier of the Baden region, braved nationalist threats in accepting the Democratic International's invitation to speak at the opening session. German participants had to be intrepid in light of transport chaos in the country. Of the estimated 7000 participants, many were obliged to take the rack railway over the hills of the Black Forest, a mere tourist attraction normally, as the occupation of Offenburg had severed the rail link between north and south Baden. One 16-year-old German Catholic, Wilhelm Solzbacher, left his home town of Bad Honnef, near Bonn, for Sangnier's Peace Congress in Freiburg. After defeating the odds of a rail network paralysed by the

French invasion and German resistance, and even making part of the journey by steamboat, Solzbacher wrote that he got to Freiburg with hostility to the French beating in his heart. The Freiburg congress disarmed his prejudice and 'changed his life'.[17]

The most basic aim of the congress, which opened on Saturday 4 August, was for Sangnier and his 125 fellow French to show 'the other France' to the Germans: 'France is not just her government and her newspapers. It is more, it is better than that.' 'Material and moral disarmament', the mainstays of cultural demobilization, were firmly on the agenda. Historians John F. V. Keiger and Martin S. Alexander have written of the challenges of enforcing arms limits on Germany after 1919, reflecting the broader historical debate on the many forms of interwar disarmament. A discussion at the congress, on Wednesday 8 August, on the disarmament clauses of the League Covenant, agreed that German disarmament was justified as the first stage in a general disarmament. The English Liberal MP Sir Willoughby Dickinson announced: 'either all disarm in concert or all re-arm in competition.' Delegates could not entirely duck the ongoing Ruhr crisis, however, which bubbled under the surface of the congress. In a spirit of self-censorship, Sangnier and the congress did their best to avoid such divisive questions. This was nothing new in the peace movement. The Franco-German Interparliamentary Committee meeting in Basle in June 1914 had prevented discussion of Alsace-Lorraine.[18] Referring to the Ruhr, the new elephant in the room, a British Quaker, Gertrude Giles, observer wrote of Freiburg that:

> The actual burning question of the moment was not discussed for some days, although we were all thinking about it. It almost seemed as if the members were afraid to start a discussion as they could not tell into what deep waters it might bring them. There were some fine addresses [...] but there was a hesitation to speak out upon the present state of affairs.[19]

Inevitably, some speakers broke the taboo. Joseph Joos, a nationally prominent Centre Party 'progressive', told the opening meeting that 'the Ruhr' represented 'an idea diametrically opposed to that which this movement and congress should represent in the world'. On the same occasion, regional premier Adam Remmele referred to the 'new injuries and humiliations that had been constantly inflicted on [Germany]', adding that the 'declaration of unique culpability imposed on Germany is a grave moral error'. Sangnier had no problem repudiating the Ruhr invasion *per se*. Was it possible 'to save a country while destroying another?' he asked rhetorically. For now, though, he avoided the larger issue of reparations' moral basis: 'We don't have the qualifications to revise the treaties.' It was only during a study commission, however, that a full-blown argument over the occupation erupted, pitting old-style French 'patriotic pacifism' against brash German radical pacifism. For Sandi E. Cooper, France's Association pour 'La Paix par le Droit' (founded in 1886) and its leaders, Ferdinand Buisson and Theodore Ruyssen, were the epitome of this late nineteenth-century liberal internationalism. In their old age, both men were actively involved in Sangnier's congresses and were present at this Freiburg congress. Ruyssen, veteran president of the APD, was in fact an apologist for the Ruhr intervention at the Freiburg congress, in keeping with his organization's doctrinaire legalism on the issue. This new evidence qualifies Norman Ingram's assertion that, from 1922, Ruyssen had reverted to scepticism about French government policy. Proclaiming Poincaré to be no more than the 'punctilious defender of the post-war settlement', Ruyssen dismissed as exaggerated German accounts of civilian suffering owing to the occupation. On passive resistance in the Ruhr, he allowed himself to wonder aloud just how 'passive' an act of sabotage was. He was speaking in the context of violent incidents such as the Hochfeld Bridge explosion outside Duisburg on 30 June, which killed nine Belgian soldiers and which had a large and negative impact on French public opinion. Gertrude Giles despaired of what she saw as this 'one-sided' pacifism: 'We might have been taking part in any other sort of Congress rather than be assisting at a Peace Congress.'[20]

More to the Quakers' liking was the rejoinder to Ruyssen from the German Nikolaus Ehlen (1886–1968), who called for actual German youth participation in the reconstruction of devastated regions of Belgium and France, 'not in order to execute a treaty which he criticized forcefully but to "bury hatred" '. Ehlen, a former army officer and teacher at Velbert, was to become a significant contributor to Sangnier's congresses throughout the 1920s. He was the leader of what is best described as a diffuse 'Grossdeutsche Jugend' tendency which formed the most radical pacifist fringe within German Catholic peace and youth movements of the 1920s. The Grossdeutsche Volksgemeinschaft (Greater German People's Community) provided this zealous minority with an organization to calls its own when it came into being with 300 members in 1922, as a leftist offshoot of Fr Magnus Jocham's mainstream Catholic peace association, the Friedensbund Deutscher Katholiken (FDK). Sangnier described this new avant-garde of German

Catholic peace activism as 'a strangely mystical, fraternal youth [...] adopting theories close to those of Tolstoy on non-resistance to evil'. Ehlen was also willing to raise the benighted issue of war crimes. Most German pacifists rejected the idea of German war guilt and war crimes. A few exceptions readily accepted both, blaming them on the entire militarist culture of the Kaiserreich. Ehlen was one such exception, as was the philosopher Friedrich Wilhelm Foerster, both men becoming known directly to Sangnier through their active participation in his Peace Congresses. As we saw in Chapter 1, atrocity stories were the subject of a furore in 1914 and the revived war culture of 1923 re-ignited the controversy, with French and Germans attempting to put each other in the dock. Ehlen criticized his own country for not 'proclaiming openly enough' its complicity in war crimes. 'Quickly,' he opined, 'we no longer thought about the odious invasion of Belgium.' But he proceeded to relativize the events of 1914 in light of ongoing French 'harsh methods' in the Ruhr: 'Brute force is taking vengeance on children, the sick and loads of innocents, poisoning their hearts with hatred.' (In point of fact, it is attested that in 1923 the French did indeed make widespread use of civilian hostages as human shields on the railways.) Such talk left Sangnier open to the charge, back in France, that he had indirectly given solace to the traducers of France. Before parliament, Sangnier later defended himself by saying that he had asked the complainants for documentary evidence precisely as he wished to 'refute a calumny'.[21]

In light of these disputes, liturgy and symbolism played a crucial unifying role, given that politics divided delegates. Thus verbal exchanges were matched by a strong liturgical element. As at Paris in 1921, the Catholic Mass amplified the theme of redemptive sacrifice and provided a sacred space for intra-Catholic reconciliation. While Protestant congress delegates gathered simultaneously in a nearby Lutheran church for an act of worship in accordance with their tradition, Catholic delegates attended a special requiem Mass celebrated in Freiburg Cathedral by the local archbishop. The chaplain of Berlin University Franziskus Stratmann (1883–1971), who had also served time as a military chaplain during the war, preached. The homily of this noted German Dominican and pacifist took as its theme the motto of Pope Pius XI 'Pax Christi in Regno Christi' and made several apt references to the recent papal encyclical *Ubi Arcano Dei Consilio* of Christmas 1922. Fittingly, for a community in mourning, turned towards reconciliation, the setting of the mass sung was *Missa in honorem BMV Matris dolorosae*, composed by the resident kapellmeister. Later, addressing German youth, Sangnier would allude to kneeling at the cathedral altar receiving the body of Christ in a sacrament that consubstantiated French and German souls: 'We want to conclude a fraternal pact. And God will bless us [...] Hatred is a spent force. Only Love endures forever, since Love is greater than Hatred.' However, the most impressive prepared symbolic act of the congress was the secular 'Sacrifice of Reconciliation', a symbolic material act of atonement by Germany in the form of a monetary gift to France. The strongly left-wing WILPF (discussed in Chapter 3) had floated the idea in March 1923. There was also a direct link with the atrocities controversy that Ehlen had raised at the congress. Lilly Jannasch, a key female German pacifist activist, was the driving force of the Sacrifice of Reconciliation campaign. Jannasch was an associate of Foerster's and a member of the editorial staff at his paper *Menschheit*. At the time of the congress she was preparing a book, published in 1924, in which she marshalled the available evidence to show that German war crimes had indeed occurred. Only the 'courageous proclamation of the truth', however unpopular, could save Germany.[22] The Sacrifice of Reconciliation, though it preceded the book's publication, reflected this radical form of cultural demobilization.

However, in an economy ravaged by hyperinflation what was a sincere German to give? The overwhelmingly female donors offered items of jewellery, whose proceeds were to be used for reconstruction of invaded regions. At a ceremony where the assorted valuables were presented to the French, Germaine Malaterre-Sellier, a moderate Catholic feminist and pacifist, accepted the German women's donation 'much less for its intrinsic value than as a symbol of your desire to make reparation, your ardent desire for fraternal reconciliation'.[23] For the Quaker Gertrude Giles, the collection of trinkets and bracelets, all that many could give, represented a release of emotion:

> Of course, there were cynical voices to be heard saying that the whole affair was worked up in a theatrical fashion and had no real value at all. Those of us who experienced the revulsion of feeling that had come over the Congress, however, were deeply thankful that for half-an-hour at least all the speakers had forgotten politics and had been just human beings.[24]

Pilgrimage was another traditional means of showing repentance. It would be used repeatedly over the course of the congresses, particularly in a German 'pilgrimage of peace' to the invaded regions, including Reims, in the week before the Bierville congress of 1926. In 1923 'invasion' was foremost in the popular consciousness, on account of the

Ruhr. The afternoon excursion to the mountaintop of Mont Sainte-Odile, 80 kilometres distant and across the border in French Alsace (but within the Kaiserreich until 1918), represented an audacious pacifist 'invasion' by the Germans, reversing the French pacifist invasion of Freiburg of a few days before. This mountain shrine had long been revered by French nationalists such as Maurice Barrès – who rejected the German-ness of Alsace-Lorraine – as a 'Gallo-Roman and Catholic outpost against Germany'. There French and German delegates basked in the summer sun, with even Sangnier's nonagenarian father, Felix, joining in! This was a nice reminder of the father–son journeys they had made together across the German frontier when Marc had been just a boy. Now, here, in August 1923, within sight of that contested Rhine, the thunderbolt of affection for the German youth movements hit the middle-aged Sangnier. Hands joined, eyes closed, Sangnier invoked the Almighty before addressing the 'young people of Germany': 'I feel your heart so close to mine that I cannot understand how one could fail to love you [...] If I did not share your desire for peace, I would no longer have the right to say that I truly love France.'[25]

These folkloric youth movements, along with the various left-wing and Catholic youth groups at the congress, represented for Sangnier *l'autre Allemagne*. Whereas the classic 'good Germany' of the French left was very specifically bound up with the good faith of the SPD, Sangnier's alternative Germany was a much more elastic concept, extending unremarkably to liberals but also to Catholics and other youth groups. Fischer's definition of that ' "other Germany" of the French left [... as] less a class-based or party political entity and more a moral and geopolitical option which found varying levels of expression in surprising and less surprising quarters of German society' is very apt. Sangnier's networking was one expression of this sensibility. Related but separate was the Socialist outlook on Germany, preponderant on the French left.[26] If Sangnier was taken with the politically diverse youth movements he met in Freiburg, the admiration was mutual, coming at a pivotal moment in European youth culture.

Youth, according to Prost, has not existed as a stable entity throughout history but rather as 'a social condition [...] the result of a social management of the life cycle'. Sangnier's role as a charismatic leader of youth, so clearly seen first in the Sillon and now at the congresses, highlights the progressive emergence of an autonomous youth culture and the social category of adolescence in the interwar period in Europe. These German youth movements, described above, were part of what Peter Stachura calls 'youth's demand to be recognized as an independent estate'. The idea of a congress dedicated entirely to youth – which came to pass at Bierville in 1926 – was a response to this. Yet what exactly was the nature of this allegedly 'new' youth culture? Over the preceding half-century a distinct social category of youth had emerged. Across Europe the offspring of the bourgeoisie, at least, were remaining in school longer and had just a little more pocket money to spend. This sociological change accentuated *fin-de-siècle* disenchantment with their bourgeois parents' boring world. This meant less for young people in working-class or peasant families, however, who made a brusque transition to the world of work at the end of primary school, awaiting the emergence to full adulthood through military service or marriage. The Wandervögel, made up of middle-class German Protestant youth and formalized by Karl Fischer in 1900, was part of a broader and even more diffuse phenomenon, that of Free German Youth. Though not monochromatic in their politics, the vegetarian, teetotal Wandervögel were generally anti-industrial, anti-urban and *völkisch*. Splintered by the trauma of 1918, those who engaged with Sangnier represented an impressive, pacifist minority, very different from the 'non-demobilized' Wandervögel who had joined the right-wing paramilitary Freikorps in 1919.[27]

Catholic equivalents of the Wandervögel, such as the Quickborn and Grossdeutschen, influenced by the theologian Romano Guardini, were even more congenial to Sangnier. The Quickborn's origins in 1909 were clerical and opposed to the Wandervögel's social libertarianism. Formalized in 1917, the Quickborn (meaning 'gushing source') had a mixed membership of 6500 in 1921. Sangnier's praise for this 'new' German youth knew no bounds: 'they have understood that it is the old order in Germany and the world that must be overthrown and destroyed. They wish to create something totally new.' Within German Catholic youth, therefore, a religious–socialist and internationalist wing, led by Nikolaus Ehlen, and a nationalist right wing tussled for supremacy. As Guido Grüneweld points out, Catholic radicals such as Ehlen consciously swam in the waters of aggressive pacifism inhabited by the German affiliates of the War Resisters' International. These German antimilitarists rallied around the journal of Fritz Küster, entitled *Das Andere Deutschland*. More broadly, this phenomenon of mass youth regimentation was by no means limited to Germany or the pacifist movement. Soon all ideological and political groups, not least the Catholic Church, were consolidating centralized auxiliary youth wings. Sangnier's youth movement existed in the shadows of the startlingly successful Jeunesse Ouvrière Chrétienne (JOC). A youth movement for Catholic workers, the JOC attempted to bring Christ to the factory floor and was brought to France in 1926 by Fr Georges Guérin, a veteran of the Sillon.[28]

However, the abiding political divisions at Freiburg had a way of marring the declarations of fraternity. Real divisions emerged when it came to adopting the congress's final motions at the concluding plenary session. As would often happen at these congresses, the motions adopted attempted to keep a fine balance between competing national interests and between radical and moderate pacifists. Unsurprisingly, given the political context, it was the issue of reparations and territorial occupations that provided the flashpoint on this occasion, whereas in 1926 at Bierville it would be the issue of conscientious objection. The congress of 1923 expressed hope that 'the recent occupations of territory, fount of distrust and new conflict, be reduced as soon as Germany has given guarantees on the execution of her obligations'. In his closing speech Sangnier contented himself with a pious declaration against sin, hoping that the League of Nations could broker an end to the 'cruel burden' of military occupation. However, such was the depth of feeling on the German side, and so acute was their wish to be seen as patriotic, that German delegates made a separate and unanimous declaration which they insisted be written into the congress's official record alongside the more anodyne motions that had won the acquiescence of both sides. It was a tacit admission that full Franco-German consensus was impossible on the issue of the Ruhr, even amongst pacifists. While recognizing their country's obligation to make reparations and asking their own government to pursue a 'policy of execution' – in itself a principle too far for many nationalists – the Germans delegates stoutly defended the legitimacy of non-violent 'passive resistance' in the Ruhr, particularly in light of the immoral, 'violent' sanctions used by the French, in an unjust breach of German sovereignty. However, for Georges Hoog, the mere occurrence of such discussions, in a comparatively civilized manner, between French and Germans was enough grounds for hope:

> Because these events took place, let us insist on this, at the most difficult moment for Franco-German relations [... And] without wishing to ignore or underestimate nationalist power across the Rhine, does not such an event attest that, in certain regions of the Reich at least, the desire for rapprochement is strongly rooted in people's minds?[29]

Sangnier returned from Freiburg more determined than ever to make known the 'other Germany'. But what did the 'other Germany' think of him? A French police report which claimed it drew on information from a German source gave a very dismissive evaluation of the Freiburg event. The German hosts accorded a 'slightly disdainful sympathy' to the French pacifists. The German participants, the contemptuous and misogynist missive droned on, were mainly women and generally of little stature: 'in sum, we can say that this meeting, pretentiously called a Congress by its organizers, was not of the least importance and that its consequences will be nil.'[30]

Even if Sangnier had not converted the German masses, a number of intangible but significant gains accrued to his movement from the Freiburg congress. Firstly, the Democratic International made new enthusiastic friends in hitherto untouched parts of the German peace movement. The propaganda effect of the congress was manifested in three ways: firstly, in the recruitment of new high-profile 'big names' to the congresses; secondly, in the firing up of activists at the base; and finally, in the confirmation of the Democratic International as a key player in transnational peace networks.

What big names? The most prestigious catch for the Freiburg congress was Ludwig Quidde, historian and elder statesman of German liberal pacifism. Vilified by the far right, from the 1890s, as an anti-patriot, Quidde was a Francophile whose tracts were unsurprisingly banned during the First World War. Later to be co-recipient of the Nobel Peace Prize in 1927 (alongside Frenchman Buisson), Quidde was president of the German Peace Society from 1914 to 1929. Quidde's speech at Freiburg saw the start of his active collaboration with Sangnier. When he was imprisoned less than a year later, in Bavaria in March 1924, for speaking out against the paramilitary organizations of Hitler and Ludendorff, his captivity galvanized the Jeune République into staging a large public rally in Paris demanding his release. 'Who now can doubt their sincerity?' Sangnier asked the Paris crowd, stressing that his German friends were neither nationalists in disguise nor 'hypocrites camouflaged as pacifists'. Conversely, the French peace movement's profile was heightened by Freiburg amongst German anti-militarist movements federated, since 1923, into a German peace cartel that would represent up to 100,000 members by 1928.[31] So much for the 'nil' impact the police had suggested after Freiburg.

Second in the record of achievement at that congress was the zeal kindled by Sangnier in a young generation of itinerant peace activists. As we saw at the Paris congress of 1921, Sangnier mobilized Catholic internationalist networks pioneered by Fr Jocham Metztger's IKA, or Catholic International. Freiburg amplified the symbiotic relationship between the Democratic International and the IKA. The personal journey in August 1923 of young German activist Wilhelm Solzbacher, whose adventure in getting to Freiburg was adverted to earlier, proves this point. As a follower of the nascent Catholic peace movement, Solzbacher would become used to spending parts of his summers travelling Europe on a shoestring to attend Catholic peace camps. His memoir, written in the 1980s, recalls the closing meeting before 3000 people at Freiburg's municipal Festival Hall on the night of 9 August 1923: 'The impression of Marc Sangnier's speech was overwhelming, even for those who did not understand French and had to wait for translation. I had never heard anyone speak about "democracy," "peace," and "brotherhood" with such religious fervour and deep sincerity.'[32]

Using his modest stipend from the World League of Catholic Youth, the youth section of Metzger's IKA, Solzbacher left Freiburg for Constance on the German-Swiss border to present a report to the IKA meeting there. On the train journey south were others who had just attended Sangnier's congress, including the IKA founder Fr Metzger himself and his comrade Sandór Giesswein, the Hungarian priest–politician. These charismatic priests enthused the young travellers by seeking their help in realizing plans for a fully transnational Catholic youth body. Sangnier's annual congresses were but one punctual fixture on a pacifist calendar and circuit that criss-crossed Europe. The proceedings of the IKA that followed on immediately after at Constance simply amplified, in a particularly Catholic key, the notes stuck at Freiburg. For instance, the IKA wished to generalize the devotional practice then promoted amongst Catholic former POWs of taking monthly communion for the intention of European peace. Blessed by the Catholic Church, this became known as the 'Messe du Premier Dimanche' ('Mass of the First Sunday'). Common to both Sangnier's and Metzger's meetings were personalities such as Don Vercesi, who had been Sangnier's prompter in the newspaper appeal of 1920, Giesswein of Hungary and Maurice Lacroix, close to the Jeune République in France, where he worked with Sangnier. The common spirit of both sets of congresses was summarized by the motion passed at the IKA Constance congress of 1923 that 'durable reconciliation between France and Germany is an urgent duty for the salvation of civilization as a whole. It is not simply a political and economic problem but above all a human, moral and religious one.'[33]

As Sangnier's train pulled out of Freiburg, the dusk rang with young German voices calling 'Vive Marc Sangnier'. Sangnier, the deputy, had repeatedly promised the enthusiastic young German delegates that he would bear witness at home to that 'other Germany' they represented. The moneys contributed by them at Freiburg offered tangible proof of their sincerity. The Sacrifice of Reconciliation money, Sangnier announced in October 1923, would be spent on materials for rebuilding the village of Arvillers (in the Somme), whose mayor was willing to accept the gift. Meanwhile, events in the Ruhr had not remained static. When Stresemann called off German passive resistance, in late September, he handed Poincaré a win which, according to Sally Marks, the French leader mishandled: 'within months he lost the war, because once again he had no plans.'[34] Prospects of proper Franco-German negotiation were complicated, moreover, by the digression of French policy into a confused flirtation with the forces of Rhenish separatism, which did much to damage France's international reputation. This confirmed German suspicions of Poincaré's desired endgame, adding further heat, if not light, to the electric political atmosphere at home in France.

With parliamentary scrutiny muted by government appeals to patriotic solidarity, it was only on 16 November 1923 that Sangnier could query the government. He told Poincaré: 'How I regret that *M. le président du Conseil* [the prime minister] could not have attended the Freiburg congress incognito!' For Sangnier, alongside the old Germany was a new one where Germans 'wanted to reject the venom of Prussian militarism and imperialism'. German youth had 'swept away his fears' as it 'applauded not alone the idea of Franco-German reconciliation but affirmed the necessity of the reparations Germany owed France'. Sangnier reminded his listeners of the 7000 Germans present at the congress's closing meeting in Freiburg and emphasized the youth movements he had observed there, dwelling in particular on Ehlen's initiative to bring a symbolic force of German volunteers to France to carry out reconstruction work. With emotion, Sangnier recalled Frenchman Léonard Constant, a follower of the Sillon and a teacher in the French *lycée* in Mainz. Committed to the imperative of reconciliation, Constant had recently been killed in crossfire during a Rhenish separatist protest while assisting an old person, a literal martyr to the cause. When Sangnier gave an emotional description of the requiem Mass for all the war's fallen at Freiburg Cathedral, the right-wing deputy Henry Ferrette could bear no more: 'No thanks! Our dead have no need of such prayers!' Sangnier also attempted to read into the record some of the pacifist letters of German mothers and schoolteachers who had contributed to the Sacrifice of Reconciliation. The letters drew sniggers from the extreme right but won the applause of the far left. Poincaré was unmoved by all this tear-jerking do-gooderism, suggesting dryly the personal items donated to this vaunted Sacrifice of Reconciliation should be given to the Minister for Liberated Regions. Poincaré also told the same session that the occupation of the Ruhr was in profit at last. Deliveries to France and Belgium from Ruhr industrialists were about to return to full capacity. Equally undeterred, Sangnier concluded his speech by warning the government that 'a France that is loved will more easily get payment than a misunderstood, calumniated and hated France.'[35]

Within France itself, a near warlike spirit gripped politics in 1923 in response to the Ruhr invasion. As we have seen this spilled over into street violence against the 'internal enemy' in which Sangnier, victim of nationalist taunts and assaults, earned additional battle scars for the peace movement's sake. However, beyond his pragmatic rationale in favour of a French foreign policy whose ambition matched its circumscribed power and demographic weakness, the Freiburg congress converted Sangnier to an unbounded enthusiasm for the new youth movements he encountered there. Though, as we have seen, the attachment of groups such as the Wandervögel, Quickborn and Grossdeutschen to Sangnier's idealized and abstracted 'other Germany' was over-simplified in Sangnier's rhetoric, his genuine attachment to them moved his pacifism from his head to his heart. Returning from Germany in the autumn of 1923, like the prophet armed, Sangnier confronted Poincaré directly with what he perceived as a failed punitive policy, a set-piece parliamentary storm that linked Sangnier to the changing political tides which were turning against Poincaré and pointing ahead to the victory of the Cartel des Gauches coalition in 1924. Nineteen twenty-three, therefore, catalysed in Sangnier's case an embrace of 'moral disarmament' that brought him even further away from his starting-point of 1919 as a pragmatic supporter of the Versailles treaty. The improved diplomatic context after the London Conference's acceptance of the Dawes Plan on reparations in 1924 set the stage for a Fourth International Democratic Peace Congress, where Sangnier would take another step towards treaty revisionism by questioning the war guilt of Germany and the very ideological foundation of the Versailles treaty itself.

5
Pacem in Terris: The Politics and Theology of Peace, 1924–5

The Ruhr occupation may have brought some material compensation for France, but it came at a high political cost. Poincaré, who as Prime Minister was identified with the hard line taken against Germany in 1923, argued at the beginning of 1924 that he had restored France to a position of relative strength in Europe. In early 1924, however, doubts over the Ruhr policy grew, and the French public mood turned against the fever-pitch war spirit and towards the centre-left's alternative coalition the Cartel des Gauches. Marc Sangnier's movement was at the heart of this more general metanoia in the French psyche. The progress of the Democratic International in the years 1924–5 helps track the infiltration of a new spirit into European politics and civil society more broadly. The campaign of the broad left, including Sangnier, for a new beginning in Franco-German relations played its part in this process. The London Accords of August 1924 marked that change in European diplomacy, and Sangnier's fourth congress, held in that same city of London, reflected that same change, both in its intensive discussion of proposals for collective security and in its evolution on the question of German war guilt. The figure of French statesman Aristide Briand came to represent such hopes for a new future by 1925, the year in which Sangnier travelled to Luxembourg with his congress and Briand went to Switzerland to negotiate a new bilateral pact with his German counterpart, Gustav Stresemann, at Locarno. In this new context, then, cultural and social issues relevant to the pursuit of lasting peace, such as the legitimate demands of international labour and moral disarmament through reformed education, took centre-stage in the congresses' deliberations.

There were several reasons for Poincaré's defeat at the polls in 1924, encompassing both war-weariness and economic anxieties. Outwardly, Poincaré was in a strong position with regard to the Germans at the end of 1923, which was undone by some of his own miscalculations and by external factors. He had forced Germany to retreat from resisting French occupation to engaging in a new round of negotiations on reparations. Poincaré contrasted his willingness to take territorial guarantees from Germany with his recent predecessors' pursuit of an unworkable collective security, an implicit attack on Briand's policy as Prime Minister in 1921–2. Such condescension played to the stereotype of Poincaré, though he was more hesitant an imperialist than his caricature suggests. In 1924 he could have forced a new bilateral reparations agreement on Germany, using phased withdrawals to extract specific reparations in kind from the Germans. His own caution, however, and fear of a further break with Britain, averted him from taking a course of action that would be 'as revisionist of the Versailles Treaty as any German recalcitrance since 1919'.[1] For all its frustrations, Poincaré judged it better to return to the Reparations Commission now that he had made the German government willing to discharge its debts, as he saw it. As early as 19 October 1923, Poincaré accepted in principle a British proposal for the constitution of another expert committee, to be chaired by American banker Charles Dawes, thus opening the way for decisive American financial intervention. This committee, acting under the aegis of the Reparations Commission, would examine the question of German payment, determining how Germany would pay rather than whether she should pay, Poincaré added. However, by keeping his options open for so long, and through his apparent flirtation with separatism in the Rhineland, the Prime Minister had undermined what would otherwise have been a position of French strength.

Simultaneously, Poincaré's stock with the French public was going into decline. With an international charitable mobilization for Germany under way amongst women's groups and Quakers, the French public were becoming aware of the damage that the country's reputation for 'imperialism' was doing to France abroad. Sangnier's appeal to France's good name in the world began to sound less like naïve bleating and to have more popular political purchase. Corroboration of this comes (oddly) from a packet of letters addressed to Sangnier found randomly on the street in Paris in early 1924, which came to the attention of the intelligence services. In them, French women reportedly supported his charity work for German families in distress and, furthermore, blamed France for German misery. Stephen Schuker writes of a shift within France to internal concerns in 1924, with the tired electorate reacting 'against the atmosphere of tension, sacrifice and eternal vigilance in defense of the Versailles treaty'. In February, Sangnier declared he was sick of the slogan 'le boche paiera'. The report of the Dawes committee on 9 April 1924, which internationalized the reparations issue, concluded that Germany could and should pay, albeit after a four-year partial moratorium. Economic guarantees seized in plant and materials in the Ruhr should return to German control. Under financial pressure from America, the French government accepted the Dawes proposals on 18 April 1924. France now had the prospect of regular revenue but, in Zara Steiner's words, also had to concede 'the first revision of the Versailles status quo in the German direction'. Sangnier felt vindicated, telling an election rally that the experts 'have only specified the solutions we have been proposing for two years. Re-read my speeches in the Chamber of Deputies, re-read those I gave in the country [...] It is exactly as we have said.'[2]

Domestic issues also worked against Poincaré as the elections approached, but they also complicated Sangnier's strategy in those same elections. The left harnessed economic anxieties against Poincaré. France was living on borrowed money from abroad, buying coal to make up for what the Ruhr had yet to yield. The political system would not deliver serious fiscal reform and a more progressive taxation system to meet costs. Inflation stalked the middle classes. In January 1924 the currency was coming under attack. Sangnier touched on these anxieties in a speech in early 1924 on the squeezed middle classes, whom he termed 'the new poor'.[3] This and the nationalist violence discussed in the previous chapter had alienated a large part of the Radical Party from Poincaré and pushed them toward the Socialists, who had long criticized his foreign policy. Belatedly, Edouard Herriot and the Radicals began to criticize the Ruhr too. Sensational confirmation of a shift to the left came in a speech by Briand at Carcassonne on 24 February 1924, when he broke with the government and called for votes for the putative Cartel des Gauches. Using precisely Sangnier's phrase, he counselled that such a government would reveal the 'true face' of France to the world.

The moving political tectonic plates forced Sangnier, as a deputy hoping for re-election, to make a choice. His support for the Bloc National was long since over, and his isolation from other Christian Democrats was nearly complete. The question for Sangnier was whether he should side in the coming elections with the Cartel des Gauches, whose foreign policy was his own. Schuker characterizes the Cartel des Gauches government as a reversion to the type of coalition that had often governed the Third Republic before 1914. This meant a government drawn from the Radical Party's ranks but with the guarded support of the more truly left-wing SFIO, the official French Socialist party. They were divided over the scope of state economic intervention and welfare provision. By pledging to dis-establish the Vatican embassy and reverse the Bloc's policy of accommodation of Catholics, this coalition of the Radicals and the Socialists found in boilerplate anticlerical rhetoric a common battle-cry and something of a useful distraction. Sangnier again showed how peace, as an overriding moral issue, brought him to countenance acts of political ecumenism that would upset some of his own Catholic base. At the annual congress of the Jeune République in Bordeaux on 21 January 1924, Sangnier said he was willing to stand in his Paris constituency on the same Cartel ticket as his anticlerical friend Ferdinand Buisson and the Socialist Paul Painlevé, in spite of the 'clerical question'. This declaration caused great unease at the congress, and ultimately the Jeune République ran an independent slate of candidates separate from the Cartel's but fully in tune with the mood for change. The campaign he ran under the banner Union Républicaine pour la Paix was in direct competition with the Bloc National list Sangnier had been on five years earlier. Where the right still used the Germans as political whipping boys, Sangnier flaunted the peace congresses and his solidarity with the imprisoned German pacifist Ludwig Quidde. Appealing directly to the voters of the 3e secteur of the Seine département on a platform of peace at home and abroad, Sangnier's list's manifesto stressed the need to 'disarm hatred and to develop the true League of Nations'.[4]

Poincaré attempted to salvage the Bloc National's campaign by spreading fear of the Socialists. He also rattled skeletons in the Radicals' closet, especially Joseph Caillaux's, the colourful former Prime Minister associated, in the public mind, with pro-German intrigues. Both Caillaux and former Radical Interior Minister, Louis Malvy, had been in disgrace since their Senate convictions on political charges in 1920. Caillaux, unlike Malvy, was not made to leave France but had instead an (impractical) five-year ban from entering large French cities imposed on him. Poincaré insinuated that the left, by treating Caillaux as a martyr, was unpatriotic. Sangnier in turn said the government was bereft of ideas and was abusing the spirit of 'sacred union' to pursue an attack on Bolshevism. If France's true face was not now recognized abroad, it was because for too long Poincaré's majority had pinned onto France's face 'a mask of militarism that has disfigured it'. On 12 May the right was beaten, and the Cartel des Gauches won a slender majority. The cruellest cut of all for Poincaré may well have been the interpretation put on this reversal of the 1919 results by Gustave Hervé. The one-time anti-militarist wrote in his paper *La Victoire* of 'the revenge of Joseph Caillaux'. Cut off from the electoral raft of the Cartel, however, Sangnier was not able to save his own seat, his vote dropping from 76,653 in 1919 to 15,063.[5]

The Radical-led Cartel des Gauches government installed in June 1924 came to power determined to liquidate the record of the Bloc National. Briand, who had hedged his bets in the last weeks before the elections, was snubbed by the new Prime Minister, Herriot, who took the Foreign Affairs portfolio for himself. Herriot was left to negotiate the treaty changes implied in the Dawes Plan. Such a treaty change necessitated an international conference, which opened in London in July 1924 and dragged on for a month, at the end of which France was forced to abandon the right to impose physical sanctions in the event of German default. France saved some face, but not a lot, by getting until 1925 to evacuate French troops from the Ruhr. Herriot, outclassed by the clever diplomacy of German Foreign Minister, Stresemann, and outfoxed by American bankers, might well have felt ill-used by Britain's Labour government as he left London without the guarantees he had hoped for, not least on German disarmament. He accepted the London accords of 1924 as he was anxious to retain British goodwill. In the autumn Herriot would spearhead attempts at Geneva to give teeth to League collective security through the so-called Geneva Protocol. Patrick Cohrs contends that while the London agreement was 'doubtless originally regarded as a defeat in France [...] in fact neither Herriot nor Poincaré but only a minority of nationalist elites and public opinion-makers took this line'. Cohrs further argues that this agreement marked an effectively new peace settlement of stabilization after the sinuous interpretations of Versailles. For the peace lobby, Sangnier prominent amongst them, the London agreement represented a vindication. In words that would delight the Germans – and Sangnier – Ramsay MacDonald, Britain's Prime Minister, spoke from the chair at the end of the London conference to signal explicitly a shift away from the war culture. He declared: 'This agreement may be regarded as the first Peace Treaty, because we sign it with a feeling that we have turned our backs on the terrible years of the war and war mentality.'[6]

A new spirit was clearly abroad. Sangnier told an audience at Central Hall, Westminster, on 18 September 1924: 'These London accords have lightened some of the dark clouds which, to our eyes, obscured the future of the peoples.' In France and Europe there emerged in 1924 a new spirit in favour of collective security and disarmament, reflected in high politics but also in civic peace movements like Sangnier's. Voluntary and diplomatic efforts co-existed in harmony rather than in competition. Carl Bouchard's study of the submissions to the Franco-American Peace Competition of 1923–4, a transatlantic civic peace effort backed by American philanthropic moneys, demonstrates the renewed faith in internationalist solutions to diplomatic problems in these years. Peter Jackson writes of France's delayed reaction to the war, from which 'a powerful current of anti-war sentiment emerged, coalesced and was given public expression during the mid-1920s by the overlapping politics of veterans' organizations, pacifist associations, the feminist movement and teachers' unions'. Jackson goes on: 'The transformation of attitudes was particularly pronounced in the centre left of the French political spectrum. Growing opposition to war led inevitably to movements within French (and German) civil society for Franco-German reconciliation.' The pioneering transnational peace congresses of Sangnier and Metzger began to appear less as isolated lights and more as part of a broader constellation of peace initiatives whose moment had come. As Benjamin F. Martin puts it, 'There could be no turning back. The "era of reconciliation" supplanted the "era of confrontation".'[7]

The Fourth International Democratic Peace Congress was held in London in September 1924 in this new climate, which set an entirely new diplomatic and political context for the civic peace movement represented by the Democratic International. The origins of this London congress (held in Central Hall, Westminster, from 16 to 19 September 1924) lay in the British Quaker presence at the celebrated Freiburg congress of 1923. Upon Gertrude Giles's return to Friends House in London, the Friends' Peace Committee saluted the 'Marc Sangnier Conference at Freiburg' as 'this most heartening effort towards Franco-German understanding'. Through the Fellowship of Reconciliation (FOR), an Anglophone and broadly Protestant pacifism had been a small but vocal presence at Sangnier's congresses from the first. Founded in 1919, the FOR fused British- and Dutch-based Christian peace activists whose networks of dissent, such as that of English Quaker and MP Henry Hodgkin, originated in 1914. The FOR had a mixed support base of Protestants and Quakers. It rejected all military service, trusting in a 'superior moral power [...] the law of God and of conscience'. The FOR Secretary-General, Revd Oliver Dryer, was Britain's sole representative at the Paris congress of 1921 before Henri Roser established a French affiliate of the FOR. While the initiative to host the Fourth International Democratic Peace Congress in London came from the FOR, it was the Quakers' Peace Committee that became the event's driving organizing force.[8] The Protestant and Quaker imprint would put conscientious objection firmly on the Democratic International's agenda: it would become a recurring flashpoint within Sangnier's movement and the broader peace movement in the years ahead.

In mid-1924, through the Friends' Peace Committee, two dedicated Quaker women, Edith Pye and Ruth Fry, began their remarkable contribution to the Democratic International. Unmarried, both were wedded to humanitarian endeavour. The intrepid pair became fixtures on the congresses' circuit, as unstinting in their support of Sangnier as they were uncompromising in their absolute pacifism. The women who came to prominence at the Vienna congress of 1922, such as Germaine Malaterre-Sellier and Klara Seibert, were associated with maternalist feminism and suffragism. Pye and Fry were more engaged as peace activists than suffragists, but, like the other women discussed, they were indelibly marked by direct experience of the war as nurses. Moreover, their brand of peace activism exemplified traditionally feminine roles of nurturing and care-giving. The figure of the wartime nurse as humanitarian witness was reinforced in British culture in the interwar period by the success of the memoir *Testament of Youth* (1933) by writer and former nurse Vera Brittain. While Pye and Fry were heavily influenced by their Quaker origins, they were also part of a broader category of women whose vocations were changed by the war.

In their own rights, these two women achieved much. Edith Pye was awarded the French Légion d'Honneur for her work as a midwife in war-torn France. She had visited the Ruhr on a humanitarian mission in 1923 to see the impact of French occupation on German civilians. Ruth Fry was a veteran of Red Cross work in wartime France who went on three humanitarian visits to Russia in the early 1920s. Thus, Pye's and Fry's endeavours were part of a pattern of women's reconciliation work in the 1920s identified by Erika Kuhlman, who writes of the presiding essentialist assumptions that marked such activism. In this sense, women were argued to be 'more pacifistic than men and therefore better suited to orchestrate a peaceful, post-war world'. Of the two women, Fry remained the more actively engaged in Sangnier's movement: indeed, it was Fry who largely organized the London congress. As a result, another strand was added to the transnational web of Christian pacifist activists. Great personal warmth developed between Fry and Sangnier: her diary records how, at a later date, she dined privately and informally in Paris with the Sangnier family, including their three children, Jean, Madeleine and Paul. At the family dinner table she marvelled at 'Paul of nine [years of age] coping with his wine in true French style'.[9] Fry remembered with special affection the eldest son, Jean (1912–2011), who, at age 12, accompanied his father to London in 1924 to get a child's-eye view of history.

The mood at the London gathering was indeed both familial and upbeat, as the ideas of Sangnier's movement had become mainstream. Sangnier told the opening meeting in Central Hall, Westminster, that the French election results told of 'the revenge of a people angry with a Government that carried out a policy of distrust and hatred, which was not the policy or the mind of the people'.[10] However, in order to be credible actors in this transnational peace lobby, the Democratic International had to do more than ooze diffuse sentiments of peace and love if they were to chivvy the politicians further along the path to lasting peace; it also had to address seriously controversial political issues such as war guilt while networking at London with the vibrant and diverse British peace movement. The Democratic International and Sangnier's leadership role within it developed in the years 1924–5, against the backdrop of intensified multilateral diplomacy, focusing on the League at Geneva and culminating in the Locarno Accords of October 1925. Sangnier's movement was both spectator and actor in this Franco-German thaw. Moreover, as well as being at the forefront of advocating and supporting such multilateral efforts, the Democratic International was also an international civic sounding board for broader issues of consolidating peace. These went way beyond the passing diplomatic compromises of the day. Ambitiously, and gaining in confidence from the diplomatic thaw, the congresses of London (1924) and Luxembourg (1925) reflected systematically on the material and moral conditions of lasting peace by examining in depth the place of education and social justice in their project for cultural demobilization. Even to the eyes of the British hosts at London it was the Franco-German couple that were the dynamic core of this peace movement. The unfinished business of war responsibility had to be faced from the start at London, as it went to the very heart of German concerns and of the concerns the French felt about Germany.

Writing of the German delegates to the congresses, Georges Hoog wrote that 'none of them, not even the most pacifist, ever accepted the idea of exclusive responsibility inscribed into the Treaty of Versailles.' In 1924 the issue of German war guilt was still a topic of scorching controversy bedevilling Franco-German movements and even dividing the German peace movement itself. The concept of co-responsibility – the belief that the war of 1914 was the fault of a generalized breakdown in the 'old diplomacy' of alliances – was the predominant belief amongst followers of the German peace movement. Nonetheless, as stated in earlier chapters, a few peace activists, such as F. W. Foerster, conducted an 'examination of conscience' that put most of the blame squarely on German policy. This line of thinking was robustly contested by the revered Ludwig Quidde, who had been in contact with Sangnier since 1921. In 1922 Quidde's pamphlet *Die Schuldfrage* raised many eyebrows amongst his French admirers for its unabashed patriotic tone. All governments had been imperialists and irresponsible, he argued, but having rid themselves of the old elite in 1918, the German people were blameless. The way forward lay in Germany's integration into the League of Nations, not flagellatory self-accusation. Quidde's pacifism, like that of many in the mainstream German peace movement, included advancing the German national interest. In truth, this made it not that different from liberal French pacifism. Released from gaol in Bavaria in early 1924, Quidde travelled to the London congress in September, in time to witness an important semantic shift in Sangnier's discourse due in no small part to his own persistent prodding. In advance of London, Quidde wrote to Sangnier: 'Has not the moment come to discuss in our groups the problem of responsibility for the outbreak of the war? Which one could not do in a congress held in Germany or in France.'[11]

For many of his German interlocutors coming to London in 1924, therefore, Sangnier's stance on German 'war guilt' was the litmus test of his sincerity. Sangnier's own evolution on this question was a gradual one. It will be recalled how, in Paris in 1921, he declared his respect for German sensitivities but confirmed his own belief that German foreign policy of the pre-war period stood condemned. In 1924, at the London congress's opening session, Sangnier went further. At that meeting in Westminster, reported in *The Times* under the heading 'Unity of Europe', Dr Stocky, a Cologne journalist, spoke on the Germans' behalf about their relationship with the League. Stocky appealed to the concept of the unity of western Europe as the defence of Christendom against the Bolshevik east. This defensive mentality, which conceived of peace between France and Germany as the bedrock for a kind of 'fortress Europe' united against the Moscow menace, had been an implicit aspect of the Democratic International's vision of Europe from the beginning, notwithstanding Sangnier's rhetoric of openness to the moderate left. A generation later, exclusion of Communism would become a linchpin of the Christian Democratic consensus for European integration in the polarized context of the Cold War. Stocky declared that

> Germany was a part of Europe in a sense that Russia was not, and it was of the greatest importance that everything should be done to

> emphasize the unity of Western Europe. (Cheers) It would be fatal for the inclusion of Germany to be dependent on Germany's signing any so-called acknowledgement of guilt. The question of responsibility for the war should be allowed to lie: and we should look to the future rather than the past.

Sangnier responded to Stocky by evading the direct question of blame. Instead, he declared that the French could only impose the conviction of responsibility on the Germans by persuasion rather than by legal sanction: 'It is undoubtedly [...] one of the weaknesses and errors of the treaty of Versailles to have wished to march into the domain of conscience by attempting to force the signature of an affirmation not accepted by German consciences. This is up to history to do.' This still represented an important semantic shift from 1921. In the same spirit of delegating the issue to the historians, the London congress's final motions echoed the calls of similar meetings in France and Germany by calling for the full opening of the relevant archives. A corollary of such rehabilitation was giving Germany full status in the world. Not only should Germany join the League, Sangnier continued, but she should have a seat on the League Council, the standing executive drawn from the Assembly, given its objective importance: 'To pose the question is to resolve it.'[12]

Though Franco-German understanding remained central, the British peace movement left its mark on Sangnier's movement too. Surprisingly, histories of British pacifism have ignored this important French connection. Martin Ceadel's survey of the topic excludes Marc Sangnier's Democratic International altogether, despite the contemporary importance British pacifists evidently attached to it. Sangnier was welcomed by the disparate political families of British pacifism, including Quakers, Socialists, Liberals and the radical anti-militarists of the international No More War Movement. Sangnier was accorded respect and taken seriously by Britain's Labour government. The politicians who fêted Sangnier were almost all adherents of the Union of Democratic Control (UDC), a British political group active since 1914 which had been the most significant group dissenting from British policy during the First World War. Founded by Liberal MP George Trevelyan, the grouping grew from a convergence of thinking between radical Liberal politicians and the Independent Labour Party on war and diplomacy. From 1917 the UDC campaigned for democratic war aims and a negotiated peace. Indeed, by the end of the war and with the eclipse of the Liberal Party, many of the UDC's leading lights migrated to the Labour Party, such as publicist Norman Angell, author of the best-selling anti-war tract *The Great Illusion* (1910), who spoke at the London congress to praise Sangnier's pioneering 'civic courage'. The Socialist MP and prominent Anglican George Lansbury and social reformer Sir William Beveridge lent their support. Nine UDC members were present in MacDonald's cabinet. This helps accounts for the official government reception held at Lancaster House on the morning of Tuesday 16 September to mark the congress. Under-Secretary of State for the Colonies Lord Sydney Arnold, a former Liberal, played host to Sangnier and 500 delegates. In reciprocation for this official gesture, the congress acted on a suggestion from the floor to send a telegram of congratulations to the Prime Ministers of Britain, France and Germany on 'the happy results already obtained at the London Conference which has oriented Europe toward the light of peace and turned it away from the darkness of the war and the post-war era'.[13]

A measure of the respect for Sangnier amongst the British civic peace movement was his honoured role as speaker in the 'No More War' demonstrations of the weekend of 20–1 September, which, by happy coincidence, occurred just at the end of the congress and for which Sangnier made impromptu orations to socialist youths from an improvised platform of lorries draped in 'No More War' banners in Hyde Park. This was the last in a series of genuinely international annual anti-war demonstrations held in major European cities, which brought together moderate and advanced pacifists, from the League of Nations Union on the right to War Resisters International on the left. These 'No More War' demonstrations were the British adaptation of a short-lived German veterans' movement. In Germany, in the years 1920–2, the 'Nie wieder Krieg' movement organized annual mass demonstrations each August. These impressive 'No More War' rallies were briefly imitated in Britain, the USA and France but were in decline between 1922 and 1924. Nonetheless, the rallies did much to cement Franco-German pacifist links around the slogan of 'never again war'. In London, in 1924, in front of a working-class audience at the Holborn Empire theatre, Sangnier declared that 'to kill war, we must give birth to love and justice in the hearts of men'. He was presented to the audience by a Labour MP called Oswald Mosley, who had yet to exchange the red flag for the black shirt! (Mosley went on, in the 1930s, to become leader of the British Union of Fascists.) At the same meeting, Quidde, behind-the-scenes ringmaster of the discussion of war guilt, gravely prophesied that 'a future war would completely destroy everything dear and sacred to humanity.' The Democratic International had been taken to the bosom of the British pacifist movement, which would enliven future congresses with its often radical perspectives.[14]

The year between the end of the London congress in September 1924 and the next congress, in Luxembourg in September 1925, saw intensive diplomatic activity and further controversy over the moral bases of the Versailles settlement, a broader polemic in which Sangnier was directly implicated. The new left-wing Cartel des Gauches government had to adjust to the new diplomatic environment after the London Accords of the summer of 1924. On 1 October 1924, Prime Minister Herriot committed the French government to internationalism in a keynote speech at the Fifth Assembly of the League at Geneva, outlining the triple-formula of 'arbitration, security, disarmament' that would henceforth be the watchwords of French interwar foreign policy. Herriot's invocation of disarmament related France's pursuit of security intimately to ongoing discussions of German disarmament which had been originally envisaged as the prelude to a more general arms reduction. The 1920s were marked by a strong sense that the arms race of the early twentieth century had contributed independently to the environment of distrust from which the war itself had exploded. Speaking on disarmament at the London congress, Sangnier had said that 'disarming Germany alone, without disarming the victorious countries, is not sufficient. All Europe must be disarmed.' However, like most French, he made national security an absolute precondition of such disarmament, having defended vigorously, during the recent election campaign, his consistent parliamentary votes for the annual defence budget. Disarming France without the League having a viable 'international gendarmerie' in situ would be criminal folly, he maintained.[15]

Herriot's public embrace of multilateralism at Geneva in October 1924 was prefigured by earlier essays in multilateral security. Liberal internationalists, such as those in France's Association pour 'La Paix par le Droit' (APD), who generally supported the Cartel des Gauches government, had advocated the concept of compulsory arbitration from well before the First World War. During Poincaré's premiership the French government was already party to arms reduction talks in Geneva. Even as the Ruhr débâcle unfolded, the French resisted what they deemed premature calls for general disarmament by shaping the course of the debate, rather than ignoring it. From late 1922 French governments used disarmament proposals as a means to seek security guarantees. In 1923 the French proposed a novel Draft Treaty of Mutual Assistance, which paired security with disarmament. Regional accords with military conventions would allow each nation to determine what arms reductions might be in accordance with security guarantees obtained. The Draft Treaty touched off a vogue for multilateral solutions that would come into its own the summer of 1924. With Britain's Labour government pushing for Franco-German understanding and arms limitation, it rejected the Draft Treaty as a re-edition of the old balance of power, forcing France to begin considering the inconceivable, some type of pact that might include Germany.

The decisive shift in the French national mood in 1924, and France's precarious finances, concentrated the minds of France's foreign policy makers. As Jacques Bariéty and Raymond Poidevin point out, Herriot's next proposal, the Geneva Protocol for the Pacific Settlement of International Disputes, presented at the same session of the League Assembly in Geneva in 1924, drew heavily on the Draft Treaty of Mutual Assistance of the previous government. Privileging political and legal obligations over military pledges, the Geneva Protocol provided for compulsory arbitration in the event of disputes through which the League could identify an aggressor state. Such a determination would trigger security accords that could sanction the errant state.[16] British suspicion that the French were merely cloaking in the language of Geneva a binding British commitment to a traditional Franco-British alliance meant that, in the event, the Geneva Protocol remained a dead letter. Nonetheless, spurred on by public opinion and fear of the jibe of militarism abroad, Herriot had performed a volte-face in French policy by premising French security on disarmament instead of a military guarantee.

The public campaigns of French Socialists and of Sangnier since 1923 had played their part in promoting France's policy shift. The French military and the political right considered such sentimentalism weak in the face of German revisionism. In 1925 treaty revisionism, amending the Versailles settlement to right wrongs towards the defeated powers, came to the fore as a political issue, with potential for grave divisions on the French left and amongst peace movements internationally. William Lee Blackwood argues that German revisionist opinion was propagated very effectively by German participants in the Socialist International in the 1920s, even arguing that it helped set the stage for the democracies' later appeasement of Hitler. No doubt, the example of the negotiated revision of the Ottoman settlement with the new Turkey of Attatürk at Lausanne in 1924 set an important precedent. The French Socialist leader Léon Blum, who disassociated himself from the proponents of radical revisionism, also pleaded in the 1920s for a peaceful evolution of international law in relation to Germany, although he later came around to defending the status quo.[17]

Sangnier entered this political minefield by publicly associating himself with the peace manifesto instigated by Victor Margueritte in July 1925. Margueritte, who would go on to animate the revisionist review *L'Evolution* from 1926 to 1933, was an integral pacifist and the notorious author of the racy novel *La Garçonne* (1922). The manifesto he issued in 1925 called for 'moral disarmament' and denied the Allies had fought a just war. War was the real atrocity; war crimes trials represented a 'derisory perpetuation of hatred'. Sangnier was one of 103 eclectic left pacifist signatories, along with the writers Henri Barbusse and Romain Rolland, anti-colonial activist Félicien Challaye and anti-war activist Georges Demartial. At the APD, Théodore Ruyssen was genuinely shocked that this Margueritte's *Appel aux consciences* had been signed not just by the usual suspects like Demartial but also by moderates such as Victor Basch, of the League of the Rights of Man, and Sangnier. Ruyssen left them under no illusion as to 'the danger that their campaign is causing to the present peace: [an] imperfect peace [...] but real peace, and [a] just peace on many points'. Conscious of the criticism of his friends, Sangnier told *Jeune République* readers that the appeal was not meant to give succour to German nationalism but was an act of justice: Germany had been tried before the world by a 'tribunal [...] exclusively composed of the victors'. There was some merit in Sangnier's contention. In the Versailles treaty of 1919, which the German government had signed through gritted teeth, a moral judgement about the guilt for the outbreak of the war had been written into international law. Alongside clauses about possible trials of the Kaiser and of those accused of war crimes in the field, the German delegation also accepted the infamous Article 231, which was inserted in part to establish German legal liability for reparations payments. In this article the Allies affirmed, and Germany accepted, that Germany and her allies had responsibility for all war damages and that it was the aggression of Germany and her allies that had imposed war upon the Allies in the first place. An immediate and enduring source of resentment for a great majority of Germans in the 1920s, this article also became the focus of criticism among non-German critics of the treaty, especially in the Anglophone world. Though a similar clause had been written into the treaties with the former allies, such as Austria and Hungary, it was its presence in the Versailles text that was generally viewed in this period as the most egregious provocation. Accordingly, in July 1925, in defending his signature of Margueritte's manifesto (which questioned the moral basis of Article 231 and thus of the treaty as a whole), Sangnier could not fail to refer to what his German friends had repeated endlessly at the International Democratic Peace Congresses since 1921. He wrote that Germans 'manifestly believe' Article 231 to be 'in opposition to the truth'. Therefore, Sangnier concluded, it should be modified to be acceptable to all.[18]

When, two months after the controversy over the Margueritte manifesto, the Fifth International Democratic Peace Congress was held in Luxembourg between 9 and 14 September 1925, the moral and political issues raised by the rehabilitation of Germany and the failed Geneva Protocol headlined proceedings. In Luxembourg, though, Sangnier's peace movement had to face an awkward reality that imperilled its unity and that of the broader peace constituency. Behind all the schemes for collective security in vogue in 1925 lay the vexed issue of legitimate force. League of Nations liberals such as Sangnier had repeatedly expressed their willingness to see the monopoly of armed force pass to an international, democratically mandated international police force. In the last resort these liberals countenanced an army taking up arms against aggressors, which was intrinsically offensive to the pieties of absolutist pacifists. The Geneva Protocol, for instance, permitted the League Council to name and shame an aggressor, against whom a military response could be activated. In the deliberations of the Fifth International Democratic Peace Congress in Luxembourg in 1925 these divisions came into the open, with the new recruits from English pacifism defending the extreme anti-militarist position and clashing with representatives of liberal pacifism.

Professor Louis Rolland of the Paris Law Faculty, who declared he had been a supporter of the Geneva Protocol, felt that 'in the present state of the world, it would compromise international justice, and consequently peace, not to envisage sanctions aimed at any nations which rose up against the international order.' Both he and Charles Richet, the old liberal pacifist, conceded the League could legitimately make war on an aggressor. For Ruth Fry, attending her second congress, this was muddled thinking. If war was wrong (as she believed it was), then it should never be used, not even as a sanction: 'Our ideal can only be a world without war. That is the Quaker ideal; one has to choose between being a Christian and being bellicose.' Fry continued by castigating economic sanctions, citing her first-hand knowledge of the suffering of innocent Germans at the hands of the Allied blockade during the war. Her position was extreme even by the standards of her own milieu, rejecting not just armed force but economic force too. The exchanges between Rolland and Fry were so heated that Sangnier had to defuse them with meaningless bluster. When, six months later in Paris, Rolland and Fry were about to share a speaking platform again, Sangnier whispered roguishly to Fry that she was about to bait '[her] adversary' again.[19] For Fry, pacifism was a matter of faith rather than practical politics.

Taken as a whole, the Democratic International's peace congresses addressed the 'moral conditions' for peace in their deliberations. Central to this, throughout their 12-year existence, was the pursuit of the pedagogy of peace. The congresses themselves were meant to be didactic, to educate participants and public opinion more generally in the 'disarmament of hatred'. In this regard, Sangnier was keeping faith with the educative mission he had begun with the Sillon, which had consciously modelled its study circles not just on Catholic groups but also on pre-war socialist experiments with 'popular universities', open to the working class. Both sets of efforts reflected Sangnier's belief in democracy as a morally virtuous system of government whose vigour depended on the extension of political reflection and virtuous civic engagement to the common man and woman. Such generalization of virtue made democracy into the antithesis of aristocracy and autocracy. Education moulded democratic citizens. Linking education and peace in the 1920s, Sangnier saw education for peace as critical to the formation of morally perfectible citizens for an interdependent world. Inevitably, therefore, between 1921 and 1932, the Democratic International repeatedly addressed itself to the pacifist education of the young. By no means the only one of the 12 congresses to deal with education, the Luxembourg congress of 1925 paid particular attention to the place of war and peace in the school curriculum. By mid-decade the discourse of reconciliation was becoming more generalized in Europe and, more specifically, debates on national bias in school texts had gained traction within France and on a transnational level, making the Luxembourg congress the key moment in the education debates within the Democratic International.

Mona Siegel's study of French primary teachers in the interwar period alludes to a generalized reaction against the traditional figure of the patriotic schoolmaster in the aftermath of the First World War. While not universally shared in any country, this sentiment was equally not specifically French. First published in German in 1928 before multiple translations, Erich Maria Remarque's *All Quiet on the Western Front* was a runaway success. One strand of the book memorably portrays the bitterness of Paul Baumer, the novel's chief protagonist, with the armchair war lust of his German schoolmaster, a disillusioning depiction that soon passed onto the silver screen through a Hollywood hit movie. A report on schoolbooks, with particular reference to France and Germany, was submitted to the European Centre of the Carnegie Foundation for International Peace in 1923, explicitly calling for vigilance against schoolbook chauvinism in the name of 'disarming hatred'. Was it not inevitable, the report asked, that teaching children about the recent war would create obstacles to this same disarmament? Anticipating the discussion in Luxembourg, the London congress of 1924 had officially deplored how 'our different national educations are, usually, simple national apologetics'. Sangnier expressed his hope there that, in a new pacific age, children would be taught to admire new heroes such as the philosopher Pascal and the scientist Louis Pasteur rather than the generalissimo Napoleon. Siegel's argument is that French teachers, especially women inspired by wartime dissident Hélène Brion, moved away from the cultural mobilization of wartime and the reflex patriotism of the first generation of Republican *instituteurs*, formed under the Ferry Laws of 1881, to embrace internationalism and a horror of war. Impelled by this moral imperative, Siegel argues that in French classrooms of the interwar period many such teachers 'slowly and patiently sought to disarm the French people of the stories, stereotypes, and images that might once again lead them unknowingly into war'.[20]

Luxembourg made Sangnier's congress a pitch-battle in a transnational 'textbook war' that was already under way. In these years the left-leaning Syndicat National teachers' union ran a campaign in France, endorsed by writers such as Henri Barbusse and Anatole France, for the eradication of bellicose schoolbooks which perpetuated the dehumanization of the Germans as 'les Boches'. Moreover, following the trail set by movements such as Sangnier's, French teachers reached out to German colleagues, inviting representatives to their congresses and co-founding a transnational teachers' federation in 1926. These contacts led to the first steps in the elaboration of agreed Franco-German history textbooks, efforts cut short by the coming of the Nazis in 1933. Meanwhile, in Luxembourg in 1925, a pioneering local woman politician, Catherine Schleimer-Kill, wanted history abolished altogether from the primary school syllabus rather than let it continue 'deforming the minds of children'. Other voices rejected this disparagement of history as inherent warmongering. Maurice Lacroix, a prominent member of Jeune République and a lecturer in literature at Paris's prestigious Collège Henri IV, managed to dissuade delegates from any condemnation of history *per se*. Properly taught, he declared, history could help children 'conceive of the possibility of an international society' such as the League of Nations rather than teach them hatred. History, then, was a prerequisite for peace, necessitating the 'reform and not the abolition of history textbooks'. Reform should be the joint endeavour of university conferences and teachers' congresses, where texts were examined and 'books infested with nationalist spirit denounced'.[21] Lacroix echoed the Carnegie philanthropists who had concluded in 1923 that the Institute of Intellectual Co-operation (based in Paris since 1921 and affiliated to the League of Nations) should monitor schoolbooks. The Carnegie enquiry cited the German educationalist F. W. Foerster, an associate of Sangnier's, who had argued that history should be used to show the compatibility of national and supranational entities.[22]

Ferdinand Buisson (1841–1932), who attended most of Sangnier's congresses in the 1920s, was a figure of real substance on the French left and in French secular education whose presence lent weight to the discussion on education at Luxembourg. A freethinker and a Freemason, Buisson had been appointed director of primary education in 1879 by Minister of Public Instruction Jules Ferry. In 15 years Buisson had laid the bedrock of the secular schools system, making him anathema to Catholics. Buisson espoused a brand of civic education that was impeccably patriotic. His manual of civic instruction for schools in 1905 aimed at forming a Frenchman who will make war but will curse it upon returning home and will work to eliminate it. Between 1913 and 1926 Buisson was president of the League of the Rights of Man, a militantly secular organization formed in 1898 in response to the Dreyfus Affair. In 1927 Buisson shared the Nobel Peace Prize with the German Quidde. While not involving himself directly in the textbook debate, Buisson's contribution here tends to confirm Siegel's broader thesis that, outside the extremes, 'a fundamentally patriotic message was embedded in many of French teachers' most pacifist lessons.' The recent war was retold as having been tragic for all fatherlands, while the narratives maintained the moral that the good Frenchman would defend his land if necessary. This was contrary to what conservatives like Marshal Pétain would later claim in 1940 about the rot beginning with pacifist teachers, a negative view of schoolteachers' patriotism that has even influenced the history-writing of the 'strange defeat' of 1940. Buisson exemplified this patriotic internationalism at Luxembourg, where he intoned that 'today, we must inspire in children the feeling of what they owe the fatherland and what the fatherland owes to humanity.' The Luxembourg congress called for 'the generalization to all countries of the annual lesson devoted to the League of Nations already given in certain countries', such as the host country Luxembourg.[23] The emphasis on the League of Nations and education reflected an optimistic belief in moral perfectibility and human progress. Education might yet bring secular salvation through law and reason.

Even more fundamental than history to a transnational movement like the Democratic International was language itself. Sangnier did not lead by example here; failing to acquire sufficient German to speak in it, he remained dependent on young German interpreters to translate his speeches at their meetings. (His son Jean learned it, though.) The broader issue had been raised by Fr Metzger, one of the presiding actors in the first congress at Paris in 1921. Metzger, as we have seen, founded the IKA, which hoped to use Esperanto as a common European language. Others, such as Maurice Lacroix, did not share his zeal, defending linguistic particularism. The Freiburg congress in 1923 urged that chauvinism and narrow nationalism should be avoided in the teaching of foreign grammar! More pertinently, as the autobiography of Wilhelm Solzbacher, the young German converted to the cause at Freiburg in 1923, makes clear, young German interpreters themselves became essential spokespeople for Sangnier both in interpreting his words and spreading his word. Solzbacher, who remained true to Metzger's Esperantist vision, was in America as an anti-Nazi exile during the Second World War (where he changed his first name to William) and earned his living as an interpreter. He eventually worked as an interpreter for the new United Nations Organization after 1945 and featured on the airwaves of the Voice of America radio station.

Language as a key to understanding was also the inspiration behind an international summer school hosted at Sangnier's Bierville estate near Paris in 1927. Though not emphasized in the existing literature on Sangnier's congresses, this educational gathering of young people, including Sangnier's 15-year-old son Jean, was significant as an effort to address the potential for misunderstanding in ignorance of foreign languages. At Bierville, 50 French boys and girls and a similar number of German and English children assembled for classes taught by teachers of the three nationalities. The summer school allowed the children to get to know one another and to increase their proficiency in a foreign language as an act of faith in the new generation and an investment in its future.[24]

At the Luxembourg congress in 1925, the visits of congress delegates to various social works such as sanatoriums and specially aerated anti-TB schools in Luxembourg showed the Democratic International's commitment to social inclusion. Social reform went hand in hand with international solidarity. A year before, in January 1924, in a speech in Paris on the 'new poor', Sangnier had bemoaned the impoverishing effects of 'la vie chère' on the middle classes – a familiar complaint in French politics up to 1926 – and of the abandonment by the French government of the 'franc fort' policy. In this same speech, Sangnier had pointed to the Jeune République's persistent highlighting of the scandal of urban slums and its recent campaign for better conditions for women workers in the clothing industry. Like the Sillon, the Democratic International married a political cause with Social Catholic activism. Co-operating with the French Catholic trade union movement, the CFTC, the congresses made an explicit link between implementation of the economic terms of the Treaty of Versailles on the dignity of workers and the church's social teaching since Leo XIII. Part XIII of the Versailles treaty provided for the establishment of an independent International Labour Organization (ILO), linked to the League of Nations, to defend workers and lessen the appeal of Communism. Established in 1919 under the leadership of former French Munitions Minister and reformist socialist Albert Thomas, the ILO, based in Geneva, brought a series of international labour conventions into being, thereby internationalizing reforms Sangnier and the workers' movement had long fought for, including regulation of the working week, of night work and of the employment of women and children. Thomas ensured that the ILO was represented at each of Sangnier's peace congresses and wrote supportively to Sangnier when he was under attack in parliament. Another advocate of moderate redistributive politics was economics professor Charles Gide, who spoke at the Luxembourg congress. Associated with the Ecole de Nîmes school, which sought a peaceful middle way between capitalism and collectivism by means of the co-operative movement, Gide's ideas had been influential on the Sillon, which had run workers' co-operatives across France before 1910 in an effort to create a type of social democracy in the workplace. Sangnier declared to the International Democratic Peace Congresses in the 1920s that the co-operative sector was 'a more democratic organization of relations between capital and labour which progressively links the latter to the management and profits of the business'. The Luxembourg congress therefore simply confirmed the intrinsic connection Sangnier's movement made between social justice and the peace and solidarity of nations.[25]

The London Accords of 1924 may have lightened the clouds of European diplomacy, but many occluded fronts remained at the beginning of 1925. As Jon Jacobson points out, the failure of League attempts at universal or near universal collective security (in particular the stillbirth of the Geneva Protocol of 1924) led to acceptance of the principle that peace was best organized by means of a regional pact in which western Europe 'identified itself as an independent region of interdependent states' that was separate from eastern Europe, Soviet Russia and the United States. In early 1925, fearing that ongoing French security concerns might lead to more intrusive enforcement of German disarmament by the League, German Foreign Minister Stresemann seized the initiative to launch a German 'peace offensive' that culminated in the Locarno Accords of October 1925. Depicted by his biographer, Jonathan Wright, as a 'creative pragmatist' rather than the unscrupulous nationalist or good European of caricature, Stresemann aimed at peaceful revision of the Versailles settlement in Europe underpinned by a nationalist consensus within Germany capable of neutering the extremes of right and left.[26] In April 1925 the new French prime minister, Paul Painlevé, made a significant appointment in restoring Aristide Briand to the Foreign Ministry, a post Briand would hold with virtually no interruption until January 1932, a month before his death.

Neither Stresemann nor Briand was a sentimental pacifist. Briand's foreign policy was not a total rupture with that of Poincaré, even though the received wisdom long drew a stark contrast between their policies, pitting Poincaré the 'nationalist' against Briand the 'father of Europe'. Rather, as Keiger puts it, 'they represented two sides of the same coin, whose currency was security. Throughout the 1920s both sought in not dissimilar ways – often overlapping – to reach an agreement with Germany that would provide France with the European security it desperately craved.' Just as Sangnier had argued from 1920, Briand quite openly defended the policy of binding Germany to a multilateral system of security as a sensible and pragmatic policy consonant with France's lower birth rate. These competing French and German objectives lay behind the Locarno Accords negotiated directly by Briand and Stresemann in Switzerland between 5 and 16 October 1925. In the Rhineland Pact, initialled as the centrepiece of the Locarno Accords on 16 October, Germany recognized its borders with France and Belgium and accepted the demilitarized left bank of the Rhine stipulated in the Versailles treaty. Britain and Italy acted as guarantors who would act against aggressors in the event of the Pact being violated. Renouncing force in the west, Germany agreed to arbitration about its borders with the Poles and the Czechs. Crucially, Locarno provided for the acceptance back into the family of nations of Germany, with a permanent seat on the Council of the League of Nations. The negotiators had a conscious sense of history, seeing the 'need to create a watershed between the era of war and a new era of peace and for the demarcation to be clear and written into international law'.[27]

Briand's rhetoric upon his return home emphasized the psychological liberation of Locarno, where a true peace process based on mutual consent had begun. Peppering his speeches with references to a 'European' destiny for the Franco-German couple (and anticipating his memorandum on European unity of 1929), Briand became France's 'pilgrim of peace', establishing almost a cult following amongst the peace movement and a French public that was thirsting for the promise of 'no more war'. Moreover, invoking the shade of Victor Hugo and the 1848 revolution, Briand operated from the belief that 'true French republicanism contained a worldwide promise of peace'. Briand made of Geneva, accordingly, 'the principal locus of a restored moral status for France'.[28] Within the peace movement itself, Briand was close to, and closely supported by, the moderate, old-school APD pacifists. Such movements were indeed precursors of the Briand policy of Franco-German rapprochement at Locarno rather than merely its heirs. Briand's multilateralism owed as much of a debt to their juridical pacifism and activism as to the pragmatism of the politician himself. Briand and the French Foreign Ministry gave money to movements such as the APD and the League of the Rights of Man, which supported government policy, actively rejecting requests for subsidy from more radical peace groups.

As Elana Passman and Sylvain Schirmann show, Briand-style multilateralism added lustre to Franco-German movements for co-operation, of which Sangnier's movement for peace through youth was but one. Sangnier's movement co-operated with and often even shared membership with other such pro-Briand groups, while remaining distinct within this eclectic bunch of fellow-travellers. In the economic sphere there was Charles Gide's movement for customs union. Louise Weiss's paper *L'Europe Nouvelle* echoed Briand's declarations of a new European moment. There also began in 1926 a new journal called *Notre Temps*. – established by young left-wing activists Jean Luchaire, Pierre Brossolette and Pierre Mendès-France – dedicated to communicating Briand's policy. In this age of the press and mass politics Briand could not, and did not, formulate foreign policy insulated from domestic opinion. Rather, as Andrew Barros argues, 'a major concern and one of Briand's objectives was to get public support for his policies within France and, at the same time, within her allies. Popular approval could translate itself into political support.'[29]

Christian Democrats such as Sangnier also benefited from their support of Briand's Locarno diplomacy; the Democratic International, in turn, reified and radiated the message that the real post-war era had begun. Indeed, as Philippe Chenaux shows, Locarno diplomacy helped thaw the Vatican's initial coldness towards the Geneva-inspired diplomacy of the League of Nations (though, technically, the Locarno Accords were only tangentially related to the League, unlike the earlier Geneva Protocol, which had proposed the League Council as world arbiter of peace and war). The spirit of fraternity between victor and vanquished that Locarno appeared to represent was pleasing to the Vatican as it seemed to vindicate the late Pope Benedict XV's exhortation to Christian charity in the affairs of nations as well as in the affairs of men. This conjunction of Briand's policies and official Catholic endorsement of internationalist diplomacy would unsettle ultra-conservative Catholics in France and elsewhere, which in turn would put Sangnier's peace movement in the front line of a looming clash between the radical right and papal policy.

In October 1925 Sangnier also felt considerable personal vindication for the political choices he had made since the first Peace Congress in 1921 in reaching out to the former enemy, at the cost of initial unpopularity and misunderstanding. The headline in *Jeune République,* above Sangnier's leading article, announced simply 'A Victory'. 'We were not mistaken,' he wrote, 'we have the right to rejoice.' Savouring this moment of public affirmation for his policies, he recalled how his French opponents had dismissed the Democratic International as 'cranks', accusing its members of 'betraying the very interests of [their] country'. Now, though, with the 'disarmament of hatred' the order of the day, the stone that the builders rejected had become the cornerstone. Sangnier explicitly recalled his pleas to Poincaré in parliament to reveal the 'true face' of France, which had met with the then prime minister's 'haranguing brusqueness'. Nor did Sangnier forget 'the indignant scandal' of his more conservative Christian Democratic colleagues in the PDP at his support for the more constructive policy of Briand.[30] These barbs aside, the Locarno moment was one for joy but not for complacency, according to Sangnier. He continued by saying how he still would have preferred the Geneva Protocol to have been adopted, as it would have been a more generalized instrument for peace under direct League management rather than the regional pacts concluded at Locarno. However, he was not willing to let the perfect become the enemy of the good. Instead, it was a challenge to redouble the efforts for the disarmament of hatred which alone could give solidity and lasting legitimacy to this diplomatic détente. The Democratic International's job was far from done if it was to achieve definitively the millenarian goal of liberal internationalism since the nineteenth century of a self-regulating society of nations; 'Therefore if we wish international anarchy to end and for there to be, at last, law-bound relations between states, public opinion must be able to recognize and even demand such previously unknown legality.'[31] The agenda of moulding that same transnational public opinion was firmly set as the guiding star for the next peace congress, which would be held in France in 1926.

The rapid succession of Sangnier's Luxembourg congress and the political breakthrough at Locarno brought to a close the paroxysm of protest and counter-mobilization on the French left against the nation's foreign policy. Politically, Sangnier had helped prepare the victory of the French left in 1924 and thus helped alter the political climate fundamentally. As the rhetoric of Briand showed, the discourse of pacification and accommodation had won the day. On the inside, Sangnier's peace movement had grown accordingly in domestic appeal and transnational breadth, including, from London in 1924, an influential current of British pacifist and Quaker opinion. Such breadth also increased the potential for internal disagreements, though, as seen in the discussion of the legitimacy of League sanctions at the Luxembourg congress of 1925. Locarno also meant that Sangnier's peace movement moved from the margins to the heart of the political world with direct access to government and support from the coffers of the French Foreign Ministry. In the years immediately following Locarno, Briand represented a new consensus in France in favour of magnifying French prestige through Geneva diplomacy. Sangnier would relay that message to the coming generation of French and Germans in a spectacular extravaganza at Bierville in France in 1926. The presence of Ferdinand Buisson at the Luxembourg congress had shown how the Democratic International brought together in the name of peace Frenchmen and women from across traditional political and religious divides. At Bierville in August 1926 this pattern of political ecumenism, between the French and the Germans and between the diverse spiritual families of France itself , was to reach its apotheosis.

6
Bierville and the Liturgy of Peace, 1926

In the chronology of the interwar European peace movement, activist bodies, like the Democratic International, forged ahead on the path of moral disarmament where governments lagged and eventually followed. By 1926, though, through the Locarno Accords, politics had caught up with the pioneers. In a political climate more favourable than at any time since the war, Marc Sangnier, having been an individual pioneer of cultural demobilization, wished, by 1926, to show the world the visible popular support that existed for the policy of reconciliation between France and Germany. To be effective, such a demonstration had to be staged in a spectacular manner that would lend further legitimacy and ballast to the political project of Locarno. At the month-long Bierville congress of August 1926, French and German youths celebrated their friendship across borders and lived up to the declared theme of the event – *La Paix par la Jeunesse* ('Peace through Youth'). Sangnier sponsored, supervised and even dominated the event, to the point of policing debates that threatened the transnational movement's fragile consensus. As bridge-builder within French politics, he also believed he held a sacred trust to uphold the so-called 'sacred union for peace' that brought together the political centre in support of *fraternité* and tolerance at home and peace abroad.

The congresses as a whole placed enormous emphasis on youth as the hope of the world. Sangnier already believed he had established a special bond with the German youth movements so prominent at Freiburg in 1923, which mirrored his long-standing role as a tribune of French Catholic youth. Though fully engaged in the affairs of the world, Sangnier, like the German youth of the Wandervögel and the Quickborn, saw retreat for reflection as a necessary part of an active mission. Like them, he idealized the countryside and the moral fibre that contact with it instilled, in camps, hostels and physical labour. Speaking at Luxembourg in 1925, Sangnier had spoken of his wish that a future congress be dedicated especially to 'a great fraternal communion amongst all the pacifist youths of the world' far away from the battlefields, 'in peaceful and calm environs, under the great pacific trees, near to the pure and moving springs, that you might know one another, love one another'.[1] Clearly, Sangnier already had his own country estate of Bierville in mind as a venue. Comprising approximately 40 hectares and including parkland, woods, prairie and three small rivers, the Bierville estate was located in the Juisne valley of the Beauce region, in the département of Seine-et-Oise. It enjoyed a decent rail link from Boissy-la-Rivière to nearby Paris. Purchased in 1922, thanks in part to his wife, Renée Sangnier (*née* Bezanson), who had lately come into her own mother's estate, the Sangnier family weekend home was also at the disposition of various political and youth movements Sangnier was active in. The Bierville estate even had its own separate guesthouse. From 1925 Sangnier was the elected mayor of the commune.

Ever before the congress, the Bierville estate was littered with tangible-monuments coupling piety with the disarmament of hatred. Le Calvaire de la Paix (Calvary of Peace) was of a piece with an outdoor Way of the Cross, dating from 1923, whose 14 stations punctuated the hillside opposite the house. It was the work of an 80-strong volunteer corps whose labours were united with Jesus's example 'to all men and races'. Atop the hill up which the Way of the Cross climbed, the Calvary of Peace dominated the plateau where the congress delegates of August 1926 would stay in a purpose-built camp. The Calvary of Peace provided a suitable focal point during the high Mass celebrated there on Sunday 22 August. The grottos of Saint Francis of Assisi were reminders of the Franciscan model of pacifism. The local bishop, Mgr Charles Gibier of Versailles, who had been a consistent episcopal ally to Sangnier in dark and bright days since 1910, had come to impart a special papal blessing on the two shrines in November 1924, on which occasion Sangnier gave a remarkable meditation on Saint Francis's example of imitating Christ in the love of enemies and patience with those who err. Similarly, Sangnier declared, Catholics must offer love instead of spiteful hostility to the anticlericalist. Recalling Pascal, Sangnier repeated his favourite writer's aphorism that 'before proving to men the truth of religion, they had to make men desire it be so'. Nearby these Catholic monuments stood a less elaborate but even more striking memorial, 'la Croix de la Réconciliation'. After the Freiburg congress of 1923, the municipality of Freiburg made a gift to Sangnier of two robust Black Forest pines, which were made into this Cross of Reconciliation. The Cross was rudimentary as bark still covered the two tree trunks it was made of; its power lay in its simplicity and its tangible expression of Christian fellowship by the old German enemy towards the French they had met in Freiburg. Fitted to the plinth on which stood the Cross was a marble plaque, a gift from the Prince of Saxony on the occasion of his entry to the seminary. It bore this inscription: 'May the Peace amongst peoples that the Saviour of the World was willing to earn for the world, by the way of the Cross, become as solid as this Saxon marble.'[2] This Cross stood quite separately from the Calvary of Peace previously described. This wooden Cross of Reconciliation bore no figure of Jesus (unlike a crucifix) and therefore was acceptable to both Catholic and Protestant aesthetics.

If Bierville had been turned into a sacred site, a living memorial without war graves, then the congress as a whole used the site to enact real and symbolic reconciliation. Though the dead were honoured, this was no mausoleum but a site where the living turned towards the future. Thus, during the congress, the unadorned Cross of Reconciliation, itself a German gift, was a perfect backdrop for a live tableau of reconciled French and German youth that was turned into an allegorical photograph. This staged photo showed a French scout and a German youth, both in shorts, forming an arc underneath the Cross of Reconciliation with the flags of France and Weimar Germany, while a few steps lower down, at the foot of the plinth, a French girl and a German girl completed a symmetrical image of harmony between the two nations. Whereas the girls faced one another at an angle for the camera and gently touched hands, the flags borne by the two boys above them completed this human circle. More even than photos of the Camp de la Paix (or Peace Camp), this photograph of two French and two German youths communicated a useful allegory of the Bierville congress to the general public, especially when the image featured in the mass-circulation *France-Soir* newspaper. Towers also dotted the landscape at Bierville, with monuments to Saints Paul, John the Evangelist and Catherine of Siena. The most prominent was that of Notre Dame de la Paix, completed just in time for the congress to honour the Virgin Mary, whom, in the words of Sangnier's impromptu public prayer at the foot of the new monument, Catholic hearts 'spontaneously recognized as the Queen of Peace'. This was a deliberate echo of the wartime popularization of this Marian title by Pope Benedict XV himself, who had added the title to the centuries-old Litany of Loreto, a Marian prayer often recited in conjunction with the rosary. As Francisque Gay, a key supporter of Sangnier's, remarked in his paper *La Vie Catholique* of the

Bierville sanctuary: 'How can we not place hope in this peace that is taking shape in the shadow of the Cross and under the Virgin's smile?'[3]

The period of the Locarno honeymoon, especially the years 1926–8, has been described by Serge Berstein as the 'golden age of consensus' in interwar French politics, drawing a line under both the Ruhr episode of 1923 and the left's revival of anticlericalism in 1924–5. Pragmatically accommodating himself to the new foreign policy of détente with Germany, Raymond Poincaré, who returned to power as Prime Minister in July 1926, symbolically retained Briand as Foreign Minister and governed from the centre, to the exclusion of Socialists, Communists and the far right. His programme took reconciliation with Germany and the stabilization of the currency, underpinned by renewed economic growth, as its twin foundations. An interlude between the convulsions of the first half of the 1920s and the more familiar tale of fear and loathing in 1930s' France, this metaphorical summer of grace helped put Sangnier and his Bierville congress of August 1926 centre-stage.[4] At the start of 1926, when Sangnier acted on his intuition that such a congress was desirable, he was confronted with divers practical and diplomatic challenges, but the new consensual atmosphere allowed him to call on both public opinion and friends in high places to make straight the path to Bierville.

As early as January 1926, donors to a subscription in aid of the coming congress in the *Jeune République* newspaper had given some 10,659 francs with dedications to the memory of the war dead or simply 'so that Marc Sangnier will obtain the Nobel peace prize'. Unlike previous congresses, Bierville attracted advance high-level political patronage. At the French Foreign Ministry on 27 January, Briand assured Sangnier of 'his entire sympathy for the Congress' work', promising all possible co-operation from government. Meeting again on 1 June, Briand promised to receive the delegates formally at his office, the Quai d'Orsay itself. Though, as we have already seen, Sangnier himself organized preparations of the Bierville estate, his resources and organizational reach were not limitless. The estate had already welcomed campers and friends of Sangnier's political party the Jeune République, but not on the scale of the projected August event expected to draw over a thousand Germans and others over the best part of a month. Here Sangnier's state patrons came to his aid. For the special 'Camp de la Paix' or Peace Camp, which would dominate the Bierville estate, Paul Painlevé, Minister of War, agreed to allow use of large army tents and military field kitchens as logistical support to the peace congress. When the congress took place in August, Painlevé, sorry he could not attend, wrote to Sangnier to acknowledge this pleasing irony and to invert the idea of military preparedness. The minister declared the Bierville congress an eminently patriotic enterprise because 'rapprochement between peoples' was one of the essential 'facets of National Defence'.[5]

In early June, the Democratic International displayed some 3000 posters across France inviting the French population to extend a good welcome to the young Germans whose inscriptions, encouraged by long-term German partners of Sangnier such as Joseph Probst, were arriving daily at *La Démocratie*. Crucially, this manifesto appealed to a new domestic consensus within France congruent with the lowering of the political temperature expressed in a 'sacred union for peace', a conscious echo of Poincaré's famous appeal of August 1914. The imminent congress aimed to 'educate international public opinion in the spirit of peace', it continued, linking its welcome of the Germans to Briand's rhetoric of the 'new spirit' of Locarno and the new 'era of confidence and collaboration.' The message concluded with an impressive list of 117 national politicians who declared their support for the Sangnier initiative headed by Painlevé as War Minister and by two former Prime Ministers, Edouard Herriot and Joseph Caillaux. Herriot was by then Minister of Public Instruction whereas Caillaux, frozen out of politics in 1920 thanks to the political hostility to his wartime peace endeavours, was now in from the cold and acting as Finance Minister in June 1926. Overall markedly left-wing, 42 per cent of the signatories were Radicals or Radical-Socialists (thus coming from the two wings of the same Radical Party) while 15 per cent were Socialist. Ironically, therefore, the Bierville congress occurred with state backing under a Prime Minister, Poincaré, whose trenchant critic Sangnier had been in 1922–4. Adapting to the new political climate, Poincaré was prepared to tolerate or ignore these marks of official endorsement, not least seeing as the tents and the official reception were comparatively small beer politically. All the same, for reasons that are unclear, he did make one personal intervention, to refuse a last-minute request, channelled through the Prefect of the Somme, for extra military sleeping accommodation at Amiens for the incoming German delegates.[6]

In July 1926, with state support secure and an average of 81 letters of registration arriving daily, Sangnier set about securing support from prominent French Catholic opinion-makers. A prominent French Catholic journalist who reflected faithfully the ambivalence felt by many traditional French Catholics about Sangnier's politics was Jean Guiraud, joint editor-in-chief of *La Croix* since 1919. A traditionalist, this historian and former lecturer at the University of Besançon was initially hesitant about going to Bierville but relented after a lunch with Sangnier. Alain Fleury points out that his decision to cover personally the Bierville congress alarmed other conservatives at the paper.[7] *La Croix* was the quasi-official newspaper of French Catholicism in this period, and Guiraud's coverage of Bierville came at a critical juncture in the paper's history. Founded by the Assumptionist order in the 1880s and associated with hard-line anti-Dreyfus politics at the turn of the century, by 1926 *La Croix* hesitated between the Catholic internationalism of the popes and the integral nationalism of Charles Maurras, which, as will be discussed later, was on the point of Roman condemnation. In the event, Guiraud gave the congress mixed reviews while reporting its core message to a broad Catholic readership.

Pilgrimage has long been as essential part of Christian ritual, an external manifestation of the inner desire for purification, change of heart and amendment of life. The journey undertaken by the 900 German 'peace pilgrims' in the first week of August 1926 reconnected with that tradition. Don Sturzo, by now an Italian political émigré out of favour in his own land, wrote to Sangnier that while 'international capitalism and nationalism are united in the work of paganism against all the ideals of pacification, the Pilgrims of Peace, coming from north and south, with all different flags, are the voice of humanity that suffers, hopes and prays'. Different German contingents, coming from Strasbourg, Maubeuge and Saarbrücken, fused at Metz in Lorraine to form a single, pacifist convoy. The sacred union for peace was active with an ecumenical 'Comité d'union sacrée pour la paix' at each port of call, such as at Reims, Laon and Rouen. The pilgrimage of peace was a self-conscious reversal of the events of 1914. At Amiens City Hall, Sangnier contrasted their peaceful 'procession' through France with the 'march to war' 12 years before along the very same routes, 'to accomplish a work of murder and devastation'. The rail journey was one of reflection and self-examination for the Germans, as Joseph Probst's feelings indicate: 'Our hearts are rent as we traverse the front. Verdun, the great killing field, with the poignant memory of its forts, Vaux and Douaumont, flashes across the screen of our memory the most awful hours of the war, whose anniversary, to the day, it was.'[8]

Having penetrated France's eastern frontiers, over 900 German pacifist pilgrims arrived at the city of Reims at about 11 p.m. on 1 August 1926. Despite the late hour, the probable exhaustion of the travellers and the banality of a railway station, there was a *frisson* of excitement tinged with nervousness in the air. The prefect worried that 'the planned demonstration [...] is contrary to public opinion which lumps all the pacifists in with the same German nationality.' In the Allied propaganda of 1914, of course, Reims had meant the martyred cathedral shelled and destroyed by German artillery. Before they could proceed to Bierville, the German pacifists had to fulfil two crucial criteria of Christian pilgrimage: penance and firm purpose of amendment. Jacques Le Goff writes that Reims, a site of memory *par excellence*, was for the French 'a city, a cathedral and a ceremony'. Significant to the nation as the millennial site of regal anointment, Catholics referred in addition to the baptism of Clovis in AD 496 as the christening of France as the 'Eldest Daughter of the Church'. Unsurprisingly, the task of reconstruction, completed in 1938, was a national project, patronized by church and state. The German pilgrims stepped into Reims Cathedral on the morning of 2 August. Probst wrote how priests from the German delegation said Mass under the watch of Joan of Arc while 'the past, majestic and sorrowful, weighs on this place'. It was an act loaded with symbolism, as striking, in its own way, as the occasion in 1962 when Konrad Adenauer and Charles de Gaulle heard Mass there together. As the pilgrims of 1926 stood outside afterwards, Dr Baur, a barrister from Constance, verbalized his compatriots' feelings about the building's 'lesson in peace'. If the diaries of Alfred Baudrillart, rector of the Catholic Institute of Paris, are to be believed, though, the visit to the cathedral was not quite as edifying an occasion as the official account tells us: 'At Reims, the Germans dare show themselves. Two [German] priests wanted to say Mass in the cathedral; the archdeacon Mgr Camu asked them to remember the authors of its destruction and turned his back on them.'[9] Even if apocryphal, the anecdote shows how bitterly resentful of Germany some of the local clergy were.

The centrepiece of the visit, the reception at the Hôtel de Ville on 2 August, moved indoors for security, was a potential flashpoint which had to be carefully choreographed. On Monday 2 August, at 3 p.m., the provisional Hôtel de Ville (the original having been destroyed in the war!) played host to 1200 Germans. Mayor Laurent and ten other municipal councillors hosted the reception. 'Youth wants peace', declared Sangnier, and will fight the 'violent and hateful state of mind'. The mayor accepted the German pilgrims' gift of 10,000 francs to the municipality as an act of restitution to aid reconstruction, originating with the 'Sacrifice de la Réconciliation' collection begun at the Freiburg congress of 1923. The local paper *Le Nord-Est* called the gift sincere but 'hardly enough to raise up the most modest house from its ruins'. German delegate Baur said the destruction and enormous cemeteries thereabout were 'an invitation to look for new ways'. The Reims ceremony concluded when a single sapling was planted by eight German youths. Designated 'Arbre de la Paix' (or 'Tree of Peace'), this was a variation on the French Republican symbolism of Trees of Liberty 'planted by our fathers' in 1793 and 1848. Moreover, mutilation of trees and the poisoned earth policy undertaken during the German withdrawal to the Siegfried Line on the Western Front in 1917 had hurt local civic pride and blackened the German Army's name. As the assembled crowd began to throw soil on its roots, Sangnier prayed aloud that 'this Tree of Peace, planted by the pacific youth of Germany in the generous earth of France, may grow strong and shelter, in its shade, the Fraternity and Love of the reconciled peoples'. Again, there was to be no sentimental ending. Baudrillart remarked sourly in his diary; 'the Germans planted, with some French socialists, a "Peace Tree." It was cut down the next day, like the fruit trees cut down by the Germans.' On the train after Reims, some German youths expressed a sorrow at the thought of what had happened there in August 1914. They now believed they had begun to redeem such sad episodes by their August 1926 'demonstration, full of hope, at the City Hall of this martyred town'. The people of Reims, according to police, were more reserved: 'In summary, no enthusiasm greeted them, no regret at their departure.'[10]

At the pilgrimage's end, around a thousand German delegates found themselves in Paris, where a packed and tumultuous reception was held on Friday 6 August at the site of the 1921 congress in the offices of *La Démocratie*. Next day they left Paris on a fleet of 30 buses that, in an hour and a half, brought the delegates to Bierville, where they were initiated into a temporary world city under white military canvas. The Peace Camp accommodated some 5410 registered delegates, representing 33 nations. At registration, which cost 10 francs, most youths paid a sum of 15 francs for each day of their stay, covering bed and board. For larger sums, less rustic guests could rent the limited number of rooms available on the estate. The gathering was the type of cosmopolitan Babel the nationalists hated. Seven delegates had come from Asia. It was predominantly a German invasion, though, with some 59 per cent of the delegates coming from across the Rhine, almost double the proportion of French delegates. British and Americans made up about 5 per cent of the delegates. Border officials had remarked upon the strong clerical and teacher presence on the German side. The second week saw the *congressistes* settle down at Bierville for a week of 'international education classes' given by French and foreign university lecturers, amongst others. The third week was that of the congress itself. The journalistic doldrums of the August holidays magnified press

Figure 2 Delegates at the Calvary of Peace, Bierville Peace Congress, August 1926 (Courtesy of the Institut Marc Sangnier, Paris). Note the presence of women leaders in the Congress, such as Germaine Malaterre-Sellier, seated in front row on the left in a white dress and matching broad-brimmed hat.

coverage. Public and politicians looked ahead with expectancy to the September League of Nations Assembly at Geneva, where Briand would preside over Germany's re-entry into the family of nations. A smiling group photograph, bathed in sunshine and taken at the same Calvaire de la Paix, shows something of the event's diversity and *joie de vivre* (see Figure 2). An England–Germany soccer challenge game showed the ludic nature of the event. Others splashed about in the modest outdoor swimming pool. The idyllic vacation from a tormented world was evoked especially well in the colour article of journalist Henry de Korab at *Le Matin*:

> [These are] not professional pacifists. It seems as if they have come to Bierville to make peace in privacy, a kind of familial peace outside of politics [...]. In the park of the chateau, a commission session takes place in the open air. Men, women and even some children make a circle, sitting hither and yon or stretched out on the ground. A goodly and unvexing public [...] Behold a charming little river where a young Englishman has asked an equally young German woman to

> do some canoeing [...] And while a coloured man of deepest black took a photo of this idyllic scene, two priests, oblivious, followed the bank reading their breviaries.[11]

The most resonant political message of Bierville was the possibility of a Franco-German reconciliation that was moral and popular as well as legal. Therefore positive impressions of German guests mattered. Bierville was in this month a kaleidoscope of activists and curious onlookers. Women were again prominent, and the French press was impressed by the fluent French of Adele Schreiber, feminist and former Socialist member of the Reichstag. From the German literary world, poet Kurt Tucholsky attended Bierville. One of the 'cultural Bolsheviks' associated with the *Weltbühne* literary and satirical review, Tucholsky had moved to Paris to spread his dream of a cosmopolitan European polity whose later destruction by the Nazis drove him to despair and death in 1935. What mattered most, though, was individual friendship forged through habituation to the foreigner. Joseph Folliet, a young Social Catholic activist from Lyon, took to heart the Franciscan message of the bucolic retreat. Together with the remarkable German seminarian Franz Stock, destined for an illustrious priestly ministry spent in Paris in the 1930s and '40s, Folliet set up the Compagnons de Saint-François as a (Franciscan lay auxiliary) 'Third Order of the roads' which promoted joint acts of pilgrimage between French and German youths. Though Sangnier was never invited to the Katholikentag which was the official annual gathering of the German Catholic, nonetheless, the French consul in Nuremberg said Bierville was the first 'fissure' in the wall of German Catholic prejudice against 'irreligious' France. A whole generation of Catholic exchanges between France and Germany would appeal to the 'spirit of Bierville'. Folliet recalled this inspirational moment:

> Bierville 1926. I am ashamed to use the cliché: an unforgettable memory. But nothing else says it as well. The long, white lines of tents, where the pilgrims of peace are staying, drawn form all over the world and each with their own tongue [...] And like a loud-hailer commanding the murmur of a human crowd, sounded the clear, lively vibrant eloquence of Marc Sangnier.[12]

The political ecumenism celebrated at Bierville was both long in gestation and extremely perilous for a Catholic like Sangnier. The liberal peace movement in France had a large overlap in membership with the

League of the Rights of Man and the Masonic lodges. Strange bedfellows for a good Catholic like Sangnier. Was he not dabbling in syncretism? After all, mixing the Gospel and Socialism had been one of the charges levelled against him in Pope Pius X's apostolic letter of 1910 that had ended the Sillon movement. Sangnier's response to this was invariably the same, a variation on the wartime theme of the 'sacred union'. He argued consistently that those Masons who were secular without being sectarian deserved the chance to be comrades for peace just as they (and the priests) had been comrades in the war. In this regard, some ecumenical links were established in the interwar peace movement that would bear fruit in an utterly different context a decade and a half later during the Occupation of France. Geoffrey Adams's study of the political ecumenism of the Free French movement shows how real fellowship in the common cause of resisting the Nazis united those once set apart by religion or political ideology. Like the later Resistance, therefore, the Bierville moment in French politics was diverse and inclusive. Several secular luminaries of the future Resistance passed through Bierville in August 1926. As a 19-year-old activist in the left-leaning Ligue d'Action Républicaine et Socialiste, Pierre Mendès-France, the future Prime Minister of the French Fourth Republic, also attended. Sangnier's Catholic-inspired political ecumenism did not alienate this assimilated French Jew.[13]

Equally, veterans were a crucial arc in this same rainbow 'sacred union for peace'. René Cassin, 14 years Sangnier's junior, spoke at Bierville on behalf of the centre-left Union Fédérale des Mutilés (UFM) veterans' organization and its newspaper *La France Mutilée*. His painful war wound obliged him to wear an orthopaedic cincture for the rest of his life but it also added to his moral authority. Since 1924 Cassin and other veterans' leaders had been touring France in support of arbitration, security and disarmament through the League of Nations. (Cassin also served at this time as a French delegate to the League of Nations and would in later life become a Nobel peace laureate for his human rights activism, having been in the Resistance network of the Free French.) Antoine Prost has written of how, in the context of 1926, when the dark days of the '30s and '40s could not be foreseen, these men saw in the Locarno reconciliation project the best testament to the death and suffering of comrades giving substance to a 'sensible' and patriotic pacifism that took Aristide Briand for its hero. Veterans present at Bierville 'saluted the memory of their comrades who had fallen on the field of battle [...] affirming their horror of war and their desire for universal peace [and] gave to the pacifist groups the moral surety of their sufferings and injuries'.[14]

As if to prove Sangnier's idea of a 'sacred union for peace' with the internal enemy, Ferdinand Buisson, President of the League of the Rights of Man, was involved in a remarkable incident at the congress's opening ceremony on 18 August. Mgr Léon-Adolphe Julien was the impeccably patriotic bishop of Arras who was also the author of a Catholic tract that was broadly positive about the idea of the League of Nations. For the congress organizers, the bishop represented a good choice of ecclesiastic to make a speech on the Christian attitude to peace and war. Julien was no leftist and had only come to Bierville after persuasion. However, he shared with Sangnier a determination that the memory of the war which had devastated his diocese had to become a vehicle not of division but of reconciliation. The idea that 'they died for peace' was a sentiment that lay at the heart of his most enduring achievement, the construction of the war memorial at Lorette. Moved by the bishop's eloquent speech on Catholics and peace, Buisson, nicknamed 'the pontiff of secularism' in the press, replied generously. Surprised by the old anticlericalist's kind words, the bishop rose spontaneously, crossed the podium and shook hands with the old enemy. As the official account puts it: 'At this manifestation of internal peace, on the terrain of peace that unites such eminent and exemplary men of goodwill, there was a new wave of prolonged applause.' Charity began at home, even before the Germans. The secular press cheered the gesture. In private, even the Vatican smiled on Buisson's mellowness in his old age. Julien had given scandal to many of his own flock, however. Hate mail poured in to the bishop for consorting with Germans and Freemasons. In his diary Baudrillart wrote acidly: 'Mgr Julien and Ferdinand Buisson fraternize and embrace one another. How infinitely touching!' Julien tried to limit the damage with an explanation in a newspaper article in *Le Correspondant*. Acknowledging the pope's directives that Catholics avoid 'rationalist' congresses in favour of strictly Catholic movements, Julien nonetheless pleaded indulgence. He explained that:

> If any question should be exempted from this rule of conduct, it is that of the peace of the world. If the hard law of war demands all citizens to rally to the same flag, in spite of spiritual divergences, why should it not be permitted to all to collaborate [...] in the universal work of peace?[15]

The rhetorical question posed by the senior ecclesiastic Julien appeared to legitimate such ecumenical overtures to former enemies in the 'culture wars' in France. On Sunday 22 August, in the same spirit of tolerant pluralism within the Peace Camp, Quakers, Lutherans and Free Christians held their own services, while a large congregation gathered at the summit of the same Calvary of Peace seen in the group photograph to hear Bishop Gibier of Versailles celebrate a special Mass. More than the bishop's homily, or his reading of the pope's message of approval, it was the common, Tridentine rubric that made the occasion truly catholic: 'The Holy Sacrifice continues while French and German choirs alternate. Above these thousands of bowed heads [...] the arms of the blessed Crucified One extend widely in a boundless gesture of Love, Reconciliation and Fraternity.'[16]

Writing to her fellow Quakers in 1927, Ruth Fry took as one of the great lessons of Bierville the need 'to enlist pageantry on the side on the angels'. Sangnier believed totally in the power of sacred drama:

> Let us have panache! There are enough military reviews with bands, bugles, drums, and assemblies of young men, slaves to brute force. Let us, for our part, place all this radiant enthusiasm and passion, which were the monopoly of the forces of war, at the service of the great power of love and peace.

During the Bierville weeks, these same hills were alive with the sound of music. The free-spirited musicality of the German Wandervögel caught the ears of their French hosts and was part of the acoustic reality of the Peace Camp. Here also the anticlerical troubadour Xavier Privas performed alongside Henri Colas, the Catholic hymnist whose political aesthetic we shall revisit in Chapter 7. Colas, songwriter for 'the cause' since Sillon days, composed a special bilingual theme song for the 1926 congress. Its strains echoed around the campfires that were burned late into the night at the Peace Camp and which were burned in turn into the memory of the participants. Entitled *Brisons nos chaînes* ('Let us break our fetters'), Colas's secular hymn called on peoples to arise and to 'set upon hatred's tomb/ The happy cradle of Peace.'[17]

The Théâtre de Verdure, the estate's specially constructed liturgical space, was ideal for showcasing the liturgy of peace. The site of both the opening and closing plenary sessions of the congress, its tiered platforms were built into the hill to create the illusion of a natural, tree-bound amphitheatre. The first major liturgy held there was a celebration of the anniversary of the adoption of the Weimar constitution of 11 August 1919, which fell during the congress. That evening, after nightfall, there was a quasi-military procession led by guitar-strumming young Germans of the Wandervögel bearing the pennants of the French and German republics from the Peace Camp to the Théâtre de Verdure. Here at the Bierville congress politics and pageantry met. The Wandervögel's folk music and popular unison reflected their anti-conformist and original brand of German popular culture, though national renewal was an abiding concern in its discourse. At the Bierville amphitheatre the 500 torchbearers fanned out along the three elevated platforms of the stage: 'Magical illumination like a great chandelier alive with three rungs of flames. In the centre were the flags. To the crowd Marc Sangnier then made some brief and enthusiastic remarks, cut off by the cries of "heil," "bravo" and by applause.' The speech (in German) by youth Kurt Döbler betrayed fervour for Sangnier, whose sincerity had won over even the sceptics amongst them: 'Marc Sangnier believes in us and trusts in the young German Republic.'[18]

The congress's grandiose *séance d'ouverture,* which set ablaze the Juisne valley on Tuesday 17 August, was an even grander nocturnal spectacle. Attended by some 9000 people, the vigil made use of technical means inconceivable before the war. For instance, the Théâtre de Verdure was illuminated by electric searchlights. The loudspeakers amplified the oratory. The opening ceremony thus belonged to a new type of mass meeting of the 1920s made possible by technical advances originally made for military purposes in wartime. Searchlights, developed so as to identify enemy aircraft at night, were now been used to floodlight a pacifist vigil. Cameramen, not least those of Pathé, came to Bierville to film during this month. On this opening night Sangnier led a torch-lit procession of a thousand *congressistes* from the hilltop Peace Camp, amidst singing and a profusion of national flags over which an enormous blue PAX banner took precedence. With due reverence, this river of light processed downhill, spellbinding onlookers with the 'near-fairylike sight of this long ribbon unrolling in the night. Conifer torches [... like] golden stars, hugging the hillside of Bierville.' Crossing the parkland in front of the château, the procession duly ascended the steep slope that led to the packed and expectant amphitheatre. Each of the three levels of the large tiered rostrum was then filled, the top two with national flags and their bearers, all deferring to the central blue PAX banner, thus forming an enchanted backdrop for the speakers on the raised dais below. Ritualizing the rehabilitation of Germany through her youth, the ceremony also showed how 'torchlight processions, running in relay and shouting in unison were all new forms of expression in this period'.[19]

The closing ceremony reiterated the theme of Franco-German reconciliation. The so-called Fête de la Paix took place at the same venue on the afternoon of Saturday 21 August. It was a spectacular affair and by far the most elaborate liturgical representation of cultural demobilization. Accompanied by a scattering of lyric and dramatic artists from Parisian theatres such as the Odéon, the Opéra-Comique and the Comédie-Française, the performing artist Firmin Gémier and his director Pierre Aldebert conceived of the pageant as a 'fête populaire', a variation on the medieval mystery play with popular participation. At the Théâtre de Verdure a representative of each nationality took his or her place on the terraces. As the ceremony proper began, attention turned to rings of children shouting for joy at the reign of Peace. Suddenly their play was stilled by the arrival of the bereaved of the war, mothers and widows, clad in large symbolic capes in mournful black: 'the joy of childhood makes way for the sorrow of the generations most cruelly tested by the war.' The dramatic use of widow-actresses to represent sorrowing mothers recalled the hand-picked fictional grieving 'family', representing the nation, that had headed the cortège at the funeral of France's Unknown Soldier in November 1920. At Bierville the women knelt at the foot of a border-post, symbol of man's sinful division, which was immediately transformed into the Cross the symbol of pardon. The two grieving mothers – one French, the other German – having been reconciled with one another at the foot of this improvised Cross advanced together towards the future. At this juncture a young woman clad in the brilliant white of the Angel of Peace emerged miraculously from behind the tree cover to complete the tableau (see Figure 3). Captured for posterity by the photographer, this was 'a moment of general reconciliation, a joyous fusion of all the delegations, the great, reconstituted human family hailing Peace, Work, Love'.[20]

In his discussion of French narratives of the First World War, Leonard V. Smith emphasizes the scholarly consensus around the intrinsic link between (male) citizenship and military service in the French republican tradition, a tradition into which Sangnier and his fellow French liberal pacifists must be inserted. The controversy at Bierville on this question of military service should be understood as part of a transnational debate dividing the peace movement. The late Peter Brock's final collection of essays attempted to compare such culture clashes over time and national contexts, but generally scholars have approached the conscientious objection issue from the national perspective, which is to underplay international influences. For instance, at Freiburg in 1923, John Stephens, an English Quaker, said that 'it would be a great day for France and her pacifist movement when Marc Sangnier found himself in prison as a conscientious objector to all war.' Having grown up in the shadow of the defeat of France in 1870 and wedded to the

Figure 3 The Angel of Peace at the Fête de la Paix, Bierville Peace Congress (Seine-et-Oise), 21 August 1926 (Courtesy of the Institut Marc Sangnier, Paris).

foundation myth of the nation-in-arms, Sangnier (and many French participants of different generations) found Anglophone and German integral pacifism discomfiting. Conscientious objection was the most contentious issue at Bierville, as it was for the peace movement generally: Buisson himself had been central to brokering a compromise declaration on it at the Universal Peace Congress in Paris in 1925. The Bierville congress's own assembly of veterans deliberately avoided the subject altogether. Separately, on Friday 13 August, during a session of the congress's preparatory week dedicated to 'National Youths and the Problem of Peace', the German radical Catholic Nikolaus Ehlen raised the issue of military service. Ehlen, a former soldier who had featured in heated debates on the Ruhr in Freiburg in 1923, declared that youth rebelled against generalized military service and its violation of the divine spark of human conscience. Gospel simplicity marked Ehlen's pacifism: ' "He who lives by the sword, perishes by the sword." [...] The way to triumph is through freely accepted suffering, like we saw at Golgotha.'[21]

Ehlen pursued the issue relentlessly in the deliberations of the Moral Commission of the congress, which was obliged to hold two extra afternoon sessions on Friday 20 and Saturday 21 in order to reach a compromise. Ehlen's motion was philosophical but brief, denouncing obligatory military service as morally illegitimate. It had, broadly speaking, the support of young German delegates, though moderate German Catholic pacifists in the Friedensbund Deutscher Katholiken (FDK) were opposed to Ehlen. The French were generally hostile. The main spokesmen for the median position were Sangnier's secular friend Buisson and Maurice Lacroix, a younger activist in the Jeune République party who also wrote for the party's newspaper that bore the same name. Though Buisson was a French Freemason and Lacroix a French Catholic, both accepted that conscientious objection existed and was based on eminently respectable convictions which for liberalism's sake should be respected, on condition that its sincerity was verifiable. Going further, they felt that in the case of an illegitimate war, citizens had both the right and the duty to refuse to bear arms. However, for many such 'old-style' pacifists, objection to military service in general represented an unacceptable individualization of pacifism. The mutual incomprehension was worsened by the linguistic factor, with the objectors being mostly German-speaking or English-speaking and their opponents French. However, caution is required here, as Ehlen represented a radical fringe of German Catholic youth within the Quickborn, which was already at odds with the patriotic pacifism of the FDK. Franziskus Stratmann, the theologian and Dominican priest who had preached at the Freiburg congress in 1923, had elsewhere accused Ehlen of dangerous sentimentalism.[22] Informing this opposition to unconditional pacifism was a traditional Christian understanding of the morality of war developed, with all manner of subtle gradations, by Thomas Aquinas. Ehlen was one of those Christians who begged to differ. He implied that the doctor of the church's work served as a comfort blanket for conservative Catholics or establishment Protestants conjoined to the state. At Bierville nearly all of the Anglophone dissenters from military service were Quakers.

In the animated sub-commission debate, a majority was sympathetic to Ehlen with a sizeable minority fiercely opposed. Louis Rolland, of the Law Faculty of Paris, who had clashed with the Quakers at Luxembourg a year earlier, was again to the fore defending the concept of the citizen-soldier. The continuing deadlock is described in great detail in a private memorandum of the event kept by Georges Blanchot. A follower of the Sillon before the war, Blanchot, a *mutilé de guerre*, was increasingly estranged from the movement in the 1920s as he felt its pacifism was not clear-cut enough. Blanchot records the clashes between Ehlen and Fr Bach, a chaplain in the Sillon Catholique, the clerically controlled successor of the old Sillon. As refusal of arms afforded no means of defence to the weak, Bach wondered if such a stance was quite simply 'killing by allowing killing?' Refusing to budge from his absolutist position, Ehlen retorted that in that case 'you would always make war because the press, government and opinion would always present the war they are planning as good and legitimate.' Raising the issue of the 'competent authority' in the declaration of war, Bach wondered if a Christian could rightfully serve in such an international army created by the League? Most integral pacifists, not just at Bierville, said no League of Nations sanction legitimized killing: 'a Christian is not a gendarme.'[23]

In the end the sub-commission could not avoid a vote. The moderate Lacroix motion was adopted almost unanimously, that of Ehlen passed narrowly. Both motions were sent forward to the final plenary session of the congress, which met on Sunday 22 August for final ratification. With Sangnier's connivance, the plenary session deliberately overlooked the Ehlen motion and approved the moderate Lacroix motion as the collective and consensual judgement of the congress. Sangnier showed he did not like his personal authority to be questioned: an anonymous German youth wrote of him 'raging' and 'fulminating' against Ehlen's motion. In Lacroix's consensual motion, the congress 'denied the right of the State [...] to violate the dignity of individual conscience', reaffirming 'the right and the duty' of every citizen of a rogue state to 'refuse to bear arms'. In other states, 'until obligatory military service is generally abolished, it is desirable that States where it exists should arrange for civil service for conscientious objectors which might well exceed military service in duration, in hardship and in dangers.' However, at the plenary session an addendum proposed by Buisson was added as a further rider. Insisting that objectors would have to prove their bona fides by means of rigorous civil national service, the Buisson amendment's final lines hardened the tone appreciably by 'declaring itself against recognition of the absolute right of all citizens individually to escape military service on their mere *ipse dixit*, without anything in substitution, while their fellow-countrymen have to bear the whole burden'.[24]

Traditional republicans like Buisson and traditional Catholics such as journalist Jean Guiraud were deeply suspicious, for their own reasons, of the reification of individual conscience. A generation earlier, writer Leon Tolstoy, as a Christian anarchist, had indeed identified universal military service as 'the keystone of the arch holding up the edifice' of the state. Guiraud saw dangerous individualism at work in conscientious objection: 'individual interpretation of the Gospel can lead, in these matters, to the worst errors.' A certain ideological conservatism and anti-individualism on the matter of military service was another, less edifying aspect of the much vaunted political ecumenism and 'sacred union' between Catholics and the French Republic at Bierville. In light of Bierville, the socialist feminist cinema actress Fanny Clar had written an open letter to Bishop Julien in the centre-left *Ere Nouvelle* accusing him and his church of relativizing murder. Julien responded publicly to her charges, arguing that she was an extremist individualist who wanted to turn the natural social order upside down: 'God, having created it as it is, cannot then destroy it.' Julien went on to label conscientious objection as the Trojan horse of subjectivist individualism, declaring: 'I see Tolstoy coming [...] careful now! Shall individualism compromise the very fabric of States? [...] Reasons of conscience can be covers for bad faith and pure cowardice.'[25]

Similar scorn was poured by moderates on a speech given at Bierville on 19 August by General Martial-Justin Verraux, a former wartime correspondent of the left-wing *L'Oeuvre* who had accompanied Buisson on secular peace delegations to Germany in 1924. After a long colonial career and home command of an army corps in 1914, Verraux's current views – outright rejection of legitimate national defence – were an embarrassment to some people. Verraux wanted the demobilization of childhood as the logical extension of school book reform, declaring: 'Let us not teach children to play at war; let us not habituate them to handling arms and guns, even in the form of inoffensive toys.' Historian Stéphane Audoin-Rouzeau has identified a reaction in the interwar years in some sections of the French peace movement against the anti-German guerrilla sentiments that had been inculcated through games, books and schooling during the war itself. Verraux was in tune with those activist teachers who removed war toys from children and lobbied manufacturers to replace toy soldiers with innocuous tram conductors and postmen! In *La Croix*, Guiraud ridiculed Verraux as a renegade bent on 'the destruction of the army'. The whole Bierville congress was ridiculed by the Communists, whose newspaper *L'Humanité* referred to bourgeois dupes and their 'odious palaver'. Recalling France's ongoing military campaigns against the Rifs (Moroccan insurgents led by Abd-el-Krim) and in Syria, mandated to France under the League of Nations, *L'Humanité* asked if the 'peace tourists' were 'so busy planting "peace trees" ' the delegates failed to notice 'while Herriot, Briand and Painlevé imprisoned, by the hundred, the brave who stood out against colonial brigandage?' The sarcasm of the Communist paper highlights a blind spot we can identify in Sangnier's views; while courageously outspoken on Irish self-determination in 1921, Sangnier remained ambivalent about applying the same principles in the French Empire. The erstwhile anti-militarist turned patriot Gustave Hervé took a more benign view of proceedings in *La Victoire*. Recalling wistfully his own pacifist youth, Hervé issued a caution rather than a rebuke: 'Let us be pacific, then, with Marc Sangnier [...] but, at the same time, let us be strong, armed to the teeth [...] Preserve the warlike virtues of our race if we do not wish to be cruelly grilled sometime for being pacific!'[26]

By proposing a sacred union for peace (and against the exaggerated nationalism that Pope Pius XI had warned of), Sangnier was suggesting Catholics collaborate with some of their sworn enemies. The peace project left Sangnier and his Catholic supporters exposed to attack by nationalists such as Charles Maurras of the Action Française which claimed to defend a 'national' Catholicism they regarded as tied with an umbilical cord to political authoritarianism. This movement kept up an unrelenting hostility to Sangnier and his Christian Democratic errors, just as they had since 1904. In the run-up to Bierville, anonymous pamphlets – whose authors were suspected to be members of the integrist Catholic Benigni clique close to the Maurras movement – alleged the Paris nunciature was conspiring with the Sillon against both France and the true faith. The nationalist right duly attacked Bierville as unpatriotic and risible. In a comparison with the American circus impresario (whose tours had become a household name in France in the 1890s), the *Action Française* newspaper sneered relentlessly at 'Barnum-Sangnier', master of the three-ringed circus at 'Barnumville'. Throughout this period, the paper insisted on misspelling their opponent's first name, Germanizing Marc to Mark. The cartoon 'Les Adieux de Bierville' reinforced the point (see Figure 4). Against the background of a recognizable drawing of the château of Bierville and the Peace Camp, Sangnier gave his Valentine, an enlarged heart, to a crudely stereotyped figure representing the hated 'Boche': 'German delegate: "Farewell, Herr Sangnier. Until next year. Next time, you'll be Germany's guest ..." Sangnier: "Bravo! In Berlin?" German: "*Nein, ici.*" '[27] However, with the pope approving of Bierville, the event was also bound up with church politics and the Vatican's next move – against the Maurras movement.

The papacy was also attempting to navigate various competing currents at this time. Having indicated at the time of the Ruhr occupation his church's distrust of national chauvinism, Pope Pius XI had thrown his support behind the new Locarno spirit of Franco-German détente. To say the least, traditionalist Catholics in France were lukewarm about this part of papal policy. At Bierville, when a young priest told him how he had been obliged to ask permission to attend, Bishop Julien

Figure 4 'Les Adieux de Bierville', cartoon, *Action Française* (25 August 1926) (Courtesy of the Bibliothèque de Documentation Internationale Contemporaire, Nanterre)

smiled ruefully and quipped: 'What impudence [...] You don't ask a bishop's permission to enter such a dangerous milieu!' Anxious to resume, after the anticlerical Herriot government of 1924, the path of conciliation between the Vatican and the French republic that had marked the immediate post-war period, the pope and his secretary of state, Cardinal Gasparri, found the monarchism and Germanophobia of Charles Maurras distasteful and politically inconvenient. There had long been doubts amongst some Catholic leaders about the orthodoxy of Maurras, who instrumentalized religion as a bulwark of reaction rather than professing it as a faith. In the words of critic and philosopher Maurice Blondel, Maurras was an atheist who turned Catholicism into 'a war machine, an instrument of earthly reign', suppressing the soul for the sake of a tyrannical 'order'. Though Maurras's books were placed on the Index in 1914, the Vatican had not publicly corrected the Action Française in contrast to Pius X's public rebuke of Sangnier in 1910. By 1926, though, Pope Pius XI was preparing for a confrontation with Maurras sympathizers in the French church, who were reputed to include no fewer than 11 of France's 17 cardinals.[28]

Sangnier's filial address to the pontiff seeking a renewed papal blessing on the congress's work emphasized the Democratic International's role in weaning youth away from aggressive nationalism and its 'false ideals of hatred'. The request had been transmitted to the Secretariat of State – which handled the Holy See's relations with governments – by the papal nuncio to France, based in Paris. A diplomatic cable from the Paris nunciature reminded the Secretariat of State that, like past meetings of Sangnier's peace movement, 'the Congress does have a democratic character' so Rome reacted cautiously. The Secretariat of State requested Valerio Valeri, assistant to the nuncio, to make further enquiries in Paris; the fact that only three French bishops – Julien (Arras), Gibier (Versailles) and Bruley de Varennes (archbishop of Troyes) – had agreed to attend initially created a bad impression, Valeri wrote back to Secretary of State Gasparri. However, Valeri proceeded to give an up-to-date (and positive) estimate of Bierville's political significance, stressing the political consensus in favour of the event and the broadmindedness of the Briand policy it reflected. Appealing to the Vatican's own foreign policy agenda, Valeri declared that 'this will be, without any doubt, the most important Congress ever held in France since the war in favour of ideas such as peace and the coming together of peoples.' Ecclesiastically, Valeri found Archbishop Dubois of Paris unenthusiastic for the event but not opposed to an official blessing. Anxious not to implicate the pope in a rationalist, syncretistic congress or in the ecumenical movement from which the ultramontane church held itself aloof until the Second Vatican Council of the 1960s, Valeri weighed a papal blessing for Bierville in the diplomatic balance:

> With regard to this matter – in my humble opinion – there are pros and cons. The Congress is not confessional, just as the previous ones were not; instead, there will be representatives of every party and

> belief. [...] On the other hand, to say the whole truth, the opposition by a large majority of Catholics to these Congresses is due, more than anything else, to an exaggerated nationalism.[29]

In the final analysis, Gasparri approved the blessing, read out at Bierville, but one addressed only to the Catholic participants and calling for prayers for the church in Mexico, then under violent attack from anticlerical forces: a subtle hint to Catholic democrats not to get too cosy with the forces of secularism, who might look the innocent flower but remain the serpent underneath. The idea of any papal blessing for a congress with prominent Masons as headline acts led to severe criticism of Catholic dignitaries and the Vatican for giving religious unction at all to Bierville. Like the movement they attacked, Bierville's right-wing critics acted out their attacks transnationally as the universal Catholic Church was now implicated in a leftist conspiracy, they claimed. In France, an ex-priest wrote to Jean Guiraud at *La Croix* under the sinister pen-name 'Miles Christi' to denounce 'aberrant Catholics' for their 'puerile' desire to ape the 'Protestant and Masonic pontiffs of the modern international ideology'. In Italy, where the Fascist state's hostility to left-wing internationalism fed a strong vein of anti-Masonic rhetoric, the presence of former Italian Prime Minister Francesco Saverio Nitti was a red rag to a bull. Nitti, who served as Italian prime minister in 1919–20, was a Radical, a Mason and, from 1924, an anti-Fascist émigré. French police said the speech at Bierville of this 'known Francophobe' reminded the French press of his pro-German policies and increasingly pointed attacks on the Versailles settlement and the thesis of Germany's responsibility. The Italian newspaper *Il Tevere*, meanwhile, saw a sinister Franco-Italian internationalist front at work. Nitti, they pounced, was a kind of witch-doctor who had assembled the spiritual forces present at Bierville into an unholy alliance, 'a type of superior and unheard of Trinity, one at once Anglican-Masonic-Catholic'. *Il Tevere* dripped sarcasm also about Bierville's French hosts:

> It is a miracle of pacifism that allows us to see humanity being moved by an exchange of messages between the Papal Secretary and the old Sillonist organizer Sangnier; this event has led to the extolling, in the shade of St. Peter's dome, of the virtues of that Congress that was led by Ferdinand Buisson.

The Vatican was sufficiently stung by the article and the accompanying cartoon, replete with Judaeo-Masonic insinuations, to issue a clarification in the pages of its official paper *L'Osservatore Romano*. It stressed that the pope's telegram had been above party politics, avoiding the term 'democratic peace' that the congress used in favour of the papal endorsement of social and international peace 'in the reign of Christ'.[30]

By this stage, papal foreign policy and the correct doctrinal understanding of patriotism required that Catholic nationalism in France be brought to heel. At precisely the moment that the last tents came down at Bierville, the singularly reluctant Cardinal Andrieu of Bordeaux was made to break the bad news from the Holy Office. In a reply to the written questions of young Catholics, Andrieu declared an anathema against Maurras's movement: 'Catholics by calculation, not by conviction, the men who lead the Action Française use the Church [...] but they do not serve it, since they reject the divine message which it is the Church's mission to propagate.' There followed a protracted crisis in the French episcopate and amongst royalist Catholics, by the end of which the formidable Pius XI had reconfigured Catholic leadership in France to root out nationalist insubordinates in a manner that showed the papacy was fully in charge of the French church. The pope even instigated an editorial cull at *La Croix* – which Jean Guiraud survived – to give it a new, more moderate line. Soon Maurras's paper *Action Française* drew connections between the papacy's enthusiasm for events such as Bierville and the condemnation. In the 16 years since 1910 the roles had been reversed, with the Christian Democrats now getting succour rather than censure. Maurras was indicted for the same heresy as Sangnier in 1910: seeming to subordinate revealed religion to a political creed. The papal censure of Maurras was confirmed on 25 August 1926, the anniversary of the condemnation of the Sillon, a roundabout vindication of the Sangnier movement's loyalty to the pope. As Eugen Weber puts it: 'revenge is a dish that even Christians can eat cold.'[31]

At Bierville in August 1926, Sangnier's Democratic International reached its apotheosis, acting as a site of sacred drama and a moment of *rassemblement* for the whole centrist and centre-left European peace movement. Within France, the Bierville phenomenon consecrated a peace coalition of moderate Catholics and moderate secularists which Sangnier called the ' "union sacrée" on the field of human endeavour for the reconstruction of the world', in contrast to the sacred union for national defence during the war.[32] These August days made of Sangnier one of the pole stars of a new political consensus. Though its detractors dismissed it as a holiday camp for the criminally naïve, Bierville garnered mainstream support and was, and came to be remembered as, a moment of hope in Franco-German relations. Understanding politics as part performance-art, the organizers of the Bierville congress tried to make pageantry and shared camp life not just symbolic of international reconciliation but constitutive of it. At another level, Aristide Briand shared the same insight, as his rhetoric of new beginnings and new hope at the League of Nations Assembly of September 1926 in Geneva shows. At the meeting which admitted Germany to the halls of the League on 10 September, Briand gave a famous speech that tried to draw a line under France and Germany's bloody encounters of the past, announcing: 'Away with rifles, with machine guns and with canons! Make way for conciliation, for arbitration and for peace.'[33] Both Briand and Sangnier were sometimes guilty of an overdone lyricism in their speeches but in both cases it served a political purpose; to move the audience and thus create an ambience congenial to the resolution of conflict. Moreover, where Sangnier had led with French and German youths in breaking bread at camp dinners, the politicians followed in the autumn of 1926 with the celebrated meal taken together by Briand and Stresemann at Thoiry in Switzerland, at talks following German entry to the League. In the remaining years of the Briand–Stresemann axis, Sangnier's movement faced the challenge of maintaining transnational contacts at the same pitch. Importation of German models of youth organization into the French sister peace movement and redoubled engagement by the cross-border Democratic International itself in transnational campaigns, on issues from disarmament to a united European continent, would constitute the new frontiers of this pioneer movement.

7
Crusade of Youth, 1927–32

With the award of the Nobel Peace Prize to Aristide Briand and Gustav Stresemann in 1926 for their work in restoring the concert of Europe, a veritable mystique of reconciliation enfolded Franco-German relations and coloured the civic peace activism of entities like the Democratic International. However, as the French poet and patriot Charles Péguy had warned, the descent from *mystique* into *politique* would bring its share of disillusionment. Tribune of this mystical message of peace, drawing on the imagery and ritual of his faith, Sangnier innovated in the late 1920s by imitating German youth and hostelling movements in France, literally redressing the fabric of youth culture. However, politics snagged his civic pacifism at home and abroad. Germany's official pacifists grew wary of his meetings, but radicals in Germany attacked him for his moderation. At the heart of an imaginative, global campaign for disarmament in the early 1930s, the ambient radicalization of politics attendant on the economic crisis led Sangnier to move outside the political mainstream and to embrace France's new wave of radical anti-militarism after 1930.

From 4 to 7 September 1927 the peace congresses returned to Germany for the first time since the Freiburg congress of 1923. However, it proved impossible to match the excitement of August 1926 at Bierville, with a mere 90 French youths travelling to Würzburg.[1] At the opening meeting, held at the Plätzchen Garten meeting hall, a resilient Sangnier self-consciously addressed a transnational constituency: 'Young French scouts, German Quickborn, republican socialists of many lands [. . .] we recognize them all as they are all part of the same spiritual family as ourselves.' Imitative of the Peace Pilgrimage of German delegates in France a year before, Sangnier led a 'Peace Circuit' of southern German cities after the congress which allowed him to speak directly to the German public. At Frankfurt on Saturday 10 September, at an open-air meeting, he declared that 'we are working to hasten the day when all peoples disarm, when to guarantee the security of states there won't be so many guns, canons or fortresses [...] as a real Society of Peoples will uphold right.' None of this could hide the disappointment of Würzburg for Sangnier. Numerically dominant, German concerns won out at Würzburg with a markedly revisionist attack on the peace treaties. In the same month, Sangnier's paper *La Démocratie* called for the evacuation of the Rhineland in the context of verifiable German disarmament but the lack of movement by the French government caused tempers to flare at Würzburg – a southern city that Sangnier had been warned was a hotbed of radical anti-militarism. Radical pacifists such as Vitus Heller, founder of the pro-Marxist Christian Social Party, prominent at the meeting, alienated moderate German Catholic spokespeople, and the bishop of Würzburg snubbed the congress.

On the credit side, the Würzburg congress was the first to include a Race Commission, following on from the head-turning presence of several non-European delegates at Bierville. Wilhelm Solzbacher, the young German translator who had fallen in love with Sangnier's message, recalled how, at the already fabled Bierville congress of 1926, he had shared his canvas lodgings with Mohammed Hatta, the future Prime Minister of Indonesia, and K. M. Panikkar, a British-educated Indian intellectual who would later become independent India's first ambassador to Communist China. Panikkar returned to the Democratic International for the Würzburg congress in 1927, where, along with nationalist delegate Van Giao of Indochina (Vietnam), he led the charge against colonialism. The congress repudiated ideas of race inequality while colonial delegates went further and called, separately, 'in the name of morality and democracy, for the peace of our consciences and for material peace: No More Colonies!' The Race Commission showed just how transnational the Democratic International had become and how a movement like Sangnier's became a forum for a new global anti-imperialism after the First World War. As we saw in Chapter 2, hopes had been raised high in the 'Wilsonian moment' of 1919, but even if colonial self-government did not suit the hegemonic powers, the ideas legitimized by Wilson's rhetoric of self-determination had a powerful impact beyond Europe all the same. Non-European elites emerged with charismatic leaders who became household names in Europe, such as Ho Chi Minh of Indochina and Gandhi of India. Loved or reviled in Europe, they came to that continent to claim national self-determination, as seen in the 1927 Congress of the Suppressed Nations in Brussels.

Communist-associated unrest in French and Dutch colonies in South-East Asia and the non-violent mass disobedience of the Congress Party in British India added to the ferment of discontent in Europe's colonies in the interwar years. In Sangnier's movement, though, many French found it difficult to conceive of their own imperialism as other than benign. The Marxist analysis of Panikkar at Würzburg linking imperialism with capitalism and war and calling for the abolition of League mandates (such as that France enjoyed in Syria) riled many French delegates, who spluttered that his proposal was 'extreme' and 'impractical'. Sangnier agreed to endorse only the '*pacific* liberation of all oppressed peoples', as distinct from liberation by force of arms, which he had supported for Ireland.[2]

However, the Würzburg congress also revealed some of the new, structural impediments that would affect the Democratic International in the second half of the 1920s. As the debates at Würzburg showed, German pacifism was itself increasingly divided, making Sangnier's attempts at a broad front more difficult. In these years the Deutsche Friedensgesellschaft [DFG], the umbrella organization for peace leagues within Germany, was debilitated by internal rivalries: the patriotic pacifism of Quidde was eclipsed by a more radical and disciplined anti-militarism, represented by Fritz Küster, which privileged collective activism over the liberal legalism of Geneva-style pacifism. In the Catholic Friedensbund Deutscher Katholiken (FDK) a new radicalism was also afoot, much as the leadership sought to temper it. The radical embrace of conscientious objection by German delegates under Vitus Heller's influence at the Würzburg congress was typical of the type of factionalism emerging inside the Catholic peace league. At Würzburg, Sangnier arbitrated between the camps by means of procedural dirigisme which alienated the German radicals, who felt his insistence on near-unanimity was designed to defend French interests and thwart the principled opponents of military service. Even if, in October 1927, Sangnier's periodical *La Démocratie* stated that the thesis of German premeditation of the war in 1914 had become 'unsustainable', Sangnier's Jeune République party could never go far enough for its new radical interlocutors across the Rhine.

In the late 1920s, meanwhile, many German Catholic peace activists and the Centre Party itself sidelined Sangnier, turning instead to the safer, dignitary-dominated and formal Franco-German Catholic Conferences held first in Paris in July 1928 and in Berlin in December 1929, safer meetings which were dominated by conservatives. In parallel to this, the European meetings of the Christian Democrat parties attracted increasing attention. These European gatherings were held under the aegis of the Sécrétariat International des Partis Démocratiques d'Inspiration Chrétienne (SIPDIC), a pan-European entity founded in 1925 with the help of France's centrist Christian Democrat party, the Parti Démocrate Populaire (PDP). The PDP were the sibling rivals of Sangnier's Jeune République party. The SIPDIC held a transnational congress on German soil for the first time in July 1927, at Cologne. The SIPDIC rapidly became a transnational reservoir of policy ideas and contacts but one that was not open to Sangnier or his party. Notwithstanding the frostiness Sangnier was beginning to experience from moderate German Catholic opinion, in 1927–8 the Democratic International remained a serious contributor to the global civic peace movement allied to the League of Nations. In one respect there was an advance in 1927 on the matter of co-ordinating the growing wave of civic peace pacifism across Europe. Previous to this, on the margins of Sangnier's Vienna congress in 1922, efforts to co-ordinate civic peace movements on a transnational basis had begun with the creation of a steering group, including Sangnier, Fr Metzger of the IKA and the British MP Sir Willoughby Dickinson, representing the Protestant-led World Alliance for Friendship Through the Churches. Astonishingly (or perhaps not astonishingly given the often fractious nature of committees), it took nine meetings and four years before a report outlining the nature of a new body came before the XXV Universal Peace Congress in Geneva in 1926. It then took another year before an International Committee for the Coordination of Pacifist Forces was founded. A well-meaning initiative, it had no outstanding impact, as its pooling of information seemed to duplicate the long-standing work of the International Peace Bureau in Geneva. In the flowering of such bodies in the aftermath of Locarno, a few endured, but many proved ephemeral.[3]

By September 1928 the Democratic International's annual rhythm of meetings meant it was time for another congress, and an eye-catching one at that. Held at Geneva and Bierville and dedicated to 'the peoples' peace through the League of Nations', it was in many ways the crowning glory of the Democratic International's transnational activism. The official account opened with the following declaration: 'Geneva-Bierville! The mere linking of these two names is wholly symbolic.' By holding its congresses in August or September of each year, the Democratic International managed to shadow the annual autumn session of the League Assembly. One event complemented the other, making the peace congresses part of a rhythmic, annual mobilization of a global civil society meant both to support and to cajole diplomats and governments.

As Susan Pedersen points out, the League itself 'fed off and promoted popular mobilization'. Thomas Davies argues that the transnational campaign for a world disarmament conference which was gathering pace worldwide in 1928 demonstrates the vitality of such links between the national League of Nations movements, mobilizing organizations that (in name at least) represented millions across the globe. A key figure in that campaign and a veteran of several of Sangnier's peace congresses was the old English Liberal MP Sir Willoughby Dickinson, who spoke at the inaugural session of the 1928 congress at Victoria Hall, Geneva, to congratulate the League on 'muzzling the dogs of war'. Next day, 14 September, after visiting the League's home at the Palais des Nations, delegates declared that they 'better understood what hopes were founded on our efforts'. Joseph Avenol, Assistant Secretary-General of the League, praised the Democratic International for its courage since 1921, when the 'very first intimate Franco-German rapprochement happened in your meetings'. Germaine Malaterre-Sellier, vice-president of the Jeune République, served as a French delegate to the League of Nations Assembly. She and Sangnier led a delegation of congress delegates to a reception on the same day at the International Labour Organization's offices. There, in a spirit of political ecumenism, Albert Thomas, the Secretary-General of the ILO who was himself a French reformist Socialist, paid generous tribute to the Democratic International's work for peace and to Sangnier's defence of workers' hard-won gains, such as the eight-hour day:

> You, in particular, represent the great social reform tradition of the Catholic Church. Without the least reserve and whatever our individual beliefs or our personal private faith, we salute in you one of the great moral forces that, with fifty years, has helped modern society achieve essential reforms.[4]

Buoyed by such international endorsement, the Democratic International assembled after Geneva at Bierville to endorse a streamlined organizational structure under the title 'Action Internationale Démocratique pour la Paix', whose new charter and constitution codified the practice of seeking overwhelming consensus (set at a three-quarters majority opinion) for policy decisions. An international executive with national representatives governed, with Sangnier as president of the movement, assisted by three vice-presidents: the Germans Ludwig Quidde and Joseph Joos, and the British Quaker Ruth Fry. However, it was through a new youth movement at home in France that

Sangnier would make the most significant innovations of 1928. At the Freiburg and Bierville congresses, German youth movements such as the Wandervögel and Quickborn had blazed a trail through their organization and *mise-en-scène*. As a transnational youth movement, associated with Franco-German rapprochement, Sangnier's movement, in its turn, reflected the timbre of the times and the ubiquitous militarization of politics, even pacifist politics. Sangnier's German guests, with their uniformed, serried ranks of young acolytes in torch-lit processions, reflect Mitterauer's statement that, in the 1920s, 'youth groups were no longer wandering hordes; they were marching columns'. Sangnier attributed a messianic role to youth in the disarmament of hatred, increasing his fixation on the formation of a new generation of pacifists.[5]

Created in July 1928, the Volontaires de la Paix were a scout movement founded by Sangnier in an attempt to perpetuate the 'spirit of Bierville' – 'Peace through Youth' – and to imitate German youth by institutionalizing this new relationship between military organization and pacifist youth culture.[6] They recruited males aged between 15 and 25. With time, the age cohort was redefined downwards to include a junior branch for boys. Tammy Proctor has analysed the international influence of the booming scouting world of the period. In these movements, uniforms were meant to 'erase otherness'. But neither could scout organizers ignore differences in nationality, and the French and Germans at Sangnier's congresses remained sartorially distinguishable. The non-confessional Volontaires were decked out in a navy blue beret with a distinctive insignia bearing the word PAX emblazoned upon a golden sun and the letter V (for victory) in red, for the blood that was shed for the sake of peace (see Figure 5). Once deemed suitable, the postulant recited a pledge to the movement, including a commitment 'to be strong, loyal, pure, courageous and disciplined to labour in the work of peace'. As Don Sturzo wrote to congratulate Sangnier on this crusader youth: 'it is youth that can operate this transformation in minds because it is generous and has the future before it.'[7]

Like contemporary youth movements elsewhere, the rigorous tests for aspirants, the role of charismatic leadership and a 'millenarian sense of need for the heroic and for self-sacrifice' all coalesced in 'a secularized form of a religious order'. The young man took his place in a team or *équipe* and a whole paramilitary system of rank and symbols. Proposing a toast at the end of the eighth congress at Bierville in September 1928, 16-year-old Jean Sangnier acknowledged this self-conscious use of martial trappings as 'a bit revolutionary', but, he said, 'there is a

Figure 5 Les Volontaires de la Paix, 1929. The peace scouts march along the Juisne valley from Boissy-la-Rivière to Bierville (Seine-et-Oise) (Courtesy of the Institut Marc Sangnier, Paris)

certain beauty in military things, a terrible beauty, a hateful beauty, but they [the Volontaires] have transformed it into a sublime and still greater glory'. This phenomenon of mass youth regimentation was by no means limited to Germany or the pacifist movement. All ideological and political groups, not least the Catholic Church, were consolidating centralized auxiliary youth wings at this time. Through Catholic Action, Pope Pius XI encouraged unified Catholic youth movements under clerical guidance. Sangnier's youth movement existed in the shadows of the startlingly successful Jeunesse Ouvrière Chrétienne (JOC). A youth movement for Catholic workers, the JOC attempted to bring Christ to the factory floor. Founded in Belgium by Fr Joseph Cardijn in 1919, the JOC came to France in 1926, with its first section at Clichy in the 'red' suburbs of Paris, instituted by Fr Georges Guérin, a veteran of Sangnier's Sillon: in fact, the JOC revered the former youth movement Sangnier had led in the first decade of the century. Intimately bound up with this mass organization of youth was a deep concern across Europe and across the political spectrum with social hygiene. Virtually all groups donned uniforms and espoused healthy minds in healthy bodies. Given the Volontaires de la Paix's military style, part of the rigorous tests for aspirants included a physical and medical examination. Physical training was inseparable from moral formation. At admission, Sangnier often administered the pledge before dubbing the new knights-apprentice of peace.[8]

However, it is in the related cult of outdoor life and in the foundation of the French youth hostelling movement in 1930 that Sangnier calibrated most enduringly the development of youth culture in the interwar period. The hostelling initiative also provided tangible means for French and German youths to meet and forms bonds of reconciliation. In founding hostels, Sangnier was acting out of the generalized predilection for fresh air and holiday camps, which, as Laura Lee Downs shows, he shared with co-religionists and secularists alike. From the time of the great pacifist summer camp he had hosted in 1926, Sangnier was deeply concerned with keeping the spirit of Bierville alive. To this end, he proposed that a permanent Foyer de la Paix be established there, which was completed in August 1930. A centrepiece of the Foyer was the Epi d'Or, France's first youth hostel, inaugurated in 1929. The German hostel pioneer Richard Schirmann, with whom Sangnier had personal contact, encouraged this development of the hostelling movement in France. Each hostel had a Père or Mère Aubergiste, who set down the limits of youth autonomy. Sangnier's faith in the idealism of youth led him to believe that hostelling, 'through the closeness it fostered between youths of all backgrounds and nations and the fecund vigour it developed in mind and body, will well serve the same cause of peace and democracy'. The original French hostelling league, the Ligue Française des Auberges de Jeunesse (LFAJ), followed in 1930, with Sangnier in a central role. Recent historical writing has re-emphasized the crucial role of Social Catholics in the 'invention of leisure' in the period 1900–40, coinciding with the advent of more free time and the phenomenon of adolescence. Indeed, in terms of organized team sports (particularly soccer) and of scouting, like the Volontaires, Catholics were often cast as pioneers in giving an urbanized population new leisure opportunities and a new educative relationship to the countryside. (For example, Jules Rimet, a former Sillon activist from the Franche-Comté, was a key figure in world football history as the organizer of the first World Cup in 1930 in a spirit of fraternity through sport: the competition trophy later bore his name.) Sport and leisure were no politics-free zone though. The secularist wing of the French hostelling movement left Sangnier's LFAJ in schism in 1933 to found the Centre Laïque des Auberges de Jeunesse (CLAJ), while Catholic bishops were none too happy at the mixing of the sexes under the same roof at the hostels! However, Sangnier's pioneering efforts contributed to a general invention of leisure that would blossom in the France of the 1930s.[9]

The suitably named Crusade of Youth held across France in September 1929 marked a coming of age for the new Volontaires de la Paix. Held from 16 August to 1 September 1929, this ninth peace congress was an attempt to conquer the entire country by means of a German pacifist 'invasion'. Jay Winter observes that such pilgrimages 'drew upon and added to the kinship bonds already forged by war victims and their families'. In its planning and execution it resembled a military operation. The organization of the young 'crusaders' into self-conscious 'columns' testifies to the truth of Tammy M. Proctor's statement that all social and political movements of the 1920s had an interest in the regimentation of youth, 'in mass rallies and spectacles, parading their aspirations on the backs of the young'. The French Volontaires de la Paix went to meet their German guests at various border crossings. The different columns were to meet up at Amiens and from thence proceed to Paris on Saturday 31 August for a grand finale. Of all the columns, it was the eastern one which best recalled the celebrated 'pilgrimage of peace' of early August 1926. Now, three years later, in 1929, German youth was back in the north of France in a renewed peaceful invasion. Now, shoulder to shoulder, they would confront the memory of the war, as mediated by their elders. On the Monday evening, 19 August, in the erstwhile war zone at Halluin (north of Lille and just inside the French border with Belgium), the local Jeune République organized a showing of the film *Verdun, visions d'histoire*, made in 1928 by Léon Poirier in an attempt to reconstruct the battle as an epic event that dwarfed its participants. At Hénin-Liétard, on Thursday 22 August, Jean Sangnier was master of ceremonies when a 'German comrade', Paul Feltrin, whose father had died at Verdun, 'protested his hatred of war'. (The eastern column visited the Douaumont ossuary at Verdun, itself the focal point of 'silent marches' by veterans.) The young German's embrace of a French colleague epitomized mutual pardon and brought cries of 'Vive la paix, guerre à la guerre!'[10]

There was fun too, however. The shared quarters in country barns broke down barriers. Joseph Probst divined the presence of that 'common soul' which had moved the Sillon: 'We are already like members of the same family. Last night we read a page of the Gospels together.' Liturgical singing – the pilgrims had a special songbook prepared by Sillon songwriter Henri Colas – built up *esprit de corps*. Despite the language barrier, Jean Sangnier recalls the Germans playing guitar and general good humour. The role of music was again vital: special songbooks were issued (one in bilingual translation) bringing together the anthems of Henri Colas and the German pacifist repertoire. This was not art music, but the words and music are certainly evocative and betimes affecting. Resolutely uncommercial, Henri Colas's minstrel compositions were distinctly French, with the same bucolic affinity to 'douce France' that would soon be woven in more contemporary style into the *chanson* of the hugely popular (and commercially successful) singer Charles Trenet. Colas's early output of religious hymns at the turn of the century, such as the *Prière du matin* (sung by the Sillon), may be appreciated as popular Romantic melody, but with the potential for sentimentality and syrupy arrangements, as was then fashionable in late Victorian English Catholic hymns also. The secular marching songs written for the peace scouts of the 1920s were more direct, in fast tempo but not goose-stepping. The texts (often from Colas's pen too) were edifying but provided credible space for emotions of sadness and loss, as in the evocative 'La Paix sur le Rhin' (a knowing reference to the patriotic song title 'Die Wacht am Rhein'). Here the dead fathers of the French and German scouts observe their sons' oath of friendship, their paternal shades urging them on. Designed for straightforward unaccompanied singing, musical settings accentuated the pathos of the lyrics often with a palindrome within the octave. Bright high notes at beginning and end framed a middle descent to the lower register to emphasize the pity of war.[11]

The crusade itself was also part of the growing wave of battlefield tourism in the 1920s. French and German 'Crusaders' in the northern column jointly visited the ossuary and war cemetery at Lorette. Lorette, Douaumont, Dormans and Hartmannswillerkopf (today known as Vieil Armand) were four national battlefield ossuaries that 'blended the cult of the dead with an affirmation of religious faith'. They were examples of how 'national memories are crystallized in historic sites'. The Lorette monument was built by Mgr Julien of Arras, patriotic bishop of the partially occupied diocese from 1917. However, his visit to the Bierville congress in 1926 had been the object of heated controversy, showing how much at odds Sangnier's movement was with mainstream conservative Catholicism. Invited in 1929 to this new ceremony, the bishop was obliged to keep his distance, confessing to Sangnier in private correspondence how badly his own flock had taken his public appearance with the secularist Buisson three years before and how Christian pacifism infuriated them. Rumoured to have been passed over for promotion to the archbishopric of Besançon in 1927 on account of Bierville, Julien was pinioned by the Action Française and by enduring and sincere sensitivities of people in a region where reconstruction was so extensive that it officially ended only in 1927. The bishop concluded wistfully:

> I would prefer to renounce the honour of enjoying your company in posterity and having a share in your glory when your ideas will have at last triumphed. I need [...] to tend souls, all souls, getting them to bear only as much of tomorrow's truth as they are able to.[12]

All the same, at Lorette in August 1929 German and French youths proffered their hands to one another in a peace pledge while pressing around the grave of a Sillon war hero, Amédée Guiard, to hear Joseph Probst mourn his pre-war French friend from the Sillon that had welcomed him, a German Catholic youth, to Paris before the great tragedy of the war.[13]

The apotheosis of this crusade took place on Saturday 31 August in Paris, where the various columns converged. Far from ignoring it, official France gave its imprimatur to Sangnier's endeavour, with a luncheon at the Quai d'Orsay. Beating protocol, the Wandervögel wore shorts. Briand, indisposed, had the Agriculture Minister Jean Hennessy act as host. Also president of the French League of Nations movement and an enthusiast for European federalism, Hennessy spoke again that same evening at the Fête de la Jeunesse et de la Paix, the crusade's closing rally, at the Palais du Trocadéro, praising the gathering as a fine preface to the attempt of politicians like Briand 'to bring the peoples of Europe together'. Ludwig Quidde, the German anti-militarist of long standing, spoke with the moral authority of the Nobel Peace Prize. As at Lorette, a 'peace oath' was renewed by youths of both nationalities at the Trocadéro, in front of the ubiquitous blue flags bearing the word PAX.[14] It declared:

> We, the young, swear by the dead of the world war, of whatever nationality, to place our activity and energy at the service of peace and international justice [...] Victims of the world war, sleep in peace. We will be faithful to our oath. *A bas la guerre! Vive la paix!*[15]

After the discussions between Briand and Stresemann at Thoiry in September 1926, a veritable mystique of rapprochement had grown up, in which Sangnier and centrist Catholics, assisted by the simultaneous condemnation of the Action Française, played a key role. This mystique obscured for a while the underlying differences that remained between France and Germany. Rapidly, however, the limits of personal diplomacy were discerned behind the rhetoric and the Nobel prizes awarded to the two statesmen in 1926. Big questions lurked in the shadows of the feast. What was the omega point of Locarno diplomacy: the consolidation of the *status quo*, as France wished, or the revision of the Versailles settlement, as Germany wished? The issue of reparations, the subject of a new and purportedly long-term settlement in the Young Plan of 1929, continued to dog Franco-German relations in 1927–29. The German government, just like German delegates to Sangnier's congresses in the late '20s, linked German fulfilment of these debts to an accelerated Allied withdrawal from the Rhineland. (The Young Plan's ratification, itself the subject of intense Nazi propaganda in Germany, in fact led to French troop withdrawal five years early, on 30 June 1930.) A multilateral pact like the Briand-Kellog Pact of August 1928 pleased the peace lobby with its pious renunciation of war but did little to fulfil Briand's hopes that such a pact would create collective security or draw America out of isolation.

Conscious of German concern for German minorities in Eastern Europe and German desires to revise their eastern frontiers, including possible union with Austria, Briand seized on the intellectual fashion for European federalism. In these years, the most seriously committed 'Europeist' enthusiasts were to be found in the Pan-Europa Union. The movement's founder Count Richard Coudenhove-Kalergi was an Austrian politician and aristocrat who had grown up as a multilingual subject of the Habsburg Empire. Son of a Japanese mother, Coudenhove-Kalergi considered himself a European unburdened by exclusive national identities of the sort that characterized Europe's nation-states after 1918. As a pamphleteer and as leader of the Pan-Europa movement, he favoured a united Europe with a Franco-German motor acting as its driving force. The formation of an international steel entente in 1926 and a Franco-German commercial treaty in 1927 gave the federalists heart. The private attraction of 'a federal link' within Europe for Briand when he floated it at the League in September 1929 was as a counterweight to demands for territorial revision by internationalizing such disputes. Stresemann's death intervened in 1929, before Briand fleshed out his ideas in a memorandum on European unity within the League framework that was unveiled on 1 May 1930. Though by then the German response emphasized just how far apart the two governments were, Briand's forlorn attempt to tie Germany into peaceful co-existence with her neighbours sparked off a whole wave of enthusiastic debates on European unity within the peace movement.[16]

Electrified by Aristide Briand's ideas of a European parliament and a common market, Sangnier's Democratic International dedicated its tenth congress, held in Brussels, Ostend and Bierville in September

1930, to the European idea. At Brussels, Sangnier declared that 'the United States of Europe is a must'. Georges Hoog's opening report to the congress anticipated German calls for border changes. Marie-Emmanuelle Reytier shows that when such calls emanated specifically from German Catholics they represented a Catholic variant of a broader sentiment in favour of 'Greater Germany', usually articulated in this Catholic variant as a feeling of fellowship with German-speaking Catholics in neighbouring lands and a nostalgic desire for unity with Catholic Austria. At the Brussels congress, Hoog responded to disputes of this type by declaring that European federation would help ease tensions by lowering the frontiers rather than displacing them. In anticipation of the congress, Hoog had gone so far as to write of the necessity of a 'truly European mentality, a European civics, what we would dare call a European patriotism'.[17] The meetings in Belgium managed to paper over disputes over the admission of Fascist Italy to such a European federation. The exiled Don Sturzo refused to countenance Mussolini having a seat in such a European entity. Corresponding with Sangnier in advance of the Brussels meeting, prepared against the backdrop of the economic crash of 1930, Sturzo anticipated calls at the congress for free movement of labour and capital within an overarching ethical and European context:

> One thing is worth affirming; that one cannot have a European federation with economic parameters, unless it is also and contemporaneously present in political and moral spheres. As the free economy is better adapted to concentrating the interests of the various states, so too democratic politics are the best adapted to overcoming national egotisms while Christian morals are the best suited to the fraternity of peoples.[18]

As in 1920, this correspondence put Sangnier once more at the heart of a pan-European Christian Democrat republic of letters whose general contours are outlined in Wolfram Kaiser's recent study. (Indeed, in 1932, the SIPDIC, representing Christian Democrats, borrowed ideas from liberals in the movement for a European customs union and agreed a resolution in favour of market integration and farmer support in Europe akin to what transpired in the European Economic Community after the Second World War.) Sangnier's European programme, therefore, reflected and amplified diverse impulses for Europe which co-existed with Christian Democrat utopianism about a new Christendom. Therefore, the final resolutions of the International Democratic Peace Congress at Brussels in September 1930 endorsed the desirability of supranational organization of Europe in which national sovereignty would be 'subordinated, through voluntarily agreed restrictions, to international public order, alone susceptible to ending European anarchy'.[19]

Martin Ceadel maintains that 'peace movements fare best when optimism is seasoned with a dash of pessimism.' The challenges of the early '30s bred a new radicalism in the international peace movement. As Norman Ingram shows in the French case, a new brand of radical anti-militarism came to the fore in France in the early 1930s to rival and outshine the liberal League of Nations pacifism, which had dominated the movement in the '20s. This European radicalization was in part a product of the impact of the Depression but also reflected the dramatic emergence of threats to world peace from authoritarian regimes, beginning with the Japanese invasion in Manchuria in 1931 and continuing with the aggressive strokes of Germany and Italy in the mid-'30s. In France, debates about the length of national service and the defensive Maginot Line begun in 1930 fuelled such fevered activism. Moreover, as Thomas Davies demonstrates, the years 1930–32 marked the noisy climax of a substantial non-governmental campaign, across borders, for international disarmament led by peace activists (and veterans in particular) who anticipated with fervent hope the World Disarmament Conference at Geneva finally set for 2 February 1932. Ceadel adds that, subsequently, in light of the Munich crisis of 1938, there was a 'subconscious rewriting of history' amongst pacifists about the date of their conversion to 'containment' of fascist foreign policy. For all that, though, talk of sanctions and enforcement measures against rogue states was virtually taboo in left-wing and pacifist circles in 1931–32 lest it jeopardize the Disarmament Conference. Sangnier interacted with these new dynamics in the peace movement in two ways. First, within France, he found himself spearheading a broad national front of peace activists in a pro-disarmament campaign that formed part of the simultaneous transnational effort. Second, Sangnier radicalized his own pacifist rhetoric, bringing it more into sympathy with the new radical anti-militarists, who were on the rise in the European peace movement.[20]

Sangnier had an ambiguous relationship with this new brand of pacifism. In the French case, this new style pacifism was represented by the Ligue Internationale des Combattants de la Paix (LICP), founded in 1931 by Victor Méric. This new organization disseminated extreme pacifist views through its paper *La Patrie Humaine*. The LICP contested the whole moderate pacifist canon of modern French history that portrayed French diplomacy as benign and the war of 1914 as a 'war of right'. They rubbished the very same moderate positions Sangnier had spent the previous decade defending while he promoted Franco-German brotherhood. Heavily criticized for signing the manifesto penned by the advanced pacifists in 1925, Sangnier, by 1932, seemed to have few qualms about sharing a pro-disarmament public platform with integral pacifists such as Méric and the anti-colonialist Félicien Challaye. By openly siding with such groups at this point, Sangnier cut himself adrift from the political centre, where the major political camps were divided on the disarmament conference between 'realists,' wanting 'security first', and moderate pacifists such as Charles Richet, who called for 'arbitration, security, disarmament', in that order. Independent accounts of Sangnier's speeches, often from the platforms of meetings of the LICP itself, as distinct from the edited (and sanitized) speeches published by *La Démocratie,* show Sangnier's violent rejection of nationalism in favour of a new pacifism that now combined anti-militarism with criticism of the League of Nations for failing to preserve peace. In March 1931, similarly, Sangnier told an LICP audience that their purpose was to 'rouse peoples from their apathy' and to 'show public opinion that they did not have to think war inevitable'. Humanity, he said, should realize 'the small case made to it while it was sent "to the slaughter" to defend the cause of the mercantilists'. The speakers Sangnier now associated himself included Georges Pioch, who expressed similar faith in proletarian peace instincts over the politicians of the League, who were 'but puppets in the hands of the Schneiders, the Krupps and the Deterlings'.[21]

On platforms Sangnier shared in 1931–32, he became associated with views well outside the moderate mainstream that he had represented at Bierville in 1926. On 11 November 1931, a sensitive day in the calendar, Sangnier took part in a meeting at the Salle Wagram against the war in the Far East. However, Victor Méric also used the occasion to protest against police scuppering of the attempts by his LICP movement to disrupt the simultaneous commemorative ceremony at the tomb of the Unknown Soldier at the nearby Arc de Triomphe. Sangnier's denunciation of the lack of an international response to the Japanese invasion of Manchuria threw into sharp relief the inconsistencies of the 'war on war' mindset, which berated the League of Nations for failing to protect the weak while pouncing on the idea of sanctions as warmongering. Sangnier said he was tired of 'verbal pacifism': 'The League cannot fail to act without revealing its impotence. That will be the admission that governments took us for fools.' However, in spite of his evident desire to bring Japan to heel, Sangnier elided the question of using force, preferring instead a heightened appeal to international morality, giving implicit support for political sanctions short of war:

> We must have means other than the great disorder of war. If we were not pacifists, every failure of the League would incite us to social war to change things. Perhaps it will suffice to confront governments with the might of enlightened consciences. Maybe that way we can attain our goals if we are resolute soldiers of Peace.[22]

While flirting with the extreme anti-militarists, Sangnier's prescriptions remained sufficiently moralistic and imprecise not to lose him all respectability with the partisans of moderate League of Nations pacifism. The 'Peace or War Museum' tour of 1931, initiated by Sangnier's supporters, was a central part in the broader public information campaign undertaken by the French peace movement in advance of the Geneva Disarmament Conference and the forthcoming French elections of 1932. Well used to collaboration with secular and left groups, the Jeune République had helped to organize the 'peace week' in localities across the land to coincide with Armistice Day 1930. Inspired by this same spirit of common purpose, Georges Lanfry, a Rouen-based party activist, set about devising the striking 'Musée "paix ou guerre" ' ('Peace or War Museum') exhibition, which opened in Rouen in early 1931, before embarking on a nationwide tour. British Quaker Edith Pye wrote of the exhibition as a 'remarkable contribution to disarmament and peace [...] a travelling exhibition of cartoons designed by a member, fastened on screens which fold up and pack into a special motor van'. The six stands, aimed primarily at young people, were didactic and made stark use of text and image to shock and provoke an immediate emotional response, playing especially on fears of aerial bombardment and gas attacks both of which, as Dennis Showalter shows, gave an apocalyptic edge to the literature of war prediction in the 1920s and 1930s. The 'Peace or War Museum' was in perfect sync with popular anxieties, reflected dramatically in the special issue of the popular magazine *VU* issued in February 1931, during its tour of France. Dedicated to the next war, *VU* made the public's blood run cold with playful but ominous photomontages (such as gas-masked figures on the Arc de Triomphe frieze or at a cocktail party). As Roxanne Panchasi puts it, no Maginot Line, then under construction, could save civilians from 'intrusion' and 'violation' at home. Sharing some of the same themes, Sangnier's 'Peace or War Museum' shocked most by means of images relating to the last war.[23]

The mobile museum's most arresting images were not imaginary at all but real photographs of men's facial disfigurements sustained during the past war. The 'gueules cassées' haunted interwar society, a physical reminder of those from the last war who could never forget. The text beneath these truly shocking images goaded viewers to look at them:

> Don't run away so fast [...] Children, look at them, fill your gaze with this awful vision and when you read in your history books that war generates beauty and glory, you will remember their poor faces and you'll recall the truth that war, like hatred, is incapable of producing anything but ugliness, destruction and ruin.[24]

When it came to Sangnier's headquarters in Paris, the exhibition formed the centrepiece of the broader French peace movement's 'Disarmament Week', held between 14 and 22 March 1931. Publicized throughout France on Paris-PTT radio, the museum received 200,000 visitors nationwide. Amongst the prominent veterans assisting Sangnier in this particular initiative was Union Fédérale des Mutilés leader René Cassin, a participant at Bierville in 1926. As his recent biographers Prost and Winter recount, Cassin's transnational activism had continued to develop through the Conférence Internationale des Associations de Mutilés et Anciens Combattants [International Conference of Disabled Soldiers and Ex-Servicemen] (CIAMAC) which he had helped found in 1925 and through his role as a member of the French delegation to the annual League of Nations Assembly in Geneva, from 1924 to 1938. In keeping with this ecumenical spirit, the 'cartels pour la paix' established town by town to welcome the travelling exhibition cast the Jeune République party organization as a catalyst for larger developments in French pacifism that helped to unite Catholic and secular peace movements. Ingram points to the importance of these *ad hoc* local 'cartels de la paix' in bringing about some semblance of co-ordination in the balkanized French peace movement in the run-up to the Geneva disarmament conference. A good example of its broad appeal was the Caen stop, where speakers welcoming the museum included the moderate Jules Prudhommeaux, Secretary-General of the Association pour 'la Paix par le Droit' (APD), and Léon Jouhaux, Secretary-General of the Confédération Générale du Travail (CGT), a prominent trade unionist and national political figure.[25]

The Democratic International's eleventh congress, held at Freiburg-Konstanz on the Swiss-German border in August 1931, served as a refuelling break in the parallel French and German international disarmament campaigns. It was also the last grand rally of Sangnier's Franco-German peace movement. Preceding it, the militarized pacifism of the Crusade of Youth of 1929 was revived and put on display for a week, albeit in miniature, with a march by French and German youths in Alsace. Along the way in that province, some two thousand signatures were collected for a Disarmament Declaration. Sangnier wanted to repeat at the Swiss Freiburg the *coup de théâtre* he had orchestrated many miles north of the Swiss border at Freiburg-im-Breisgau, in Germany's Black Forest, back in 1923. It was not to be. The pacifist youth movements of Germany were in retreat in the Reich, where the Nazi party had won 107 seats in the general election of September 1930. Sangnier alluded to the ambient violence when he spoke to the Germans of 'the Hitlerites and the "steel helmets" ', whose growth had 'profoundly saddened your French friends'. The peace movement now faced an increasingly empowered and emboldened opposition to its efforts from these same *Stahlhelme* and the whole gamut of disaffected nationalist veterans representing men who, in Richard J. Evans's words, were 'incapable of adapting to a world without the Kaiser'. In response, Sangnier placed his faith in the moderate veterans' movement of the Reichsbanner, represented at this new congress, as antidote. However, on a boat trip around Lake Constance, vividly recalled by Jean Sangnier, then aged 19, some delegates had an eerie premonition of the impending storm when Nazi youths paddled a kayak up close to the pack boat on which they knew the peace delegates to be aboard. The adolescent Nazis then unfurled their red flag, complete with swastika, an incident which the pacifists' German hosts tried to laugh off, nervously.[26]

National divisions over the diplomacy of disarmament spilled over – again – into the Democratic International's discussions at this Freiburg-Konstanz congress. In the real (and sometimes unreal) world of diplomacy, the Geneva Disarmament Conference drew closer, by now just six months away. An international 'Preparatory Commission' had spent six years preparing a Draft Convention, which was supposed to act as the basis for an international disarmament agreement at Geneva, where the grand conference was set for February 1932. At the time, and in much subsequent history writing, French policy has been regarded as intransigent and niggardly in its response to this supposedly grand opportunity for disarming Europe. The French War Minister, André Tardieu, made France the first country to declare its hand on the issue when he published a memorandum on 21 July 1931 that claimed French armaments were at 'the lowest point consistent with her national security' before putting the onus on the British and Americans to supply firmer guarantees of collective security if further French disarmament was to be considered. Though this cast France as unyielding, especially in British and American eyes, French historian Maurice Vaïsse asks how it could have been otherwise, given France's vulnerability and its certain knowledge of German violation of the arms limitation terms set down at Versailles. By his statements at Freiburg in August 1931, Sangnier sided with minority opinion in France, represented by the Socialists and the Communists, which promoted unconditional arms limitation and argued the French government was being obstructive. At the opening of his congress in Freiburg, Sangnier declared himself to be against the construction of the defensive Maginot Line along France's eastern frontier and France's commissioning of new battleships, as these policies were inconsistent with a policy of general disarmament: 'We cannot ask others to do what we don't do ourselves.' The Quaker representative Edith Pye spoke of the 'necessary success of the [forthcoming] Disarmament Conference at Geneva'. This she envisaged as a prelude to the total abolition of armies, a statement at which French delegates demurred. This congress witnessed the most strident exchanges between French and German delegates on the question of revising the Versailles settlement. The German delegates moved the Democratic International in a more explicitly revisionist direction than ever before leaving some French delegates to fume in their replies to German delegates at the recent proposal floated by some German and Austrian politicians for an Austro-German customs union. For some French this was but the backdoor to Anschluss, the political union (or absorption) of Austria with Germany, explicitly ruled out in the 1919 treaties. At the promptings of Ludwig Quidde, by then the waning star of German pacifism, Sangnier endorsed final motions at the Freiburg-Konstanz congress which asked that 'no principled objection should be put in the way of the revision of treaties'.[27]

As 1931 drew to a close and the World Disarmament Conference and the French parliamentary elections came into direct view, the tempo of the popular campaign for disarmament quickened, as did the temper of its opponents. An international pro-disarmament rally at the Trocadéro in Paris in November 1931 descended into a riot when infiltrated by 700 members of the nationalist veterans' movement the Croix de Feu, a pattern soon to be replicated in a wave of assaults on peace activists. The sense of militant antipathy to the disarmament cause further constrained French political leaders in the concessions they felt it possible to make at Geneva. Faced with renewed physical violence from their political opponents, Sangnier implied in a speech in Paris in January

1932 that it was time for the pacifists to take the gloves off. Referring to opponents on the far right, Sangnier announced: 'their strength [...] is a product of our weakness.' After invoking the martyrdom of Jean Jaurès in 1914, Sangnier referred to the attacks by the *camelots du roi* on pacifist newspaper vendors, recommending that 'the latter fight with the same weapons as their adversaries.' At this same juncture, Méric and the LICP instituted their own Jeune Garde Pacifique, who were willing to give as good as they got in street brawls.[28] Similarly, Sangnier's rhetoric was increasingly that of combat and violence for the sake of peace, mirroring the near-Armageddon syndrome of a beleaguered peace movement.

The ideological civil war also hung over Sangnier's last interwar election campaign in 1932. Having lost his parliamentary seat in Paris in 1924, Sangnier failed again at the polls in the 1928 elections. Squeezed by the appeal of the new centrist Christian Democrat PDP, the Jeune République fared poorly overall in 1928, the election of law professor Louis Rolland in the Maine-et-Loire département representing one of the party's few successes. Despite this, the party prevailed upon a reluctant Sangnier to stand again in the 1932 election on an independent platform that included a commitment to 'controlled simultaneous disarmament of all nations', in keeping with the theme of the 1931 congress at Freiburg-Konstanz and the 'Peace or War Museum' campaign. This time, however, in an act of daring, he was nominated for the Roche-sur-Yon seat, deep in the conservative Catholic heartland of the Vendée. A hostile electorate did not take Sangnier to its heart. The *Action Française* newspaper took great pleasure in describing how a peace meeting Sangnier held in the Vendée in December 1931 descended into farce. Joseph Delest, a local royalist, roundly criticized the policies of Aristide Briand, 'whose loyal supporter Marc Sangnier is', calling it a 'policy of treason' which had 'handed over the ramparts of security and the fatherland' to German ambition and desire for revenge, inciting the local mob to disavow Sangnier, his 'murderous doctrines of peace' and 'the suicidal theories of the Sillon'. Sangnier lost the election while repeating ad nauseam his message on 'the moral conditions of peace'. Though not quite ostracized by the establishment, he had become tainted by association with the LICP. By the 1932 elections, such a link with militant anti-militarists was something of a liability. Viewed as unreliable patriots, the LICP seemed to be calling for 'peace by all means'. To avoid further ire, both Sangnier and the LICP kept a careful distance from the ultimate pariahs, the Communists. Recession bit hard at the spirit of charity too: in March 1932, at a moment of severe economic dislocation in Germany, French police noted how 'some Catholics who until now had unreservedly supported Marc Sangnier's peace efforts find that he is going too far in asking for godfathers and godmothers for the children of the German unemployed. These are being asked to send to the latter delicacies and clothes.'[29]

When the Disarmament Conference did not live up to the high hopes invested in it, a general pacifist disillusionment with traditional politics set in around 1932. Sangnier's announcement after the May elections of 1932 that he was walking away from party politics stunned his party, the Jeune République. Wishing to lead his followers into a peace activism outside electoral politics, like that of the radicals with whom he had become associated, Sangnier's imperiousness split the party executive on 29 May, when 112 delegates voted against the new orientation and a mere 16 backed him. Sangnier resigned from his own party, taking 32 key activists with him, including Georges Blanchot, Gustave Salmon and Maurice Coquelin. Painfully, he bade adieu to intimates such as Georges Hoog and Maurice Lacroix, who took the Jeune République to new premises and into the competitive electoral politics of the 1930s. Sangnier addressed his last editorial for *Jeune République* simply 'to our friends', in the sure hope that 'a separation for practical work need not seem cruel as it does not affect our ideas or our friendship'.[30] In the summer of 1932 there were external blows too. At the Lausanne conference, Germany effectively used the economic crisis to annul the greatest part of its pending reparations payments. This was hardly likely to make it easier for the French negotiators at the ongoing Disarmament Conference. Hovering around the hard questions without squaring them, the conference agreed to equal military status for Germany in December 1932. In January 1933 Germany got a new chancellor, in the person of Adolf Hitler. From then until the 'Night of the Long Knives' in June 1934, when Hitler eliminated alternative power bases amongst the old conservative German elite and within in his own Nazi movement, Hitler moved cautiously. However, his bold move on the League of Nations in that first year gave an early signal of his revisionist intent in Europe. Hitler pulled the plug on the whole Disarmament Conference pantomime in October 1933 by withdrawing Germany from both it and the League of Nations.

From the early 1930s on, Sangnier vehemently denounced the idea that the peace policy had failed, a heresy he said should be fought with a pacifism of action and not just words. Sangnier's rhetoric reflected the entry of pacifism into a new combative phase from 1932, when the ship of the League began to list perceptibly. The high summer of Geneva optimism, seen at the 1928 congress, was long past. The Freiburg-Konstanz congress of 1931 was to be the last such meeting with the German peace movement, rapidly decapitated by Hitler after 1933. For all his initial caution in Germany, Hitler had introduced quite quickly new categories of preventative political detention (in camps) for awkward political activists on the left, such as pacifists. In France, meanwhile, deprived of his political party from 1932, Sangnier mobilized his Volontaires de la Paix in peace campaigns that struggled to keep hope alive without abdicating their principles to the demands of Fascism. At home, Sangnier hailed the Popular Front victory of 1936, though it put him yet again at the forefront of the culture wars within French Catholicism. Spain, the Rhineland and Munich offered excruciating political choices in which Sangnier was as consistent or inconsistent as many others. Whether peace was worth 'appeasement' or legitimated 'collaboration' was a pressing question that pervaded the bitter struggles of the pacifist movement from 1933 to the end of the Second World War.

8

Marc Sangnier and the Pacifist Conundrum, 1932–45

The spiral of ideological politics in Europe in the 1930s made it a decade of national and international crises in which political pluralism and consensus went into retreat. The confrontation of totalitarian 'sacred causes' – Communist and Fascist – made politics an extension of war, with each side fighting for maximalist aims of re-ordering the map of Europe and the re-ordering of humanity itself, in the name of class struggle or racial purity. While there has been heated debate amongst historians about whether there was a viable French Fascism in the 1930s, the formation and qualified successes of the French Popular Front of the centre and centre-left in the mid-1930s does attest to the sense of a liberal democracy under strain in that country. The Catholic generation of which Sangnier was an ageing but active representative shared fully in this turmoil and the divisions it wrought. The unflinching encyclicals of Pope Pius XI showed a Catholic Church engaged in an ideological war on two fronts – against Communism and Nazism – even if the 'red scare' had more resonance for some Catholics than the threat from the right. Similarly, the peace movement was dragged in contradictory directions by events. Franco-German détente took on a new and divisive meaning once Hitler came to power. For some, resistance to Fascism meant reassessing the absolute value of peace; for others peace legitimated a Faustian pact with the dictators. So searing were the divisions and so turbulent the times that some peace activists, such as Sangnier himself, defended both stances at different junctures in the 1930s.

The failure of the World Disarmament Conference in the spring of 1932 and Sangnier's choice to leave the Jeune République in May 1932 marked a crucial turning point both for Sangnier's own movement and for the broader peace movement, with Sangnier drawn further down the path of integral pacifism sketched out in the previous chapter.

A symbolic moment for this eclipse of moderate pacifism came with the death of an architect of the Locarno Accords, French Foreign Minister Aristide Briand, on 7 March 1932. Support for Briandism came from the centre-left of French politics, from the liberal pacifists of the Association pour 'la Paix par le Droit' (APD) and, beyond France's shores, from the Vatican. As Yves Santamaria puts it, Briandism was 'a substitute Wilsonianism for the democratic left [...] who made of the French statesman the symbol of a foreign policy that turned the page on nationalism so as to enter the era of conciliation'.[1] Sangnier's movement was close to this consensus and it was valued politically by Briand himself, as his support for its various initiatives, at Bierville in 1926 and the Crusade of Peace in 1929, showed. This closeness was spectacularly recalled at Briand's national obsequies in Paris. While his remains lay in state in the vestibule inside the Quai d'Orsay, Volontaires de la Paix stood guard at the catafalque, as Briand had requested. The teenage boys took relays in the guard of honour. In a serendipitous accident and departure from strict protocol, the last two boys to stand guard by the catafalque, Sangnier's son Jean and Bernard Rivière, were present when the wreathed coffin was brought to the front railings of the Foreign Ministry, the Quai d'Orsay, for the military salute and funeral march. While Sangnier looked on from the official tribune, his Volontaires de la Paix, his own son included, stood to attention in an image that was relayed immediately in press photographs of the national event.

This coincidence is more than just a sentimental detail. The prominence of the Volontaires de la Paix, whose ecumenical and pacifist purpose was discussed in Chapter 7, highlights two crucially important aspects of Briand's political legacy. Firstly, as we have already seen, his policies of rapprochement turned him, in his own lifetime, into a symbol of hope for the peace movement. Secondly, his legacy legitimated domestic political ecumenism and a coming-together of the centre-left and moderate Catholics in the cause of peace, in a manner consistent with his own career. From 1905, when as a parliamentary rapporteur he had helped broker the law separating church and state, Briand pursued a policy of accommodation rather than confrontation with the Catholic Church, determined, in the words of his biographer Gérard Unger, to uphold the separate spheres of church and state while giving the Catholic Church its place – but no more than its place – in the public square. The archbishop of Paris came to the Quai d'Orsay to pronounce absolution over the remains of Briand the Freethinker. As René Rémond reminds us, when Briand made the Gourdon speech of June 1931, in which he pleaded for a policy of European reconciliation and was roundly criticized for it in the Chamber, 'it was Catholic democrats like Francisque Gay and Georges Hoog who sprung most vigorously to his defence'. Sangnier had been a key supporter, whom Briand in turn had supported. The 'new-style' pacifists of the early 1930s, advocates of unilateral disarmament, did not join the mourning. They rejected Briand as a fraudulent pacifist. Georges Demartial, one of their chief propagandists, denounced the 'Gospel of the Quai d'Orsay', the 'myth' of legitimate national defence. Victor Méric, founder of the Ligue International des Combattants pour la Paix (LICP), reflected stingingly on the funeral of the Briand he perceived as a traitor to the socialist anti-militarism of his youth: 'A pacifist, he departs amidst flags, soldiers, the tears of [former Prime Minister André] Tardieu and the holy water of Cardinal Verdier.' In death, though, the star of Briand's cult rose exponentially until the mid-1930s. The interment of his remains near Pacy-sur-Eure on 2 July 1932 was another national event. His name appeared in street names nationally, his image on stamps, and the anniversary of his death made the Normandy village of Cocherel the focus of pilgrimages and speeches such as the generous tribute paid by Prime Minister Léon Blum in March 1937.[2]

With Briand gone and Sangnier's own leadership of the Jeune République at an end, the Democratic International for Peace and its founder, Sangnier, were at a crossroads. After the Eleventh International Democratic Peace Congress held at Freiburg-Konstanz on the borders of Switzerland and Germany in September 1931, Spain was mooted as host for a twelfth congress in 1932. However, the peace movement was deflated after all the energy spent on the apparently failed disarmament campaign. In the event, a much scaled-down twelfth congress was held at Bierville in September 1932, a faint cadenza in an unfinished symphony, not even yielding its own official account.[3] The Volontaires de la Paix (whose Crusade of Youth in 1929 had been such a propaganda coup) now seemed to offer Sangnier the most effective means to re-launch a popular propaganda campaign for peace and against militarism. This was the impetus that lay behind the 'Journées d'Espérance' or 'Days of Hope' which Sangnier's core supporters organized as a month-long nationwide series of themed events from 11 to 28 August 1932. Even if liberal pacifists such as Ruyssen collaborated, Sangnier's company in the mid-1930s was increasingly of the 'new-style' pacifist persuasion. For all of the problems besetting the peace movement, the 'Journées d'Espérance' succeeded in making the news in France and in re-capturing some of the imagination and talent for publicity coups of the movement's heyday in the mid-1920s.

The multiple 'Journées d'Espérance' events showed an adept understanding of politics as performance. Germaine Malaterre-Sellier, Jeune République leader and suffragist whom we first met in Chapter 3, opened up her summer home at Hossegor, near Biarritz, to a piano recital by composer and virtuoso Maurice Ravel that was relayed on national radio. In a more political sense, on 24 August 1932, Sangnier reflected the cult of Briand discussed above by leading a pilgrimage to Briand's grave in Cocherel. In the presence of Briand's nephew and niece, children placed flowers on the grave. Long before his death, Briand was popularly endowed with the image of the 'pilgrim of peace', touching on the deep desires of veterans, young people and women who worried for their children's future. Sangnier spoke directly to the children and their parents at nearby Pacy-sur-Eure on the meaning of Briand's life. Its greatness came not only from his being a talented statesman but above all from 'having created a mystique of peace in the world'. Briand had communicated intimately with the peoples he inspired, especially the unlettered and the children, who responded instinctively to his appeal to the better angels of human nature:

> It is because Briand is the apostle of peace that he truly is your elder brother, your father, to all you little children of France [...] to all the children of the world, and most of all to you young German pacifists whom we should love all the more as you have the greater merit of fighting.

The 'Journées d'Espérance' simultaneously honoured at Port-Royal the French Catholic philosopher Blaise Pascal, a formative writer for the young Sangnier. Now, at Briand's tomb, he invoked Pascal's appeal to souls and hearts. Sangnier again addressed directly the children surrounding him. Diplomats could only make peace, he declared, if they, the children, remained true to this simple message:

> The peace of the world [...] can only be achieved in an atmosphere of peace, and this atmosphere of peace, it is this atmosphere of your souls and your hearts, children of France, because we who are growing old, we are leaving behind this world, our souls all anxious and tensed towards the worries of future days, but it is you who shall make the future, it is you who bear it in your hearts.

The shade of Briand wanted not pomp nor 'bugle [nor] the dazzling display of military steel' but instead, 'the simple and devout gift of mothers' hearts, of women's hearts, of children's souls. Peace cannot be made any other way.'[4]

In the same month, Sangnier similarly stood over the tomb of the recently deceased Ferdinand Buisson at Thieuloy in the Oise in a gesture of political ecumenism that recalled the fellowship between Catholics and Freethinkers exemplified by Buisson's embrace of Bishop Julien at Bierville in 1926. Veterans were placed at the heart of the 'Journées d'Espérance' so as to pass on the torch to the young. Police noted how its first event was a visit to Geneva on 11 August, when in the presence of the League secretariat, veterans and *mutilés* would meet with young people attending an international school. On the same day, the advocates of 'peace at any price', as *Action Française* called them, went on pilgrimage to Rethondes, site of the armistice of November 1918. There, in front of the railway carriage used in 1918, Colonel Picot, president of the association of the *gueules cassées*, the victims of facial disfigurement, made a highly emotional address describing what the moment of ceasefire had meant for men in the trenches. The Pensions Minister, Aimé Berthod, spoke of preventing the 'great madness' that was war.

The conservative daily *Le Figaro* bracketed Sangnier's events with the campaigns of defeatist primary schoolteachers, commenting that 'the pontiffs of our pacifism ignore what is going on in Germany.' Catholic critics of Sangnier such as Mgr Alfred Baudrillart described as 'ridiculous' and 'odious' Sangnier's prayers at Briand's and Buisson's graves, but all joined the chorus of disapproval of the Action Française movement when persons associated with it attacked the finale of the month at Bierville. On 28 August, a crowd of almost 3000, including 400 children, packed into the Théâtre de Verdure, the focal point of the 1926 congress. Firecrackers thrown into the arena caused a stampede. Six children were treated for burns, up to second-degree in severity. While the authors of the incident (praised by the *Action Française* newspaper for 'shutting up the valets of the Germans') escaped by car, some Volontaires de la Paix gave chase. The royalist press gloated at Georges Hoog's alleged loss of his temper. When Christian Frogé, a local Action Française supporter, was found out walking in the vicinity in the immediate aftermath of the incident, suspicions were aroused and Hoog was reported to have told the pacifist scouts to 'take a firm grip of him so that I can punch him in the face'. However, it was the tardy and apparently fruitless police pursuit of the malfeasants that led Victor Basch, vice-president of the League of the Rights of Man, to write to Prime Minster Edouard Herriot to complain of the seeming impunity for 'serious breaches of the law, when they come from certain quarters'.[5]

Nonetheless, the appeal to a pacifist mystique (rather than a practical political programme that inspired the 'Journées d'Espérance') had some resonance in the country. It was 'startling proof that we were not mistaken and that it was possible to unite many and diverse people of goodwill all fixed on the same goal, animated by the same spirit'. This encouraged Sangnier to launch a new enterprise for grassroots pacifism – *L'Eveil des Peuples*. The new newspaper of the same name first appeared as a special edition of *Le Volontaire* in September 1932. The first full independent issue of *L'Eveil des Peuples* appeared on 6 November 1932, selling 50,000 issues. Jean Carlu's *art déco* large-format design and impressive blue masthead struck a thoroughly modern note. Carlu was one of the foremost graphic designers of the time, having created advertisements for household-name products, such as 'Banania' and 'Mon Savon'; it was he who had designed a striking abstract poster for the 'Journées d'Espérance'. Sangnier wrote in the new paper's first edition about 'Our Efforts' and about the need to speak out against peace activists who used bellicose language to make 'war on war'. He argued that peace too needs 'strength and violence, but not that of arms. It requires the force of reason and the violence of love.' Such a 'dynamic pacifism' marked a closer embrace of integral pacifism and a loss of faith in jaded liberal pacifism.

Meanwhile, as we have already seen, the Twelfth International Democratic Peace Congress at Bierville in September 1932 was, in contrast to the 'Journées d'Espérance', an apologetic and anti-climactic affair. It led Sangnier to conclude that the peace congresses, in their 1920s' form, were unsustainable. Accordingly, the Action Internationale, the organizing body of the congresses, had the desultory task of dissolving itself in March 1933, weeks after Hitler entered government in Germany. Surprisingly, though, Sangnier did not cast the decision in terms of a defeat. Without the support of the Jeune République, Sangnier considered it unrealistic to maintain the Democratic International in its original form. The final message declared:

> Since 1921, we can congratulate ourselves for having been part of and having contributed to the essential restoration of international relations. However, since then, Congresses have been held, in all areas, and international associations have been created. The impetus that we gave has been followed in all domains: political, social, moral and educational, etc. It now appears to us that our task is accomplished and that we have attained our goal. [...] We propose therefore, so as not to risk duplication with more specialized organizations, to wind up the Action Internationale Démocratique pour la Paix.

Seeing as Hitler was now Chancellor, such a statement might seem hopelessly naïve and even deluded. However, as Ilde Gorguet maintains, the statement merely reflected Sangnier's sense that the time had come to pass the pacifist torch on to a new set of groups, among which he had his own movements – the youth hostels, the scouts and *L'Eveil des Peuples* newspaper – firmly in mind.[6]

'Pacifist depression' was a term coined in the 1930s by the Francophile Greek diplomat Nicolas Politis to describe the broader conundrum posed for the peace movement by the rise of Fascism. Yves Santamaria makes use of it to analyse their dilemma. It was difficult for French pacifists in particular to make the semantic shift towards seeing an external threat, in the form of Fascist expansionism, as the major danger to peace, rather than blaming the nationalist bloodhounds at home. In the immediate aftermath of 1933, preventative measures in the diplomatic realm against Hitler were portrayed as illegitimate because Hitler, though distasteful, was the product of an unjust policy pursued against Germany by the other powers. New-style pacifists persuaded themselves that the principal enemy of peace was the enduring effect of Versailles and the pursuit of traditional French foreign policy since then. Singling out Germany as the sole culprit of 1914 was therefore unacceptable. Hitler's clever appeal to veterans, at home and abroad, allowed the Nazis to be re-branded as friends of reconciliation. Scathing of the old legalist pacifists who defended the previous war as just, advocates of the new pacifism, such as Georges Demartial, advocated purist isolation and a sectarian withdrawal from mainstream society. A pacifist critique of anti-Fascism in the 1930s countered that liberty was not exported at the point of a bayonet and that the costs of modern war discredited war as a means of resisting Fascism. Norman Ingram points out that old-school pacifists such as Théodore Ruyssen were more prescient in discerning that Hitler spoke with a forked tongue on peace. The warnings published in France from Hellmut von Gerlach and Friedrich Wilhelm Foerster sensitized the APD to the bellicose intentions of Nazism and the consequent perils of Tolstoyan non-resistance in the face of this ideology. Félicien Challaye, who led the integrist minority in the League of the Rights of Man, took a different stance and issued a pamphlet in December 1933 'for a disarmed peace even in the face of Hitler'. Without excluding the just grounds for individual acts of resistance in the event of a hypothetical German occupation, he still argued that France should treat with Hitler to right the wrongs of the treaties as 'war, all war between peoples, is stupidity, a crime, the worst of evils, absolute evil'.[7]

Sangnier's own evolution towards integral pacifism and the related public polemic on conscientious objection put him in the front line of these debates in France in 1933. Disagreement with German and British delegates on the issue of national service had marred Sangnier's congress at Bierville in 1926, as we have seen. French political culture was not hospitable to the cause. As Norman Ingram points out, 'conscientious objection was no wildfire malignancy' in the body politic in the early 1930s, but a series of court cases against individual objectors and a leaked government investigation into the issue in mid-1933 showed that the French government suddenly perceived itself to have a problem. By the early 1930s Sangnier's position on objectors was more ambivalent. He conceded their point but felt it to be a politically futile gesture. He declared in 1931 that the objectors' 'only crime is to be ahead of a revolution'. Camille Chautemps, the Minister of the Interior, and the War Minister, Edouard Daladier, ordered an investigation into non-Communist conscientious objection in January 1933, singling out religious movements, not least the reformed churches, teachers and posts and telegraph workers, for observation by the prefects. Leaked to the conservative *Echo de Paris*, the document shocked the political establishment by purporting to show the infiltration of conscientious objection outside the normal Communist constituency. Sangnier featured on the list on account of his unsuccessful pleading in May 1932 for a young Protestant primary schoolteacher and objector, Camille Rambaud. The leak coincided with Sangnier's appearance before the Military Tribunal at Orléans as a character witness for Armand Rolland, a Catholic turned anarchist and conscientious objector who declared he did not want to die for the industrialists and that '[his] body is [his] own'. Sangnier was emphatically agnostic: 'I am not a conscientious objector and I have proven it.' However, like Théodore Ruyssen and the cautious liberals of the APD, he argued that the law should allow for moral as well as physical inaptitude. Sangnier cited the example of two other famous objectors such as the contemporary German-born scientist Albert Einstein and the nineteenth-century French country priest Jean-Marie Vianney, a Catholic saint better known by the title of the 'curé d'Ars', who had deserted the Napoleonic army to follow his vocation.[8]

Sangnier did not save Rolland from gaol, but *Action Française* gloated at seeing Sangnier holding himself up to public ridicule now that, as the royalist paper claimed, 'the Sillon [sic] is working for conscientious objection'. Sangnier, however, operated within the context of Catholic thinking on this issue. Peter Farrugia points out that, as a Catholic, Sangnier was obliged by denominational constraints to 'avoid open praise of the objectors as this would imply criticism of the Catholic hierarchy which opposed them'. Dieter Reisenberger has elucidated the debates within German Catholicism on military service which were touched on in the discussion of the Bierville congress of 1926 (in Chapter 6). German Catholic writers on the subject, such as the Dominican Franziskus Stratmann, author of *The Church and War* (1929), were sympathetic to the pacifist cause but, like the bishops, stood back from the endorsement of personal conscience over national service. In Paris, in December 1932, the French Dominican theologian J. V. Ducatillon delivered a series of controversial lectures on 'true patriotism' to the Institut Pie XI, the young study circle attached to Francisque Gay's Volontaires du Pape, attacking the 'neo-pagan' nationalism of Maurras. Having begun the lecture series with pronouncements tending towards an endorsement of objection on Catholic grounds, Ducatillon drew back, appealing to Aquinas and the duty of obedience to civil rulers against the abolition of military service: 'For a country to abandon it, pure and simple, could be dangerous, a morally unacceptable act of imprudence [...] we de not have the right to inconsiderately expose ourselves to death.' Sangnier's position was unlike that of the Protestant pastor Henri Roser, who featured prominently in the state inquiry of 1933. Roser was a central figure in the French branch of the Fellowship of Reconciliation (FOR), whose British parent organization had been active in Sangnier's London congress of 1924. The trainee pastor Roser shocked the Missionary Society, for whom he worked in 1922–3, by returning his military papers, but, while he met a series of institutional obstacles, French Protestantism still allowed him relative independence in his writings on conscientious objection in his paper, *Cahiers de la Réconciliation*. Roser clashed with liberal pacifist Théodore Ruyssen on the issue at the Boulogne-sur-Mer congress of the APD in 1930. Interestingly, Ruyssen appealed to precisely the same Pascal that Sangnier used repeatedly to counter religious appeals to complete non-violence: 'Justice is impotent without Force and Force is tyrannical without Justice. Since we cannot make Force just, let us make sure that Justice is strong.'[9]

In the years 1933–5 Sangnier was faced with the withdrawal of Germany by Hitler from both the League of Nations Disarmament Conference and then from the League itself, moves which showed a new purpose in German foreign policy. The flight into Parisian exile of some of Sangnier's German associates, such as the pacifist Hellmut von Gerlach, who left as early as 1933, also alerted him to the persecution of dissidents in Germany. Philo-Semitic and an outspoken anti-Fascist, Sangnier was happy to serve on the honorary committee of the Ligue

Internationale contre le Racisme et l'Anti-sémitisme (LICRA), along with Socialists such as Henri Sellier. A shadow from the past must be acknowledged at this point. Vicki Caron, in her examination of the turn-of-the-century 'democratic priests' and their Catholic defence congresses – in which the young Sangnier participated – correctly draws attention to the anti-Semitic commentary associated with them at the time of the Dreyfus Affair. In this context, and citing evidence from police reports, she asserts that 'although Sangnier later became a fierce opponent of anti-Semitism, during the Dreyfus Affair, he frequently voiced anti-Semitic sentiments.' This is a jarring finding but it should not be totally surprising. Hardly any young Catholic could have escaped the reactionary mentalities of those years when church and state were engaged in a fierce 'culture war'. However many countervailing liberal influences Sangnier may have had in his youth, it would be almost too good to be true if he had never entertained the ambient conservative Catholic conspiracy theory about Jews and Freemasons in league together. However, it is equally clear that Sangnier's mindset evolved rapidly and irrevocably in the direction of tolerance and inclusivity, in decades during which many of his contemporaries went from bad to worse in their prejudices against Jews, culminating either in indifference to their fate or in active racist hostility towards them. As Mathieu Noli makes clear, when the crux came, in the 1930s, Sangnier was involved early on in supporting refugees from the Nazi Germany who arrived in France (including Jews), establishing along with Bernard Lecache the Comité d'Aide aux Victimes du Fascisme Hitlérien. The Foyer de la Paix, the permanent foundation at Bierville, dating from the halcyon days of the congresses, was the focus of such humanitarian endeavour. Greg Burgess reminds us how, after an initial welcome, French state policy towards these German (often Jewish) refugees evolved from sympathy to a regime of exclusion and antipathy when public disquiet at an 'invasion' grew. This coolness deflected onto precisely these same private charitable organizations the task of refugee solidarity. Sangnier's paper *L'Eveil des Peuples* meanwhile relayed vigilantly news of the ongoing attacks on liberty in the early Third Reich. Maurice Coquelin kept a beady eye on the tense relations between the Nazis and the Catholic Church in Germany. In June 1933, though, the Foyer at Bierville was the focus of an editorial crisis at *L'Eveil des Peuples* when some young French socialists, led by Jean Luchaire and André Bossin, insisted on a meeting with members of the Hitler Youth there. The gesture scandalized many of the older generation, including Luchaire's own father, Julien Luchaire, former director of the League of Nations-affiliated and Paris-based Institute for International

Intellectual Co-operation. Luchaire senior upbraided his son by name in the columns of *L'Eveil des Peuples*, asking how he could seriously tell German refugees he was wholeheartedly with them 'if they knew [he] was in friendly contact with their persecutors'. In the following decade and a half, there would be plenty more in the younger Luchaire's career to break his father's heart.[10]

Sensing the new menace in German foreign policy in the 1930s, Sangnier's rhetoric changed emphasis from 'disarming hatred' to what he called 'the pacifism of action'. The Foyer de la Paix at Bierville became the focus of the movement's practical and moral efforts through the so-called Relèves de la Paix. In keeping with the social hygienist inspiration of the Volunteers in 1929, the Relèves de la Paix promoted physical labour and the spirit of self-sacrifice, while also easing the maintenance costs of the Foyer de la Paix. While appealing in the first instance to the same Volunteers, this 'social service of peace' was open to older adults and young children too, every summer and every Easter vacation. Days spent building pathways, draining marshes and restoring dormitories were followed by campfires and peace meetings in the evenings. In the 'difficult birth of peace', Sangnier declared in 1936, 'nothing unites more than being bowed under the weight of the same hard work.'[11]

Faced with this most disorientating of decades, Sangnier's rhetoric was not always self-evidently consistent. The pulling of his heart in more than one direction throughout the 1930s is understandable in his case, and in those of many others who combined visceral anti-Fascism with a horror of the past war and fear of what a future war would mean. These anxieties are recorded in a 1936 compilation of his speeches and articles from the early 1930s. Like others of the 'génération du feu', he was fearful that the younger generation were jaded with warnings against war 'like old men's groaning':

> Their eyes have not been shocked by visions of horror; their shoulders have never been stooped under the ever deforming weight of dismal waiting and the desperate boredom of the trenches; they do not recall the bitter taste of drinking to the lees the chalice of a disappointing heroism.

To combat the lure for the younger generation of the dynamic totalitarian regimes, Sangnier called for a new self-confidence in 'constructive pacifism' and a reassertion of the mystique of democracy, whose genius was that it allowed people 'to develop the conscience and civic responsibility of all'. This rhetoric was related to what Tom Buchanan has identified as a more generalized discourse of renewal amongst European anti-Fascists of the 1930s, who responded to the threats of Bolshevism and Fascism by defending liberal democracy while arguing that democracy itself needed to be fundamentally transformed for the sake of efficiency, economic planning and redistributive social justice.[12]

In these early years of Hitler, Sangnier's editorials still referred to the idealized and strengthened League of Nations, which had been his favoured theme in the 1920s. He was also still critical of the bellicose tone of the confessed integral pacifists who wrote in *Patrie Humaine*. Pinpointing what he called the 'singular illogicality' of the extreme 'war on war' position, he wrote that they mimicked 'the temperament [...] and even the same brutal violent methods they excoriate in their adversaries [...] Peace will not be made through revolution in the manner of the dictators.' Returning to the war experience, Sangnier wrote that 'the soldier is great, not because he kills but because he dies', giving a harrowing description of the hail of bullets and the 'vile mud of the trenches'. It was time to rescue the 'manly virtues' war brought forth from war itself (and from the warlike Fascists and Communists): 'these rare and sublime virtues of courage, valour, tenacity, order, discipline, self-sacrifice' which war used to 'crown the work of violence, hatred and death. Let us seize back these magnificent virtues from the charnel house of destruction! Let us purify them, activate them for the work of life!'[13]

Fascism would soon confront pacifists with a less abstract war to grapple with. The attack by Mussolini on Abyssinia in October 1935 brought advocates of League of Nations pacifism face to face with the impotence of the League in the face of aggression. *L'Eveil des Peuples* noted and deplored the attack on a member state. The French Federation of Associations for the League of Nations had lobbied the Laval government in France to take a strong stance against Italian aggression and initially placed great faith in the efficacy of economic and financial sanctions rapidly taken by the League Council and Assembly against Italy. In the event, these proved a dead letter, but, as Jean-Michel Guieu points out, Abyssinia helped clarify pacifists' positions, distancing moderates from the temptation to be indulgent towards German and Italian demands for the sake of peace. They showed themselves unimpressed by the 'neo-pacifists' of the right who condemned every attempted sanction against Italy as a step towards war while also confronting those left-wing pacifists who opposed sanctions because they were 'warmongering'. Sangnier's own ambiguity grew in 1935–6, faced with a worsening international situation and the even more present danger of Fascism in France in light of the rise of right-wing leagues and the bloodshed on the streets of Paris during the events of 6 February 1934. In November 1935 Sangnier lent his support to the campaign against the much publicized detention of conscientious objector Gérard Leretour. From the same platform as Henri Roser, he called for objection to be legally recognized as 'a moral defect' overriding national service while also denouncing the indigenous Fascist leagues and calling for republican solidarity: 'in the present state of the world, society [has] to be ready to defend justice and right.' While the rhetoric echoes the mainstream liberal position of 'peace through justice', Sangnier was moving in circles including Félicien Challaye and Marcel Déat, where anti-Fascism and pacifism parted company. Whereas in the 1920s pacifists and anti-Fascists had been generally on the same side, now the idea took root on the pacifist far left that Franco-German entente was still possible, even with Hitler, prompting Félicien Challaye to go to Germany on cultural exchanges. This new conjunction of the right and the far left in French politics meant integral pacifists often found themselves 'arm in arm with the sworn enemies of their class', as Marc Bloch reflected ruefully in 1940.[14]

As the international landscape darkened, 'the gulf tended to widen between partisans of firmness and the apostles of appeasement.' Confronted in March 1936 with Hitler's thunderbolt remilitarization of the Rhineland in defiance of the Treaty of Versailles, there was shock in the League of Nations movement, but prominent figures such as Jules Prudhommeaux were quick to write that it did not merit war and to counsel against the tough talking of the French government about protecting Strasbourg from German canons. More forcefully, Théodore Ruyssen wrote of Hitler's bad faith and how Nazi *raison d'état* had torn asunder the shared concept of international law that had underpinned the Locarno agreement and the left's faith in Franco-German understanding since 1925. As Ruyssen saw it, there no longer existed a common language of morality between France and the regime in Germany. He called in the columns of the APD's paper *La Paix par le Droit* not for a new war but for eternal vigilance and 'a sort of moral quarantine' for Germany. At this point, though, Sangnier aligned himself even more clearly with the pacifist far left. In his paper *L'Eveil des Peuples* André Bossin said the French government, having given Mussolini free rein in Africa, could hardly 'inflict fire and (the) sword on Europe to prevent a few German battalions from occupying German towns'. In early March 1936, at a meeting of the LICP at the Salle Susset in Paris, Sangnier joined Félicien Challaye and Robert Jospin, who took pride in the title of 'pacifistes intégraux'. In their view, French failure to disarm had given

Hitler the excuses he needed. Sangnier rowed in to 'put on trial the policy of successive governments of our country', before declaring, strikingly, that 'we must respond to Hitler's unspeakable act with a sincere offer to disarm, even unilaterally, if needs be.'[15]

The coming to power of a left-wing government in France in May 1936, in the form of the Popular Front, was welcomed by Sangnier. However, Spain and divisions over rearmament complicated the attitude of Sangnier and others in the pacifist camp towards that government. While Sangnier had condemned parts of the 'war on war' movement for its rhetorical violence, it is likely that this was aimed more at the Communist-linked Amsterdam-Pleyel movement, for whom anti-militarism was a tactic rather than a core belief in the struggle to overthrow capitalism. The embrace of national defence and the Popular Front strategy by the Comintern in Moscow isolated integral pacifists and mystical pacifists such as Sangnier even more in their radical anti-militarism. Many Communists now moved away from tactical opposition to capitalist war to an offensive militarized strategy against the Fascist powers. In this polarized climate the LICP, whose members used Bierville for gatherings in 1936, had two other attractions for Sangnier. First of all, it gave him an audience for his mystical and sometimes esoteric speeches against war. His rhetoric was sufficiently nebulous not to offend far-left sensibilities. More importantly, in terms of organization and methods, the LICP copied Sangnier's example of populist propaganda, which brought pacifism out of the fusty conference hall and into the music theatre, the street, the popular press and the radio. Whereas Sangnier had the pageantry of peace at Bierville, the LICP recruited the singer Edith Piaf, as one example, so as to entertain and convince at the same time through festivity. While the outbreak of civil war in Spain in July 1936 posed the question of force and Fascism starkly, the integral pacifists continued to focus on the threat of militarism within France, even from the left-wing government itself. This was in the context of the heated debate on the left about rearmament, in which Léon Blum defended building up armaments, as sometimes one had to prepare war to secure peace. On 3 December 1936 Sangnier spoke along with Challaye and Jospin at a rally against the militarization of France. Posters for the meeting stoked fears of the high command and their alleged plans for military camps for women and children. Whereas Challaye and Jospin attacked the Popular Front's Defence Minister Edouard Daladier, Sangnier fell back on his usual mystical rhetoric against war.[16]

As René Rémond and Paul Christophe have shown, the year 1936 and the election of the Popular Front forced Catholics to choose sides between right and left but in so doing the Popular Front phenomenon also confirmed the emergence of political pluralism amongst Catholics. Even French Christian Democrats were divided, as the left wing associated with Marc Sangnier and Francisque Gay showed a general sympathy for the left whereas the centrists represented by the Parti Démocrate Populaire (PDP) remained in opposition to the new government headed by Socialist politician and intellectual Léon Blum. Intra-Catholic divisions mirrored the polarization of French politics into a state of rhetorical civil war. Serge Berstein argues that after the broad consensus around the Locarno détente and internal fiscal stability that characterized the late 1920s, when Poincaré returned to power and accepted the Briand policy in 1926–8, the Depression caused a regression of French politics in the 1930s to a state of putative civil war which stretched through the Occupation. In this period, political debate was once again a zero-sum game whose goal was the political, or even the physical, elimination of political adversaries. In the 1930s ideological disagreements admitted of 'no compromise' or possibility of consensus. Berstein cites as evidence the violence of anti-Semitism (as seen in the verbal and physical attacks on Blum) and the 'visceral hatred that set pacifist hard-liners against alleged "bellicists" '. The growth of unemployment to over 1 million by 1935 and the perceived threat from French Fascist leagues encouraged a common front amongst Socialists, Communists and Radicals, launched on 14 July 1935, that became known as the Popular Front. In the run-up to the elections of late April and early May 1936, the leader of the Communist Party, Maurice Thorez, gave a speech on national radio in which, in the spirit of national solidarity dictated by the Comintern, he told Catholics, 'we hold out our hand to you, Catholic [...] because you are our brother'. Most Catholics and their bishops were scornful of this 'main tendue'. Sangnier and Francisque Gay, editor of the Christian Democrat paper *L'Aube*, were more in touch with the mood of the working class. Both were ideologically opposed to Communism but were open to cautious co-operation with Communists to advance social reform and to resist Fascism.[17]

Where the bishops and conservative Catholics saw the horror of the revolutionary crowd, socially engaged Catholics in the JOC and the Confédération Française des Travailleurs Chrétiens (CFTC) trade union and Sangnier himself shared the left's faith in the people, even representing them as a political 'mystical body'. So too did the anticonformist Catholic intellectuals associated with Emmanuel Mounier and the new *Esprit* journal. Thus, when the left won a famous victory at the polls, including a breakthrough for the Communists, Sangnier applauded 'the victory of the popular masses'. Sangnier's former party, the Jeune République, unlike the PDP, had joined the Popular Front alliance, and had three deputies elected, one of whom, Philippe Serre, was appointed Under-Secretary for Labour by Blum in a reshuffle in 1937. The advanced Social Catholics shared Sangnier's sympathy for the mass strikes movement that occurred spontaneously during the interregnum between the election results and Blum's accession to power in June 1936. The Matignon Accords, conceded by a fearful and resentful bourgeoisie, held the tangible promise of improved working-class conditions. Blum himself pointed out the commonality between these socialist reforms and Catholic social teaching in an interview with the Catholic journal *Sept* in 1937, in another indication of his own moderation. The granting of paid holidays to the workers went hand in hand with the democratization of leisure attempted by the Popular Front's Minister of Youth, Sports and Leisure, Léo Lagrange, a social hygienist endeavour which built on existing private initiatives such as Sangnier's youth hostel movement. Recalling the initial struggles of Sangnier's hostels to establish themselves, a later police report cited 1936 as crucial to their implantation, because in that year the paid holidays and the creation of a Ministry of Leisure 'allowed them a success unequalled up to then'. In response to the sudden demand for cheap accommodation, the number of hostels expanded from 250 in June 1936 to 400 by the year's end, albeit largely to the benefit of the rival Centre Laïque des Auberges de Jeunesse (CLAJ). Nonetheless, Sangnier's hostels became integral elements of the *Zeitgeist* of the summer of 1936 by mirroring, in Julian Jackson's words, the 'optimism, the anti-elitism [and] the appeal to fraternity and solidarity' that defined the Popular Front.[18]

Linked to this ambience of anti-Fascist solidarity was the emergence in 1935–6 of a new international movement, the Rassemblement Universel pour la Paix (RUP), which offered the kiss of life to the beleaguered League of Nations movement in France. As Jean-Michel Guieu points out, in the early 1930s the moderate French League of Nations movement underwent a crisis of confidence, not helped by its division into numerous groups vying for the same members. A former French delegate to Geneva and a serving government minister, Joseph Paul-Boncour, succeeded in bringing about some better co-ordination of France's League of Nations movement. However, throughout the interwar period, the French movement remained very much the poor relation of its sister organization in Britain, where the League of Nations Union enjoyed a large membership and an enviable degree of popular and political impact. In spite of its own internal problems, the British movement staged a massive publicity coup in 1935, when some

11.5 million Britons participated in a major public consultation on disarmament and security entitled the Peace Ballot. The French League of Nations movement had no comparable moment of glory. Indeed, just when the French League of Nations Association appeared to be emerging as chief voice of the movement advocating strengthened collective security in 1936, it faced an attractive competitor in the form of the Rassemblement Universel pour la Paix (RUP). Though originating with Louis Dolivet, a member of the Swiss Communist Party, in the 'Comité mondiale contre la guerre et le fascisme', the RUP's sometime Communist instigators were overlooked by many, so that it rapidly attracted support from across the political spectrum, with the reassuring figures of Lord Robert Cecil, the British peer, and French politician Pierre Cot as presidents. (For reason of the RUP's origins, Cecil's participation unsettled and upset many of his colleagues in the British League of Nations Union of which he was president.) Like Sangnier's movement, the RUP held public rallies, but on a grander scale. Its Universal Peace Congress at the Heysel Stadium in Brussels in September 1936 was one such glittering occasion. The RUP attracted the support of prominent non-Communists, such as René Cassin and Germaine Malaterre-Sellier.[19]

For all this apparent renewal in the rival wings of the French peace movement, international events exacerbated debilitating divisions. Throughout the Spanish Civil War, which broke out in July 1936, Sangnier opened up Bierville to Catalan refugees. His own newspaper *L'Eveil des Peuples* was marked by the left's passionate divisions between advocates of aid to Republican Spain and integral pacifists who wanted to contain the war by means of non-intervention. The liberals of the APD were instinctively pro-Republican. Léon Blum's government itself hesitated, going from supplying arms to the Spanish government at the start of the conflict to initiating, with Britain, a policy of international non-intervention, which Italy and Germany blatantly flouted. However, rather than entering the lists for Spain, the suasion of the League on Germany and Italy should be tried, the APD reasoned. Charles Rousseau argued in *La Paix par le Droit* in autumn 1936 for 'prudence' over 'proselytism', lest the 'powder-keg which is the Europe of 1936' ignite. On the far left, though, Spain brought forward a growing divorce between anti-Fascism and pacifism. Already put on their guard by the Stalin–Laval military agreement of 1935 between France and the Soviet Union, integrists such as Challaye warned, notwithstanding their antipathy to Franco, against a Communist 'Red Fascism' that would spill blood in foreign wars for the sake of the revolution. The French Communists and the international Amsterdam-Pleyel movement (which had acted as a Communist front) glided from their tactic of 'opportunistic anti-militarism' to advocating armed intervention in Spain, a policy to which Blum's government would not consent. Uncompromising pacifists in the LICP (who were termed 'Tolstoyans') rejected even armed self-defence by Spanish Republicans. Others, such as René Gerin, conceded that, if he were Spanish, he would take up arms to uphold the democratic government of his country. Indicative of the strain within French pacifism was the schism at the annual congress of the League of the Rights of Man in Tours in July 1937, when – defeated in a bitter debate on 'how to defend peace and democracy' that was overshadowed by Spain – the integrist minority walked away, led by Challaye, René Gerin and Georges Pioch, who resigned in protest at the congress's vote. Ingram judges the Tours congress as being characteristic of a growing enfeeblement of the League of the Rights of Man, this touchstone Republican lobby group, well in advance of 1940. After the German destruction of the Basque town of Guernica in May 1937, which confirmed the most apocalyptic nightmares of modern aerial war propagated by the integral pacifists since the late 1920s, containment was the watchword of the integrists. As René Gerin wrote in May 1937: 'the most clear-sighted and effective pacifism in these troubled times is undoubtedly not that which refuses all wars, but rather that which refuses to transform localized civil conflicts into universal butchery.'[20]

The issue of national defence continued to divide the left. In the era of détente, French military service had been reduced to a single year. In March 1935 Hitler unilaterally reintroduced conscription in Germany. When, in that same year, the Flandin government in France tried to return French military service to two years in response, it was opposed by the Socialists and the Communists as the thin end of the militarist wedge. Léon Blum had retorted that the Maginot Line had been built precisely to reduce the need for manpower, though when he assumed office in 1936 he altered his position. Blum won a debate about rearmament within the Socialist party in 1937 when he argued that, in order to preserve peace, France would have to be prepared for war. Hitler's flagrant disregard not just for Versailles but also for the Locarno agreement which Germany had negotiated on equal terms with France in 1925 prompted a reassessment of priorities by many supporters of the Popular Front. By 1937–8, when the Popular Front government fell and power passed from the left to the conservative centre-right under Edouard Daladier and a revived Radical party, the mood had changed. The era of concessions to Hitler was far from over, but French governments had a new interest in shoring up the nation's defences. Precisely this cautious acceptance of the possibility of war by the main parties, especially those of the left, heightened the anger of French integral pacifists, who continued to conceive of the Fascist threat as jingoism at home rather than the aggressive foreign policy of the Nazis. On 8 March 1938 Sangnier spoke in Paris at a meeting 'against the arms race' called by the LICP, where he defended a very hard-line stance, calling for 'collective conscientious objection by the peoples of the world' and the people's fight for peace. He continued by noting that 'the government and parties of the left have taken up the old rhetoric of the nationalists.' Sangnier expressed regret that 'some who used to call themselves pacifist' (i.e., the Communists) were today bent on 'the preparation of ideological crusades. This is a strange conversion for those who used to vilify the army and who now express their honour at being good soldiers of France.' Supporting the motion against a new sacred union, he again turned the lens in on France itself: 'We are paying for the mistakes made since the Armistice. It is we who forged the omnipotence of Mussolini and of Hitler [...] If France had embarked more boldly on the path of peace, we would not be two steps away from war.'[21]

In 1938, in reaction to the polarization of French politics, the directors of the Christian Democrat newspaper *L'Aube*, Francisque Gay and Georges Bidault, attempted to overcome the fragmentation of the Christian Democrats by reorganizing the 'Christian-inspired' political centre, including the left Catholicism of Sangnier, through the creation of the 'Nouvelles Equipes Françaises'. At the group's opening congress in Paris in November 1938, Sangnier stood alongside Emmanuel Mounier, the Catholic philosopher, and Robert Garric, founder of the Equipes Sociales that since 1919 put into practice the socially aware faith that had inspired the Sillon. Such displays of unity could not hide the contrasting attitudes of Christian Democrats to the intervening Munich crisis, at the end of which, in September 1938, France and Britain agreed to Hitler's demands for the German-speaking Sudetenland to be taken from Czechoslovakia and added to the Reich. At *L'Aube*, Catholic journalist Georges Bidault took a very strong line against appeasement, showing the same independence of spirit that had put him off-side with the church hierarchy over Abyssinia and Spain. Sangnier, in contrast, was reeling from these political body blows. Writing on the Anschluss of Germany and Austria in March 1938, he acknowledged the paralysis he shared with many veterans:

> We still have such a horror of war that we are unable to acknowledge that because of the attachment of Austria to Germany, or even

> of the imperialist designs of Hitler on Czechoslovakia, millions of our sons should be condemned to die. This is the origin of our disquiet, and of the disarray in our internal politics [...] We content ourselves with a week-by-week policy, so very happy if we succeed each morning in postponing each morning the terrible eventuality of an imminent war.[22]

The Munich accords were a political trial of conscience for many in Britain and France. Welcomed as breathing space by a majority initially, the consensus stretched from right to centre-left, excluding the Communists. In France, the 'neo-pacifism' of the conservatives and of the extreme right was striking in pitting the traditional nationalists in favour of concessions to what were presented, mistakenly, as Hitler's final demands in September 1938. Many pacifists also took this position, with the most committed seeming to desire peace at virtually any price. Challaye at this point defended his recent visit to Germany and said in October 1938 that it was still possible to find common ground with the German people. However, as Daniel Hucker argues, to regard Munich as the retreat into 'a pacifist shell or defeatist mindset' that partially accounts for the failures of 1940 is a distortion of history. Preferring the term 'war anxiety' to distinguish mainstream opinion from the *outré* stances of Challaye and the LICP, Hucker argues support for Munich was, 'above all, an expression of relief' that soon hardened into an acceptance of a future firmness in face of Hitler. Munich was rather the apogee of a generalized 'war anxiety' that remained 'compatible with a determination to fight'.[23]

Sangnier, in a speech entitled 'Pour Sauver la Paix' delivered at *La Démocratie* press at boulevard Raspail in Paris on 6 November 1938, clung to the battered ideal of collective security rejecting what he termed the 'militarist solution' of rearmament. His 'pacifist solution' was threefold: 'disarmament, peaceful revision of the treaties on each occasion it is legitimately claimed and, finally, economic collaboration'. The last point – on economic collaboration – may well seem bizarre given the context but, as Olivier Prat points out, Sangnier saw this as a means of neutralizing Nazi Germany and it was consistent with the calls of the International Democratic Peace Congresses between 1921 and 1932 for supranational European economic solidarity. Indeed, Prat goes so far as to say that such an idea was also the basis of the Monnet–Schuman Plan of 1950 for coal and steel co-operation, albeit in a radically different context. In November 1938 erstwhile friends found themselves divided. As is revealed by the letters written to the outspokenly anti-Munich editor of the review *Esprit* the philosopher Emmanuel Mounier, recently published in edited form by Michel Winock, readers and contributors were not slow to voice agreement or disgust on this topic. Similarly, Sangnier's rationalization of 'saving the peace' proved too much for Albert Bayet, a contributor to *L'Eveil des Peuples*. Professor at the Ecole des Hautes Etudes in Paris and vice-president of the League of the Rights of Man, Bayet had been instrumental in confronting Challaye and Gerin at the League's Tours meeting the year before. Bayet now denounced Sangnier as a dangerous defeatist. His published letter of resignation from Sangnier's paper was brutally direct. Sangnier's manner of saving the peace imperilled France and 'the ideal of the Rights of Man' itself: 'Will we abandon that too under the threat of the canons? The day we are called upon to choose between fascism and war, are we to choose fascism?'[24]

The year 1939 was one of personal and political trials for Sangnier. After the seizure of Czechoslovakia by Hitler in March 1939, Sangnier clarified his position on the rightful recourse to arms. The nation had a duty to resist the imposition 'through the brutal violence of arms, a regime of totalitarian dictatorship'. Sacrifices could be made to 'the exigencies of peace' but not under such duress. Days later, tragedy struck the Sangnier family. Their youngest son, Paul, a promising anthropologist, was drowned in a canoeing accident in the Dordogne at the age of 21. The family waited two weeks for his remains to be found. A *Paris-Match* report in late September 1939, ironically on the Foyer de la Paix at Bierville, featured a photograph of a disconsolate Sangnier, alone on the abandoned estate, contemplating his grievous loss and the end of the Bierville dream. With Poland in flames and Europe at war, Sangnier wrote a final editorial for *L'Eveil des Peuples* dated 10 September, accepting the war imposed on France by the violence of Hitler. However, paradoxically, Sangnier turned defiance of Hitler through arms into a defiant re-statement of faith that Love was greater than Hate;

> [Hitler] may, of course, in his sickly fever of domination, condemn men to slaughter, but there is something he cannot do [...] and that is affect our souls [...] Do not say that the work of Peace and love that was ours has been extinguished today. It is not true. Sooner or later, the seeds that we have sown will germinate for future harvests, even if the furrows where they have been planted are flooded with blood.[25]

Though the direct political impact of Sangnier's 'pacifism of action' in the 1930s was often limited to the moral elite that foregathered around him, indirectly the imaginative pacifist campaigns of *L'Eveil des Peuples* and those of the LICP kept alive in the French public an acute fear of the 'next war'. However, beyond pious declarations against sin, their political programme of compromise with Hitler divided them from the Communists on the issue of peace and war and sowed confusion on the left more generally. Sangnier could not sustain a truly transnational movement when his German interlocutors were either scared or exiled. Anti-Fascism, of which the Popular Fronts in Spain and France were key components, seemed like the new, vibrant internationalism. In contrast, some far-left pacifist circles in France even greeted some refugees' warnings about Nazi Germany as self-serving warmongering. Such a wish for French national self-preservation had broader reverberations in public opinion, encouraging acquiescence in the compromises of Munich. Finally, the internecine quarrels of conditional and integral pacifists showed that pacifism was itself subject to the ambient polarization of politics. The defeat of France in 1940 brought the issue of peace and resisting Fascism to a crux in everyday life. The contortions of the 1930s made it certain that the choices made in Vichy France by Sangnier and others from the interwar peace movement would be neither obvious nor clear-cut.

In 1940 Marc Sangnier and his youth hostel movement shared fully in the national trauma of invasion, exodus and defeat. During the Phoney War, Bierville and the 400 hostels affiliated to Sangnier's LFAJ hosted the children of fathers absent in the army. With Hitler's invasion of the west in May–June 1940 and the bewildering collapse of French military resistance, millions of internal refugees took to the roads of France in a biblical movement of populations unprecedented in size. The same hostels were again mobilized to give succour to refugees. The radio address of the new Prime Minister, Philippe Pétain, on 17 June announcing an armistice and an imminent end to hostilities and making the 'gift' of his person to the French people struck a deep chord with the displaced. In this confused environment, flight into exile and an appeal to continued resistance to the Germans, such as that issued in General Charles de Gaulle's BBC broadcast from London on 18 June, were unattractive. Patriotism seemed to rhyme with Pétainism. The rigid application of polarized categories of resistance and collaboration to French reactions to the new Vichy regime installed in the summer of 1940 is perilous. Even those like Sangnier and his Christian Democratic colleagues who emerged after the war with impeccable (and merited) Resistance credentials were often as confused as everyone else in the summer of 1940. Some few, such as the Catholic Edmond Michelet, engaged in underground activity from the first hour, but many others in what became the family of the Resistance took time to shed ingrained loyalty to 'the Marshal' – as the veteran general Pétain was known - and to reject his Vichy government as a regime of collaborators. A huge volume of ink has been spilt in the debate over the attitudes of French Catholics and their leadership to the Vichy regime and collaboration with the Germans. Many Catholics and their bishops saw in the events of 1940 the wages of 'decadence' but also a unique opportunity for regeneration, nationally and pastorally. While Thomas Kselman writes that 'insertion of Pétain into this salvation history could produce a kind of syncretism between Catholicism and Vichy', equally the diverse tendencies within French Catholicism in the 1930s meant there could be no single Catholic response to Vichy. The French hierarchy was overwhelmingly loyal to Pétain while simultaneously sponsoring pastoral innovations such as the worker-priests of the Mission of France that held the promise of future renewal for the church.[26]

The National Revolution promoted by Vichy advocated a return to the land and a reinvigoration of youth. Youth policy was an aspect of the Vichy regime where Social Catholics exercised great influence.[27] Pétain appointed Georges Lamirand, an engineer and veteran of Robert Garric's Equipes Sociales, to head the Secrétariat General de la Jeunesse (SGJ), which sponsored a series of youth training efforts such as the Chantiers de la Jeunesse, a labour service corps that drew on existing scouting practice. Crucially, though, Lamirand and the Catholic bishops successfully resisted efforts to replace the multiple Catholic youth groups with a 'jeunesse unique' or unified state youth movement as desired by the advocates of collaborationism. These calls came most often from Paris-based Nazi sympathizers and renegade leftists associated with Marcel Déat and Jacques Doriot who derided Vichy for its 'clericalism'. However mixed the church's record was under the Occupation, its resistance on this point was crucial. Wilfrid D. Halls correctly points out that, had the church failed to uphold its sectional interests against the mooted national youth movement, its broader defence of Christian ideals would have been catastrophically compromised. Within Vichy and the French Catholic youth movement, though, there was, unsurprisingly, a mutual attraction between the projects of Lamirand for a French youth policy independent of the Germans and Sangnier's youth hostels movement. In 1941 Sangnier was happy to co-operate with Lamirand in the project of amalgamating the Catholic and secularist wings of the hostel movement. Both men were Social Catholics, both trained as engineers. At this point, Vichy rhetoric and Sangnier's converged. 'Redressement national' or 'national recovery', as Sangnier called it in a message to the hostels movement in the unoccupied zone in 1941, meant reconnecting French youth through the hostels with 'our land' and 'the simple joys of rude and healthy life' in a resurrected France. Blurring further the ambiguous border between collaboration with Vichy and resistance, in July 1941 Sangnier travelled to Vichy itself in connection with a 'strictly confidential' mission that Lamirand had entrusted to him in resuscitating the youth hostel movement. When 'neo-socialists' or renegade socialists who were bent on collaboration with the Nazis forcibly seized control of the secular Mouvement Laïque des Auberges de Jeunesse, successor of the CLAJ, in 1940, orphaned members of that same secular hostelling movement turned to Sangnier's Vichy-sponsored hostel organization as an alternative home. Sangnier displayed the calculus of accommodation rather than collaboration in the years 1940–1.[28]

By mid-1942 it was becoming increasingly difficult for Sangnier and the cadres of the hostelling movement, and for the French more generally, to regard the Vichy regime as an independent French government. The crux for Sangnier and the hostels came in 1942, when the Germans forced the issue of Aryanization. The Vichy regime, in the exclusionary laws enacted from 1940 and in its rhetoric, both responded to and fostered a strong strain of domestic anti-Semitism which the German occupation had merely allowed to come out from under the carpet. Julian Jackson has referred to Vichy's 'emulative zeal' on the Jewish question, whereby a morally dubious determination to protect sovereignty saw French and foreign Jews sacrificed to the Nazis for the sake of collaboration. When Sangnier wrote to demur at the German request that Jews be expelled from the hostels movement, Lamirand encouraged acquiescence in the German demands: 'in the interests of the League itself, it is necessary that you take all measures to the ends of excluding Israelite members.'[29] At a painful meeting on 6 May 1942, Sangnier and the LFAJ central committee conceded this exclusion, while in practice issuing false membership to Jewish members. Two months later, in July 1942, the notorious 'Vél d'Hiv' round-up of Jews jolted public opinion out of resigned passivity. Though not the first round-up of Jews in wartime France, these highly visible arrests brought forth forceful denunciations from a vocal minority of French ecclesiastics, led by Archbishop Jules Saliège of Toulouse. Within months, evasion by young Frenchmen of the Service du Travail Obligatoire (STO) or compulsory labour service in Germany swelled the ranks of the Vichy regime's critics and those of the Resistance networks. Meanwhile, the German occupiers were not fooled by the half-hearted expulsion of Jews from the hostels movement and promptly banned it. The activities of Sangnier's movement moved further into illegality from 1942 and turned away from Vichy.

Christians were prominent in the Resistance. Already, at Vichy in July 1940, three deputies from the Jeune République and most of the PDP deputies were amongst the minority of 80 deputies who voted against giving full powers to Pétain. The Resistance cell centred on the rue de Lille in Paris led by Emilien Amaury contained veterans of the Sillon such as Ernest Pezet and, from the younger generation, Sangnier's own son Jean. The premises at *La Démocratie* were continually used for printing clandestine papers and counterfeit papers literally only metres away from the sometime German military headquarters in Paris the Hôtel Lutétia, also on boulevard Raspail. Resisters circulated between this old seat of the Sillon and the offices of Francisque Gay's *L'Aube* newspaper at the nearby rue Garancière. In Lyon the old Sillon activist and printer Eugène Pons was deported to his death for publishing the tracts of the underground Resistance journal *Témoignage chrétien*. In such an ambiance of clandestinity did Francisque Gay and the student activist Gilbert Dru (who was later arrested and executed) formulate plans for a broad, post-war Christian Democrat political movement which was to become the Mouvement Républicain Populaire (MRP). Meanwhile, in Paris, at 4 p.m. on Friday 18 February 1944, the Gestapo interrupted the printing of the paper *Défense de la France* at *La Démocratie*. Sangnier was arrested in his apartment and the premises searched. Three printers – Charles Geraert, veteran of the Sillon, Gustave van Weert and Pierre Lepetit – were arrested, as was the secretary, Mlle Triboult. Sangnier remained in German custody at Paris's Fresnes prison until 16 March, when he was released after questioning; the four others were deported to Germany. Triboult returned alive from imprisonment in Ravensbrück in 1945. The three men had died in Buchenwald prison camp. Like the victims of the First World War, their names were inscribed in *La Démocratie*'s crypt.[30]

Beyond this direct involvement in the Resistance was Sangnier's place in its mystique and ideology. The importance of Sangnier as an inspiration to Christian Democrat resisters in the Vichy period is borne out by the personal testimonies contained in Roderick Kedward's study of motivations for resistance after 1940. Their collaboration with other French men and women of different faiths and of none in the common cause of resistance was indicative of what Geoffrey Adams has called the 'political ecumenism' of Free France and of the internal Resistance. A contemporary account aimed at an American audience stressed this inclusivity: 'On this secular ground, on this will of the citizens, a cooperation has been established between Catholics and non-Catholics. In their common illegal action, they have had the occasion to know each other, to count on each other, to trust each other.'[31] At his first ever meeting with General de Gaulle, in London in 1940, René Cassin, the veterans' leader who had participated in Sangnier's Bierville congress, broached awkwardly the issue of his own Jewishness with the General, who promptly swept it aside as irrelevant. Following up this positive beginning to his interview with the leader of the Free French, Cassin emphasized his own long-standing admiration for the democratic Catholicism of Marc Sangnier, marking out a practical ecumenism amongst the opponents of collaboration and highlighting a bridge between republican secularism and De Gaulle's own brand of patriotic Social Catholicism. De Gaulle subsequently made Cassin chief jurist to the Free French. In the interwar period, even if unwittingly, Sangnier's International Democratic Peace Congresses had helped prepare this domestic civic truce and renewed sacred union. The Bierville congress in particular had prefigured a civic tolerance that departed from the waxing and waning secular–religious sectarianism that had marred the Third Republic. Remarkably, the same secular collaborators present at Bierville recur as key non-Catholic players in the Resistance, such as Cassin himself and Pierre Mendès-France, the Radical Party politician and future Prime Minister of the Fourth Republic.

Not everyone from the interwar French peace movement and from the Christian Democratic movement returned to the public stage in 1945 amidst universal applause. The MRP, the new Christian Democratic party that had emerged from the Resistance and of which Sangnier was the honorary president, was attacked by the Communists as a refuge for old Pétainists. Sangnier was accused of being a Vichyite anti-Semite due to the exclusion of Jews from the hostels. Veterans of the hostels movement sprung to its defence, citing the deportation of 200 members who were patriotic resisters; they dismissed the caricature of Sangnier the racist as risible. The hostelling movement initially remained united under Sangnier before distinct political and confessional elements reasserted themselves. As for the pacifist movement, the picture was mixed. Peter Farrugia refers to 'pacifism on the cross' during the Occupation. Traditional League of Nations peace activists in the Association pour 'la Paix par le Droit' had supported the French war effort in 1939–40 as a just cause, just as they had supported the war of 1914. By remaining largely silent during the Occupation, the APD emerged from the war relatively uncompromised, its activists becoming supporters of the new United Nations Organization from 1945 and advocates of a united Europe, reconnecting with the message of the federalist movement of the late 1920s. However, integral pacifists of the

LICP (with whom Sangnier had worked in the 1930s) were self-conscious dissenters from the militarized, republican political narrative that valorized armed service of the 'fatherland in peril'. Georges Demartial, Victor Margueritte and Félicien Challaye wrote indefatigably in the collaborationist press to indict French imperialism as inimical to peace and to support Vichy's integration into a peaceful (Nazi) Europe. For such *outré* stances, several of them were arraigned and marginalized after the Liberation. Christian (especially Protestant) fellow-travellers of their movement remained opposed to violence but resisted courageously Nazi persecution of the Jews. Some erstwhile pacifists, such as Yves Farge, made the transition to active resistance. Amongst pro-Locarno politicians and activists, though, there was, as Julian Jackson reminds us, a pragmatic tradition in French foreign policy that pushed for 'rational' accommodation with Germany. Stretching back to the then Prime Minister Joseph Caillaux's policy of accommodation during the Agadir crisis in 1911, this pragmatism also informed Briand's Locarno diplomacy. French collaborationist head of government Pierre Laval, who considered himself a man in the pragmatic Briand mould, could justify the 1940 Montoire summit between Pétain and Hitler in light of this tradition. Other veterans of the Briand camp of the 1920s, including figures such as Sangnier, Cassin and Mendès-France, ultimately drew an utterly different lesson, rejecting as dishonourable any peace gained through submission to the Germans as represented by the Nazi regime.[32]

Conclusion

Throughout his activism with the Democratic International, Marc Sangnier invoked the common humanity of formerly warring nationalities. As a moral witness, he told the assembled French and German youths at the Palais du Trocadéro in Paris in August 1929 how he recalled vividly the pitiful sight of the 'poor German soldier' coming over the top into the wasteland of barbed wire. Yet, he added, 'we hadn't a word of hatred for him. The poor French *poilu* saw in him a victim of the same misery.'[1] While idealizing his own position in retrospect, fundamentally Sangnier was right. Long before the 'Locarno honeymoon', even when a combatant and a war propagandist, Sangnier had already posited the millenarian task of reconciliation with the foe whose resolution lay in the future. What is true for Sangnier is true for interwar pacifists generally: it was impossible to divorce personal experience and memory of the war from subsequent pacifist stances. Studies that fail to take this into account have a gaping hole at the centre. Adopting that lesson, that is why this study chooses to begin with the war experience as an integral part of the subsequent peace activism of Marc Sangnier.

The First World War had brought together patriotism and religion in a striking 'war religion' in which adherents felt their violence was both sanctioned and sacralized. The president of the secular French Republic, Raymond Poincaré, had made this linkage clear in August 1914 with his coining of the term 'sacred union' to describe the covenant binding the diverse spiritual families of France to her flag. In marked contrast, the new pope, Benedict XV, echoed the disenchantment of the dissenting pacifist minority identified with Swiss-based Romain Rolland, rebel of the French world of letters. While the pope's moralistic view of the war as the wages of egotism and sin was calibrated differently from that of the minority socialists, he shared their refusal to behave passively in the face of what he called 'useless slaughter'. The head of the Catholic Church conducted a parallel diplomacy to that of the socialists aimed at the restoration of international peace. Men that would later figure prominently in the Democratic International and its Peace Congresses, such as the German Fr Metzger, were prominent messengers of this papal policy. Suspended midway between the anti-war message of the pope and the pull of patriotism was Marc Sangnier, who was trusted by both Foreign Minister Aristide Briand and the French government, on the one hand, and by the pope, on the other. Implacable on the need for national defence, Sangnier tried very hard to reconcile these two poles of his belief system. He did so, in his propaganda lectures of 1918–19, by investing the war, intrinsically tragic as it was, with a redemptive quality: it could yet, through the achievement of those 'democratic' war aims encapsulated in Wilson's 14 Points, usher in a new era of hope, based on open diplomacy and inter-state arbitration. This sense of messianic mission was to inform Sangnier's activism after the official cessation of hostilities in 1919.

The transition from war to peace was far from clear-cut, though. After the sacramental camaraderie of the trenches, many returning French troops, including Sangnier, were afflicted with a sense of anomie: the 'real absence' of erstwhile colleagues and friends, those who had not survived the trenches, afflicted many demobbed soldiers acutely. War also seemed to continue on the home front; Sangnier was elected to parliament in 1919 as part of a broad, centre-right anti-Communist front. However, the strategy of tension that underlay the process of implementing the Versailles treaty soon began to grate on Sangnier: his faith in a different 'peace' (which was more than the absence of war) compelled him to look for a route to re-establish dialogue with Germany. Sangnier argued from 1921 that, in order to complete the passage from war to real peace, a true 'disarmament of hatred' was necessary. Already an emissary between the pope and Paris during the war, Sangnier's sense of the transnational possibilities of rapprochement grew in 1920, when Benedict XV completed the church rehabilitation of Sangnier and the pope expressly encouraged him in his cautious first steps towards peace activism. A republic of letters developed across Europe between Christian Democrats after the sad Catholic divisions of the Great War. This new transnational body of opinion put Sangnier at the heart of a European constituency that included the German and Italian Christian Democrats. The Democratic International that held its first congress in Paris in December 1921 was a crucial component of what Wolfram Kaiser calls the 'left-Catholic cooperation' of the 1920s, so vital in linking personalities such as Sturzo and Sangnier with German counterparts like Joseph Wirth.

The French writer François Mauriac is reported to have remarked at the height of the Cold War that he liked Germany so much that he was happy there were two of them. The 'German question', in its recurring forms, was one of the most vexing for the French throughout Sangnier's lifetime. Having fought the war against one type of authoritarian Germany, in the 1920s Sangnier put his faith in the 'other Germany' of the left and the democrats. Within French politics, and on the European stage, Sangnier acted as an itinerant goodwill ambassador, activating and making visible the Catholic and democratic variant of the French left's belief in the Weimar Republic and the good faith of its leaders. What drew German Catholics and pacifists to him – his willingness to question French reparations policy – turned him into a lightning rod for French nationalist hostility to the rhetoric of internationalism. From his Vienna congress of 1922, with its symbolic visit to a decommissioned arsenal, the pacifist import of this movement was clear, as it girded unto itself the untapped political resource of women's peace activism. The great test of Sangnier's mettle and of the unity of the Democratic International in the early 1920s, though, was, without doubt, the Ruhr crisis of 1923–4. A near warlike ambience pervaded France as supporters and opponents of Poincaré's direct action clashed. The mere occurrence of the Freiburg congress of August 1923 as well as the controversial topics discussed such as reparations and atrocities put Sangnier at odds with his own government in Paris, just as had his regular speeches in the Chamber of Deputies and the country in 1923. However, it is important to note that the German participants at the Peace Congresses were not just passive recipients of Sangnier's brimming over-enthusiasm. Rather, their genuine peace efforts coincided with a national – if not quite nationalist – agenda that wanted to efface aspects of the Versailles settlement that they viewed as insulting to their national honour. German pacifists, especially Ludwig Quidde, were very savvy in this regard. Quidde, who had once enraged right-thinking Germans with a covert and clever satire of the young Wilhelm II as the mad-dog Emperor Caligula, was quite willing, in the 1920s, to act on the guilty conscience of French figures such as Sangnier to advance a revisionist agenda. This does not imply insincerity but rather that most – but not all – of the German peace movement shared in the 'realist' appreciation of national interests articulated by the mainstream German parties.

In 1924 Sangnier's brand of internationalist solidarity moved from the margins to the mainstream. Sangnier can no doubt be credited with helping change the political climate within France and contributing to the swing to the left in that year's election, even though he lost his own seat. With the London Accords, which promised a negotiated way out of the reparations impasse, a new spirit of moral disarmament seemed to be infiltrating European politics and civil society. When the fourth International Democratic Peace Congress was held in London in 1924, the message of the Democratic International was in sync with the new political landscape. Having survived the Franco-German proxy war in the Ruhr in 1923, the Democratic International was able to grow in depth and breadth in 1924–5, in tempo with the diplomatic rapprochement achieved at Locarno in October 1925 by Aristide Briand and Gustav Stresemann. Taking on board the 'peace testimony' of British Quakers like Ruth Fry added dynamism to the Democratic International but also challenged the dominant 'just war' tradition within the movement. This tension was both divisive and creative for the movement. In a related field, through its debates on education and a pedagogy of peace, the place of the Democratic International in the search for moral disarmament in the 1920s is clear. (The message sent by educator Ferdinand Buisson when accepting the 1927 Nobel Peace Prize – which he shared with Quidde – emphasized the same message of 'peace through education' he had extolled at Sangnier's congresses.) The 'Bierville moment' of August 1926, the largest extravaganza of the Democratic International, was the epitome of this new spirit in Franco-German relations, offering a youthful and festive consecration of the work of the politicians at Locarno. With its elaborate Catholic symbols and ritual, popular theatre and sacred drama, the Bierville congress was in the tradition of performance politics which all groups used in the interwar period. The secularist Buisson's cordiality with the Catholics at Bierville showed that, as well as bringing together French and Germans, Sangnier had brokered a 'sacred union for peace' of the centre and centre-left within France, transcending the old Catholic–secular divide. In the cycle of conflict and conciliation in French domestic politics, the staged reconciliation at Bierville in 1926 stands out as a moment of convergence between church and republic, one confirmed neatly by the Vatican's condemnation of the 'exaggerated' nationalism of the Action Française quite literally in the days following the Bierville congress.

In keeping with the process of cultural transfer alluded to at the outset of this study of cross-national movements, Sangnier acted in the second half of the 1920s as a conduit for aspects of German youth culture which he imitated in France as part of a more general movement for the regimentation of youth and adolescence in the interwar period. The examples of the Wandervögel and Quickborn which he had first met in Freiburg in 1923 lent colour to the subsequent Bierville and Würzburg meetings, prompting Sangnier to create his own Volontaires de la Paix in 1928. Honoured that same year at the League of Nations institutions in Geneva, Sangnier's movement now surfed the wave of transnational movements, especially those advocating world disarmament or the cause of a united Europe. However, from 1931, as the political tide began to turn against Sangnier's project of Franco-German friendship, Sangnier moved once again out of the mainstream and re-entered the political margins which he shared with a new brand of integral pacifists associated with Victor Méric and the Ligue Internationale des Combattants de la Paix (LICP). Sangnier's call to a 'pacifism of action' in the wake of his last major peace congresses at Freiburg-Konstanz in August 1931 was an admission that pacifist debating societies had failed and that a new and more combative phase in the struggle for peace was beginning. His withdrawal from the Jeune République and the electoral fray in 1932 confirmed this shift in Sangnier's career.

In the spiral of ideological confrontation in the Europe of the 1930s, pacifists like Sangnier were dragged in different directions by events and were monthly confronted with painful political choices. The failure of the World Disarmament Conference of 1932–3 dashed hopes for a Geneva-led peaceful Europe. The German peace movement Sangnier had worked with was politically decapitated, and actively persecuted, by the Nazis after 1933. The shock of expansionist strokes by German and Italian Fascist regimes, and the inscrutable and self-interested priorities of the Soviet Union, produced sharp divisions on the pacifist left. Sangnier drifted towards a revisionist position on the Versailles settlement in these years, sharing platforms with groups that endorsed concessions to Hitler as but the correction of wrongs inflicted by France in 1919. We can see this especially in Sangnier's reaction to the reoccupation of the Rhineland in March 1936. By this point, though, the Communists had shown how tactical their pacifism was. Communist advocacy of a crusade by the workers of the world in Spain's civil war in 1936 confirmed their change of policy. The French Popular Front's common programme of anti-Fascism and social reform leavened Sangnier's views on defence with practicality. A sometime critic of the military budget, Sangnier called for French acquiescence in the supply of arms to Spain's republican government during the civil war, a public position Léon Blum felt prevented from taking, notwithstanding the covert solidarity shown by his government with the other Popular Front in Madrid. The ill-starred olive branch or 'outstretched hand' of the French

Communists to the Catholics in 1936 had in mind precisely those Catholics imbued with Sangnier's Social Catholic republicanism. Sharing the guilty relief of the masses at the Munich conference of March 1938, Sangnier was forced, by stinging criticism from some of his own supporters, to reassess his advocacy of peace. By 1939, unlike some of the LICP activists that had courted him successfully over the preceding nine years, Sangnier had reached a bottom line below which he would not go in acquiescence to German demands.

Sangnier's experience of the Occupation from 1940 to 1944 demonstrates the complexity of the times. He was sympathetic at first to the moral hygiene agenda of the Vichy regime insofar as it chimed with advancing Social Catholic youth projects, such as his own youth hostels. However, initial contact belied his deep disquiet at the chimerical nature of the regime as a 'shield' against the German occupation, a clear-sightedness that guarded Sangnier from the vertigo of Vichy. He was not playing Vichy's alleged 'double game' – the excuse of pretending to collude in German occupation policies so as to undermine them. Sangnier shared fully in the real-life ambiguity of the political choices to be made inside Occupied France, as his visit to Vichy in 1941 demonstrates. This does not disqualify him from inclusion in the roll of honour of the Christian Democratic Resistance, whose activities led to his own arrest in 1944, and the sacrifice of their lives by associates such as Eugène Pons. It was the Fourth Republic (1946–58) that saw Sangnier's political family enter the lists of mass politics as a challenger for executive authority in the guise of the MRP. For all its tawdry compromises and for all the conflicts some of its ministers presided over in France's dirty wars of decolonization, from Indochina to Algeria, the MRP did pay homage to Sangnier's ideas in its elaboration from 1948 of projects for Franco-German partnership. Not only did the Christian Democratic networks so crucial to European integration around 1950 owe much to the transnational trend and cross-national constituency Sangnier had helped initiate in the 1920s, but Sangnier's peace congresses had also helped to plant in the European imagination the vision of a peaceful Europe with Franco-German friendship at its heart.

Writing on the challenge of completing the new *Palgrave Dictionary of Transnational History* (2009), co-editor Pierre-Yves Saunier described it as process of 'learning by doing'. This book has been guided by insights from a variety of scholarly approaches, including the 'transnational turn' itself. As well as considerations of method, if we turn slightly to one side to consider the linked area of interpretation, my introduction set out a number of the current concerns in European history-writing to which this book is addressed. The first of these is the question of how nations and peoples exited war in Europe after 1918. My narrative of the International Democratic Peace Congresses has interrogated the book's presiding idea: that alongside the persistence of a stubborn hatred there were French, Germans and others who undertook a parallel peace process of 'cultural demobilization' in the interwar period. They did so through a transnational peace movement in which Marc Sangnier played an important part, one acknowledged even by those who refused to demobilize. This book has also been a work-in-progress in transnational history, using its insights while probing its frontiers. Thirdly, the role of religion – and of Catholicism is particular – in contemporary European history has animated these pages and formed a clear subtext to this study. At the end of this book, it is fair to ask if after narrating the Sangnier movement, its 'learning by doing' can yield the beginnings of answers to these broader questions.

To deal first with transnationalism, this study has shown how vibrant the transnational sphere was in the interwar period. Even allowing for the ultranationalism of the 1930s, peace groups, Catholic movements and a myriad of other non-governmental organizations met at international congresses, exchanged ideas and pooled resources the better to influence the international sphere. These early NGOs bolstered sub-state dynamics in international relations, creating a web of 'border crossings' both above and below nation-state level. The European constituency that answered Sangnier's proposal for a Democratic International in 1920–1 began with just such bottom-up activism. A decentralized core of activists responded, writing letters to Paris. The offers of help came as often from the regions of France, Austria and Germany and elsewhere as from the capitals of Europe or from Europe's Catholic elites. Energized by the creation of the League of Nations, such networks of knowledge became European bodies of opinion, sometimes officially recognized as lobby groups by the League institutions. European encounters therefore meant more than just the diplomats' meetings, as activists like Sangnier co-ordinated the soft power of the peace movement to influence the political decision-makers. (He did this, for example, in his high-level political meetings at the Genoa economic conference of 1922.) The supporters of Sangnier were hardly ever self-regarding cosmopolitans who looked down on patriotism. In contrast, most of the French and Germans in his movement were absolutely certain their primary allegiance was to their own country, within a true Society of Nations. Patricia Clavin's comments on recent historical research in the field are a helpful reminder that interwar transnationalism is a force 'that takes life inside nation-states. [...] The histories of transnational encounters in the interwar period tell us as much about the national contexts [...] as they do about the world they seek to reshape.'[2]

Examining the theme of 'demobilizing the mind', John Horne has reminded us that if other types of demobilization were preconditions of peace, then 'cultural demobilization (or its absence) determined what type of peace it would be.'[3] As seen here in Chapters 1 and 2, the return of peace after 'total' conflict in 1919 was the highpoint of the war culture, not its end. Against a backdrop of continuing popular hostility to Germany in France, the vanquished Germans had to accept – officially at least – the victors' version of history in the peace settlement. Having adopted, with nuances, the premise that there was indeed a cultural mobilization for war from 1914, this book has shown how, according to his own lights, Sangnier fought the First World War in order to make the world safe for democracy. Around him, general French public opinion remained 'mobilized' until 1924 and the aftermath of the Ruhr invasion, before the season of grace for détente. Sangnier's programme and early campaign 'to disarm hatred' enunciated from 1921 stands in contrast to this. His case thus illustrates some of the subtler gradations of cultural demobilization at work. Not for Sangnier the rejection of the war he had just fought: as he made clear again and again, particularly in the early 1920s, he was aligned with the liberal pacifist tradition which saw the war of 1914 as just and as having given new birth to 'old-style pacifism' through the League of Nations. Unlike the dissident Socialists and the pacifist minority who had demobilized themselves during the war itself, Sangnier's cultural demobilization was conjugated in the present and future tenses and turned primarily against a future war.

The most salient features of this same cultural demobilization are the mainstay of this study. Thus the experience and passions of the Great War, as it was termed, drove both wings of the peace movement. Horne represents the war culture itself as two axes of a graph. One axis places at one end of the spectrum the (dehumanized) enemy and at the other an idealized collective self of the nation (for Sangnier, French civilization). Another axis relates individuals to the violence and brutality of the war. The intersection of these lines is in 'sacrifice'. Very baldly, for combatants like Sangnier, this meant being party to violence, killing and being killed for the fatherland. 'Sacrifice' thus became the key value of the war culture and the key theme of its rhetoric. How was French society to deal, though, with the pivotal issue of 'sacrifice' once it began to dismantle the war culture? The rhetoric of Marc Sangnier is almost preternaturally fixated on the rehabilitation of 'sacrifice' by investing it with a new meaning.

Well ahead of the vogue for cultural demobilization in the mid-1920s, Sangnier activated and acted out its most distinctive features. The series of International Democratic Peace Congresses held successively at Paris, Vienna and Freiburg-im-Breisgau in the years 1921–3 startled many by dismantling the enemy, restoring his humanity and meeting the Germans as equals. Sangnier's movement began as a lonely pioneer, but the theme of 'disarming hatred' it espoused became a pressing moral imperative for many French and Europeans with the Locarno Accords of 1925. Sangnier's non-governmental organizations both influenced and held up a mirror to the broader search for meaning in the 'sacrifice'. The rhetoric of activists like Sangnier might, taken in isolation, seem a pious historical curiosity, with no hard power behind it to change the world or really to 'disarm hatred'. However, when taken in conjunction with that of statesmen like Briand, we can see that, in the Locarno period, the power of 'the word' itself was historically significant. *Realpolitik* had by no means died: as the diplomatic context provided at each stage in this book shows, very down-to-earth geopolitical realities conditioned French and German leaders to seek accommodation rather than unremitting antagonism after the Ruhr crisis. However, the rhetoric of 'disarming hatred' – in its various declensions – meant words themselves took on transformative power, moving electorates to believe it was possible to imagine and start building a peaceful Europe.

Sangnier's public compassion in his speeches for both the German and French soldiers he had fought with and against unlocks for us a crucial rhetorical device of cultural demobilization. It now reinvested the sacrifice of the trenches in the cause of peace without repudiating the heroism of the front-line soldier. French Foreign Minister Briand, though not himself a combat veteran, spoke of the two countries' veterans in his speech welcoming Germany to the League of Nations at Geneva in September 1926, to say that 'both have reaped an ample harvest of glory in combat. Henceforth, they can seek successes in other fields.' More psychologically, moral disarmament created a disjuncture in personal memory for veterans, one perhaps common to most wars. War was horrific, it was agreed, but one's personal acts of violence within war remained generally taboo. Sangnier's 1929 declaration that his unit of soldiers had not had a word of hatred for the boys on the other side might be touching, but, as he never advocated desertion from the madness, such veterans, German and French, now shoulder to shoulder as brothers, must have spilt one another's blood, if the casualty lists were true. To quiet this ethical and emotional qualm, which must have affected at least some of those who spoke up through the Democratic International, veterans often 'emphasized the horrors of the war and the mutual victimhood of the soldiers, rather than their part in its violence'.[4] The voice of women, insisted upon in Chapter 3, which resonated through the congresses in the testimony of former front-line nurses like Germaine Malaterre-Sellier, Ruth Fry and Edith Pye was perhaps particularly important here. Not conscripts but war volunteers, on account of their sex, their voice was welcomed by men such as Sangnier not just so as to endorse votes for women but for old-fashioned essentialist reasons too. Precisely as mothers or as nature's care-givers, these women activists could make up for stains that combat left on the men's hearts and minds.

Once veterans and politicians embarked on this reversal of their understanding of the war, the war itself became 'strangely incomprehensible', as Horne puts it. Instead of being a recent experience, with a familiar smell, the past became a truly different country, marked by a nightmarish débâcle difficult to explain to oneself and the next generation. Jean-François Sirinelli alludes to the existence of two generations in this interwar France. The younger 'generation of 1905' shared the veterans' aversion to war, but did so out of rejection of a failed adult society rather than out of direct experience.[5] Thus new narratives were both required and created, with consequences for both the blame game over the past and for the veteran's personal relationship to the war. The new condensed versions of history blackened the war culture and castigated the old balance of power, and not just the wartime enemy, for the tragedy of 1914. In France, however, new ogres emerged to replace the Hun: the rhetorical attacks at Sangnier's conferences (and across the European moral disarmament movement) on the old militarism and on present-day arms dealers were not just echoes of cultural demobilization; they partially constituted its substance. Always savvy at public relations, Sangnier's movement and his Jeune République party translated this rhetoric into material culture through its 'Peace or War' Museum which toured France in 1931, in advance of the World Disarmament Conference. As had the Sillon of old, Jeune République produced strikingly modern posters to promote its agenda of hope. Like other groups, though, they also produced lurid posters in the 1930s seething with savage indignation at named enemies in the arms industry. 'Krupp, Schneider, Armstrong, Vickers, Skoda' were made into cartoonish greedy capitalists under the poster's heading: 'the manufacturers get rich: the peoples die.'[6]

For people at the time, Horne argues, 'the full redemption of wartime sacrifice lay now in the defeat not of the enemy but of war itself.' What limits applied to the cultural demobilization project in Europe in its own time? Even more pertinently, what challenges arise for historians wishing to avail of cultural demobilization as an interpretative tool today? Sangnier's campaign to 'disarm hatred' can instruct us on some such limitations. The approach (and this study) necessarily incorporates those who refused to 'demobilize', the critics of 'moral disarmament'. In this regard, the whole project met particular stumbling blocks in Germany itself. Consensus on what Germans had died for was nigh on impossible after 1919, when the so-called 'peace' so bitterly divided the people of Germany. In spite of such political impediments, it was Germans, whether they were moderate liberals or conscientious objectors, who were the indispensable actors in the Sangnier peace congresses, without whom he could have achieved nothing since 1921. However, as their frequent touchiness in congress rows with the French showed, these Germans operated under more vexing constraints than their French friends did. More generally, cultural demobilization was a destination towards which groups and individuals travelled in zigzag lines. Sangnier's intellectual itinerary had a pattern, but we should beware over-determination in studying political ideas. As Matt Perry writes of the socialist pacifists, there were 'trigger events' but rarely do 'individuals conveniently obey general trends'.[7]

A final consideration on cultural demobilization occurs here. Could it not be argued that, paradoxically, Sangnier's youth movement with its military-style rhetoric and organization actually contributed to a militarization of youth in interwar France in accordance with the law of unintended consequence? The idea that the First World War represented a 'rupture in civility' which engendered a new strain of rhetorical and physical violence in domestic politics has marked much scholarship on the interwar period, not least that of Michael Geyer and George Mosse.[8] Geyer contends that the war domesticated violence and prepared the way for its use as a political instrument in the interwar years. Antoine Prost argues that French *anciens combattants* were marked, to a large degree, by respect for the precepts of morality and legality. Though the undercurrent of violence in French public life became more obvious in the 1930s, with the growing prominence of right-wing leagues, French politics in the 1920s was already quite robust. The violence, both rhetorical and actual, unleashed against Sangnier's movement by the nationalist right amply shows this. The International Democratic Peace Congresses themselves, notwithstanding Sangnier's well-known liking for having his own way, were democratic in spirit and practice. Dissonant voices were given space, even when they irritated the Democratic International's leaders such as Sangnier or tested the patience of the majority of delegates. The Bierville congress, for instance, scandalized the French right in 1926 by giving the rostrum to Francesco Nitti, the exiled anti-Fascist Italian politician who, to their lights, had been no friend to France, not to mention the hearing given by the naïve do-gooders of Bierville to a pitiful renegade like the French general Verraux, who wanted to banish toy soldiers. Motions at the congresses were passed by means of democratic votes. Where lively disputes arose, as at Bierville, over the issue of conscientious objection, a special sub-commission was established which allowed for exhaustive debate.

This ardent desire to achieve consensus eschewed authoritarianism, but it did give rise to a stage-managed consensus at times, as with the sidelining of the hard-line anti-war 'Ehlen motion' at Bierville. However, a procedural stroke does not militarization make. The Volontaires de la Paix are at first sight a more ambiguous entity. As volunteer Louis Primet wrote to Sangnier in 1931: 'We want to be young revolutionaries in the pacific sense of the word. That's what puts fire in our bellies.'[9] They were undoubtedly a highly organized and disciplined youth movement who were part of the ubiquitous formation of youth culture into marching columns in these years. However, if their garb was martial, the Volontaires were militarized but not anti-democratic. The fundamental purpose of these 'Volunteers of Peace' was the formation of adult citizens who would work for peace. Their discipline and strict organization were made consistent with a fundamentally liberal outlook. In the face of banners and uniforms, we must resist the lure of hindsight history, seeing the spectre of Fascism (or totalitarian Communism) everywhere.

Turning finally and briefly to Catholicism, the secondary literature underpinning this book places 'Catholic history' firmly in the context of transnational history. The Sangnier experiment shows how the peace movement and Christian Democracy travelled a significant length of road together in interwar Europe. The new perspectives offered here on Vatican policy in the First World War and the 1920s illuminate the papacy's cautious cohabitation with the peace movement itself. How, though, might this study relate to recent and highly ambitious interpretations of religion's place in modern European history writ large? The historical problem of the ideological roots of political totalitarianism has encouraged historians of Europe to return to religion as an avenue of historical enquiry on this vexed issue. Thus, for Emilio Gentile, a constitutive element of Italian Fascism was the 'sacralization of politics'. Secular movements became endowed with the trappings of religion, seeing the world in terms of good and evil and brooking no opposition. Related, but pitched on an even more ambitious scale, is Michael Burleigh's endeavour to write the history of Europe since the French Revolution while placing religion back centre-stage. In the face of harassment and an allegedly irresistible secularizing modernity, Burleigh argues, in the course of two books, that a dogged resilience has characterized religious faith in Europe over the past two centuries. However, his presiding idea is not this alone. Rather, as Gentile has done, Burleigh deploys the concept of 'political religion' to explain the power of secular creeds: not just Fascism but also Marxism and the related 'secular religion' of nationalism in its various guises. Far from universally 'progressive', though, Burleigh sees these 'Earthly Powers' and 'Sacred Causes' as double-edged phenomena, capable of bearing both good and bad fruit. Within them also were the seeds of potential fanaticism and human misery. They could become religious dogma, without mercy.

'Political religion' is an attractive explanation in certain respects, not least in framing the Catholic Church's principled hostility to both Nazism and Bolshevism in the 1930s, even if Burleigh's emphasis on the left-wing origins of political religions, stretching back to 1789 via Romantic nationalism, is more debatable. Kevin Passmore wisely notes that totalitarianism was but one possible development that emerged out of the tangled 'shared roots' of ideology, 'leading in multiple directions as contexts changed'.[10] The rhetoric and ideology of Sangnier's movement may be called as witness here in support of this more nuanced picture. As the 'political religion' of the Sillon had shown, Sangnier was a son of the Romantic nationalism of France's 1848 Revolution, with its Liberty Trees and its inclusion of Catholics. Like the Sillon, Sangnier's whole project integrating Catholicism, patriotism and internationalism in the 1920s shows how a more tolerant application of political religion was conceivable. (In fairness, this possibility is acknowledged by Burleigh himself, not least in his sympathetic discussion of the French Christian Democrat intelligentsia in the interwar and Occupation years.) The political idealism that prompted Sangnier, as a Catholic democrat, to support new nations against old empires in the 1920s should be understood, therefore, as fully internationalist rather than as Romantic totem-pole worship. Conviction does not equal bigotry.

Though not a biography of Sangnier, this study has had to keep one eye on the mercurial relationship between 'the Catholic left' and the official church that marked his career. The question of how far a Catholic 'democrat' or socialist should go in integrating the 'social Gospel' with revealed religion is a recurring controversy in modern Catholicism. As documented in this book, his close relations with the papacy show Sangnier's brand of Social Catholicism was radical but utterly loyal to church authority. In the interwar period the Christian Democrats looked to the magisterium of the church for support against Catholic conservatives. Oscar Arnal has written of how the 'Mission of France', which attempted the renewal of French parish life in the 1940s, drew on this Social Catholic heritage to create a new dynamic apostolate, the 'worker-priests'. The example of the JOC and of Sangnier's Sillon informed this daring initiative even if, for the worker-priests themselves, their most formative experience was often ministry to French deportees in the labour camps of Germany during the Second World War. Over time, the worker-priests' proximity to Marxism through the labour unions at the height of the Cold War prompted trouble for them as a movement; a major crisis of French 'progressive' Catholicism occurred in the 1950s, when the worker-priest experiment was shut down by the pope for its Modernist errors or was cruelly betrayed by the Vatican, depending on one's point of view. Philippe Chenaux has recently and provocatively reinterpreted Eric Hobsbawm's thesis about 'the short twentieth century' (from 1917 to 1989) as not just a Catholic clash with the external enemy – Marxism – but also as a bitter internalized confrontation with Marxism as the last great Christian 'heresy'. In light of this scheme of interpretation, Sangnier and the worker-priests encountered a similar dilemma to that which painfully confronted the movement for liberation theology in the global south after the Second Vatican Council (1962–5) on the correct balance between faith and politics. Sangnier's reluctance to synthesize the faith with Marxism is itself equally clear as he saw this would risk drawing his religion into unacceptable compromises. In contrast, his one-time follower Maurice Laudrain put the cross and the hammer-and-sickle on the cover of his *Terre Nouvelle* journal. The journal was condemned by Rome in 1937 for just such Communist deviation from true Catholicism.[11]

The 'mystic modernism' of 'Jazz Age Catholicism' in Paris infused the arts and church music as much as the theology of Jacques Maritain marked the Catholic intellectual realm in interwar France. It was a challenging but stimulating time to be a French Catholic in these same intellectual circles. Sangnier's politics and in particular the aesthetic of the youth gatherings he staged were part of the same spirit of the age. His Democratic International and its European Catholic network remind us that the alliance of Catholicism with authoritarianism (so apparent in Franco's Spain and elsewhere) was only one possible configuration of Catholic politics in the interwar period. If, as John W. O'Malley argues, the renewal and turning outwards of Catholicism at the Second Vatican Council came not from a void but at the end of a dynamic 'long nineteenth century' of Catholic thought, Sangnier's Social Catholicism and peace ecumenism surely have their place in that longer history.[12] We should recall in this regard his dialogue with non-Catholics, non-Christians and the secularists themselves. Disavowing blithe indifferentism, Sangnier was adamant such collaboration was not based on cowardly avoidance of philosophical differences. As he told in a meeting of Catholic women at the St Joan's Social and Political Alliance in London in 1924, Catholicism was the leaven of his peace movement. Contact with those who do not share the faith 'renders ever firmer our desire to remain, for our part, integrally Catholic'. This was orthodox faith with an opened palm rather than with a clenched fist.

Sangnier, of course, was not the only lay Catholic activist who was building such bridges in the decades before the Second Vatican Council. The Catholic Worker movement founded in this period in the United States by Dorothy Day and Peter Maurin to promote justice and peace comes to mind. Irish Catholic layman Frank Duff was apolitical by comparison with Sangnier but the Legion of Mary he founded in Dublin in the 1920s grew worldwide and gave space and dignity to the vocation of lay Catholics in the religious and social spheres, much as Sangnier had tried to do throughout his career.[13] Sangnier's open-air youth festivals equally have a relevance to the history of contemporary Catholicism, even if they also made space for many non-Catholics. Like the Jeunesse Ouvrière Chrétienne rallies of the 1930s, the Sangnier youth gatherings had a traditional Catholicism at heart; they were staged, though, in imaginative ways that showed a friendly and less forbidding face of the Catholic Church to the curious onlooker. Such a spirit of outreach to the young was rekindled strikingly during the World Youth Days that marked the pontificate of John Paul II, notably in Paris (1997) and Rome (2000), events which surprised secular Europe with images of youthful enthusiasm for a church thrown open to the world, albeit on its own particular terms. However, in both cases, though they were decades apart, it was not unknown that some 'who came to scoff, remained to pray'.

The presiding concern of this book has been the issue of peace in a Europe scarred by the First World War and made anxious by its fears for the future. Richard Overy's study of Britain between the wars shows how the League of Nations movement in that country gained a level of popular legitimacy through the Peace Ballot of 1934–5 that was the envy of the European movement. The problem of war haunted the public discourse, but war itself was constantly contested through the peace movement's vibrant 'challenge to death'. However, Overy still situates his study in what he calls a 'Morbid Age'. The thrust of my study has drawn on a reinvigorated international history to give their true weight and worth to these internationalists and their non-governmental organizations, so often categorized by historians as well-meaning but ultimately impotent. If the Locarno treaty and the League of Nations really represented what Zara Steiner calls 'the lights that failed', then the transnational Sangnier movement illuminates a whole series of questions about peace, youth and politics in Europe between the wars, opening windows onto roads taken and not taken. The 'Bierville moment' of 1926 and the mission of 'peace through youth' were an integral part of the diplomatic and cultural détente of the mid-1920s, which in turn was more than a mere truce in a new Thirty Years War. In his Nobel Peace Prize Lecture in Oslo in June 1927, Gustav Stresemann gave a remarkable speech, at least as affecting as Briand's flowery Geneva speech of September 1926. The German Foreign Minister, as he neared his concluding paragraphs, added this personal note:

> I do not think of Locarno only in terms of its consequences for Germany. Locarno means much more to me. It is the achievement of lasting peace on the Rhine [...]. *Treuga Dei*, the peace of God, shall reign where for centuries bloody wars have raged [...] The youth of Germany can be won over to the same cause.[14]

The Germans and French in Sangnier's movement shared Stresemann's faith in German (and French) youth and his hopes for the future. These hopes would not be fulfilled, though. The world itself changed after 1929, coincidentally the year of Stresemann's death. The challenge of Fascism and Nazism disaggregated the moral disarmament movement. For many, like Sangnier, cultural demobilization in the 1920s and 1930s was not inconsistent with a reluctant but resolute 'remobilization' for resistance and even for a new war in the 1940s. In those grim times, in what Mark Mazower pithily called this 'dark continent', a more resilient and humane Europe persisted, though often under cover. More than four score years on, the campfires at the Bierville Peace Camp glimmer as a past reminder of the grand – but elusive – task Marc Sangnier set for his movement, the 'disarmament of hatred'. Seen through the prism of history from our own age of anxiety, its lights – those hilltop torches in the night – represent a striking challenge to Mars and the enduring possibility, however obscured, of more hopeful horizons for humanity.

Appendix: International Democratic Peace Congresses, 1921–32

Year	Venue	Designated theme/particular feature	Dates
1921	Paris	[At Sangnier's *La Démocratie*]	4–11 December
1922	Vienna	[First Women's Section as element. Addition of 'Peace' to Congresses's titles]	26 September – 1 October
1923	Freiburg-im-Breisgau (Baden, Germany)	[Visit to Mont Sainte-Odile, Alsace]	4–10 August
1924	London	[Held at Methodist Central Hall, Westminster; Government reception, Lancaster House]	16–19 September
1925	Luxembourg	[Major 'Section' dedicated to Education]	9–14 September
1926	Bierville (Seine-et-Oise, France) [now in Essonne *département*.]	Peace through Youth [La Paix par la Jeunesse] 'Pilgrimage of Peace' by Germans in northern and eastern France.	17–22 August
1927	Würzburg	['Peace Circuit' of southern Germany]	3–7 September
1928	Geneva and Bierville	'The Peoples' Peace through the League of Nations.'	12–23 September
1929	Events across France culminating with meetings at Paris and Bierville.	'The Crusade of Youth' ['La Croisade de la Jeunesse']	16 August – 5 September
1930	Meetings at various locations in Belgium followed by closing meetings in Brussels and Bierville (Seine-et-Oise, France)	'The United States of Europe' ['Les Etats-Unis d'Europe']	24 August – 9 September
1931	Freiburg-Konstanz (Switzerland)	[Focus on treaty revision and on the Geneva Disarmament Conference set for February 1932]	4–9 September
1932	Events across France culminating with meeting at Bierville (Seine-et-Oise, France)	'Days of Hope' ['Journées d'Espérance']	11–28 August

Notes

Introduction

1. Denis Lefèvre, *Marc Sangnier: L'aventure du catholicisme social* (Paris: Mame, 2008), p. 230.
2. On Catholicism in the immediate post-war period, see Nicholas Atkin, 'Catholics and the Long Liberation: The Progressive Moment', in Andrew Knapp (ed.), *The Uncertain Foundation: France at the Liberation, 1944–1947* (Basingstoke: Palgrave Macmillan, 2007), pp. 121–38.
3. Lefèvre, *Marc Sangnier*, p. 230: Isser Woloch, 'Left, Right and Centre: The MRP and the Post-War Moment', *French History*, 21 (2007), pp. 85–106 at p. 88.
4. Ulrich Lappenküpper, 'On the Path to a "Hereditary Friendship"?', in Carine Germond & Henning Türk (eds), *A History of Franco-German Relations in Europe*, pp. 151–64 at p. 152; Wolfram Kaiser, *Christian Democracy and the Origins of European Union* (Cambridge: Cambridge University Press, 2007), pp. 191–252. See also, Marie-Thérèse Bitsch, *Robert Schuman, apôtre de l'Europe 1953–1963* (Brussels: P.I.E. Peter Lang, 2010): Richard Ayoun, 'Robert Schuman, "le père de l'Europe" ', in Hélène Fréchet & Richard Ayoun (eds), *Penser et Construire L'Europe (1919–1992)* (Nantes: Temps, 2007), pp. 177–212: Philippe Chenaux, *Une Europe vaticane? Entre le plan Marshall et les traités de Rome* (Brussels: Editions Ciaco, 1990): Philippe Chenaux, *De la chrétienté à l'Europe: les catholiques et l'idée européenne au XXe siècle* (Tours: CLD, 2007).
5. Stéphane Audoin-Rouzeau & Annette Becker, *14–18, Retrouver la guerre* (Paris: Gallimard, 2000), p. 122.
6. John Horne, 'Introduction: Mobilizing for "total war", 1914–1918', in John Horne (ed.), *State, Society and Mobilization in Europe during the First World War* (Cambridge: Cambridge University Press, 1997), pp. 1–17 at p. 1.
7. Matt Perry, *Memory of War in France, 1914–45: César Fauxbras, the Voice of the Lowly* (Basingstoke: Palgrave Macmillan, 2011).
8. Georges Hoog, 'Avant le Congrès de Bierville', *La Vie catholique*, 31 July 1926.
9. John Horne, 'Introduction' in 'Démobilisations culturelles après la Grande Guerre', *14–18 aujourd'hui*, 5 (2002), pp. 45–53: John Horne, 'Film and Cultural Demobilization after the Great War: The Two Versions of "J'Accuse" by Abel Gance (1918 and 1938)', in Hanna Diamond & Simon Kitson (eds), *Vichy, Resistance, Liberation: New Perspectives on Wartime France* (Oxford: Berg, 2005), pp. 131–41.
10. Laurence van Ypersele, 'Mourning and Memory, 1919–45', in John Horne (ed.), *A Companion to World War I* (London: Wiley-Blackwell, 2010), pp. 576–90 at p. 582: On pacifism in France, see Ilde Gorguet, *Les Mouvements Pacifistes et la réconciliation franco-allemande dans les années vingt (1919–1931)* (Berne: Peter Lang, 1999); Jean-Michel Guieu, *Le Rameau et le Glaive: Les militants français pour la Société des Nations* (Paris: Presses de Sciences Po, 2008); Norman Ingram, *The Politics of Dissent: Pacifism in France, 1919–1939*

(Oxford: Clarendon, 1991); Peter Farrugia, 'The Conviction of Things Not Seen: Christian Pacifism in France, 1919–1945', in Peter Brock & T. P. Socknat (eds), *Challenge to Mars: Essays on Pacifism from 1918 to 1945* (Toronto: University of Toronto Press, 1999), pp. 101–16: Sandi E. Cooper, *Patriotic Pacifism: Waging War on War on Europe, 1815–1914* (New York: Oxford University Press, 1991).

11. Christophe Prochasson, 'Les congrès, lieux de l'échange intellectuel 1850–1914', *Mil neuf cent: Revue d'histoire intellectuelle*, 7, 1989, pp. 5–8; Christian Sorrel, 'Le prêtre et le congrès (1870–1940): un rendez-vous manqué?', *Revue d'histoire de l'Eglise de France*, 93, 1 (2007), pp. 71–88; Emiel Lamberts, 'Catholic Congresses as Amplifiers of International Catholic Opinion', in Vincent Viaene (ed.), *The Papacy and the New World Order: Vatican Diplomacy, Catholic Opinion and International Politics at the Time of Leo XIII, 1878–1903* (Leuven: KADOC, 2005), pp. 213–24.
12. Kaiser, *Christian Democracy and the Origins of European Union*, p. 19.
13. Deborah Cohen & Maura O'Connor, 'Introduction: Comparative History, Cross-national History, Transnational History – Definitions', in Deborah Cohen & Maura O'Connor (eds), *Comparison and History: Europe in Cross-National Perspective* (London: Routledge, 2004), pp. ix–xxiv at p. xii; . See also Akira Iriye & Pierre-Yves Saunier (eds), *The Palgrave Dictionary of Transnational History* (Basingstoke: Palgrave Macmillan, 2009); Nigel Young (ed.), *The Oxford International Encylopedia of Peace*, 4 vols (Oxford: Oxford University Press, 2010).
14. Heinz-Gerhard Haupt & Jürgen Kocka, 'Comparative History: Methods, Aims, Problems', in Cohen & O'Connor (eds), *Comparison and History: Europe in Cross-National Perspective* (London: Routledge, 2004), pp. 23–39, here at p. 33.
15. Cohen & O'Connor, *Comparison and History*, p. xiv.
16. Carine Germond & Henning Türk (eds), *A History of Franco-German Relations in Europe: From 'Hereditary Enemies' to Partners* (Basingstoke: Palgrave Macmillan, 2008); Jean-Jacques Becker & Gerd Krumeich, *La Grande Guerre: Une histoire franco-allemande* (Paris: Tallandier, 2008). See also; Hans Manfred Bock, *Les jeunes dans les relations transnationales: L'office franco-allemand pour la jeunesse, 1963–2008* (Paris: Presses Sorbonne Nouvelle, 2008); Guido Müller, 'France and Germany after the Great War: Business Men, Intellectuals and Artists in Non-Governmental European Networks', in Jessica C. E. Gienow-Hecht & Frank Schumacher (eds), *Culture and International History* (New York: Berghahn, 2003), pp. 97–114; Paul Weindling, ' "For the Love of Christ": Strategies of International Catholic Relief and the Allied Occupation of Germany, 1945–48', *Journal of Contemporary History*, 43 (2008), pp. 477–92; Corine Defrance, 'Les jumelages franco-allemands: Aspects d'une cooperation transnationale', *Vingtième siècle*, 99 (2008), pp. 189–201.
17. Christopher Clark & Wolfram Kaiser (eds), *Culture Wars: Secular-Catholic Conflict in Nineteenth-Century Europe* (Cambridge: Cambridge University Press, 2003); Michael Gehler & Wolfram Kaiser (eds), *Christian Democracy in Europe since 1945*, vol. 2 (London: Routledge, 2004); Jean-Dominique Durand, *L'Europe de la Démocratie chrétienne* (Paris: Editions Complexe, 1995); Martin Conway, *Catholic Politics in Europe, 1918–1945* (London: Routledge, 1997); Vincent Viaene, 'The Roman Question: Catholic Mobilization and Papal

Diplomacy during the Pontficate of Pius IX (1846–1878)' in Emiel Lamberts, (ed.), *The Black International/L'International noire 1870–1878* (Leuven: Leuven University Press, 2002), 150–6.
18. Kaiser, *Christian Democracy*, p. 12.
19. Diarmaid MacCulloch, *A History of Christianity: The First Three Thousand Years* (London: Allen Lane, 2009), pp. 826–7.
20. Kaiser, *Christian Democracy*, p. 20.
21. Kaiser, *Christian Democracy*, pp. 43–5.
22. Kaiser, *Christian Democracy*, p. 46.
23. Kaiser, *Christian Democracy*, p. 63.
24. Holger Nehring, 'Peace', in Iriye & Saunier (eds), *Palgrave Dictionary of Transnational History* (Basingstoke: Palgrave Macmillan), pp. 803–6; David Cortright, *Peace: A History of Movements and Ideas* (Cambridge: Cambridge University Press, 2008); Susan R. Grayzel, *Women and the First World War* (London: Pearson, 2002); Cooper, *Patriotic Pacifism*; Sandi E. Cooper, 'Peace as a Human Right: The Invasion of Women into the World of High International Politics', *Journal of Women's History*, 14 (2002), pp. 9–25; Sandi E. Cooper, 'Pacifism in France, 1889–1914: International Peace as a Human Right', *French Historical Studies*, 17 (1991), pp. 359–86.
25. Holger Nehring & Helge Pharo, 'Introduction: A Peaceful Europe? Negotiating Peace in the Twentieth Century', *Contemporary European History*, 17 (2008), pp. 277–99; Jay M. Winter, *Dreams of Peace and Freedom: Utopian Moments in the Twentieth Century* (New Haven, CT & London: Yale University Press, 2006), pp. 1–10; Antony Adolf, *Peace: A World History* (Cambridge: Polity, 2009); Birgitte Hamann, *Bertha Von Suttner: A Life for Peace* (New York: Syracuse University Press, 1996).
26. Raymond Poidevin & Jacques Bariéty, *Les relations franco-allemandes 1815–1975* (Paris: A. Colin, 1977), pp. 240–57; Conan Fischer & Alan Sharp (eds), *After the Versailles Treaty: Enforcement, Compliance, Contested Identities* (London: Routledge, 2008); Stanislas Jeannesson, 'French Policy in the Rhineland', *Diplomacy and Statecraft*, 16 (2005), pp. 475–86; Jeannesson, 'Pourquoi la France a-t-elle occupé la Ruhr?', *Vingtième siècle*, 51 (1996), pp. 56–7; Jean-Jacques Becker & Serge Berstein, *Victoire et frustrations, 1914–29* (Paris: Seuil, 1990), pp. 210–23; Georges-Henri Soutou, 'The French Peacemakers and their Home Front', in Manfred F. Boemke, Gerald D. Feldman, & Elisabeth Glaser (eds), *The Treaty of Versailles: A Reassessment after 75 Years* (Cambridge: Cambridge University Press, 1998), pp. 167–88.
27. Thomas R. Davies, *The Possibilities of Transnational Activism: The Campaign for Disarmament between the Two World Wars* (Leiden: Brill, 2007), pp. 4–5.
28. Martin H. Geyer & J. Paulmasnn, *The Mechanics of Internationalism: Culture, Society and Politics from the 1840s to the First World War* (Oxford: Oxford University Press, 2001), p. 22.
29. Vincent Viaene, 'International History, Religious History, Catholic History: Perspectives for Cross-Fertilization (1830–1914)', *European History Quarterly*, 38, 4 (2008), pp. 578–607, at p. 594–96; Oxford-Leuven research project on Religious Internationals in the nineteenth century, http://www.history.ox.ac.uk/mehrc/research.htm, accessed 21 June 2009. See also Daniel Gerster, Review of conference on 'New Approaches to Contemporary Religious History' [held at European University Institute Florence, 26 May 2009],

H-Soz-u-Kult, H-Net Reviews, July, 2009, URL:http://h-net.org/reviews/showrev.php?id=27561, accessed 10 July 2011.)
30. Paul Misner, *Social Catholicism in Europe: From the Onset of Industrialization to the First World War* (London: Darton, Longman & Todd, 1991), pp. 298–306.
31. Winfried Becker, 'Marc Sangnier und Hermann Platz: Eine frühe Wahrnehmung und Würdigung des "Sillon" in der Münchener Zeitschrift "Hochland"', *Zeitschrift für Bayerische Landesgeschichte,* 68 (2005), pp. 1009–29.
32. Marc Sangnier, *Autrefois* (Paris: Bloud & Gay, 1936), p. 13.
33. Sangnier, *Deux mois en Afrique et en Espagne: Notes et impressions,* ed. Roger Rubuguo Mpongo (Paris: Don Bosco, 2009); Jean-Jacques Greteau, *Marc Sangnier: Le semeur d'espérances* (Paris: Harmattan, 2009), pp. 17–29; Olivier Prat (ed.), *Alphonse Gratry (1805–1872): Marginal ou précurseur* (Paris: Cerf, 2009). On the monumental and hugely divisive scandal that split France in the years following 1898 – and the unedifying role of some Catholics in it – see the recent book by Ruth Harris, *The Man on Devil's Island: Alfred Dreyfus and the Affair that divided France* (London: Allen Lane, 2010), pp. 217–46. For a synoptic French account, see Vincent Duclert, *L'Affaire Dreyfus* (1994; New ed., Paris: Larousse, 2009).
34. Sangnier, *Albert de Mun* (Paris: Presses Universitaires de France, 1932): On religious history, Adrien Dansette (1901–76) was the author of a series of classic histories of modern French Catholicism. On Sangnier, this penetrating article endures: 'The Rejuvenation of French Catholicism: Marc Sangnier's Sillon', *The Review of Politics,* 15 (1953), pp. 34–52. On Sangnier's debt to 'first wave' Social Catholicism, see also Benjamin F. Martin, *Albert de Mun: Paladin of the Third Republic* (Chapel Hill, NC: University of North Carolina Press, 1978); and Joan L. Coffey, *Léon Harmel: Entrepreneur as Catholic Social Reformer* (Notre Dame: University of Notre Dame Press, 2003).
35. Carter Jefferson, 'Worker Education in England and France, 1800–1914', *Comparative Studies in Society and History,* 6 (1964), pp. 345–66, p. 360.
36. Dansette, 'The Rejuvenation of French Catholicism', pp. 35–8.
37. Jean Guiraud to Pierre Petit de Julleville (his brother-in-law), 18 June 1903, Jean Guiraud papers, Archives Nationales de France[AN] (Paris), 362 AP 145, dossier 2.
38. On Sangnier's relationship with the Vatican, see Gearóid Barry, 'Rehabilitating a Radical Catholic: Marc Sangnier and Pope Benedict XV', *Journal of Ecclesiastical History,* 60 (2009), pp. 514–33. On Blondel as teacher and inspiration, see Peter J. Bernardi, *Maurice Blondel, Social Catholicism, and Action Française. The Clash over the Church's Role in Society during the Modernist Era* (Washington, D.C.: Catholic University of America Press, 2009).
39. J. F. Maclear, *Church and State in the Modern Age: A Documentary History* (New York: Oxford University Press, 1995), p. 320.
40. Lefèvre, *Marc Sangnier*: Greteau, *Marc Sangnier*: Madeleine Barthélemy-Madaule, *Marc Sangnier 1873–1950* (Paris: Seuil, 1973); Jeanne Caron, *Le Sillon et la démocratie chrétienne* (Paris: Plon, 1966); Vincent Rogard, 'Marc Sangnier et la Séparation', *Revue d'histoire de l'Eglise de France,* 91 (2005), pp. 299–309; Jean-Marie Mayeur (ed.), *Le Sillon de Marc Sangnier et la démocratie sociale: Actes du colloque des 18 et 19 mars 2004 à Besançon* (Besançon: Presses Universitaires de Franche-Comté, 2006).

41. Olivier Prat, 'La Paix par la Jeunesse: Le Congrès de Bierville. Août 1926', in Michel Meslin(ed.), *Marc Sangnier, la guerre, la paix, 1914–1939. Actes de la journée d'études du 26 septembre 1997* (Paris: Institut Marc Sangnier, 1999), pp. 55–82; Peter Farrugia, 'French Religious Opposition to War, 1919–1939: The Contribution of Henri Roser and Marc Sangnier', *French History*, 6 (1992), pp. 279–302; Jean-Claude Delbreil, *Les Catholiques français et les tentatives de rapprochement franco-allemand dans l'entre-deux-guerres, 1920–1933* (Metz: Presses Universitaires de Metz, 1972); Jean-Claude Delbreil (ed.), *Marc Sangnier: Témoignages* (Paris: Beauchesne, 1997); Jean-Claude Delbreil, *La revue 'La Vie Intellectuelle': Marc Sangnier, le thomisme et le personnalisme* (Paris: Cerf, 2008); Susan B. Whitney, *Mobilizing Youth: Communists and Catholics in Interwar France* (Durham, NC: Duke University Press, 2009); Julian Wright, 'Social Reform, State Reform, and Aristide Briand's Moment of Hope in France, 1909–10', *French Historical Studies*, 28 (2005), pp. 31–67; *Histoire@Politique. Politique, Culture, Société*, 10 (2010), www.histoire-politique.fr, accessed 7 June 2011 – 'Jeune Europe, jeunes d'Europe', ed. Ludivine Bantigny & Arnaud Baubérot (special issue, especially articles by Olivier Prat & Jean-Michel Guieu); Christophe Bellon, 'Aristide Briand et la naissance d'un centrisme politique, 1905–14', Mémoire pour le DEA, Institut d'Etudes Politiques, Paris, 2002.
42. See also Roger Chickering, *Imperial Germany and a World without War: The Peace Movement and German Society, 1892–1914* (Princeton, NJ: Princeton University Press, 1975), pp. 327–83.
43. Caron, *Le Sillon et la démocratie chrétienne*, p. 426.
44. Meslin (ed.), *Marc Sangnier, la guerre, la paix*, p. 213. On the resonance of the 'lost provinces', see Karine Varley, *Under the Shadow of Defeat: The War of 1870–71 in French Memory* (Basingstoke: Palgrave Macmillan, 2008).

1 Marc Sangnier's War, 1914–19

1. French views on threat of war in this period are summarized in William Mulligan, *The Origins of the First World War* (Cambridge: Cambridge University Press, 2010), pp. 145–9. Also, on the 'nationalist revival', see Gerd Krumeich, *Armaments and Politics in France on the Eve of the First World War: The Introduction of Three-Year Conscription, 1913–1914* (Leamington Spa: Berg, 1984); and Eugen Weber, *The Nationalist Revival in France, 1905–1914* (Berkeley, CA: University of California Press, 1968).
2. Alfred Baudrillart, *Les Carnets du Cardinal Alfred Baudrillart, 1er août 1914–31 décembre 1918*, ed. Paul Christophe (Paris: Cerf, 1994), p. 30, 5 August 1914.
3. James F. McMillan, 'French Catholics: Rumeurs Infâmes and the Union Sacrée, 1914–1918', in Frans Coetzee & Marilyn Shevin-Coetzee (eds), *Authority, Identity and the Social History of the Great War* (Oxford & Providence RI: Berghahn, 1995), p. 113; Jean-Jacques Becker, *The Great War and the French People* (Leamington Spa: Berg, 1986); Becker & Krumeich, *La Grande Guerre*, pp. 77–80.
4. Both approaches have impeccable methodological credentials. For 'war cultures', see the excellent textbook by Leonard V. Smith, Stéphane Audoin-Rouzeau, & Annette Becker, *France and the Great War, 1914–1918* (Cambridge:

Cambridge University Press, 2003). For a challenge to this 'historiography of consensus', see François Bouloc, *Les profiteurs de guerre, 1914–18* (Brussels: Editions Complexe, 2008). Fair summations of these debates are found in Leonard V. Smith, 'The "culture de guerre" and French Historiography of the Great War of 1914–1918', *History Compass*, 5 (2007), pp. 1967–79.

5. Baudrillart, *Les Carnets, 1914–1918,* p. 185, entry for 29 May 1915. See also Gearóid Barry, 'Marc Sangnier's War, 1914–1919: Portrait of a Soldier, Catholic and Social Activist', in Pierre Purseigle (ed.), *Warfare and Belligerence: Perspectives in First World War Studies* (Leiden: Brill, 2005), pp. 163–88.
6. Michael S. Neiberg, *Dance of the Furies: Europe and the Outbreak of World War I* (Cambridge MA: Belknap Press, 2011), pp. 51–7; AN, F7 16005/1, Police report, 18 September 1919. Jeune République meeting, Malakoff Palace Cinema, 17 September 1919. On socialists, the military and national unity, see Paul B. Miller, *From Revolutionaries to Citizens: Antimilitarism in France, 1870–1914* (Durham, NC: Duke University Press, 2001), p. 3; John Horne, 'Socialism, Peace, and Revolution, 1917–1918', in Hew Strachan (ed.), *The Oxford Illustrated History of the First World War* (2nd ed.; Oxford: Oxford University Press, 1998), pp. 227–38.
7. On French Catholics and the First World War, see Jacques Fontana, *Les Catholiques français pendant la grande guerre* (Paris: Cerf, 1990); Nadine-Josette Chaline (ed.), *Chrétiens dans la Première Guerre mondiale* (Paris: Cerf, 1993); Annette Becker, *War and Faith: The Religious Imagination in France, 1914–30* (1994; Eng. trans.; Oxford: Berg, 1998); James F. McMillan, 'French Catholics', in Coetzee & Shevin-Coetzee (eds), *Authority, Identity and the Social History of the Great War*, pp. 113–32; Annette Becker, 'Faith, Ideologies, and the "Cultures of War"', in Horne (ed.), *Companion to World War I* (2010), pp. 234–47.
8. Horne, 'Introduction: Mobilizing for "total war", 1914–1918', in Horne (ed.), *State, Society and Mobilization*, p. 1.
9. On the Catholic Committee, see Fontana, *Les catholiques*, pp. 329–38. On French intellectuals and the war, see Martha Hanna, *The Mobilization of Intellect: French Scholars and Writers during the Great War* (Cambridge, MA: Harvard University Press, 1996); Christophe Prochasson & Anne Rasmussen, *Au Nom de la Patrie: les intellectuels et la première guerre mondiale* (Paris: Editions de la Découverte, 1996); Eric Thiers, 'Droit et culture de guerre 1914–1918: Le Comité d'études et documents sur la guerre', *Mil neuf cents: Revue d'histoire intellectuelle*, 23 (2005), pp. 23–48. Catholic Committee publications included Alfred Baudrillart (ed.), *L'Allemagne et les alliés devant la conscience chrétienne* (Paris: Bloud et Gay, 1915).
10. Georges Hoog, *Pourquoi l'Alsace-Lorraine doit redevenir française* (Paris: Bloud et Gay, 1915).
11. Baudrillart, *Les Carnets 1914–1918*, p. 398, entry for 20 July 1916.
12. Institut Marc Sangnier (Paris) [IMS], M.S. 26, Letter Sangnier-Louis Meyer (secretary accompanying him in Rome), 11 August 1916.
13. *Service Historique de l'Armée de Terre* (Vincennes) [SHAT], 6Ye 30527, 'Marc Sangnier – État des Services', Dossier Marc Sangnier, Report of Colonel Commanding Engineers at Langres, January 1915: IMS, Correspondance Générale I, Corresp. Hubert Aubert – Sangnier, 14 April 1915. (Aubert was a supporter

of the Sillon from Aube-Ste Savine, Marne. See obituary in *L'Ame commune*, December 1962.)

14. Becker, *War and Faith*, p. 111; Fontana, *Les catholiques*, pp. 268–9.
15. Becker, *War and Faith*, pp. 106–11; Fontana, *Les catholiques*, pp. 268–9.
16. Alfred Baudrillart, *Les Carnets du Cardinal Alfred Baudrillart. 1 janvier 1919–31 décembre 1921*, ed. Paul Christophe (Paris: Cerf, 2000), p. 372, entry for 19 January 1920.
17. Becker, *War and Faith*, p. 109.
18. Becker, 'Faith, Ideologies, and the "Cultures of War"', p. 235: Fontana, *Les catholiques*, p. 273. For similarities and differences with the British experience, see Edward Madigan, *Faith under Fire: Anglican Army Chaplains and the Great War* (Basingstoke: Palgrave Macmillan, 2011), and Michael Snape, *God and the British Soldier: Religion and the British Army in the First and Second World Wars* (London: Routledge, 2005).
19. Joseph F. Byrnes, *Catholic and French Forever: Religious and National Identity in Modern France* (University Park, PA: Pennsylvania State University Press, 2005), pp. xxi, 155–77.
20. Joseph F. Byrnes, 'Priests and Instituteurs in the Union Sacrée: Reconciliation and its Limits', *French Historical Studies*, 22(2) (1999), pp. 263–89, at p. 286.
21. Martha Hanna, 'A Republic of Letters: The Epistolary Tradition in France during World War I', *American Historical Review*, 108 (2003), pp. 1338–61; Martyn Lyons, 'French Soldiers and their Correspondence: Towards a History of Writing Practices in the First World War', *French History*, 17 (2003), pp. 79–95.
22. Stéphane Audoin-Rouzeau, *Men at War, 1914–1918: National Sentiment and Trench Journalism in France during the First World War* (Oxford: Berg, 1992); *Notre Étoile*, 15 February 1916.
23. Robert Cornilleau, 'Les Républicains-Démocrates (Histoire et Souvenirs) – XVIII: Les Républicains-Démocrates et la Guerre', *Le Petit Démocrate*, 11 October 1925.
24. IMS, M.S. 26, Corresp. Chapon-Sangnier, 26 December 1916.
25. IMS, M.S. 26, Corresp. Chapon-Sangnier, 26 December 1916.
26. *Nos Annales de Guerre*, 24 March 1918.
27. Georges Hoog, 'Les Pâques de la patrie', *Lettres à un soldat*, 4 April 1915.
28. Memo by Jean Sangnier on his father's wartime activities, n. d., IMS, M.S. 26.
29. McMillan, 'French Catholics', p. 114.
30. 'La Mission de Marc Sangnier en Italie', *Notre Étoile*, 24 September 1916.
31. Mgr Jules Tiberghien [writing from Paris] to Mgr Eugenio Pacelli, 29 July 1916, Vatican Secret Archives [ASV], Affari Ecclesiastici Straordinari, Francia 1916, fasc. 658. On France–Vatican relations in 1916, see Fontana, *Les catholiques*, pp. 192–7. However, Fontana does not allude to Sangnier's visit.
32. Baudrillart, *Les Carnets du Cardinal Alfred Baudrillart*, ed. Paul Christophe, pp. 388–9, entries for 6–7 July 1916.
33. John F. Pollard, *Benedict XV: The Unknown Pope and the Pursuit of Peace* (1999; 2nd ed.; London: Continuum, 2005), p. 25. See also Barry, 'Rehabilitating a Radical Catholic'; Frank J. Coppa, *Politics and the Papacy in the Modern World* (Westport, CT: Praeger, 2008); Jean-Jacques Becker, *Le Pape et la Grande Guerre* (Paris: Bayard, 2006); Nathalie Renoton-Beine, *La Colombe et les tranchées: Les tentatives de paix de Benoît XV pendant la Grande Guerre* (Paris: Cerf, 2004).

34. Pollard, *Benedict XV*, p. 27.
35. Pollard, *Benedict XV*, p. 69.
36. Account revealed in 1973 in Barthélemy-Madaule's biography of Sangnier.
37. IMS, M.S. 26, Memo, Marc Sangnier, 'Audience du Pape 1916'.
38. Eamon Duffy, *Saints and Sinners: A History of the Popes* (London & New Haven, CT: Yale University Press, 2002), p. 329.
39. Tiberghien to Pacelli, 29 July 1916, ASV, Affari Ecclesiastici Straordinari, Francia 1916, fasc. 658.
40. IMS, M.S. 26 Memo Marc Sangnier, 'Audience du Pape 1916'.
41. Sangnier to Holy See, 15 August 1916, ASV, Affari Ecclesiastici Straordinari, Francia 1916, fasc. 658.
42. John Horne & Alan Kramer, *German Atrocities, 1914: A History of Denial* (New Haven, CT & London: Yale University Press, 2001), pp. 268–9.
43. Jean-Marie Mayeur, 'Les catholiques français et Benoît XV en 1917: Brèves remarques', in Chaline (ed.), *Chrétiens dans la première guerre mondiale: Actes des journées tenues à Amiens et à Péronne les 16 mai et 22 juillet 1992* (Paris: Cerf, 1993), pp. 153–65 at p. 160.
44. IMS, M.S. 26, Sangnier, diary, August 1916.
45. IMS, M.S. 26, Memo, Marc Sangnier, 'Audience du Pape 1916'.
46. IMS, M.S. 26 Memo, Marc Sangnier, 'Audience du Pape 1916'.
47. Baudrillart, *Les Carnets 1914–18*, p. 414, entry for 22 August 1916.
48. Chapon to pope, May 1919, ASV, Affari Ecclesiastici Straordinari, Francia 1919, fasc. 697, fols. 36–48.
49. Bishop Tissier of Châlons to Gasparri, 9 October 1916, ASV, Affari Ecclesiastici Straordinari, Francia 1916, fol. 658.
50. Pacelli to Tissier, 16 October 1916, ASV, Affari Ecclesiastici Straordinari, Francia 1916, fol. 658.
51. Archives Historiques de l'Archévêché de Paris [AHAP], 1 D XI, 13, Papers of Cardinal Amette, Notes sur audiences pontificales (1906–9), fol. 32.
52. Bishop Chapon of Nice to Sangnier, 26 December 1916, IMS, M.S. 26.
53. AN, F7 16005/1, Police report, Paris, 16 May 1917.
54. AN, F7 16005/1, Police report, Paris, 16 May 1917.
55. Marc Sangnier, *Ce que savent les Jeunes Français aujourd'hui: Simple contribution à une enquête sur l'instruction. Examen passé par 661 conscrits de la classe 18 au depot du 1er Génie à Versailles* (Paris: La Démocratie, n. d.).
56. Sangnier, *Ce que savent*, p.19.
57. Sangnier, *Ce que savent*, p. 4. See also Mona L. Siegel, *The Moral Disarmament of France: Education, Pacifism and Patriotism, 1914–40* (Cambridge: Cambridge University Press, 2004), chapter 1.
58. Sangnier, *Ce que savent*, pp. 9–10.
59. Sangnier, *Ce que savent*, pp. 8–9.
60. Sangnier, *Ce que savent*, p. 12.
61. Sangnier, *Ce que savent*, pp. 14, 16.
62. John Horne, 'Remobilizing for "total war": France and Britain, 1917–1918', in Horne (ed.), *State, Society and Mobilization*, pp. 195–211; Horne, 'Socialism, Peace, and Revolution', p. 234.
63. IMS, M.S. 26 Marc Sangnier as Propagandist – Letter Captain Deuil, Cabinet of War Minister – Sangnier, 29 October 1917.
64. IMS, M.S. 26, Gen. Conneau – General D.E. du GAN, 13 May 1918.

65. IMS, M.S. 26, Memo, Jean Sangnier, n. d.
66. IMS, M.S. 26, Propaganda Conferences – Reports to War Ministry, 1918–19 (Sangnier submitted official reports to the War Ministry after each of these tours.).
67. IMS, M.S. 26, diary, 25 March 1918.
68. IMS, M.S. 26, Memo, Jean Sangnier, n. d.
69. Jay M. Winter, 'Propaganda and the Moblization of Consent', in Strachan (ed.), *The Oxford Illustrated History of the First World War*, pp. 216–26, here at pp. 216–17: David Stevenson, *French War Aims against Germany, 1914–1919* (Oxford: Oxford University Press, 1992).
70. Horne & Kramer, *German Atrocities*, part i; for summary of recent debate, see Thomas Weber, *Hitler's First War: Adolf Hitler, the Men of the List Regiment, and the First World War* (Oxford: Oxford University Press, 2011), pp. 37–41.
71. IMS, M.S. 26, Propaganda Conferences, Propaganda Conferences – Memo of conference, first tour, March–April 1918, p. 7.
72. Audoin-Rouzeau & Becker, *14–18, Retrouver la guerre*, pp. 68, 129.
73. IMS, M.S. 26, Propaganda Conferences – Memo of conference, first tour, March–April 1918, pp. 16–18.
74. Georges-Henri Soutou, '1918: la fin de la Première Guerre mondiale?', *Revue historique des armées*, 251 (2008), pp. 4–17.
75. IMS, M.S. 26, Propaganda Conferences – Marc Sangnier's private diary – Entry for 23 September 1918.
76. Walter Lippmann cited in Martin Ceadel, *Thinking about Peace and War* (Oxford: Oxford University Press, 1987), p. 51.
77. IMS, M.S. 26, Propaganda Conferences – Memo of conference, first tour of conferences, March–April 1918, pp. 36–7.
78. IMS, M.S. 26, Propaganda Conferences – Notes, 1918.
79. IMS, M.S. 26, Diary – Entry for 10 June 1918.
80. IMS, M.S. 26, entry for 6 November 1918.
81. IMS, M.S. 26, Diary – Entry for 17 January 1919.
82. Horne & Kramer, *German Atrocities*, p. 188.
83. IMS, M.S. 26, press cutting, *Réveil de la Marne*, n. d. but 31 January 1919.

2 Demobilization and Politics, 1919–21

1. Bruno Cabanes, *La Victoire endeuillée: La sortie de guerre des soldats français (1918–1920)* (Paris: Seuil, 2004), p. 56; Becker & Krumeich, *La Grande Guerre*, pp. 293–9; Bruno Cabanes, 'Les Vivants et les Morts: La France au sortir de la Grande Guerre', in Stéphane Audoin-Rouzeau & Christophe Prochasson (eds), *Sortir de la Grande Guerre: Le monde et l'après-guerre 1918* (Paris: Tallandier, 2008), pp. 27–45, at p. 28; Stéphane Audoin-Rouzeau & Annette Becker, *1914–1918: Understanding the Great War* (London: Profile Books, 2002), pp. 175–225; Stéphane Audoin-Rouzeau, *Cinq deuils de guerre, 1914–1918* (Paris: Noésis, 2001); Olivier Faron, 'Le deuil des vivants', in Stéphane Audoin-Rouzeau & Jean-Jacques Becker (eds), *Encylopédie de la Grande Guerre, 1914–1918: Histoire et culture* (Paris: Bayard, 2004), pp. 1113–22; Cabanes, *La Victoire endeuillée*, pp. 81–95. See also Cabanes & Guillaume Piketty (eds), *Retour à l'intime: au sortir de la guerre* (Paris: Tallandier, 2009).

2. Cabanes, *La Victoire endeuillée*, pp. 488–90; Antoine Prost, *Les anciens combattants, 1914–1939*, vol. 3, *Mentalités et idéologies* (Paris: Sciences Po, 1977); Jay Winter, 'Henri Barbusse and the Birth of the Moral Witness' introduction to Henri Barbusse, *Under Fire* (London: Penguin, 2003), p. vii–xix; Audoin-Rouzeau, *Cinq deuils*, pp. 9–12; Annette Becker, *Les monuments aux morts, patrimoine et mémoire de la Grande Guerre* (Paris: Errance, 1988). See also Jay Winter, *Sites of Memory, Sites of Mourning: The Great War in European Cultural History* (Cambridge: Cambridge University Press, 1995); Daniel Sherman, *The Construction of Memory in Interwar France* (Chicago, IL: Chicago University Press, 1999).
3. Georges Hoog, 'Le rappochement moral', in Georges Hoog (ed.), *France et Allemagne* (Paris, 1928), pp. 127–59, at p. 138. Souvenir card issued by newspaper *Lettres à un soldat*, c. 1918. Private collection, Mme. Dominique Laxague.
4. Marc Sangnier, *Autrefois* (Paris, 1933), pp.182, 191, 211; Guillaume Cuchet, 'L'Au-delà à l'Epreuve du Feu: La Fin du Purgatoire (1914–1935)', *Vingtième Siècle: Revue d'histoire*, 76 (2002), 117–30; Barthélemy-Madaule, *Marc Sangnier*, p. 236; IMS, Paris, M.S. 26 Handwritten memo, Paul Chatelat, Secretary to MS 'Pélerinage aux cantonnements de Marc. Guerre 1914–18'. Sangnier's reflections on combat and the front may be contrasted with the broad range explored by Leonard V. Smith in his *The Embattled Self: French Soldiers' Testimony of the Great War* (New York: Cornell, 2007). On visits to front, see David William Lloyd, *Battlefield Tourism: Pilgrimage and the Commemoration of the Great War in Britain, Australia and Canada, 1919–1939* (Oxford: Berg, 1998); Audoin-Rouzeau, *Cinq deuils*, pp. 115–19; Lisa M. Budreau, 'The Politics of Remembrance: The Gold Star Mothers' Pilgrimage and America's Fading Memory of the Great War', *The Journal of Military History*, 72, (April 2008), pp. 371–411.
5. Erez Manela, *The Wilsonian Moment: Self-Determination and the International Origins of Anticolonial Nationalism* (Oxford: Oxford University Press, 2007), p. 8; Benjamin F. Martin, *France and the Après-Guerre, 1918–1924: Illusions and Disillusionments* (Baton Rouge, LA: Louisiana State University Press, 1999), pp. 11–56.
6. Pierre Miquel, *Le traité de Versailles et l'opinion publique française* (Paris: Flammarion, 1972), pp. 62–94: See also Manela, *The Wilsonian Moment*, pp. 16–17; Margaret Macmillan, *Peacemakers: The Paris Conference of 1919 and its Attempt to End War* (London: John Murray, 2001), p. 23. See also Georges-Henri Soutou, 'The French Peacemakers and their Home Front', in Boemke, Feldman, & Glaser (eds), *The Treaty of Versailles*, pp. 167–88; M. L. Dockrill & John Fisher (eds), *The Paris Peace Conference, 1919: Peace without Victory?* (New York: Palgrave Macmillan, 2001); Alan Sharp, *The Versailles Settlement: Peacemaking after the First World War, 1919–23* (Basingstoke: Palgrave Macmillan, 2008), pp. 109–38.
7. Guieu, *Le Rameau et le Glaive*, pp. 86–8, 127–28; *La Démocratie*, 22 June 1919. See also Christian Birebent, *Militants de la paix et de la SDN: Les mouvements de soutien à la Société des Nations en France et au Royaume Uni, 1918–1925* (Paris: Harmattan, 2007).
8. AN, F7 16005/1, Police report, 18 September 1919. Jeune République meeting, Malakoff Palace Cinema, 17 September 1919. See Macmillan,

Peacemakers, pp. 310–14; Martin, *France and the Après-Guerre*, pp. 17–19; AN, F7 16005/1, Police report, 24 October 1919. Jeune République public meeting, 23 October 1919.

9. AN, F7 16005/1, Police biographical note on Marc Sangnier, 10 November 1920; Yves Santamaria, *Le pacifisme, une passion française* (Paris: Armand Colin, 2005), p. 90; Martin, *France and the Après Guerre*, pp. 20–2, 111–17, 49–53.
10. Gérard Cholvy & Yves-Marie Hilaire, *Religion et société en France, 1914–45: Au péril des guerres* (Toulouse: Privat, 2002), pp. 49–50; ASV, Affari Ecclesiastici Straordinari, Francia 1919 Elezioni, fasc.700, fol. 40, Letter Mgr Chapon of Nice- Affari Ecclesiastici Straordinari, 3 January 1920.
11. AN, F7 16005/1, Police report, 12 November 1919; Cornilleau, 'Les Républicains-Démocrates', *Le Petit Démocrate*, 11 October 1925; Barthélemy-Madaule, *Marc Sangnier*, p. 241. See also Olivier Prat, 'Marc Sangnier et la paix à la Chambre «Bleu Horizon», 1919–1924', in Claude Carlier & Georges-Henri Soutou (eds), *1918–1925: Comment faire la paix? Actes du colloque international organise à Versailles les 26 et 27 novembre 1999* (Paris: Economica, 2001), pp. 53–79.
12. AN , F7 16005/1, Police reports, 9 & 10 November 1919.
13. Archives départementales et communales, Département et Ville de Paris, [ADVP], D3 M2/12 'Propagande électorale, 1919–28'; Caron, *Le Sillon*, pp. 584–85; Sangnier, *Autrefois*, p.193; Barthélemy-Madaule, *Marc Sangnier*, p. 247.
14. Georges Hoog, *Marc Sangnier au Parlement, 1919–1924* (Paris: La Démocratie, 1924), pp.13–14. On the 'unknown soldier', see Annette Becker, 'Le culte des morts: entre mémoire et oubli', in Audoin-Rouzeau & Becker (eds), *Encylopédie de la Grande Guerre, 1914–1918: Histoire et culture*, pp. 1107–9; R. Dalisson, 'La célébration du 11 novembre ou l'enjeu de la mémoire combattante dans l'entre-deux-guerres (1918–1939)', *Guerres mondiales et conflits contemporains*, 192 (1998), pp. 5–23.
15. Cholvy & Hilaire, *Religion et société en France, 1914–1945*, pp. 47–56. James F. McMillan, 'France', in Tom Buchanan & Martin Conway (eds), *Political Catholicism in Europe 1918–65* (Oxford: Clarendon Press, 1996), pp. 34–68; Denis Pelletier, '1905–2005; Un siècle d'engagements catholiques', in Bruno Duriez et al. (eds), *Les catholiques dans la république, 1905–2005* (Paris: Editions de l'Atelier, 2005), pp. 19–50; Hoog, *MS au Parlement*, p. 30.
16. Duffy, *Saints and Sinners*, p. 335; ASV, Affari Ecclesiastici Straordinari, Francia 1919, fasc. 697. fols. 36–48, Memo Mgr Chapon of Nice-Pope, Rome, May 1919.
17. *La Démocratie*, 10 February 1922; Pollard, *Benedict XV*, p. 143. On papal diplomacy, see also J.-M. Ticchi, *Aux Frontières de la Paix. Bons offices, médiations, arbitrages du Saint-Siège (1878–1922)* (Rome: Ecole Française de Rome, 2002); Jean-Dominique Durand, 'Pie XI, la paix et la construction d'un ordre international', in Ecole Française de Rome (ed.) *Achille Ratti. Pape Pie XI: Actes du colloque organisé par l'Ecole Française de Rome (Rome, 15–18 mars 1989)* (Rome: Ecole Française de Rome, 1996), pp. 873–92. On Pius XI's politics, see also Michel Burleigh, *Sacred Causes: The Clash of Religion and Politics, from the Great War to the War on Terror* (New York: Harper Collins, 2007), pp. 160–8.
18. Frank J. Coppa, *The Modern Papacy since 1789* (London: Longman, 1998), p. 171; Harry Kessler, *The Diaries of a Cosmopolitan: Count Harry Kessler,*

1918–37 (1961, English trans., London: Weidenfeld & Nicolson, 1971), p. 142, entry for 23 Jun 1921: Hoog, 'Le rappochement moral', p. 142: Simone de Beauvoir, *Memoirs of a Dutiful Daughter* (1958; English trans., London, 1984), p. 132.

19. On certain bishops' resistance, see Baudrillart, *Les carnets du Cardinal Baudrillart*, ed. Paul Christophe, p. 470, entry for 11 May 1920; Cholvy & Hilaire, *Religion et société en France, 1914–1945*, p. 51; ASV, Segretaria di Stato, 1920, rubrica 14, fasc. 4, fol. 50, Letter Chapon-Tedeschini (Secretariat of State), 25 February 1920; ASV, Segretaria di Stato, 1920, rubrica 14, fasc. 4, fol. 139, Gasparri-Archbishop Nègre of Tours, 30 April 1920.
20. Martin, *France and the Après Guerre*, pp. 30, 112–14; Jean-Jacques Becker & Serge Berstein, *Histoire de l'anti-communisme en France*, vol. 1, *1917–40* (Paris: O. Orban, 1987), p. 77; John Horne, 'The State and Challenge of Labour in France, 1917–1920', in Chris Wrigley (ed.), *Challenges of Labour: Central and Western Europe, 1917–1920* (London: Routledge, 1993), pp. 239–61. On the strikes, see also Marjorie Millbank Farrar, *Principled Pragmatist: The Political Career of Alexandre Millerand* (New York: Berg, 1991), pp. 212–19.
21. Prat, 'Marc Sangnier et la Paix à la Chambre', p. 56; Zara S. Steiner, *The Lights That Failed: European and International History, 1919–33* (Oxford: Oxford University Press, 2005), p. 183; John Horne, 'La reconstruction du nord-est de la France après 1918', *Les chemins de la mémoire*, 173 (2007), pp. 7–10; *Jeune République*, 1 August 1920.
22. Germaine Malaterre-Sellier, 'Société des nations, Société des peuples', Jeune République, 21 July 1922. Cited in Guieu, *Le Rameau et le Glaive*, pp. 69–76; Prat, 'Marc Sangnier et la Paix à la Chambre', pp. 57–60. On the minorities system of the League, see Carole Fink, *Defending the Rights of Others: The Great Powers, the Jews, and International Minority Protection, 1878–1938* (Cambridge: Cambridge University Press, 2004).
23. Gorguet, *Les Mouvements Pacifistes*, p. 75; Donald Sassoon, *One Hundred Years of Socialism: The West European Left in the Twentieth Century* (New York: New Press, 1996), pp. 31–4; Kaiser, *Christian Democracy and the Origins of European Union*, p. 61; Delbreil, *Les catholiques français*, p. 62.
24. William Solzbacher & Josephine Solzbacher-Kennon, *Peace Movements between the Wars: One Man's Work for Peace* (Lampeter: E. Mellen Press, 1999), pp. 46–55; Frédérick Hadley, 'La Paix par la Jeunesse', *La Lettre de l'Historial* [Historial de la Grande Guerre, Péronne], 23, November 2008, p. 13; ASV, Affari Ecclesiastici Straordinari , IV, 293, fasc. 19, fol. 125. Pamphlet on Third International Catholic Congress (IKA), Constance, 10–15 August 1923; fol. 23. Letter, Metzger-Secretary of State, 1 March 1922. On Esperanto, see also Roxanne Panchasi, *Future Tense: The Culture of Anticipation in France between the Wars* (Ithaca, NY: Cornell University Press, 2009), pp. 135–59.
25. Gorguet, *Les Mouvements Pacifistes*, p. 73–4; Caron, *Le Sillon*, p. 266.
26. AN, F7 16005/1, Police biographical note on Marc Sangnier, 10 November 1920; *La Démocratie*, 25 August 1920, 10 November 1920, 25 November 1920; Horne, 'Introduction – Démoblisations Culturelles', pp. 45–53 at p. 51; *La Démocratie*, 25 December1920; Gorguet, *Les mouvements pacifistes*, p. 76.
27. *La Démocratie*, 25 December 1920; 25 November 1920; 10 January 1921.
28. Sangnier, 'Le Désarmement des haines', *La Démocratie*, 25 January 1921; *Jeune République*, 6 February 1921, cited in Olivier Prat, 'Marc Sangnier et l'idée

européenne', in Hélène Fréchet (ed.), *Penser et construire l'Europe (1919–1992)* (Nantes: Editions du Temps, 2007), p. 48; *La Démocratie*, 25 May 1921.

29. Sangnier, *Discours* (Vol. 7) *1922–23* (Paris: La Démocratie, 1925), p. 17, 24 May 1922. On Briand and Germany in 1921, see Paul Létourneau, ' "La main au collet" et le révisionisme allemande durant la période Rathenau: l'occasion ratée?', *Revue d'Allemagne et des Pays de langue allemande*, 38, 2, (2006) – 'Révisionisme allemande et puissances occidentals entre 1919 et 1939', eds. Paul Létourneau & Georges-Henri Soutou, pp. 185–96; Steiner, *The Lights That Failed*, p. 200; Jacques Néré, *The Foreign Policy of France from 1914 to 1948* (London: Routledge & Kegan Paul, 1975), p. 37.
30. Steiner, *The Lights That Failed*, p. 201; Néré, *Foreign Policy of France*, p. 37; Martin, *France and the Après-Guerre*, p. 87; Gorguet, *Les Mouvements Pacifistes*, p. 77; Martin, *France and the Après-Guerre*, p. 91.
31. Sharp, *The Versailles Settlement*, p. 131.

3 'The Traitor in Berlin': Paris, Germany and Austria, 1921–2

1. *Compte-rendu complet du Ier Congrès démocratique international, Paris, 4–11 décembre 1921* (Paris: La Démocratie, 1922), pp. 235, 237, 291–2.
2. AN, F7 16005/1, Police report, Paris, 29 November 1921; *Ier Congrès démocratique international, Paris, 4–11 décembre 1921*, p. 238; Olivier Prat, ' "La Paix par la Jeunesse": Marc Sangnier et la réconciliation franco-allemande, 1921–1939', *Histoire@Politique*, 10 (2010).
3. Gorguet, *Les Mouvements Pacifistes*, pp. 78–9.
4. *Ier Congrès démocratique international, Paris, 4–11 décembre 1921*, p. 378; Kessler, *The Diaries of a Cosmopolitan*, p. 144, entry for 11 December 1921.
5. Georges Hoog, 'Le rapprochement moral', in Hoog (ed.), *France et Allemagne*, pp. 139–40.
6. *Ier Congrès démocratique international, Paris, 4–11 décembre 1921*, pp. 249, 264, 249–50. On the German-Polish dispute, see Martin Kitchen, *Europe between the Wars* (1988; 2nd ed.: London: Pearson/Longman, 2006), chapter 5.
7. Hoog, 'Le rappochement moral', pp. 142–3; *Ier Congrès démocratique international, Paris, 4–11 décembre 1921*, pp. 300–1; 'The Covenant of the League of Nations', The Avalon Project, Yale Law School, http://avalon.law.yale.edu, accessed 9 July 2009.
8. Horne, 'Locarno et la politique de démobilization culturelle: 1925–30', *14–18 aujourd'hui*, 5, 2002, pp. 78–9; *Ier Congrès démocratique international, Paris, 4–11 décembre 1921*, pp. 347–8.
9. Gorguet, *Les Mouvements Pacifistes*, pp. 23, 24–7.
10. Prat (ed.), *Alphonse Gratry*, p. 122; *Ier Congrès démocratique international, Paris, 4–11 décembre 1921*, p. 246. Ó Ceallaigh, a veteran of the 1916 Rising and a lifelong supporter of De Valera's, served in several republican Fianna Fáil governments from 1932, before serving as President of Ireland (1945–59). The genial Dubliner was a favourite target of popular wit and polite satire in view of his short stature.
11. Marc Sangnier, *Pour l'Irlande libre: Discours prononcé à Paris le 28 juin 1920 et précédé d'une allocution de M. Gavan Duffy, délégué du Gouvernement élu de*

la République irlandaise (Paris: La Démocratie, 1920), pp. 26–35; IMS, M.S. 23, Speech, Sangnier, reception for De Valera, 28 January 1922. On Ireland and world opinion, see Maurice Walsh, *The News from Ireland: Foreign Correspondents and the Irish Revolution* (New York: I.B. Tauris, 2008).

12. *Ier Congrès démocratique international, Paris, 4–11 décembre 1921*, p. 352: AN, F7 16005/1, Police report, Paris, 12 December 1921. Report on closing meeting of first congress, 11 December 1921.
13. *Ier Congrès démocratique international, Paris, 4–11 décembre 1921*, p. 358.
14. *Ier Congrès démocratique international, Paris, 4–11 décembre 1921*, pp. 373, 359, 361, 368.
15. *La Démocratie*, 10 February 1922; *Jeune République*, 22 January 1922; 29 January 1922.
16. Martin, *France and the Après-Guerre*, pp. 101, 69.
17. AN, F7 12951, 'Notes Jean', 13 January 1922: Georges-Henri Soutou, 'L'ordre européen de Versailles à Locarno', in Carlier & Soutou (eds), *1918–1925: Comment faire la paix? Actes du colloque international organisé à Vincennes les 26 et 27 novembre 1999*, pp. 301–31, at p. 306; Sharp, *The Versailles Settlement*, pp. 87–8; Georges-Henri Soutou, *L'or et le sang: les buts de guerre économiques de la Première Guerre mondiale* (Paris: Fayard, 1989), pp. 766–7; Steiner, *The Lights That Failed*, p. 185.
18. Martin, *France and the Après-Guerre*, p. 124: Hoog, *MS au Parlement*, p. 17, 19 January 1922; Barthélemy-Madaule, *Marc Sangnier*, p. 244; John F. V. Keiger, *Raymond Poincaré* (Cambridge: Cambridge University Press, 1997), p. 288; Martin, *France and the Après-Guerre*, pp. 123–59. See also, Carole Fink, *The Genoa Conference: European Diplomacy, 1921–22* (Chapel Hill, NC: University of North Carolina Press, 1984).
19. Durand, 'Pie XI, la paix et la construction d'un ordre international', in Ecole Française de Rome (ed.), *Achille Ratti. Pape Pie XI*, pp. 873–92; *Jeune République*, 3 May 1921; 26 May 1921; 21 April 1922: Kessler, *The Diaries of a cosmopolitan*, p. 174, entry for 1 May 1922.
20. *Jeune République*, 26 May 1922; 19 May 1922: Gorguet, *Les Mouvements Pacifistes*, pp. 80, 24–29.
21. Ruyssen cited in Guieu, *Le Rameau et le Glaive*, p. 131. On the French left and Germany in the 1920s, see Yves Santamaria, *L'enfant du malheur: Le parti communiste français dans la Lutte pour la Paix (1914–1947)* (Paris: Armand Colin, 2002); Becker & Berstein, *Victoire et frustrations*, pp. 230–7; Guieu, *Le Rameau et le Glaive*, pp. 127–38.
22. On pacifism in Germany, see Guido Grünewald, 'War Resisters in Weimar Germany', in Brock & Socknat (eds), *Challenge to Mars*, pp. 68–88; Karl Holl, 'The Peace Movement in German Politics 1890–1933', in Art Cosgrove & J. I. McGuire (eds), *Parliament and Community: Papers read before the Irish Conference of Historians, Dublin 27-30 May 1981* (Belfast: Appletree Press, 1983), pp. 177–89, here at pp. 182–3; Chickering, *Imperial Germany*, p. 327; Horne & Kramer, *German Atrocities*, p. 364.
23. Magnus Jocham, 'Paroles de paix', *La Démocratie*, 25 September 1922: Marie-Emmanuelle Reytier, 'Les Katholikentage dans l'entre-deux-guerres', *14–18: Aujourd'hui*, 1, (1998), pp. 71–85, here at pp. 81–2; Gorguet, *Les Mouvements Pacifistes*, p. 87; Richard J. Evans, *The Coming of the Third Reich* (London: Penguin, 2003), p. 92. On interwar German Catholicism, see

also Marie-Emmanuelle Reytier, 'Des catholiques pacifistes: Die Katholische Friedenswarte (1924–1927) et Der Friedenskämpfer (1928–1933)', in Michel Grunewald, Uwe Puschner, & Hans-Manfred Bock (eds), *Le milieu intellectuel catholique en Allemagne, sa presse et ses résaux (1871–1960)* (Berne: Peter Lang, 2006), pp. 255–80; Karl-Egon Lönne, 'Germany' in Buchanan & Conway (eds), *Political Catholicism*, pp. 156–86.

24. *Le IIe Congrès démocratique international pour la Paix: Vienne, 26 septembre–1 octobre 1922* (Paris: La Démocratie, 1922), pp. 122, 192. On German politics, see also Detlev J. K. Peukert, *The Weimar Republic* (London: Allen Lane, 1991); Eberhard Kolb, *The Weimar Republic* (New York: Routledge, 1995).
25. Sangnier, 'Réflexions de voyageur', *Jeune République*, 26 May 1922: Sangnier, *Discours* (Vol. 7) *1922–23*, pp. 13–55 (full speech), here at pp. 18, 29, 47–9, 53–5, 24 May 1922. See also, Martin, *France and the Après-Guerre*, p. 141.
26. IMS (Paris), M.S. Correspondance Générale, Albert Thomas, ILO. Corresp. Thomas-Sangnier, 29 May 1922; Cornilleau, 'Les Républicains-Démocrates', *Le Petit Démocrate*, 18 October 1925; Ernest Pezet, *Chrétiens au service de la cité: De Léon XIII au Sillon au MRP*, 1891–1965 (Paris: Nouvelles Editions Latines, 1965), p. 94; McMillan, 'France', p. 43: On Christian Democrats in France in this period, see Delbreil, *Les catholiques français*, pp. 17–18, 53–7; Kaiser, *Christian Democracy and the Origins of European Union*, pp. 42–71.
27. *Jeune République*, 23 June 1922; *Action française*, 10 June 1922; AN, F7 16005/1, Police report, Paris, 28 June 1922. Copy of *Camelots du roi* poster.
28. Christopher Forth, *The Dreyfus Affair and the Crisis of French Manhood* (London & Baltimore: Johns Hopkins University Press, 2003), pp. 203–4; Jessica Wardhaugh, *In Pursuit of the People: Political Culture in France, 1934–39* (Basingstoke: Palgrave Macmillan, 2009), pp. 31–2; Jessica Wardhaugh, 'Un Rire Nouveau: Action Française and the art of political satire', *French History*, 22, 2008, pp. 273–307; AN, F7 16005/1, Police report, Paris, 28 June 1922. Copy of Camelots du roi poster.
29. *Le IIe Congrès démocratique international pour la Paix: Vienne, 26 septembre–1 octobre 1922* (Paris: La Démocratie, 1922), p. 242.
30. Mona Siegel, ' "To the Unknown Mother of the Unknown Soldier": Pacifism, Feminism, and the Politics of Sexual Difference among French *Institutrices* between the Wars', *French Historical Studies*, 22, 1999, pp. 421–51, here at p. 421; *Le IVè Congrès démocratique international pour la Paix. Londres, 16–19 Septembre 1924* (Paris: La Démocratie, 1924), p. 73; Winter, *Sites of Memory*, pp. 90–1. (Politically, the WILPF Hague meeting of 1915 led directly to general conferences of anti-war socialists at Swiss villages of Zimmerwald (September 1915) and Kienthal in 1916.)
31. Siegel, 'To the Unknown Mother', p. 425.
32. Sandrine Wierzbicki, 'Germaine Malaterre-Sellier: un destin aux croisés du féminisme et du pacifisme (1889–1967)' (Mémoire de Maîtrise, Université de Paris I – Panthéon-Sorbonne, 2001). See also Christine Bard, *Les filles de Marianne: Histoire des féminismes, 1914–1940* (Paris: Fayard, 1995); James F. McMillan, *Housewife or Harlot: The Place of Women in French Society, 1870–1940* (Brighton: Harvester Press, 1981); Evelyne Diebolt (ed.), *Militer au XXe siècle: Femmes, féminismes, Eglises et société: Dictionnaire biographique* (Paris: Houdiard, 2009).

33. Sandi E. Cooper, 'Pacifism, Feminism, and Fascism in Inter-War France', *International Historical Review*, 19, 1997, pp. 103–26; Erika Kuhlman, *Reconstructing Patriarchy after the Great War: Women, Gender, and Postwar Reconciliation between Nations* (Basingstoke: Palgrave Macmillan, 2008); Norman Ingram, 'Gender and the Politics of Pacifism: Feminist Pacifism and the Case of the French Section of the WILPF', in Eva Schöch-Quinteros, Anja Schüler, Annika Wilmers, & Kerstin R. Wolff (eds), *Politische Netzwerkerinnen: Internationale Zusammenarbeir bei Frauen, 1830–1960* (Berlin: Trafo Verlag, 2007), pp. 267–85; Susan Grayzel, *Women's Identities at War: Gender, Motherhood, and Politics in Britain and France during the First World War* (Chapel Hill, NC: University of North Carolina Press, 1999); William D. Irvine, 'Women's Right and the "Rights of Man"', in Martin S. Alexander & Kenneth S. Mouré (eds), *Crisis and Renewal in France, 1918–1962* (New York & Oxford: Bergahn, 2002), pp. 46–65.
34. *Jeune République*, 24 April 1921; *IIe Congrès*, p. 188.
35. Sangnier, *Discours* (Vol. 7) *1922–23*, p. 153 (Speech in Paris, 7 November 1922).
36. *IIe Congrès*, pp. 251, 197.
37. *IIe Congrès*, pp. 251, 197, 254, 190; Delbreil, *Les catholiques français*, pp. 31–5.
38. ASV, Segretaria di Stato, Epoca Moderna, 1922, Rubrica 78, fasc. 5, fol. 31. Letter, Sangnier & Hoog-Pope, 21 September 1922 (request for papal blessing for Vienna congress); ASV, Segr. di Stato (1922), Rubr. 249, fasc. 4, fol. 122. Hoog-Gasparri, 7 November 1922; Pope Pius XI, 'Ubi Arcano Dei Consilio: Encyclical of Pope Pius XI on the Peace of Christ in the Kingdom of Christ', 23 December 1922, http://www.vatican.va/holy_father/pius_xi/encyclicals/documents/hf_p-xi_enc_23121922_ubi-arcano-dei-consilio_en.html, accessed 15 November 2011.

4 From Pragmatist to Dove: Freiburg-im-Breisgau, 1923

1. Conan Fischer, *The Ruhr Crisis, 1923–1924* (Oxford: Oxford University Press, 2003), p. 15. For an overview of reparations controversy, see Fischer, *Europe between Democracy and Dictatorship, 1900–1945* (Chichester: Wiley-Blackwell, 2011), pp. 143–71.
2. Fischer, *The Ruhr Crisis*, p. 3, 170; *Jeune République*, 19 January 1923; Alan Sharp & Conan Fischer, 'The Versailles Settlement: Enforcement, Compliance, Contested Identities', *Diplomacy and Statecraft*, 16, (2005), pp. 419–22; Steiner, *The Lights That Failed*, passim: Jeannesson, 'Pourquoi la France a-t-elle occupé la Ruhr?', pp. 56–7; Sally Marks, '"Poincaré-La-Peur": France and the Ruhr Crisis of 1923', in Mouré & Alexander (eds), *Crisis and Renewal in France, 1918–1962*, pp. 28–45; Poidevin & Bariéty, *Les relations franco-allemandes*, pp. 240–57. See also Marc Trachtenburg, *Reparation in World Politics: France and European Economic Diplomacy 1916–1923* (New York: Columbia University Press, 1980); Walter McDougall, *France's Rhineland Diplomacy 1914–1924* (Princeton, NJ: Princeton University Press, 1978); Stephen Schuker, *The End of French Predominance in Europe: The Financial Crisis of 1924 and the Adoption of the Dawes Plan* (Chapel Hill, NC: University of North Carolina Press, 1976).

3. Georges-Henri Soutou, 'Les Occidentaux et l'Allemagne durant l'entre-deux-guerres', *Revue d'Allemagne et des Pays de langue allemande*, 38, (2006), pp. 165–84; Sharp & Fischer, 'The Versailles Settlement', pp. 420–1; Jeanness on, 'French Policy in the Rhineland', p. 482.
4. Gerald D. Feldman, 'The Reparations Debate', *Diplomacy and Statecraft*, 16, (2005), pp. 487–98.
5. Wardhaugh, *In Pursuit of the People*, pp. 12–13; Marks, 'Poincaré-La-Peur', p. 30; Anna-Monika Lauter, *Sicherhiet und Reparationen: Die französische Őffentlichkeit, der Rhein und die Ruhr (1919–1923)* (Essen: Klartext, 2006); Martin, *France and the Après-Guerre*, pp. 160–3.
6. Guieu, *Le Rameau et le Glaive*, pp. 131–2.
7. Sangnier, *Discours* (Vol. 7) *1922–23*, pp. 169–72, Intervention of 13 January 1923.
8. AN, F7 16005/1, Police report, 11 March 1923, Public meeting, Nantes.
9. *Le IIIe Congrès démocratique international pour la Paix. Fribourg-en-Brisgau (Allemagne), 4–10 août 1923. Compte rendu complet* (Paris: La Démocratie, 1923), p. 494.
10. AN, F7 16005/1, Police report, 11 March 1923, public meeting, Nantes; Prefect of the Rhône–Interior Minister, 20 March 1923. Public meeting, Lyon, 18 March 1923: *Jeune République*, 21 May 1923.
11. AN, F7 13196 'Agression contre Marc Sangnier, 31.5.1923', Meeting organized by Ligue des Droits de l'homme against Fascism in France, Salle des Sociétés Savantes, 31 May 1923.
12. Directeur de la Police Judiciaire to Prefect of Paris, 1 June 1923, AN, F7 13196, 'Manifestations de l'Action Française'. Manifestation contre le meeting organise par la Ligue des droits de l'homme contre le fascisme; AN, F7 13196, Report of M. Philipon, Commissaire d'Arrondisement, Police municipale, Quartier ND-des-Champs, 31 May 1923.
13. Sangnier, *Discours* (Vol. 7) *1921–23*, p. 239.
14. George L. Mosse, *Fallen Soldiers, Reshaping the Memory of the World Wars* (New York: Oxford University Press, 1990), p. 159; Audoin-Rouzeau & Becker, *1914–1918: Understanding the Great War*, pp. 35–6; Michael Geyer, 'The Militarization of Europe, 1919–39', in John R. Gillis (ed.), *The Militarization of the Western World* (New Brunswick, NJ: Rutgers University Press, 1989), p. 79. Cited in Pierre Purseigle, 'Introduction', in Purseigle (ed.), *Warfare and Belligerence: Perspectives in First World War Studies*, p. 11; Antoine Prost, 'The Impact of War on French and German Political Cultures', *The Historical Journal*, 37, (1994), pp. 209–17, at p. 215; Stanislas Jeannesson, *Poincaré, la France et la Ruhr 1922–24. Histoire d'une occupation* (Strasbourg: Presses Universitaires de Strasbourg, 1998), p. 210.
15. Conan Fischer, 'The Human Price of Reparations', *Diplomacy and Statecraft*, 16, (2005), pp. 499–514; Fischer, *The Ruhr Crisis*, p. 114; Marks, 'Poincaré-La-Peur', p. 34; Siegel, 'To the Unknown Mother', p. 438: Gorguet, *Les Mouvements Pacifistes*, pp. 65–9; Sangnier, *Discours* (Vol. 7) *1922–23*, p. 320.
16. Delbreil, *Les catholiques français*, p. 231; Jay P. Corrin, *Catholic Intellectuals and the Challenge of Democracy* (Notre Dame IN.: University of Notre Dame Press, 2002), pp. 70–80; Hoog, 'Le rapprochement moral', p. 154: *IIIe Congrès*, p. 441.

17. *IIIe Congrès*, pp. 446, 437, 615; Solzbacher & Solzbacher-Kennon, *Peace Movements between the Wars*, p. 45. The Anglicized version of his first name, Wilhelm, was adopted in later life in the USA.
18. *IIIe Congrès*, 453, 536, 547: Santamaria, *Le pacifisme*, p. 48. On the disarmament debate, see Peter Jackson, 'France and the Problems of Security and International Disarmament after the First World War', *Journal of Strategic Studies*, 29, 2006, pp. 247–80.
19. Gertrude A. Giles, 'The Third International Peace Congress', *Friends Fellowship Papers*, 1, 1923, pp. 185–89, at p. 186.
20. *IIIe Congrès*, pp. 445, 449–50, 454, 456: Cooper, *Patriotic Pacifism*, pp. 42, 183; Ingram, *The Politics of Dissent*, pp. 47–9; *IIIe Congrès*, pp. 561–2; Fischer, *The Ruhr Crisis*, p. 114; Giles, The Third International Peace Congress', p. 186.
21. *IIIe Congrès*, p. 541; Winfried Becker, 'Le pacificisme sous la République de Weimar et ses liens avec Marc Sangnier et Bierville', in Meslin (ed.), *Marc Sangnier la guerre, la paix*, pp. 174–5; Sangnier, *Discours* (Vol. 7) *1921–23*, p. 368; Horne & Kramer, *German Atrocities*, pp. 364, 358; *IIIe Congrès*, pp. 541, 556; Fischer, *The Ruhr Crisis*, p. 176; Sangnier, *Discours* (Vol. 7) *1921–23*, p. 367.
22. *IIIe Congrès*, pp. 462–70, 474–5; Wierzbicki, Germaine Malaterre-Sellier, p. 66. For the history of the WILPF's French section, see Michel Dreyfus, 'Des femmes pacifistes dans les années trente', *Matériaux pour l'histoire de notre temps*, 30, 1993, pp. 32–4; *IIIe Congrès*, p. 544; Horne & Kramer, *German Atrocities*, p. 364.
23. *IIIe Congrès*, p. 543.
24. Giles, 'The Third International Peace Congress', p. 188.
25. Robert Gildea, *The Past in French History* (New Haven, CT & London: Yale University Press, 1994), p. 194; *IIIe Congrès*, p. 474.
26. Fischer, *The Ruhr Crisis*, p. 292.
27. Antoine Prost, 'Youth in France between the Wars', in Antoine Prost (ed.), *Republican Identities in War and Peace: Representations of France in the Nineteenth and Twentieth Centuries* (Oxford: Berg, 2002), pp. 221–34, at p. 221; Peter D. Stachura, *The German Youth Movement 1900–45: An Interpretative and Documentary History* (London: Palgrave Macmillan, 1981), pp. 33, 14, 23; Walter Laqueur, *Young Germany. A History of the German Youth Movement* (London: Routledge & Kegan Paul, 1962), p. 90; Chickering, *Imperial Germany*, pp. 169–70.
28. Stachura, *The German Youth Movement*, p. 74; Sangnier, *Discours* (Vol. 7) *1921–23*, p. 368; Laqueur, *Young Germany*, p. 71; Grünewald, 'War Resisters in Weimar Germany', p. 71; Michael Mitterauer, *A History of Youth* (Oxford: Blackwell, 1992), p. 220; Joseph Débès & Émile Poulat, *L'appel de la JOC, 1926–28* (Paris: Cerf, 1986), p. 21. On the ideology of the Wandervögel members, see also John Alexander Williams, *Turning to Nature in Germany: Hiking, Nudism, and Conservation, 1900–1940* (Stanford: Stanford University Press, 2007), pp. 107–83. [Please note that in the historical literature the plural form Wandervögel is used to indicate the membership whereas the movement itself is sometimes distinguished by use of the singular form (e.g. the Wandervogel movement)].
29. *IIIe Congrès*, pp. 592, 606, 594; Hoog, 'Le rapprochement moral', p. 155.

30. AN, F7 16005/1, Police report, 5 September 1923.
31. Chickering, *Imperial Germany*, p. 304; *IVè Congrès – Londres, Septembre 1924* (Paris, La Démocratie, 1924), p. 49; *Jeune République*, 21 March 1924; Grünewald, 'War Resisters in Weimar Germany', p. 69.
32. Solzbacher & Solzbacher-Kennon, *Peace Movements*, p. 45.
33. Solzbacher & Solzbacher-Kennon, *Peace Movements*, p. 47; Delbreil, *Les catholiques français*, pp. 31–5; ASV, Affari Ecclesiastici Straordinari, IV, 293, fasc. 19, fol. 125. Pamphlet on Third International Catholic Congress (IKA), Constance, 10–15 August 1923, p. 14.
34. *III Congrès*, p. 614; AN, F7 16005/1, Police report, 27 October 1923. Jeune République meeting, Paris. [It would appear the police reporter at this meeting transcribed incorrectly as 'Avilliers', instead of Arvillers, the name of the village that became the beneficiary of the Sacrifice of Reconciliation moneys: I have located no such commune as 'Avilliers' in the Somme department or nationally but Arvillers is located 13 kilometres from the town of Montdidier]; Sally Marks, 'Poincaré-La-Peur', p. 36.
35. Sangnier, *Discours* (Vol. 7) *1921–23*, pp. 386–87; Sangnier, *Discours* (Vol. 7) *1922–23*, p. 361; *III Congrès*, p. 376; Sangnier, *Discours* (Vol. 7) *1921–23*, pp. 359–87, esp. 372–73, 387.

5 *Pacem in Terris*: The Politics and Theology of Peace, 1924–5

1. Martin, *France and the Après-Guerre*, p. 188.
2. AN, F7 16005/1, Lieutenant Bleuzet, General Staff of the Marine-Sûreté Générale, 26 February 1924; Schuker, *The End of French Predominance*, p. 122; AN, F7 16005/1, Police report, 24 February 1924, election meeting, Paris; Steiner, *The Lights That Failed*, p. 193; Sangnier, *Discours* (Vol. 8) *1923–25* (Paris: La Démocratie, 1925), pp. 299–300 (speech at Manège du Panthéon, Paris, 4 May 1924).
3. Marc Sangnier, *Discours* (Vol. 8) *1923–25*, vol. 7, pp. 173–214 (speech at the Salle des Sociétés Savantes, 30 January 1924 on 'Les Nouveaux Pauvres'). On Briand's sinuousness in 1924, see Martin, *France and the Après-Guerre*, p. 239.
4. AN, F7 16005/1, Police report, 21 January 1924, on Jeune République congress at Bordeaux; ADVP, D3 M2/ 12 'Propagande électorale 1919–28', manifesto of Liste d'Union Républicaine pour la Paix, April 1924.
5. Sangnier, *Discours* (Vol. 8) *1923–1925*, p. 292 (speech at the Manège Huyghens, Paris, 4 May 1924); Martin, *France and the Après-Guerre*, pp. 226–52; ADVP, D2 M2/52, Notices sur les députés, 'Procès-verbal – Election 1924 -3ème circonscription de la Seine.'
6. Patrick O. Cohrs, *The Unfinished Peace after World War 1: America, Britain and the Stabilisation of Europe, 1914–1932* (Cambridge: Cambridge University Press, 2006), pp. 155–6; Steiner, *The Lights That Failed*, p. 248.
7. *Le IVè Congrès – Londres, Septembre 1924*, p. 72; Carl Bouchard, 'Les Lauréats de la Paix. Les Concours Américain et Français pour la Paix de 1923–1924', *Revue d'Histoire Moderne et Contemporaine*, 54, 2007, pp. 118–37; Jackson, 'France and the Problems of Security and International Disarmament after

the First World War', pp. 247–80, at p. 269; Martin, *France and the Après-Guerre,* p. 254. See also Poidevin & Bariéty, *Les relations franco-allemandes,* pp. 258–65; Gérard Unger, *Aristide Briand, le ferme conciliateur* (Paris: Fayard, 2005), pp. 471–544.

8. Library of the Religious Society of Friends in Britain (Quakers) [LSF], MSS Vol.S.107, Peace Committee Minutes 1921–25, 6 September 1923; *Ier Congrès démocratique international, Paris, 4–11 décembre 1921,* p. 253; Jill Wallis, *Valiant for Peace: A History of the Fellowship of Reconciliation 1914–1989* (London: Fellowship of Reconciliation, 1991), pp. 36–7; LSF, MSS Vol. S.107, Peace Committee Minutes 1921–25, 1 May 1924.
9. LSF, MSS Vol.S.107, Peace Committee Minutes 1921–25, 3 July 1924. On Vera Brittain's influence, see Dan Todman, *The Great War: Myth and Memory* (London: Hambledon Continuum, 2005), pp. 183–5; Kuhlman, *Reconstructing Patriarchy after the Great War,* p. 10 (see also Chapter 4, 'Women Activists in the Postwar World: Gender, Reconcilialion, and Humanitarian Aid', pp. 105–37); LSF, TEMP MSS 481, Ruth Fry Papers, box 1, diary, 3 March 1926. On these activists, see also LSF, *Dictionary of Quaker Biography* (typescript, work in progress), Entry for Anna Ruth Fry (1878–1962); Fry, *A Quaker Adventure: The Story of Nine Years' Relief and Reconstruction* (New York: Nisbet & Co., 1926); Sybil Oldfield, 'Pye, Edith Mary (1876–1965)' in H.C.G. Matthew, Brian Howard Harrison & Lawrence Goldman (eds), *Oxford Dictionary of National Biography* (Oxford: Oxford University Press, 2004), http://www.oxforddnb.com/view/article/37871, accessed 6 August 2009.
10. 'Unity of Europe: Frenchmen and Germans at a Congress', *The Times,* 18 September 1924.
11. Hoog, 'Le rappochement moral', p. 143; Letter, Quidde-Sangnier, n. d. but 1924, Bundesarchiv Koblenz. Fonds Quidde 212/135. Cited in Sophie Lorrain, *Des pacifistes français et allemands, pionniers de l'entente franco-allemande, 1871–1925* (Paris: L'Harmattan, 1999), p. 231, n. 19.
12. 'Unity of Europe', *The Times,* 18 September 1924: *IVe Congrès,* pp. 23–24.
13. For this exclusion, see Martin Ceadel, *Semi-detached Idealists: The British Peace Movement and International Relations, 1854–1945* (Oxford: Oxford University Press, 2000), pp. 429–34; *IVe Congrès,* pp. 79, 43, 77. See also, Ceadel, 'A Legitimate Peace Movement: The Case of Britain, 1918–1945', in Brock & Socknat (eds), *Challenge to Mars,* pp. 134–48; Keith Robbins, *The Abolition of War: The Peace Movement in* Britain, *1914–1919* (Cardiff: University of Wales Press, 1976).
14. Gorguet, *Les Mouvements Pacifistes,* pp. 30–7; *IVe Congrès,* pp. 104–10: '"No More War" London Demonstrations', *The Times,* 22 September 1924.
15. *IVe Congrès,* p. 25; Sangnier, *Discours* (Vol. 8) *1923–25,* p. 214. See also Jackson, 'France and the Problems of Security', pp. 247–80; Andrew Webster, 'From Versailles to Geneva: The Many Forms of Interwar Disarmament', *The Journal of Strategic Studies,* 29, (2006), pp. 225–46.
16. Poidevin & Bariéty, *Les relations franco-allemandes,* p. 259.
17. Jackson, 'France and the Problems of Security', p. 275; William Lee Blackwood, 'German Hegemony and the Socialist International's Place in Interwar European Diplomacy', *European History Quarterly,* 31, (2001), pp. 101–40; Santamaria, *Le pacifisme,* p. 96.

18. Patrick de Villepin, 'La revue "Évolution" et le pacifisme révisionniste (1926–33)', *Matériaux pour l'histoire de notre temps,* 30, 1993, pp. 11–13; Horne & Kramer, *German Atrocities,* p. 370; Victor Margueritte, *Vers la paix; Appel aux consciences: Avec un avant-propos de Victor Margueritte* (Paris. A. Delpeuch, 1925), pp. 14–15; Théodore Ruyssen, 'Encore l'Article 231!', *La Paix par le Droit,* 35/5, May 1925, p. 203, cited in Ingram, *The Politics of Dissent,* p. 43; *Jeune République,* 24 July 1925.
19. *Indépendance luxembourgeoise,* 12 September 1925; *Le Ve Congrès démocratique internarional pour la Paix. Luxembourg, 9–14 septembre 1925* (Paris: La Démocratie, 1925), pp. 68–69; LSF, TEMP MSS 481, Ruth Fry Papers, box 1, diary, 3 March 1926.
20. European Office of the Carnegie Endowment for International Peace, *Enquête sur les livres scolaires d'après-guerre* (Paris, 1923), pp. 8, 124; IVe Congrès, pp. 62, 75–87; Siegel, *The Moral Disarmament of France,* p. 12.
21. Siegel, *The Moral Disarmament of France,* p. 43.
22. *Luxembourg 1925,* pp. 29–34, 42–3; Carnegie Endowment, *Enquête sur les livres scolaires,* pp. 120, 128.
23. Santamaria, *Le pacifisme,* p. 42; Siegel, *The Moral Disarmament of France,* pp. 125, 135–7; *Luxembourg 1925,* p. 37; *Indépendance luxembourgeoise,* 13 & 14 September 1925.
24. *Ier Congrès démocratique international, Paris, 4–11 décembre 1921,* p. 287; *IIIe Congrès,* p. 590; Solzbacher & Solzbacher-Kennon, *Peace Movements,* passim; *Xe Congrès démocratique international pour la Paix. Inauguration du Foyer de la Paix de Bierville, 24–31 août 1930. Réunions d'Ostende, Bruxelles, Anvers et Liège sur les Etats-Unis d'Europe* (Paris: La Démocratie, 1930), p. 5; interview with M. Jean Sangnier, March 2001. On Buisson and education, see also Yves Déloye, 'L'Ecole', & Jean-François Chanet, 'Apprendre', in Vincent Duclert & Christophe Prochasson (eds), *Dictionnaire Critique de la République* (Paris: Flammarion, 2002), pp. 699–704, 981–6.
25. *Luxembourg 1925,* pp. 54–5; Sangnier, *Discours* (Vol. 8) *1923–25,* pp. 173–214; *Ier Congrès démocratique international, Paris, 4–11 décembre 1921,* p. 334; *IIe Congrès,* p. 121.
26. Jon Jacobson, 'Locarno, Britain and the Security of Europe', in Gaynor Johnson (ed.), *Locarno Revisited: Europe Diplomacy, 1920–1929* (London: Routledge, 2004), pp. 11–32, at p. 11; Anthony Best, Jussi M. Hahnimäki, Joseph A. Maiolo, & Kirsten E. Schulze, *International History of the Twentieth Century and Beyond* (London: Routledge, 2008 [2004]), pp. 50–4; Jonathan Wright & Julian Wright, 'One Mind at Locarno? Aristide Briand and Gustav Stresemann', in Steven Casey & Jonathan Wright (eds), *Mental Maps in the Era of Two World Wars* (Basingstoke: Palgrave Macmillan, 2008), pp. 58–76.
27. John F. V. Keiger, 'Poincaré, Briand and Locarno: Continuity in French Diplomacy in the 1920s', in Johnson (ed.), *Locarno Revisited,* pp. 95–107; Ruth Henig, *Versailles and after, 1919–1933* (London: Routledge, 1984), p. 40; Johnson (ed.), *Locarno Revisited,* p. 3.
28. Wright & Wright, 'One Mind at Locarno?', p. 65.
29. Unger, *Aristide Briand,* pp. 545–7; Norman Ingram, 'Les pacifistes et Aristide Briand', in Jacques Bariéty (ed.), *Aristide Briand, la Société des Nations, 1919–1932* (Strasbourg: Presses Universitaires de Strasbourg, 2007), pp. 200–13; Elana Passman, 'Civic Activism and the Pursuit of Cooperation in the

Locarno Era', in Germond & Türk (eds), *A History of Franco-German Relations in Europe*, pp. 101–12; Andrew Barros, 'Briand, l'Allemagne et le "pari" de Locarno', in Bariéty (ed.), *Aristide Briand*, pp. 160–72.

30. Philippe Chenaux, 'Le Saint-Siège, l'Europe et la paix dans les années vingt', in Bariéty (ed.), *Aristide Briand*, pp. 251–63; *Jeune République*, 23 October 1925.
31. *Jeune République*, 23 October 1925.

6 Bierville and the Liturgy of Peace, 1926

1. *Luxembourg 1925*, p. 87.
2. *Xe Congrès démocratique international pour la Paix. Innauguration du Foyer de la Paix de Bierville, 24–31 août 1930. Réunions d'Ostende, Bruxelles, Anvers et Liège sur les Etats-Unis d'Europe* (Paris: La Démocratie, 1930), pp. 3–4; *La Démocratie*, November–December 1924, pp. 113–17.
3. *France-Soir*, 18 August 1926; *La Paix par la Jeunesse: Le Mois international de Bierville (août 1926). VIe Congrès démocratique international pour la Paix, 17–22 août 1926* (Paris: La Démocratie, 1926), p. 248; *La Vie catholique*, 14 August 1926.
4. Serge Berstein, 'Consensus Politique et Violences Civiles dans la France du 20e siècle', *Vingtième Siècle: Revue d'histoire*, 69, (2001), pp. 51–60.
5. *Jeune République*, 8 January 1926; 29 January 1926; 4 June 1926: *La Paix par la Jeunesse*, p. 117.; IMS, M.S. Correspondance Générale, Paul Painlevé. Corresp. Minister of War–Sangnier, 17 August 1926.
6. *La Paix par la Jeunesse*, pp. 6–7, 280–82; AN, F7 13962, 'Congrès démocratique international', Report, Commissaire special de police, Paris, 1 June 1926; AN, F7 13962 Prefect of Département of the Somme – Minister of the Interior, 29 July 1926; Prat, 'La Paix par la Jeunesse: Le Congrès de Bierville. Août 1926', p. 62.
7. Prat, 'La Paix par la Jeunesse: Le Congrès de Bierville. Août 1926', p. 62; AN, Jean Guiraud Papers, 362 AP 107, dossier 4. Corresp. Sangnier-Guiraud, n. d. but July 1926; Alain Fleury, *La Croix et l'Allemagne, 1920–30* (Paris: Cerf, 1986), p. 55.
8. Istituto Luigi Sturzo (Rome), [ILS], fasc. 436, c.1, Corresp. Sturzo-Sangnier, 27 July 1926; *La Paix par la Jeunesse*, pp. 2, 21–2, 13.
9. AN, F7 13962, Commissaire de Police (3ème arrondisement, Reims) – Interior Ministry, 31 July 1926; Note of phone call, Sous-Préfet de Reims-Ministry of the Interior, 31 July 1926; Jacques Le Goff, 'Reims, City of Coronation', in Pierre Nora (ed.), *Realms of Memory*, vol. 3, *Symbols* (New York: Columbia University Press, 1998), pp. 193–8; *La Paix par la Jeunesse*, pp. 13–14; Alfred Baudrillart, *Les Carnets du Cardinal Baudrillart, 13 avril 1925–25 décembre 1928*, ed. Paul Christophe (Paris: Cerf, 2002), pp. 444–5, entry for 19 August 1926.
10. *La Paix par la Jeunesse*, pp. 14–19; 'Sur la visite des pacifistes', *Le Nord-Est*, 3 August 1926; Horne & Kramer, *German Atrocities*, p. 307; Baudrillart, *Les Carnets 1925–1928*, p. 445, entry for 19 August 1926; *Jeune République*, 6 August 1926; AN, F7 13962, Commissaire spécial de Police (Reims)–Directeur de la Surêté Générale, Ministry of the Interior, 4 August 1926.

11. Prat, 'La Paix par la Jeunesse: Le Congrès de Bierville. Août 1926', pp. 63–5; AN, F7 13962, Commissariat Spécial des Ponts du Rhin et Port de Strasbourg (Kehl)–Directeur de Police d'Alsace et de Lorraine (Strasbourg), 31 July 1926: Henry de Korab, 'La paix par l'intimité', *Le Matin*, 18 August 1926.
12. *L'Oeuvre*, 21 August 1926; István Deák, *Weimar Germany's Left-wing Intellectuals: A Political History of the Weltbühne and its Circle* (Berkeley, CA: Univeristy of California Press, 1968), p. 38; Ministère des Affaires Étrangères, Quai d'Orsay, Paris [MAE], Série Z. Allemagne 402, 'Propagande de la France, 1924–29', ff. 24–25. Report, French Consul in Nuremberg-Briand, Minister for Foreign Affairs, 15 September 1926; Florence Denoix de Saint-Marc, 'Joseph Folliet et les Compagnons de Saint François de 1926 à 1958', Mémoire de maîtrise, Université de Lyon 2, 1986, p. 15. On Folliet at Bierville 1926, see Antoine Delery, *Joseph Folliet, 1903–1972: parcours d'un militant catholique* (Paris: Cerf, 2003), pp. 61–6; Jacques Perrier, *L'Abbé Stock (1904–48): Heureux les doux* (Paris: Cerf, 1998).
13. AN, F7 16005/1, Police report, 11 March 1923, public meeting, Nantes; Geoffrey Adams, *Political Ecumenism: Catholics, Jews, and Protestants in De Gaulle's Free France* (Montreal: McGill-Queen's University Press, 2006) [reviewed in Jessica Wardhaugh, 'Sacred Unions: Religion and Reconciliation in French Society, 1919–1945', *French Politics, Culture & Society*, 27, 2009, pp. 116–28].
14. Prost, *Les anciens combattants, 1914–1939*, p. 119. See also Prost & Jay Winter, *René Cassin et les Droits de l'Homme: Le projet d'une génération* (Paris: Fayard, 2011), pp. 43–78; Veterans' resolutions in *L'Oeuvre*, 12 & 21 August 1926.
15. *La Paix par la Jeunesse*, pp. 127–37; Philippe Chenaux, 'Monseigneur Julien et l'Allemagne', in Meslin (ed.), *Marc Sangnier, la guerre, la paix*, pp. 105–20. On Lorette memorial, see Becker, *War and Faith*, pp. 125–34; ASV, Affari Ecclesiastici Straordinari, IV, Stati Ecclesiastici, 1922–34, 293, fasc. 20, fol. 90. Letter, Valeri-Gasparri, 23 August 1926: Baudrillart, *Les Carnets 1925–1928*, p. 444, entry for 18 August 1926; Léon-Adolphe Julien, 'A propos du Congrès de Bierville', *Le Correspondant*, 25 September 1926, cited in *Documentation catholique*, 14, 1926, col. 1236.
16. *La Paix par la Jeunesse*, p. 198.
17. IMS, M.S. 38, 'Congrès de la paix', Article by Ruth Fry, 'Advance in the Peace Movement', *The World Outlook: A Quaker Survey of International Life and Service*, 7 January 1927; *La Paix par la Jeunesse*, pp. 232, 22; Jeanne Caron, *Henri Colas 1879–1968* (Le Mans: private publication, n. d. but ca. 1973), pp. 71–7; Pierre Pierrard, *Un Siècle de l'Eglise de France, 1900–2000* (Paris: Desclée, 2000), pp. 70, 96.
18. Ulrich Herrmann (ed.), *'Mit uns die neue Zeit …': Der Wandervogel in der deutschen Jugendbewegung* (Weinheim: Juventa, 2006): Monique Mombert, 'Notes de lecture: "Mit uns die neue Zeit …" ', *Revue d'Allemagne et des pays de langue allemande*, 39, 2007, pp. 609–19; Geneviève Humbert-Knitel, 'La Jeunesse allemande et le mythe du renouveau de l'Allemagne au début du XXe siècle', *Revue d'Allemagne et des pays de langue allemande*, 39, 2007, pp. 590–608; *La Paix par la Jeunesse*, p. 244; IMS, M.S. 38, Peace Congresses, manuscript notes by Kurt Döbler, 11 August 1926.
19. *La Paix par la Jeunesse*, pp. 121–2; Mitterauer, *A History of Youth*, p. 219.
20. Becker, *War and Faith*, p. 176: *La Paix par la Jeunesse*, pp. 193–4.

21. Smith, *The Embattled Self*, p. 23. On German First World War objectors, see Peter Brock, *Against the Draft: Essays on Conscientious Objection from the Radical Reformation to the Second World War* (Toronto: University of Toronto Press, 2006), pp. 281–300. See also Lois S. Bibbings, *Telling Tales about Men: Conceptions of Conscientious Objectors to Military Service during the First World War* (Manchester: Manchester University Press, 2009); Giles, 'The Third International Peace Congress', p. 187; Ingram, *The Politics of Dissent*, p. 59; *La Paix par la Jeunesse*, p. 72.
22. *La Paix par la Jeunesse*, pp. 149–50; Norman Ingram, 'Pacifisme Ancien Style', *Matériaux pour l'histoire de notre temps*, 30, 1993, p. 4; Gorguet, *Les Mouvements Pacifistes*, p. 170. See also Dieter Reisenberger, *Die katholische Friedensbewegung in der Weimarer Republik* (Düsseldorf: Droste Verlag, 1976), pp. 67–101.
23. Ernest Robidet, 'Georges Blanchot', *L'Âme commune*, March 1964, p. 18; Blanchot Papers. Memo, 'Réunion du 14 août 1926 à Bierville': Ceadel, *Thinking about Peace and War*, p. 143.
24. Unsigned German female delegate's letter, IMS, cited in Gorguet, *Les Mouvements Pacifistes*, p. 250; *La Paix par la Jeunesse*, p. 206; LSF, MSS Vol.S.107 Peace Committee Minutes, 1921–25, entry 328, fols. 99–101.
25. Peter Brock, *The Roots of War Resistance: Pacifism from the Early Church to Tolstoy* (New York: Nyack, 1981), p. 73; Jean Guiraud, 'Retour de Congrès', *La Croix*, 24 August 1926; Fanny Clar, 'Pour la communion spirituelle: Lettre ouverte à Mgr Julien, évêque d'Arras', *L'Ère nouvelle*, 25 August 1926; Jean Maitron (ed.), *Dictionnaire biographique du mouvement ouvrier français*, vol. 22 (Paris: Editions Ouvrières, 1984), p. 331; *Le Correspondant*, 25 September 1926.
26. *La Paix par la Jeunesse*, p. 166 (see also sanitized biography of Verraux, Ecole Supérieure de Guerre website, http://ecole-superieure-de-guerre.fr/promotions/biographie/422, accessed 25 July 2011); Barnett Singer, 'From Patriots to Pacifists: The French Primary School Teachers, 1880–1940', *Journal of Contemporary History*, 12 (1977), pp. 413–34, at p. 422; Stéphane Audoin-Rouzeau, *La guerre des enfants, 1914–1918: essai d'histoire culturelle* (Paris: Armand Colin, 1993), p. 43; Jean Guiraud, 'Pacifique et pacificiste', *La Croix*, 27 August 1926: *L'Humanité*, 20 August 1926; *Victoire*, 31 August 1926.
27. ASV, Arch. Nunz. Parigi, b. 454, fasc. 551 'Sillon.' Letter, Paris Nunciature-Gasparri, 5 June 1926; *Action Française*, 19 & 25 August 1926.
28. *La Nouvelle*, 20 August 1926; Bernardi, *Maurice Blondel, Social Catholicism and Action Française*, p. 132; Jacques Prévotat, *Les catholiques et l'Action Française: Histoire d'une condamnation 1899–1939* (Paris: Fayard, 2001); Michel Leymarie & Jacques Prévotat (eds), *L'Action Française: culture, société, politique* (Villeneuve d'Ascq: Presses Universitaires de Septentrion, 2008); Jean-Dominique Durand, 'Pie XI, la paix et la construction d'un ordre international', in Ecole Française de Rome (ed.) *Achille Ratti-Pape Pie XI: Actes du colloque organisé par l'Ecole Française de Rome (15–18 mars 1989)* (Rome: Ecole Française de Rome, 1997), pp. 873–91.
29. ASV, Affari Ecclesiastici Straordinari , IV, Stati Ecclesiastici, 1922–34, 293, fasc. 20, fols. 68–9. Address to pope, signed by Marc Sangnier & Georges Hoog, August 1926; fol. 70. Secretariat of State-Valeri, Paris Nunciature, 10 August

1926; fol. 77. Valeri-Gasparri, 10 August 1926; fol. 81. Valeri-Gasparri, 14 August 1926.

30. AN, 362 AP 56, dossier 4. Jean Guiraud papers. Readers' letters to *La Croix*. Corresp. 'Miles Christi'–Guiraud, 11 August 1926; AN, F7 13962 Commissaire de Police, Paris–Directeur de la Sûreté Générale, Paris, 21 August 1926: *Il Tevere*, 24–5 August 1926 & *L'Osservatore Romano*, 25 August 1926, press cuttings cited in ASV, Affari Ecclesiastici Straordinari, IV Periodo, Stati Ecclesiastici, 1922–34, fasc. 20, fol. 86; official 'clarification' in same fol. 86.
31. Eugen Weber, *Action Française: Royalism and Reaction in Twentieth-century France* (Stanford: Stanford University Press, 1962), pp. 231, 67.
32. *La Paix par la Jeunesse*, p. 137.
33. Unger, *Aristide Briand*, p. 516,

7 Crusade of Youth, 1927–32

1. Gorguet, *Les Mouvements Pacifistes*, pp. 199–202.
2. Solzbacher & Solzbacher-Kennon, *Peace Movements*, pp. 94–5; *VIIème Congrès démocratique international pour la Paix. Wurtzbourg* [sic], *3–7 Septembre 1927* (Paris: La Démocratie, 1927), pp. 100, 117 [The German spelling of the city's name Würzburg used hereinafter in references and in the text of book]. On anti-colonial context, see Best, Hahnimäki, Maiolo, & Schulze, *International History of the Twentieth Century and Beyond*, pp. 95–102; Sebastian Conrad & Dominic Sachsenmaier (eds), *Competing Visions of World Order: Global Moments and Movements, 1880s–1930s* (Basingstoke: Palgrave Macmillan, 2007), p. 11.
3. *Würzburg 1927*, pp. 74, 139, 110; Delbreil, *Les catholiques français*, pp. 115–16, 134–8; Kaiser, *Christian Democracy and the Origins of European Union*, pp. 86–91; Gorguet, *Les Mouvements Pacifistes*, pp. 199–202.
4. *VIIIème Congrès démocratique international pour la Paix, Genève-Bierville, 12–23 septembre 1928: La paix des peuples par la Société des Nations* (Paris: La Démocratie, 1928), pp. 1–2, 26, 45; Susan Pedersen, 'Back to the League of Nations', *American Historical Review*, 112, 2007, pp. 1091–117, at p. 1096; Davies, *The Possibilities of Transnational Activism*.
5. *VIIIème Congrès démocratique international pour la Paix, Genève-Bierville, 1928*, pp. 60, 103; Mitterauer, *A History of Youth*, p. 219. See also my article, '"The Crusade of Youth": Pacifism and the Militarization of Youth Culture in Marc Sangnier's Peace Congresses, 1923–32', in Jennifer D. Keene & Michael S. Neiberg (eds), *Finding Common Ground: New Directions in First World War Studies* (Leiden: Brill, 2011), pp. 239–66.
6. Barthélemy-Madaule, *Marc Sangnier*, p. 267; Mathieu Noli, '"L'Éveil des peuples" "Le Volontaire" et les "Volontaires de la Paix "', in Meslin (ed.), *Marc Sangnier, la guerre, la paix*, pp. 83–103, at p. 86.
7. Tammy M. Proctor, 'Scouts, Guides and the Fashioning of Empire, 1919–39', in Wendy Parkins (ed.), *Fashioning the Body Politic: Dress, Gender, Citizenship* (New York: Berg, 2002), pp. 125–44, at p. 127; Noli, '"L'Éveil des peuples"', p. 85; *VIIIème Congrès démocratique international pour la Paix, Genève-Bierville, 1928*, p. 67; ILS, fasc. 436, c.20, Corresp. Sturzo-Sangnier, 29 August 1929.

8. Stachura, *The German Youth Movement*, pp. 46–8; *VIIIème Congrès démocratique international pour la Paix, Genève-Bierville, 1928*, pp. 108–9; Mitterauer, *A History of Youth*, p. 220; Débès & Poulat, *L'appel de la JOC*, p. 21; *VIIIème Congrès démocratique international pour la Paix, Genève-Bierville, 1928*, p. 67.
9. IMS, Correspondance générale, CG14, Richard Schirmann- Sangnier, 22 December 1934; Laura Lee Downs, *Childhood in the Promised Land: Working-class Movements and the Colonies de Vacances in France, 1880–1960* (Durham, NC & London: Duke University Press, 2002), pp. 204–5; Barthélemy-Madaule, *Marc Sangnier*, p. 259; André Émorine & Jacques Lamoure, *Histoire des auberges de jeunesse en France 1929–51* (Paris: Ligue Française pour les Auberges de Jeunesse, 1952), p. 5; Denis Pelletier, *Les catholiques en France depuis 1815* (Paris: La Découverte, 1997), pp. 73–5; Jean-Pierre Augustin, 'Loisirs, sport et éducation populaire', in Bruno Duriez, Etienne Fouilloux, Denis Pelletier, & Nathalie Viet-Depaule (eds), *Les catholiques dans la république, 1905–2005* (Paris: Editions de l'Atelier, 2005), pp. 153–64, at p. 153; Dominique Magnant, 'Témoignage' in Michel Meslin (ed.), *Marc Sangnier, la guerre, la paix, 1914–39: Actes de la journée d'études du 26 septembre 1997* (Paris: Institut Marc Sangnier, 1999), pp. 197–212, at p. 202. [Magnant was a former president of the hostels movement league, the LFAJ.]. See also Whitney, *Mobilizing Youth*.
10. *IXè Congrès démocratique internationale pour la Paix: Croisade de la Jeunesse (16 août–1er septembre 1929). Réunion d'Etudes de Bierville (2–5 septembre 1929). Un Voyage d'Etudes Sociales et Internationales en Angleterre (7–17 septembre 1929)* (Paris: La Démocratie, 1929), p. 130; Winter, *Sites of Memory*, p. 52; Proctor, 'Scouts, Guides and the Fashioning of Empire', p. 129; *IXè Congrès démocratique internationale pour la Paix: Croisade de la Jeunesse*, p. 133; Antoine Prost, 'Verdun', in Nora (ed.), *Realms of Memory*, vol. 3, *Symbols*, pp. 377–401; *IXè Congrès démocratique internationale pour la Paix: Croisade de la Jeunesse*, pp. 161–2, 141.
11. Interview with Jean Sangnier, 5 September 2002; *IXè Congrès démocratique internationale pour la Paix: Croisade de la Jeunesse*, p. 180; Henri Colas, *Nos Chants: les Volontaires de la Paix* (Paris: La Démocratie, 1930), p. 1; Joseph Probst (ed.), *La paix par la chanson: Chants de la nouvelle jeunesse allemande* (1929). [IMS pamphlet collection].
12. IMS, M.S. Correspondance Générale, Mgr Julien-Sangnier, 9 March 1929.
13. Becker, *War and Faith*, p. 130; Horne, 'La reconstruction du nord-est de la France après 1918'; *IXè Congrès démocratique internationale pour la Paix: Croisade de la Jeunesse*, pp. 147–8.
14. *IXè Congrès démocratique internationale pour la Paix: Croisade de la Jeunesse*, pp. 207, 222, 225, 220.
15. *IXè Congrès démocratique internationale pour la Paix: Croisade de la Jeunesse*, p. 209. Text of oath at p. 198.
16. Poidevin & Bariéty, *Les relations franco-allemandes*, pp. 271–6; Sylvain Schirmann, 'Franco-German Relations, 1918–45', in Germond & Türk (eds), *A History of Franco-German Relations in Europe*, pp. 75–88, at pp. 78–80. See also Antoine Fleury & Lubor Jílek (eds), *Le Plan Briand d'Union fédérale européenne: Perspectives nationales et transnationales, avec documents: actes du colloque international tenu à Genève du 19 au 21 septembre 1991* (Bern: Peter Lang, 1998); Anita Ziegerhofer, *Botschafter Europas: Richard Nikolaus*

Coudenhove-Kalergi und die Paneuropa-Bewegung in den zwanziger und dreißiger Jahren (Vienna: Boehlau, 2004).

17. *Xe Congrès démocratique international pour la Paix. Inauguration du Foyer de la Paix de Bierville, 24–31 août 1930. Réunions d'Ostende, Bruxelles, Anvers et Liège sur les Etats-Unis d'Europe* (Paris: La Démocratie, 1930), p. 74; *Jeune République*, 13 June 1926: Prat, 'Marc Sangnier et l'idée européenne', in Fréchet (ed.), *Penser et construire l'Europe (1919–1992)*, pp. 46–62; Kaiser, *Christian Democracy and the Origins of European Union*, pp. 104–10; Marie-Emmanuelle Reytier, 'I cattolici tedeschi e l'Europa all'indomani della Prima Guerra Mondiale. L'esempio dei Katholikentage', in Alfredo Canavero & Jean-Dominique Durand (eds), *Il fattore religioso nell'integrazione europea* (Milan: Unicolpi, 1999), pp. 359–71. See also Durand, *L'Europe de la démocratie chrétienne*.
18. ILS (Rome), fasc. 309, c. 21, Corresp. Sturzo–Sangnier, 12 July 1930.
19. *Xe Congrès démocratique international pour la Paix*, p. 50.
20. Ceadel, *Thinking about Peace and War*, p. 281; Thomas R. Davies, 'France and the World Disarmament Conference of 1932–34', *Diplomacy and Statecraft*, 15, (2004), pp. 765–80; Ceadel, *Semi-detached Idealists*, p. 282.
21. Nicolas Offenstadt, 'Le pacifisme extrême à la conquête des masses: la LICP (1931–1939) et la propagande', *Matériaux pour l'histoire de notre temps*, 30, 1993, pp. 35–9; Maurice Vaïsse, *Sécurité d'abord. La politique française en matière de désarmement. 9 décembre 1930–17 avril 1934* (Paris: Pédone, 1981), p. 155; Santamaria, *Le pacifisme*, p. 104; APP, BA 1777. 'Pacifisme – LICP.' Police note on LICP meeting, Paris, 4 March 1931 (meeting held on 3 March at Salle des Sociétés Savantes); Police report on LICP meeting, 4 September 1931.
22. APP, BA 1777. 'Pacifisme – LICP.' Police report, 12 November 1932.
23. Edith M. Pye, *The Peace Movement in France* (London: Friends' Peace Committee, 1932), p. 5; Dennis Showalter, ' "Plus jamais" du moins pas comme cela: imaginer la guerre après 1918', *14–18 aujourd'hui*, 5, 2002, pp. 144–57, at p. 152; Panchasi, *Future Tense*, p. 96.
24. *Paix ou guerre: Exposition documentaire* (Paris: Jeune République, 1931), p. 13.
25. *Paix ou guerre*, p. 2; Davies, *The Possibilities of Transnational Activism*, p. 192; Pye, *The Peace Movement in France*, p. 3; Ingram, *The Politics of Dissent*, p. 82; AN, F7 16005/1, police report on national tour of Musée 'Guerre ou Paix', 30 November 1931; Prost & Winter, *René Cassin*, pp. 88–112.
26. Pye, *The Peace Movement in France*, p. 6; *Le Congrès de Fribourg-Constance, 5–9 août 1931* (Paris: La Démocratie, 1931), p. 136; Evans, *The Coming of the Third Reich*, p. 71; Interview with Jean Sangnier, 5 September 2002.
27. *Fribourg-Constance 1931*, pp. 173, 152; Vaïsse, *Sécurité*, p. 597; *Fribourg-Constance 1931*, p. 161.
28. Davies, 'France and the World Disarmament Conference', p. 771; APP, BA 1777. 'Pacifisme – LICP.' Police report on meeting at Salle des Sociétés Savantes, 21 January 1932; Police note on 'Jeune Garde pacifique', 28 January 1932.
29. *Jeune République*, 25 March 1932; *Action Française*, 21 December 1931; AN, F7 16005/1, Report of meeting in Tours, 12 January 1932; Anon. note in police files on collection taken by Sangnier in aid of German people affected by the economic crisis, 29 March 1932.

30. Helène & Simone Gaillot, *Marc Sangnier 1873–1950* (Le Mans: private publication, 1960), p. 95; *Jeune République*, 3 June 1932.

8 Marc Sangnier and the Pacifist Conundrum, 1932–45

1. Santamaria, *Le pacifisme*, pp. 103–4.
2. Unger, *Aristide Briand,* p. 594, on cult after Briand's death. See also pp. 597–602; René Rémond, *Les catholiques dans la France des années trente* (Paris: Cana, 1979), pp. 41–5; Ingram, 'Les pacifistes et Aristide Briand', p. 207.
3. *Fribourg-Constance 1931*, p. 158; *Jeune-République*, 9 September 1932. (This edition covered the two-day gathering at Bierville.)
4. Marc Sangnier, *Le Combat pour La Paix* (Paris: Foyer de la Paix, 1937), pp. 281–5.
5. AN, F7 14819, 'Groupements divers (1932–40) – Journées d'Espérance', Police note, 22 July 1932; *L'Oeuvre*, 12 August 1932; *Le Figaro*, 17 August 1932; Alfred Baudrillart, *Les Carnets du Cardinal Alfred Baudrillart. 13 février 1932–19 novembre 1935,* ed. Paul Christophe (Paris: Cerf, 2003), p. 271, entry for 30 August 1932; *Action Française*, 29 August & 1 September 1932; AN, F7 14819, 'Journées d'Espérance', Letter, Victor Basch–Prime Minister, 28 September 1932.
6. *Le Volontaire*, 11 September 1932; Noli, '"L'Éveil des peuples"', p. 51; Sangnier, 'Notre effort', *L'Éveil des peuples*, 6 November 1932; IMS, M.S. 38, Peace Congresses, Folder on XIII Congress, 23 March 1933. Dissolution, 'procès-verbal de dissolution de l'Action Internationale'; Gorguet, *Les Mouvements Pacifistes*, pp. 248–9.
7. Santamaria, *Le pacifisme*, p. 121; Jean-Pierre Biondi, *La Mêlée des Pacifistes, 1914–1945* (Paris: Maisonneuve & Larose, 2000), pp. 105–17; Ingram, *The Politics of Dissent,* pp. 93–109, 179–93; Patrick de Villepin, 'Le Pacifisme Intégral et l'Allemagne nazie (1933–1939)', in Hans Manfred Bock, Reinhart Meyer-Kalkus & Michel Trebitsch (eds), *Entre Locarno et Vichy: Les relations culturelles franco-allemandes dans les années 1930,* vol. 1 (Paris: CNRS Editions, 1993), pp. 161–73.
8. Norman Ingram, 'The « Circulaire Chautemps », 1933: The Third Republic discovers conscientious objection', *French Historical Studies*, 17, (1991), pp. 387–409, at p. 391; *Fribourg-Constance 1931*, p. 156; AN, F7 13352, 'Objection de conscience', Minister of the Interior-Prime Minister, 9 January 1933; 'Liste des objecteurs de conscience et des personnes ayant défendu l'objection, 15.4.1933[sic].'; *La France du Centre*, 11 May 1933.
9. *Action Française*, 12 May 1933; Farrugia, 'French Religious Opposition', p. 297; Reisenberger, *Die Katholische Friedensbewegung in der Weimarer Republik*, pp. 182–5; Franiskus Stratmann, *The Church and War* (New York: P.J. Kenedy & Sons, 1928); J.-V. Ducatillon, *Le vrai et le faux patriotisme* (Paris: Spes, 1933), p. 249; Ingram, *The Politics of Dissent*, p. 63.
10. BDIC, Fonds LICRA, F delta rés. 798/44. Réunions publiques (1924–36); Vicki Caron, 'Catholic Political Mobilization and Anti-Semitic Violence in France', *The Journal of Modern History*, 81, (2009), pp. 294–346, at p. 331; Greg Burgess,

'France and the German Refugee Crisis of 1933', *French History*, 16, (2002), pp. 203–29; Noli, ' "L'Éveil des peuples" ', p. 98. The left eventually disowned Jean Luchaire, who persisted in such contacts with the Germans to the extent that in 1946 he was executed by the French state for his collaboration during the Occupation.

11. Sangnier, *Le pacifisme d'action* (Paris: Foyer de la Paix, 1936), pp. 97, 100.
12. Sangnier, *Le pacifisme d'action*, pp. 41–5; Tom Buchanan, 'Anti-Fascism and Democracy in the 1930s', *European History Quarterly*, 32, (2002), pp. 39–57.
13. Sangnier, *Le pacifisme d'action* (Paris: Le Foyer de la Paix, 1936), pp. 35–39, 9–12.
14. Guieu, *Le Rameau et le Glaive*, p. 227; Santamaria, *Le pacifisme*, p. 123; Marc Bloch, *Strange Defeat: A Statement of Evidence Written in 1940* (London & New York: W. W. Norton, 1999), p. 142.
15. Guieu, *Le Rameau et le Glaive*, p. 240; Ingram, *The Politics of Dissent*, pp. 103–5; *L'Éveil des peuples*, 22 March 1936. Cited in Guieu, *Le Rameau et le Glaive*, pp. 241–2; APP, BA 1777. 'Pacifisme – LICP.' Police report, 11 March 1936.
16. Nicolas Offenstadt, 'Le pacifisme extrême à la conquête des masses: la LICP (1931–1939) et la propagande', *Matériaux pour l'histoire de notre temps*, 30, 1993, pp. 35–9; APP, BA 1777. 'Pacifisme – LICP.' Police report, 4 December 1936.
17. Rémond, *Les catholiques*, pp. 205–41; Paul Christophe, *1936: les catholiques et le Front Populaire* (Paris: Desclée, 1979); Berstein, 'Consensus Politique et Violences Civiles dans la France du 20e siècle', pp. 51–60. See also Pierrard, *Un Siècle*, pp. 121–4.
18. On JOC and the representation of 'the people' in this period, see Wardhaugh, *In Pursuit of the People*, pp. 172–82; AN, F7 15313, Memo of the director of the Renseignements Généraux on Mouvement Laïque des Auberges de Jeunesse, Paris, 18 December 1947; Julian Jackson, *The Popular Front in France: Defending Democracy, 1934–38* (Cambridge: Cambridge University Press, 1988), pp. 132–5. On Sangnier and Lagrange, see also David Pompfret, 'The City of Evil and the Great Outdoors: The Modern Health Movement and the Urban Young, 1918–40', *Urban History*, 28, (2001), pp. 405–27.
19. Guieu, *Le Rameau et le Glaive*, pp. 233–8; Rachel Mazuy, 'Le Rassemblement Universel pour la Paix (1935–1939): une organization de masse?', *Matériaux pour l'histoire de notre temps*, 30, (1993), pp. 40–4; Richard Overy, *The Morbid Age: Britain between the Wars* (London: Allen Lane, 2009), pp. 255–61.
20. Ingram, *The Politics of Dissent*, pp. 106–8, 218–22; Ingram, 'Selbsmord or Euthanasia? Who killed the Ligue des Droits de l'Homme?', *French History*, 22, (2008), pp. 337–57; William D. Irvine, *Between Justice and Politics: The Ligue des Droits de l'Homme, 1898–1945* (Stanford: Stanford University Press, 2007), pp. 160–93; Ingram, 'Defending the Rights of Man: The Ligue des Droits de l'Homme and the Problem of Peace', in Brock & Socknat (eds), *Challenge to Mars*, pp. 117–33.
21. Anthony Adamthwaite, *France and the Coming of the Second World War* (London: Frank Cass, 1977), p. 26; APP, BA 1777. 'Pacifisme – LICP.' Police report, 11 March 1936, on meeting at Salle Susset, 8 March 1936.
22. Kaiser, *Christian Democracy and the Origins of European Union*, p. 52; Jean-Michel Cadiot, *Francisque Gay et les démocrates d'inspiration chrétienne*,

1885–1963 (Paris: Salvator, 2006), pp. 302–7; Marc Sangnier, 'Quand la paix en déroute', *Éveil des peuples*, 3 April 1938. Cited in Noli, '"L'Éveil des peuples"', p. 100.

23. APP, BA 1777. 'Pacifisme – LICP.' Police report, 11 October 1938; Daniel Hucker, 'French Public Attitudes towards the Prospect of War in 1938–1939; "Pacifism" or "War Anxiety"', *French History*, 21, (2007), pp. 431–49, at p. 449. Developed in Hucker, *Public Opinion and the End of Appeasement in Britain and France* (Farnham: Ashgate, 2011), pp. 23–62. For the literature questioned by Hucker, see also Jean-Baptiste Duroselle, *France and the Nazi Threat: The Collapse of French Diplomacy 1932–39* (New York: Enigma, 2004 [1979]), pp. 287–301; Jean-Pierre Azéma, *From Munich to the Liberation, 1938–1944* (Cambridge: Cambridge University Press, 1984 [1979]), pp. 1–20.
24. Marc Sangnier, *Pour Sauver la Paix: Compte-rendu sténotypé du discours prononcé dans la grande salle de La Démocratie le 6 novembre 1938* (Paris: Foyer de la Paix, 1938), p. 13. Cited in Prat, 'Marc Sangnier et l'idée européenne', p. 55; Michel Winock, *La trahison de Munich: Emmanuel Mounier et la grande débâcle des intellectuels* (Paris: CNRS, 2008); *Éveil des peuples*, 13 November 1938.
25. Marc Sangnier, 'Précisions', *L'Éveil des peuples*, 2 April 1939. Cited in Prat, 'Marc Sangnier et l'idée européenne', p. 52; Sangnier, 'À nos amis', *Éveil des peuples*, 10 September 1939. Cited in Noli, '"L'Éveil des peuples"', p. 102.
26. Thomas Kselman, 'Catholicism, Christianity and Vichy', *French Historical Studies*, 23, (2000), pp. 513–30, at p. 522; Etienne Fouilloux, *Les chrétiens entre crise et libération 1937–1947* (Paris: Seuil, 1997), p. 231; Richard Francis Crane, '"La Croix" and the Swastika: The Ambiguities of Catholic Responses to the Fall of France', *The Catholic Historical Review*, 90, (2004), pp. 45–66; Jacques Duquesne, *Les Catholiques français sous 1'Occupation* (Paris: Grasset, 1966), pp. 39–60, 204–12; Michèle Cointet, *L'Église sous Vichy. 1940–1945: La repentance en question* (Paris: Perrin, 1998), pp. 140–61; Michael Curtis, *Verdict on Vichy: Power and Prejudice in the Vichy France Regime* (London: Phoenix, 2004). pp. 322–43. See also Frédéric Le Moigne, *Les évêques français de Verdun à Vatican II: une génération en mal d'héroïsme* (Rennes: Presses Universitaires de Rennes, 2005); Vesna Drapac, *War and Religion: Catholics in the Churches of Occupied Paris* (Washington, D.C.: Catholic University of America Press, 1998); Renée Bédarida, *Les catholiques dans la guerre, 1939–1945: entre Vichy et la Résistance* (Paris: Hachette, 1998); Philippe Burrin, *Living with Defeat: France under the German Occupation,1940–1944* (London: Arnold, 1996).
27. Wilfrid D. Halls, *The Youth of Vichy France* (Oxford: Clarendon, 1981), pp. 342–3; Halls, *Politics, Society and Christianity in Vichy France* (Oxford: Berg, 1995), pp. 269–310; Philip Nord, 'Catholic Culture in Interwar France', *French Politics, Culture & Society*, 21, (2003), pp. 1–20, at pp. 12–13. See also Lucette Heller-Goldenberg, 'Histoire des Auberges de Jeunesse en France des origines à la Libération (1929–45)', PhD thesis, Université de Nice, 1985.
28. Halls, *Politics, Society and Christianity*, p. 284; AN, F7 16005/1. Prefect of the Gard (Nîmes)–Minister of the Interior (Vichy), 11 July 1941. 'Amalgamation of Youth Hostels movement'; IMS, M.S. 43, Marc Sangnier–LFAJ in unoccupied zone, 31 December 1941. On the general complexity of 'living with the enemy', see also Richard Vinen, *The Unfree French: Life Under the Occupation* (London: Allen Lane, 2006), pp. 99–132.

29. IMS, M.S. 43, Lamirand-Sangnier, 29 April 1942. On Vichy and anti-Semitism, see Julian Jackson, *France: The Dark Years, 1940–44* (Oxford: Oxford University Press, 2001), pp. 354–81; Michael Marrus & Robert Paxton, *Vichy France and the Jews* (New York: Basic Books, 1981).
30. On this Resistance network, see Guillaume Piketty, 'Groupe de la rue de Lille', in François Mascot, Bruno Leroux, & Christine Levisse-Touzé (eds), *Dictionnaire historique de la Résistance: Résistance Intérieure et France Libre* (Paris: Robert Laffont, 2006), pp. 190–1; Renée Bédarida, 'Eugene Pons (1886–1945)', in Mascot, Leroux, & Levisse-Touzé (eds), *Dictionnaire historique de la Résistance,* pp. 506–7; IMS, M54, Vie quotidienne, Agendas personnels, 1904–49; AN, F7 16005; Anon. note on German arrest of Sangnier, 21 February 1944. See also Barthélemy-Madaule, *Marc Sangnier,* pp. 276–8. For names of all four persons arrested at La Démocratie in February 1944, see Lefèvre, *Marc Sangnier,* p. 228. [Please note that Lefèvre spells one of their surnames differently from others. I have preferred to use the spelling that is employed most consistently in the sources available to me i.e. Geraert].

    On Catholics and the Resistance, see Bernard Comte, *L'Honneur et la conscience: catholiques français en résistance (1940–44)* (Paris: Editions de l'Atelier, 1998); François & Renée Bédarida, *La Résistance Spirituelle, 1941–1944: Les Cahiers Clandestins du Témoignage Chrétien* (Paris: Albin Michel, 2001), pp. 9–32. See also Limor Yagil, *Chrétiens et Juifs sous Vichy, 1940–44: sauvetage et désobéissance civile* (Paris: Cerf, 2005). pp. 91–120.
31. H. R. Kedward, *Resistance in Vichy France: A Study of Ideas and Motivation in the Southern Zone, 1940–1942* (Oxford: Oxford University Press, 1978), pp. 253, 259; Adams, *Political Ecumenism,* pp. 69–83; Georgette Vignaux, 'The Catholics in France since the Armistice', *The Review of Politics,* 5, (1943), pp. 194–215, at p. 215.
32. IMS, M.S. 43, press cutting, *L'Avant-Garde,* 17 & 23 October 1945; Typed response to allegations (anonymous), 1945; Farrugia, 'The Conviction of Things Not Seen', pp. 108–11; Jackson, *The Dark Years,* pp. 81–5; Norman Ingram, '"Nous allons vers les monastères": French Pacifism and the Crisis of the Second World War', in Mouré & Alexander (eds), *Crisis and Renewal in France, 1918–1962,* pp. 132–51.

Conclusion

1. *IXè Congrès démocratique internationale pour la Paix: Croisade de la Jeunesse,* p. 238.
2. Patricia Clavin, 'Introduction: Conceptualising Internationalism between the World Wars', in Daniel Laqua (ed.), *Internationalism Reconfigured: Transnational Ideas and Movements between the World Wars* (London: I.B. Tauris, 2011), pp. 1–14.
3. John Horne, 'Demobilizing the Mind: France and the Legacy of the Great War, 1919–1939', *French History and Civilization. Papers from the George Rudé Seminar,* 2, 2009, pp. 100–19. At George Rudé Society website: http://www.h-france.net/rude/rudepapers.html/, accessed 10 August 2011.

4. Horne, 'Demobilizing the Mind', pp. 114–15.
5. Jean-François Sirinelli, 'La France de l'entre-deux-guerres: un "trend" pacifiste?', in Maurice Vaisse (ed.), *Le pacifisme en Europe des années 1920 aux années 1950: Actes du colloque tenu à Reims du 3 au 5 décembre 1992 par le Centre ARPEGE* (Brussels: Bruylant, 1993), p. 45.
6. Gilles Morin (ed.), *Les deux Frances du Front Populaire: chocs et contre-chocs* (Paris: L'Harmattan, 2008), p. 12.
7. Horne, 'Demobilizing the Mind', p. 116; Perry, *Memory of War in France, 1914–45*, p. 98.
8. Geyer, 'The Militarization of Europe, 1919–39', in Gillis (ed.), *The Militarization of the Western World*, p. 75. See also Mosse, *Fallen Soldiers*. On this debate, I am indebted to the introduction by editor Pierre Purseigle to *Warfare and Belligerence: Perspectives in First World War Studies* (Leiden: Brill, 2005), pp. 10–18.
9. Louis Primet to Sangnier, n. d. but March 1931, IMS, CG 10.
10. For this debate, see Kevin Passmore, 'The Ideological Origins of Fascism', in R. J .B. Bosworth (ed.), *The Oxford Handbook of Fascism* (Oxford: Oxford University Press, 2009), pp. 11–31, here p. 14. See also Emilio Gentile, *The Sacralization of Politics in Fascist Italy* (Cambridge, MA: Harvard University Press, 1996) and Michael Burleigh, *Earthly Powers: Religion and Politics in Europe from the Enlightenment to the Great War* (London: Harper Collins, 2005) and *Sacred Causes* (2007).
11. Oscar L. Arnal, 'A Missionary "Main Tendue" toward French Communists: The "Témoignages" of the Worker-Priests, 1943–54', *French Historical Studies*, 13, (1984), pp. 529–56; Philippe Chenaux, *L'Église catholique et le communisme en Europe, 1917–1989: De Lénine à Jean-Paul II* (Paris: Cerf, 2009), pp. 97–100.
12. Stephen Schloesser, *Jazz Age Catholicism: Mystic Modernism in Postwar Paris, 1919–1933* (Buffalo, NY: University of Toronto Press, 2005): John W. O'Malley, *What Happened at Vatican II* (Cambridge MA: Harvard University Press, 2008).
13. *IVè Congrès – Londres, Septembre 1924,* p. 98; William J. Thorn, Phillip M. Runkel & Susan Mountin, *Dorothy Day and the Catholic Worker movement: centenary essays* (Milwaukee WI: Marquette University Press, 2001). [It is worth noting that Day's co-founder, Peter Maurin, was in fact French-born and that his first contact with Social Catholicism came through his activities in Sangnier's Sillon movement.]; Finola Kennedy, *Frank Duff: A Life Story* (London: Continuum, 2011).
14. 'Gustav Stresemann: Nobel Lecture, 29 June 1927', http://nobelprize.org/nobel_prizes/peace/laureates/1926, accessed 10 August 2011.

Bibliography

Primary sources

Archives and libraries

Institut Marc Sangnier, Paris [IMS]

Francisque Gay papers
FG6 (Correspondance).

Jean Sangnier papers
JS 1

Marc Sangnier papers
MS 4
MS 32 (formerly MS 23).
MS 35 (formerly MS 26.1).
MS 36 (formerly MS 26.2).
MS 38 (formerly MS 28).
MS 41
MS 43
MS 49
MS 50
MS 51 (formerly MS 35.2).
MS 54 (formerly MS 38).
MS 55
MS 56
MS 60
MS 67 (formerly CG 1 – [Correspondance Générale]).
MS 76 (formerly CG 10).
MS 80 (formerly CG 14).

Archives Nationales de France, Paris [AN]

Private papers (Série AP)
Paul Painlevé – Correspondance
313 AP 212–3.

Jean Guiraud – Correspondance
362 AP 25, 48, 56, 103–4, 107, 145–6 (Corresp. episcopate), 149.

General

General police surveillance – Series F7

F7 12747 Prefects' reports (Seine, 1924–28).

F7 12884 Ligue des Droits de l'Homme (1923–24).

F7 12951 'Notes Jean' (1918–22).

F7 13196 Action Française ('Agression contre Marc Sangnier, 31.5.1923').

F7 13213 Mouvement catholique (1924–27).

F7 13228 Droits des Religieux Anciens Combattants (DRAC).

F7 13254–261 Elections legislatives (1924–32).

F713352 Objection de conscience.

F7 13961 Political personalities – Victor Méric.

F7 13962 'VIe Congrès démocratique international pour la paix août 1926 & VIIe Congrès Würzburg septembre 1927.'

F7 14819 Groupements divers (1932–40) – Journées d'Espérance (1932).

F7 14880 Menées antinationales (1940).

Occupation (1940–44)

French police records

F7 15283 Libération – partis politiques – MRP.

F7 15284 Libération – partis politiques – Jeune République.

F7 15313 Relations with occupier – students/youth movement.

Occupation (1940–44)

Seized German police papers – 'Sicherheitsdienst [SD] en France, 1942–44'

F7 15146 Auberges de la Jeunesse, law of 25 Jan. 1941.

Etat Français (Vichy)

Sécretariat Général à la Jeunesse

F44 1 Cabinet Georges Lamirand, Sécrétaire Générale à la Jeunesse – Corresp.

F44 2 Sécretariat Général à la Jeunesse – Cabinet Georges Lamirand – Mouvements de jeunesse.

F44 12 Sécretariat Général à la Jeunesse – Cabinet Georges Lamirand – Courrier dep (Oct.–Nov. 1941).

F44 36 Enquiry into youth attitudes.

F44 51 Lamirand – personal correspondence, 1943.

F44 105 Requests for official approval, Auberges de la Jeunesse (1945–).

Series 'Fonds Panthéon.' Surveillance of public personalities.

F7 16005 Sangnier (Marc)

Vatican Secret Archives, Rome [ASV]

Arch. Nunz. Parigi (Nunziatura Maglione, Titolo IV, Partiti Politici, Elezioni), b. 454, Fasc. 551 ('Sillon').

Affari Ecclesiastici Straordinari, Francia, 1916, Fasc. 654, Riattivazione delle relazioni diplomatiche della Francia con la S. Sede.

Affari Ecclesiastici Straordinari, Francia, 1916, Fasc. 658 – 'Marc Sangnier'.

Affari Ecclesiastici Straordinari, Francia, 1916–19, Fasc. 667 – Progetti et Memorie di Mons. Chapon, Vescovo di Nizza.

Affari Ecclesiastici Straordinari, Francia, 1919–22, Fasc. 697 – 'Mémoire de l'Evêque de Nice au Saint Père' (1919).

Affari Ecclesiastici Straordinari, Francia, 1919–22, Fasc. 700 – Elezioni (1919).

Affari Ecclesiastici Straordinari, Francia, 1919–22, Fasc. 719 – Rapporti di Mons. Ceretti, Nunzio Apostolico in Francia.
AES, IV Periodo, Stati Ecclesiastici, Pos. 293, Fasc. 19.
AES, IV Periodo, Stati Ecclesiastici, 1922–34, 293, Fasc. 20.
Segreteria di Stato, Guerra 1914–18, 244 C 7, Fasc. 76.
Segreteria di Stato, Guerra 1914–18, 244 D 4, Fasc. 93–94.
Segretaria di Stato Epoca Moderna 1920, Rubrica 14, Fasc. 4.
Segretaria di Stato, Epoca Moderna, 1920, Rubrica 16, Fasc. 1.
Segretaria di Stato, Epoca Moderna, 1922, Rubrica 78, Fasc. 5.
Segretaria di Stato, Epoca Moderna, 1922, Rubrica 249, Fasc. 4.

Archivio Storico Istituto Luigi Sturzo, Rome [ILS]

Fondo Luigi Sturzo
Fasc. 290, c. 37, c. 60; Fasc. 291, c. 1; Fasc. 436, c. 1, c. 20 (correspondence – Sangnier).
Fasc. 753, c. 11 (Guiseppi Stragliati).
Fasc. 300, c. 74 (Ruth Fry).
Fasc. 289/1, c. 62; Fasc. 289/2, c. 176; Fasc. 290, c. 32–33, c. 58; Fasc. 291, c. 105; Fasc. 296, c. 67 (Domenico Russo).
Fasc. 313, c. 74
Fasc. BW 436, c. 5 (pacifism).

Service Historique de l'Armée de Terre, Vincennes [SHAT]

6Ye 30527
26N 1296, 1597, 1658

Département et Ville de Paris, Archives départementales et communales, Paris [ADVP]

11 AZ 2 Professions de foi. Elections 1924
D2 M2 Carton 52 Notices sur les députés.
D2 M2 Cartons 44–51, 53–56 Procès-verbaux des élections 1924–28
D3 M2 Articles 12–14 Propagande électorale 1919–28

Ministère des Affaires Etrangères, Quai d'Orsay, Paris [MAE]

Correspondance politique et commerciale, 1914–40
Série Y Affaires internationales, 1918–40
386 Action pacifiste et révolutionnaire, 1924–27.
445 Société des Nations. Associations, ligues, manifestations – 1921–39.
Série Z Europe, Allemagne 1918–29
47 Résumés de la presse allemande, 1922–25.
323 Communistes et pacifistes, 1922–25.
401 Propagande de la France, 1918–24
402 Propagande de la France, 1924–29.
413 Étude de la Presse. Compte-rendus trimestriels
Série Z Europe, Autriche 1918–40.
49 Action pacifiste, 1922–29.

Série Z Saint-Siège 1918–40
13 Relations avec la France, 1918–20.
Papiers d'Agents-Archives privées (PA–AP)
335 Aristide Briand 14 Guerre, Attitude du Saint- Siège, 1914–15.
26 Correspondance.
194 Louis Canet 30 Saint-Siège et la France, 1920–23.
62 Correspondance, 1921–45.

Bibliothèque de Documentation Internationale, Nanterre [BDIC]

Papers of Ligue Intérnationale contre le Racisme et l'Anti-sémitisme [LICRA].
F delta rés. 798/ 44. Réunions publiques (1924–36).

Archives de la Préfecture de Police de Paris, Paris [APP]

BA 1 1540 'Démocrates chrétiens: Le Sillon.'
BA (2ème partie)
BA 1775 'Pacifisme – Conférence pour la paix.'
BA 1776 'Mouvement mondiale de la jeunesse pour la paix.'
BA 1777 'Pacifisme – Ligue Internationale des combattants de la paix.'
BA 1778 R.U.P. [Rassemblement Universel pour la Paix].
BA 1780 'Propagande anti-militariste, 1914–39.'
BA 1781
BA 1788 Occupation, 1940–44 'Arrestations par l'autorité allemande.'
BA 2005 'Francisque Gay.'
BA 2300 'Journaux – Éveil des peuples.'

Archives Historiques de l'Archévêché de Paris, Paris [AHAP]

Papers of Cardinal Amette
1 D XI, 13 Le Sillon, 'Notes sur audiences pontificales, 1906–19.'
Papers of Cardinal Dubois
1 D XII, 59–60 Correspondence with episcopate, 1901–29.
1 D XII, 63–68 Correspondence, 1893–1929.
1 D XII, 84 Correspondence, 1923–29.

Library of the Religious Society of Friends in Britain (Quakers), London [LSF]

MSS Vol.S.107, Peace Committee Minutes, 1921–25.
Peace Committee Minutes, 1925–34.
Ruth Fry Papers, TEMP MSS 481.

Private collection

Papers of Georges Blanchot in possession of Mme. Dominique Laxague, Fontenay-aux-Roses.

Printed sources

Published primary sources

Baudrillart, Alfred, *Les Carnets du Cardinal Alfred Buadrillart: 1er août – 31 décembre 1918*, ed. Paul Christophe (Paris: Cerf, 1994).

Baudrillart, Alfred, *Les carnets du Cardinal Baudrillart: 1er janvier 1919–31 décembre 1921*, ed. Paul Christophe (Paris: Cerf, 2000).

Baudrillart, Alfred, *Les Carnets du Cardinal Alfred Baudrillart: 13 avril 1925–25 décembre 1928*, ed. Paul Christophe (Paris: Cerf, 2002).

Baudrillart, Alfred, *Les Carnets du Cardinal Alfred Baudrillart: 13 février 1932–19 novembre 1935*, ed. Paul Christophe (Paris: Cerf, 2003).

Baudrillart, Alfred (ed.), *La Guerre allemande et le catholicisme* (Paris: Bloud et Gay, 1915).

Baudrillart, Alfred (ed.), *L'Allemagne et les alliés devant la conscience chrétienne* (Paris: Bloud et Gay, 1915).

Bloch, Marc, *Strange Defeat: A Statement of Evidence Written in 1940* (1946; Eng. trans., London & New York: W. W. Norton, 1999).

De Beauvoir, Simone, *Memoirs of a Dutiful Daughter* (1958; Eng. trans., London: Penguin, 1986).

Hoog, Georges, *Pourquoi l'Alsace-Lorraine doit redevenir française* (Paris: Bloud et Gay, 1915).

Kessler, Harry, *The Diaries of a Cosmopolitan: Count Harry Kessler, 1918–37* (1961; Eng. trans., London: Weidenfeld & Nicolson, 1971).

Magnant, Dominique, 'Témoignage' in Michel Meslin (ed.), *Marc Sangnier, la guerre, la paix, 1914–39: Actes de la journée d'études du 26 septembre 1997* (Paris: Institut Marc Sangnier, 1999), pp. 197–212.

Pius XI, Pope, 'Ubi Arcano Dei Consilio: Encyclical of Pope Pius XI on the Peace of Christ in the Kingdom of Christ', 23 December 1922, http://www.vatican.va/holy_father/pius_xi/encyclicals/documents/hf_p-xi_enc_23121922_ubi-arcano-dei-consilio_en.html, accessed 15 November 2011.

Stresemann, Gustav, 'Nobel Lecture, 29 June 1927', http://nobelprize.org/nobel_prizes/peace/laureates/1926, accessed 10 August 2011.

'The Covenant of the League of Nations', The Avalon Project, Yale Law School (http://avalon.law.yale.edu), (accessed 9 July 2009).

Contemporary books and pamphlets

Official accounts of the International Democratic Peace Congresses

Compte-rendu complet du Ier Congrès démocratique international. Paris, 4–11 décembre 1921 (Paris: La Démocratie, 1922).

Compte-rendu complet du IIe Congrès démocratique international pour la Paix, Vienne, 26 septembre–1 octobre 1922 (Paris: La Démocratie, 1922).

IIIè Congrès démocratique international pour la Paix. Fribourg-en-Brisgau, 4–10 août 1923 (Paris: La Démocratie, 1923).

Le IVè Congrès démocratique international pour la Paix. Londres, 16–19 septembre 1924 (Paris: La Démocratie, 1924).

Le Vè Congrès démocratique international pour la Paix. Luxembourg, 9–14 septembre 1925 (Paris: La Démocratie, 1925).

La Paix par la Jeunesse. VIè Congrès Démocratique International pour la Paix, 17–22 août 1926. Le Mois International de Bierville, Août 1926 (Paris: La Démocratie, 1926).

VIIème Congrès démocratique international pour la Paix. Wurtzbourg, 3–7 septembre 1927 (Paris: La Démocratie, 1927).

VIIIème Congrès démocratique international pour la Paix, Genève-Bierville, 12–23 septembre 1928: La paix des peuples par la Société des Nations (Paris: La Démocratie, 1928).

IXè Congrès démocratique internationale pour la Paix: Croisade de la Jeunesse (16 août-1er septembre 1929). Réunion d'Etudes de Bierville (2-5 septembre 1929). Un Voyage d'Etudes Sociales et Internationales en Angleterre (7-17 septembre 1929) (Paris: La Démocratie, 1929).

Xè Congrès démocratique international pour la Paix. Inauguration du Foyer de la Paix de Bierville, 24–31 août 1930. Réunions d'Ostende, Bruxelles, Anvers et Liège sur les Etats-Unis d'Europe (Paris: La Démocratie, 1930).

Paix ou guerre: Exposition documentaire (Paris: Jeune République, 1931).

Le Congrès de Fribourg-Constance, 5–9 août 1931 (Paris: La Démocratie, 1931).

Publications of Marc Sangnier, Jeune République and/or La Démocratie

Colas, Henri, *Nos Chants – les Volontaires de la Paix* (Paris: La Démocratie, 1930).

Hoog, Georges, *Marc Sangnier au Parlement, 1919–1924* (Paris: La Démocratie, 1924).

Probst, Joseph (ed.), *La paix par la chanson. Chants de la nouvelle jeunesse allemande. Musique, paroles, traductions* (1929) [IMS pamphlet collection].

Sangnier, Marc, *Ce que savent les Jeunes Français aujourd'hui: Simple contribution à une enquête sur l'instruction. Examen passé par 661 conscrits de la classe 18 au dépot du 1er Génie à Versailles* (Paris: La Démocratie, 1918).

Sangnier, Marc, *Pour l'Irlande libre. Discours prononcé à Paris le 28 juin 1920 et précédé d'une allocution de M. Gavan Duffy, délégué du Gouvernement élu de la République irlandaise* (Paris: La Démocratie, 1920).

Sangnier, Marc, *Discours* (Vol. 7) *1922–23* (Paris, La Démocratie, 1925).

Sangnier, Marc, *Discours* (Vol. 8) *1923–25* (Paris, La Démocratie, 1925).

Sangnier, Marc, *Albert de Mun* (Paris: Presses universitaires de France, 1932).

Sangnier, Marc, *Autrefois* (Paris: La Démocratie, 1933).

Sangnier, Marc, *Le pacifisme d'action* (Paris: Le Foyer de la Paix, 1936).

Sangnier, Marc, *Le combat pour la paix* (Paris: La Démocratie, 1937).

Sangnier, Marc, *Pour sauver la paix. Compte-rendu sténotypé du discours prononcé dans la grande salle de La Démocratie le 6 novembre 1938* (Paris: Foyer de la Paix, 1938).

Sangnier, Marc, *Deux mois en Afrique et en Espagne. Notes et impressions,* ed. Roger Rubuguo Mpongo (Paris: Don Bosco, 2009).

Sangnier, Marc, *Pourquoi la France se bat par le capitaineX* (Paris: Bloud et Gay, n. d. but 1918). [Published anonymously in first instance].

Other contemporary published sources

Ducatillon, J.-V., *Le vrai et le faux patriotisme* (Paris: Spes, 1933).

Emorine, André & Jacques, Lamoure, *Histoire des auberges de jeunesse en France 1929–51* (Paris: LFAJ, 1952).

European Office of the Carnegie Foundation for International Peace, *Enquête sur les livres scolaires d'après-guerre* (Paris, 1923).
Fletcher, John P., Carl Heath & Bertram Pickard, 'Pacifists in Paris', *Friends Fellowship Papers*, 1 (1923), 7–15.
Fry, Anna Ruth, *A Quaker Adventure: The Story of Nine Years' Relief and Reconstruction* (New York: Nisbet & Co, 1926).
Giles, Gertrude A., 'The Third International Peace Congress', *Friends Fellowship Papers*, 1 (1923), 185–89.
Hoog, Georges, 'Le rappochement moral', in Georges Hoog (ed.), *France et Allemagne* (Paris: Bloud et Gay, 1928), pp. 127–59.
Julien, Mgr Léon-Adolphe, *La Société des Nations, une théorie catholique* (Paris: Bloud et Gay, 1919).
Julien, Mgr Léon-Adolphe, *L'Evangile nécessaire à l'ordre international* (Paris: Bloud et Gay, 1927).
Margueritte, Victor, *Vers la paix; Appel aux consciences: Avec un avant-propos de Victor Margueritte* (Paris: A. Delpeuch, 1925).
Pye, Edith M., *The Peace Movement in France* (London: Friends' Peace Committee, 1932).
Sadoul, Jacques, *Notes sur la révolution bolchevique* (1919; Paris, 1971).
Solzbacher, William & Josephine Solzbacher-Kennon, *Peace Movements between the Wars: One Man's Work for Peace* (Lampeter: E. Mellen Press, 1999).
Stratmann, Franziskus, *The Church and War* (New York: P.J. Kenedy & Sons, 1928).
Vignaux, Georgette, 'The Catholics in France since the Armistice', *The Review of Politics*, 5 (1943), 194–215.

Newspapers and periodicals

L'Action française
L'Âme commune
L'Aube
Badischer Beobachter
Bulletin de l'Institut catholique de Paris
Le Canard Enchainé
La Croix
La Démocratie
La Documentation catholique
L'Ère nouvelle
L'Éveil démocratique
L'Éveil des peuples (1932–)
La France catholique
La France du Centre
L'Humanité
Indépendance luxembourgeoise
La Jeune République
Le Journal
Les Lettres à un Soldat
Le Matin
Notre Étoile (1916–17)
Nos Annales de Guerre (1918–19)

Le Nord-Est
L'Oeuvre
Paris-Soir
Le Petit Démocrate
Le Temps
The Times (London)
La Vie catholique
Le Volontaire (1929–1932)
The World Outlook: a Quaker survey of international life and service

Interviews

Pierrard, Pierre (1920–2005), Professor Emeritus of History, Institut catholique de Paris, October 2000.
Sangnier, Jean (1912–2011), son of Marc Sangnier, September 2002.

Audio-visual sources

De Place, Ghislain, *Marc Sangnier, le sillon de l'Europe* (VHS, Paris: Les Films du Capricorne & Institut Marc Sangnier, 2003, 56mins.)
Centre National de Cinéma, Service des Archives du Film, Bois d'Arcy. Original Pathé film footage of the Bierville Congress (1926).

Relevant recent media items

Cadiot, Jean-Michel, 'Marc Sangnier: un message d'une extraordinaire actualité', *Le Monde*, 3 June 2010.
Tincq, Henri, 'La France et le schisme traditionaliste', *Le Monde*, 12 July 2007.

Secondary sources

Adams, Geoffrey, *Political Ecumenism: Catholics, Jews, and Protestants in De Gaulle's Free France* (Montreal: McGill-Queen's University Press, 2006).
Adamthwaite, Anthony, *France and the Coming of the Second World War* (London: Frank Cass, 1977).
Arnal [Cole-Arnal], Oscar L., 'Alternatives to the Third Republic among Catholic Leftists in the 1930s', *Historical Reflections*, 5 (1978), 177–95.
Arnal [Cole-Arnal], Oscar L., 'Why the French Christian Democrats Were Condemned', *Church History*, 49 (1980), 188–202.
Arnal [Cole-Arnal], Oscar L., 'A Missionary "Main Tendue" toward French Communists: The "Témoignages" of the Worker-Priests, 1943–54', *French Historical Studies*, 13 (1984), 529–56.
Arnal [Cole-Arnal], Oscar L., 'Shaping Young Proletarians into Militant Christians: The Pioneer Phase of the JOC in France and Canada', *Journal of Contemporary History*, 32 (1997), 509–26.
Atkin, Nicholas, 'Catholics and the Long Liberation: The Progressive Moment', in Andrew Knapp (ed.), *The Uncertain Foundation: France at the Liberation, 1944–1947* (New York: Palgrave Macmillan, 2007), pp. 121–38.

Audoin-Rouzeau, Stéphane, *Men at War, 1914–1918: National Sentiment and Trench Journalism in France during the First World War* (Oxford: Berg, 1992).

Audoin-Rouzeau, Stéphane, *La guerre des enfants, 1914–1918: essai d'histoire culturelle* (Paris: Armand Colin, 1993).

Audoin-Rouzeau, Stéphane, *Cinq deuils de guerre, 1914–1918* (Paris: Noêsis, 2001).

Audoin-Rouzeau, Stéphane & Annette Becker, 'Violence et consentement: la "culture de guerre" du premier conflit mondial', in Jean-Pierre Rioux & Jean-François Sirinelli (eds), *Pour une histoire culturelle* (Paris: Seuil, 1997), pp. 251–71.

Audoin-Rouzeau, Stéphane & Annette Becker, *14–18, Retrouver la guerre* (Paris: Gallimard, 2000).

Audoin-Rouzeau, Stéphane & Annette Becker, *1914–1918: Understanding the Great War* (London: Profile Books, 2002).

Augustin, Jean-Pierre, 'Loisirs, sport et éducation populaire', in Bruno Duriez, Etienne Fouilloux, Denis Pelletier, & Nathalie Viet-Depaule (eds), *Les catholiques dans la république, 1905–2005* (Paris: Editions de l'Atelier, 2005), pp. 153–64.

Ayoun, Richard, 'Robert Schuman, "le père de l'Europe" ', in Hélène Fréchet & Richard Ayoun (eds), *Penser et construire l'Europe (1919–1992)* (Nantes: Editions du Temps, 2007), pp. 177–212.

Azéma, Jean-Pierre, *From Munich to the Liberation, 1938–1944* (1979; Eng. trans.), Cambridge: Cambridge University Press, 1984).

Bard, Christine, *Les filles de Marianne: Histoire des féminismes, 1914–1940* (Paris: Fayard, 1995).

Bariéty, Jacques (ed.), *Aristide Briand, la Société des Nations et l'Europe, 1919–1932* (Strasbourg: Presses Universitaires de Strasbourg, 2007).

Bariéty, Jacques & Raymond Poidevin, *Les relations franco-allemands, 1815–1975* (Paris: Armand Colin, 1977).

Barros, Andrew, 'Briand, l'Allemagne et le « pari » de Locarno', in Jacques, Bariéty (ed.), *Aristide Briand, la Société des Nations et l'Europe, 1919–1932* (Strasbourg: Presses Universitaires de Strasbourg, 2007) pp. 160–72.

Barry, Gearóid, ' "The Crusade of Youth": Pacifism and the Militarization of Youth Culture in Marc Sangnier's Peace Congresses, 1923–32', in Jennifer D. Keene & Michael S. Neiberg (eds), *Finding Common Ground: New Directions in First World War Studies* (Leiden: Brill, 2011), pp. 239–66.

Barry, Gearóid, 'Marc Sangnier's War, 1914–1919: Portrait of a Soldier, Catholic and Social Activist', in Pierre Purseigle (ed.), *Warfare and Belligerence: Perspectives in First World War Studies* (Leiden: Brill, 2005), pp. 163–88.

Barry, Gearóid, 'Rehabilitating a Radical Catholic: Pope Benedict XV and Marc Sangnier, 1914–1922', *Journal of Ecclesiastical History*, 60 (2009), 514–33.

Barry, Gearóid, 'Marc Sangnier and "the Other Germany": The Freiburg International Democratic Peace Congress and the Ruhr Invasion, 1923', *European History Quarterly*, 41 (2011), 25–49.

Barthélemy-Madaule, Madeleine, *Marc Sangnier 1873–1950* (Paris: Seuil, 1973).

Beales, A.C.F., *The History of Peace: A Short Account of the Organised Movements for International Peace* (London: G. Bell, 1931).

Beales, A.C.F., *The Catholic Church and International Order* (London: Penguin, 1941).

Becker, Annette, *Les monuments aux morts, patrimoine et mémoire de la Grande Guerre* (Paris: Errance, 1988).

Becker, Annette, 'Les dévotions des soldats catholiques pendant la Grande Guerre', in Nadine-Josette Chaline (ed.), *Chrétiens dans la première guerre mondiale: Actes des journées tenues à Amiens et à Péronne les 16 mai et 22 juillet 1992* (Paris: Cerf, 1993), pp. 15–201.

Becker, Annette, *War and Faith: The Religious Imagination in France, 1914–30* (1994; Eng. trans., Oxford: Berg, 1998).

Becker, Annette, 'Le culte des morts : entre mémoire et oubli', in Stéphane Audoin-Rouzeau & Jean-Jacques Becker (eds), *Encylopédie de la Grande Guerre, 1914–1918: Histoire et culture* (Paris: Bayard, 2004), pp. 1107–09.

Becker, Annette, 'Faith, Ideologies, and the "Cultures of War"', in Horne, John (ed.), *A Companion to World War I* (London: Wiley-Blackwell, 2010), pp. 234–47.

Becker, Annette, *Les Cicatrices Rouges: France et Belgique Occupées* (Paris: Fayard, 2010).

Becker, Jean-Jacques, *The Great War and the French People* (Leamington Spa: Berg, 1984).

Becker, Jean-Jacques & Gerd Krumeich, *La Grande Guerre. Une histoire franco-allemande* (Paris: Tallandier, 2008).

Becker, Jean-Jacques & Serge Berstein, *Histoire de l'anti-communisme en France,* vol. 1, *1917–40* (Paris: O. Orban, 1987).

Becker, Jean-Jacques & Serge Berstein, *Victoire et frustrations, 1914–29* (Paris: Seuil, 1990).

Becker, Winfried, 'Le pacificisme sous la République de Weimar et ses liens avec Marc Sangnier et Bierville', in Michel Meslin (ed.), *Marc Sangnier la guerre, la paix, 1914–39. Actes de la journée d'études du 26 septembre 1997* (Paris: Institut Marc Sangnier, 1999), pp. 171–95.

Becker, Winfried, 'Marc Sangnier und Hermann Platz: Eine frühe Wahrnehmung und Würdigung des "Sillon" in der Münchener Zeitschrift "Hochland"', *Zeitschrift für Bayerische Landesgeschichte*, 68 (2005), 1009–29.

Bédarida, François & Renée Bédarida, *La Résistance Spirituelle, 1941–1944: Les Cahiers Clandestins du Témoignage Chrétien* (Paris: Albin Michel, 2001).

Bédarida, Renée, *Les catholiques dans la guerre, 1939–1945: entre Vichy et la Résistance* (Paris: Hachette, 1998).

Bédarida, Renée, 'Eugene Pons (1886–1945)', in François Mascot, Bruno Leroux & Christine Levisse-Touzé (eds), *Dictionnaire historique de la Résistance: Résistance Intérieure et France Libre* (Paris: Robert. Laffont, 2006), pp. 506–07.

Bellanger, Claude, *Histoire générale de la presse française*, 4 vols (Paris, 1969–72); Vol. 3, *De 1871–1940* (Paris, 1972).

Bernardi, Peter J., *Maurice Blondel, Social Catholicism, and Action Française: The Clash over the Church's Role in Society during the Modernist Era* (Washington D.C.: Catholic University of America Press, 2009).

Berstein, Serge, 'Le milieu genevois dans la France de l'entre-deux-guerres' in *Les Internationales et le problème de la guerre au XXe siècle. Actes du colloque organisé par l'Ecole Française de Rome, 22–24 novembre 1984* (Rome: Ecole Française de Rome, 1985), pp. 321–35.

Berstein, Serge, 'Consensus Politique et Violences Civiles dans la France du 20e siècle', *Vingtième Siècle: Revue d'histoire*, 69 (2001), 51–60.

Berthod, Bernard & Elisabeth Hardouin-Fugier, *Dictionnaire iconographique des saints* (Paris: Editions de l'Amateur, 1999).

Best, Anthony, Jussi M. Hahnimäki, Joseph A. Maiolo & Kirsten E. Schulze, *International History of the Twentieth Century and Beyond* (2004; New ed., London: Routledge, 2008).

Bibbings, Lois S., *Telling Tales about Men: Conceptions of Conscientious Objectors to Military Service during the First World War* (Manchester: Manchester University Press, 2009).

Bilis, Michel, *Socialistes et pacifistes: l'intenable dilemme des socialistes français, 1933–1939* (Paris: Editions Syros, 1979).

Biondi, Jean-Pierre, *La Mêlée des pacifistes, 1914–45* (Paris: Maisonneuve & Larose, 2000).

Bitsch, Marie-Thérèse, *Robert Schuman, apôtre de l'Europe 1953–1963* (Brussels: P.I.E. Peter Lang, 2010).

Blackwood, William Lee, 'German Hegemony and the Socialist International's Place in Interwar European Diplomacy', *European History Quarterly*, 31 (2006), 225–46.

Bock, Hans Manfred, *Les jeunes dans les relations transnationales: L'office franco-allemand pour la jeunesse, 1963–2008* (Paris: Presses Sorbonne Nouvelle, 2008).

Bonnefous, Edouard & Georges Bonnefous, *Histoire politique de la troisième république*, 8 vols (Paris: Presses universitaires de France, 1965–86); Vol. 3, *L'après-guerre (1919–1924)* (Paris: Presses universitaires de France, 1968).

Bouchard, Carl, 'Les Lauréats de la Paix: Les Concours Américain et Français pour la Paix de 1923–1924', *Revue d'Histoire Moderne et Contemporaine,* 54 (2007), 118–37.

Bouchard, Carl, *Le citoyen et l'ordre mondial (1914–1919): Le rêve d'une paix durable au lendemain de la Grande Guerre, en France, en Grande-Bretagne et aux États-Unis* (Paris: Pedone, 2008).

Boudon, Jacques-Olivier, Jean-Claude Caron & Jean-Claude Yon (eds), *Religion et culture en Europe au 19e siècle (1800–1914)* (Paris: Armand Colin, 2001).

Bouloc, François, *Les profiteurs de guerre, 1914–18* (Brussels: Editions Complexe, 2008).

Brandt, Suzanne, 'Le voyage aux champs de bataille', in Jean-Jacques Becker, Gerd Krumeich, Jay Winter, Annette Becker & Stéphane Audoin-Rouzeau (eds), *Guerre et cultures, 1914–1918* (Paris: Armand Colin, 1994), pp. 411–16.

Brennan, Brian, 'Visiting "Peter in Chains": French Pilgrimage to Rome, 1873–93', *Journal of Ecclesiastical History*, 51 (2000), 741–65.

Brock, Peter, *The Roots of War Resistance: Pacifism from the Early Church to Tolstoy* (New York: Nyack, 1981).

Brock, Peter, *Pacifism to 1914: An Overview* (Toronto: private publication, 1994).

Brock, Peter, *Against the Draft: Essays on Conscientious Objection from the Radical Reformation to the Second World War* (Toronto: University of Toronto Press, 2006).

Brock, Peter & Thomas P. Socknat (eds), *Challenge to Mars: Essays on Pacifism from 1918 to 1945* (Toronto: University of Toronto Press, 1999).

Buchanan, Tom, 'Anti-Fascism and Democracy in the 1930s', *European History Quarterly*, 32 (2002), 39–57.

Buchanan, Tom & Martin Conway (eds), *Political Catholicism in Europe 1918–65* (Oxford: Clarendon, 1996).

Budreau, Lisa M., 'The Politics of Remembrance: The Gold Star Mothers' Pilgrimage and America's Fading Memory of the Great War', *The Journal of Military History*, 72 (April 2008), 371–411.

Burgess, Greg, 'France and the German Refugee Crisis of 1933', *French History*, 16 (2002), 203–29.

Burleigh, Michael, *Earthly Powers: Religion and Politics in Europe from the Enlightenment to the Great War* (London: Harper Collins, 2005).

Burleigh, Michael, *Sacred Causes: The Clash of Religion and Politics, from the Great War to the War on Terror* (New York: Harper Collins, 2007).

Burrin, Philippe, *Living with Defeat: France under the German Occupation, 1940–1944* (London: Arnold, 1996).

Byrnes, Joseph F., *Catholic and French Forever: Religious and National Identity in Modern France* (University Park, PA: Pennsylvania State University Press, 2005).

Cabanes, Bruno, *La Victoire endeuillée: La sortie de guerre des soldats français (1918–1920)* (Paris: Seuil, 2004).

Cabanes, Bruno, 'Les Vivants et les Morts: La France au sortir de la Grande Guerre', in Stéphane Audoin-Rouzeau & Christophe Prochasson (eds), *Sortir de la Grande Guerre: Le monde et l'après-guerre 1918* (Paris: Tallandier, 2008), pp. 27–45.

Cabanes, Bruno & Guillaume Piketty (eds), *Retour à l'intime: au sortir de la guerre* (Paris: Tallandier, 2009).

Cadiot, Jean-Michel, *Francisque Gay et les démocrates d'inspiration chrétienne, 1885–1963* (Paris: Salvator, 2006).

Carlier, Claude & Georges-Henri Soutou (eds), *1918–1925: Comment faire la paix? Actes du colloque international organisé à Versailles les 26 et 27 novembre 1999* (Paris: Economica, 2001), pp. 53–79.

Caron, Jeanne, *Le Sillon et la démocratie chrétienne* (Paris: Plon, 1966).

Caron, Jeanne, *Henri Colas 1879–1968* (Le Mans: private publication, n. d. but ca. 1973).

Caron, Vicki, 'Catholic Political Mobilization and Antisemitic Violence in Fin de Siècle France: The Case of the Union Nationale', *The Journal of Modern History*, 81 (2009), 294–346.

Ceadel, Martin, 'A Legitimate Peace Movement: The Case of Britain, 1918–45', in Brock, Peter & Thomas P. Socknat (eds), *Challenge to Mars: Essays on Pacifism from 1918 to 1945* (Toronto: University of Toronto Press, 1999), pp. 134–48.

Ceadel, Martin, *Living The Great Illusion: Sir Norman Angell, 1872–1967* (Oxford: Oxford University Press, 2009).

Ceadel, Martin, *Pacifism in Britain, 1914–45: The Defining of a faith* (Oxford: Clarendon, 1980).

Ceadel, Martin, *Thinking about Peace and War* (Oxford: Oxford University Press, 1987).

Ceadel, Martin, *Semi-detached Idealists: The British Peace Movement and International Relations, 1854–1945* (Oxford: Oxford University Press, 2000).

Chadwick, Kay (ed.), *Catholicism, Politics and Society in Twentieth-century France* (Liverpool: Liverpool University Press, 2000).

Chadwick, Owen, *A History of the Popes, 1830–1914* (Oxford: Oxford University Press, 1998).

Chaline, Nadine-Josette (ed.), *Chrétiens dans la première guerre mondiale: Actes des journées tenues à Amiens et à Péronne les 16 mai et 22 juillet 1992* (Paris: Cerf, 1993)

Chaline, Nadine-Josette, 'Marc Sangnier : La Jeune République et la paix', *14–18: Aujourd'hui*, 1 (1998), 86–99.

Chamouard, P. & G. Weill, *Députés et Sénateurs de la région parisienne (1848–1984)* (Nanterre: Archives départementales des Hauts-de-Seine, 1985).

Chanet, Jean-François, 'Apprendre', in Vincent Duclert & Christophe Prochasson (eds), *Dictionnaire critique de la République* (Paris: Flammarion, 2002), pp. 981–86.

Charrier, Landry, 'Le mythe de la France revancharde dans l'historiographie allemande des années 1919-1937', *Vingtième siècle. Revue d'histoire*, 110 (2011), 59–66.

Chaunu, Jean, *Christianisme et totalitarisme en France dans l'entre-deux-guerre, 1930–1940*, Vol. 1, *Esquisse d'un jugement chrétien du nazisme* (Paris: F.-X. de Guibert, 2007).

Chenaux, Philippe, *Une Europe vaticane? Entre le plan Marshall et les traités de Rome* (Brussels: Editions Ciaco, 1990).

Chenaux, Philippe, *Entre Maurras et Maritain: une génération intellectuelle catholique 1920–1930* (Paris: Cerf, 1999).

Chenaux, Philippe, 'Monseigneur Julien et l'Allemagne', in Michel Meslin (ed.), *Marc Sangnier, la guerre, la paix, 1914–1939. Actes de la journée d'études du 26 septembre 1997* (Paris: Institut Marc Sangnier, 1999), pp. 105–20.

Chenaux, Philippe, 'L'église catholique et la démocratie chrétienne en Europe, 1925–1965', in Michael Gehler, Wolfram Kaiser & Helmut Wohnout (eds), *Christian Democracy in Twentieth-century Europe* (Vienna: Böhlau, 2001), pp. 604–15.

Chenaux, Philippe, *De la chrétienté à l'Europe: les catholiques et l'idée européenne au XXe siècle* (Tours: CLD, 2007).

Chenaux, Philippe, 'Le Saint-Siège, l'Europe et la paix dans les années vingt', in Jacques Bariéty (ed.), *Aristide Briand, la Société des Nations et l'Europe, 1919–1932* (Strasbourg: Presses universitaires de Strasbourg, 2007), pp. 251–63.

Chenaux, Philippe, *L'Église catholique et le communisme en Europe, 1917–1989: De Lénine à Jean-Paul II* (Paris: Cerf, 2009).

Chickering, Roger, *Imperial Germany and a World without War: The Peace Movement and German Society, 1892–1914* (Princeton, NJ: Princeton University Press, 1975).

Cholvy, Gérard & Yves-Marie Hilaire, *Histoire religieuse de la France, 1880–1914* (Toulouse: Privat, 2000).

Cholvy, Gérard & Yves-Marie Hilaire, *Religion et société en France, 1914–45: Au péril des guerres* (Toulouse: Privat, 2002).

Christophe, Paul, *1936: les catholiques et le Front Populaire* (Paris: Desclée, 1979).

Christophe, Paul, *1939–1940: les catholiques devant la guerre* (Paris: Editions Ouvrières, 1989).

Clark, Christopher & Wolfram Kaiser (eds), *Culture Wars: Secular-Catholic Conflict in Nineteenth-Century Europe* (Cambridge: Cambridge University Press, 2003).

Clément, Jean-Louis, *La démocratie chrétienne en France: un pari à haut risque de 1900 à nos jours* (Paris: F.X. de Guibert, 2005).

Coffey, Joan L., *Léon Harmel: Entrepreneur as Catholic Social Reformer* (Notre Dame, IN: University of Notre Dame Press, 2003).

Cohen, Deborah & Maura O'Connor (eds), *Comparison and History: Europe in Cross-National Perspective* (London: Routledge, 2004).

Cohrs, Patrick O., *The Unfinished Peace after World War I: America, Britain and the Stabilisation of Europe, 1919–1932* (Cambridge: Cambridge University Press, 2006).

Cointet, Michèle, *L'Église sous Vichy, 1940–1945: La repentance en question* (Paris: Perrin, 1998), pp. 140–61.

Comte, Bernard, *L'Honneur et la conscience: catholiques français en résistance (1940–44)* (Paris: Editions de l'Atelier, 1998).

Conrad, Sebastian & Dominic Sachsenmaier (eds), *Competing Visions of World Order: Global Moments and Movements, 1800s–1930s* (Basingstoke: Palgrave Macmillan, 2007).

Conway, Martin, *Catholic Politics in Europe, 1918–45* (London: Routledge, 1997).

Conway, Martin, 'Catholic Politics or Christian Democracy?; The Evolution of Interwar Political Catholicism. A Comment', in Michael Gehler, Wolfram Kaiser & Helmut Wohnout (eds), *Christian Democracy in Twentieth-century Europe* (Vienna: Böhlau, 2001), pp. 294–309.

Cooper, Sandi E., *Patriotic Pacifism: Waging War on War in Europe, 1815–1914* (Oxford: Oxford University Press, 1991).

Cooper, Sandi E., 'Pacifism in France, 1889–1914: International Peace as a Human Right', *French Historical Studies*, 17 (1991), 359–86.

Cooper, Sandi E., 'Pacifism, Feminism, and Fascism in Inter-war France', *International Historical Review*, 19 (1997), 103–26.

Cooper, Sandi E., 'Peace as a Human Right: The Invasion of Women into the World of High International Politics', *Journal of Women's History*, 14 (2002), 9–25.

Coppa, Frank J., *The Modern Papacy since 1789* (London: Longman, 1998).

Coppa, Frank J., *Politics and the Papacy in the Modern World* (Westport, CT: Praeger, 2008).

Corrin, Jay P., *Catholic Intellectuals and the Challenge of Democracy* (Notre Dame, IN: University of Notre Dame Press, 2002).

Costley-White, Hope, *Willoughby Hyett Dickinson, 1859–1943: A Memoir* (Gloucester: J. Bellows, 1956).

Coutrot, Aline, *Un courant de la pensée catholique, l'hebdomadaire Sept, 1934–1937* (Paris: Cerf, 1961).

Coutrot, Aline, 'Youth Movements in France in the 1930s', *Journal of Contemporary History*, 5 (1970), 23–35.

Craig, Gordon A., *Germany 1866–1945* (1978; 2nd ed., Oxford: Oxford University Press, 1981).

Crane, Richard Francis, '*La Croix* and the Swastika: The Ambiguities of Catholic Responses to the Fall of France', *The Catholic Historical Review*, 90 (2004), 45–66.
Cuchet, Guillaume, 'L'Au-delà à l'Epreuve du Feu: La Fin du Purgatoire (1914-1935)', *Vingtième Siècle: Revue d'histoire*, 76 (2002), 117–30.
Curtis, Michael, *Verdict on Vichy: Power and Prejudice in the Vichy France Regime* (London: Phoenix, 2004).
Dalissson, R., 'La célébration du 11 novembre ou l'enjeu de la mémoire combattante dans l'entre-deux-guerres (1918–1939)', *Guerres mondiales et conflits contemporains*, 192 (1998), 5–23.
Dansette, Adrien 'The Rejuvenation of French Catholicism: Marc Sangnier's Sillon', *The Review of Politics*, 15 (1953), 34–52.
Dansette, Adrien, *Destin du catholicisme français, 1926–1956* (Paris: Flammarion, 1957).
Dansette, Adrien, *A Religious History of Modern France*, Vol. 2, *Under the Third Republic* (1948–51; Eng. trans., Edinburgh & London: Nelson, 1961).
Darricau, André, *Marc Sangnier* (Paris: Editions Ouvrières, 1958).
Davies, Thomas R., 'France and the World Disarmament Conference of 1932–34', *Diplomacy and Statecraft*, 15 (2004), 765–80.
Davies, Thomas R., *The Possibilities of Transnational Activism: The Campaign for Disarmament between the Two World Wars* (Leiden: Martinus Nijhoff Publishers, 2007).
Deák, István, *Weimar Germany's Left-wing Intellectuals: A Political History of the Weltbühne and its Circle* (Berkeley, CA: University of California Press, 1968).
Dèbes, Joseph & Émile Poulat, *L'appel de la JOC, 1926–28* (Paris: Cerf, 1986).
Defrance, Corine, 'Les jumelages franco-allemands: Aspects d'une coopération transnationale', *Vingtième siècle*, 99 (2008), 189–201.
Delaporte, Sophie, *Les Gueules cassées: Les blessés de la face de la Grande Guerre* (Paris: Noêsis, 1996).
Delbreil, Jean-Claude, *Les Catholiques français et les tentatives de rapprochement franco-allemand dans l'entre-deux-guerres, 1920–1933* (Metz: Presses universitaires de Metz, 1972).
Delbreil, Jean-Claude, *Centrisme et Démocratie chrétienne en France: Le Parti démocrate populaire des origines au MRP, 1919–1944* (Paris: Publications de la Sorbonne, 1990).
Delbreil, Jean-Claude (ed.), *Marc Sangnier: Témoignages* (Paris: Beauchesne,- 1997).
Delbreil, Jean-Claude, *La revue 'La Vie Intellectuelle': Marc Sangnier, le thomisme et le personnalisme* (Paris: Cerf, 2008).
Delery, Antoine, *Joseph Folliet, 1903–1972: parcours d'un militant catholique* (Paris: Cerf, 2003).
Déloye, Yves, 'L'Ecole', in Vincent Duclert & Christophe Prochasson (eds), *Dictionnaire critique de la République* (Paris: Flammarion, 2002), pp. 699–704.
Desertine, Dominique, 'La paroisse, le vicaire et les enfants: l'éducation catholique populaire en milieu urbain (1919–1939)', in Isabelle von Bueltzingloewen & Denis Pelletier (eds), *La charité en pratique: Chrétiens français et allemands sur le terrain social: xixe-xxe siècles* (Strasbourg: Presses universitaires de Strasbourg, 1999), pp. 1–217.
De Villepin, Patrick, 'Le Pacifisme Intégral et l'Allemagne nazie (1933–1939)', in Hans Manfred Bock, Reinhart Meyer-Kalkus & Michel Trebitsch, *Entre Locarno*

et Vichy: Les relations culturelles franco-allemandes dans les années 1930, Vol. 1 (Paris: CNRS Editions, 1993), pp. 161–73.
De Villepin, Patrick, 'La revue « Evolution » et le pacifisme révisionniste (1926–33)', *Matériaux pour l'histoire de notre temps*, 30 (1993), 11–13.
Diebolt, Evelyne (ed.), *Militer au XXe siècle: Femmes, féminismes, églises et société: Dictionnaire biographique* (Paris: Houdiard, 2009).
Dockrill, M. L. & John Fisher (eds), *The Paris Peace Conference, 1919: Peace without Victory?* (New York: Palgrave Macmillan, 2001).
Downs, Laura Lee, *Childhood in the Promised Land: Working-class Movements and the Colonies de vacances, 1880–1960* (Durham, NC & London: Duke University Press, 2002).
Drapac, Vesna, *War and Religion: Catholics in the Churches of Occupied Paris* (Washington D.C.: Catholic University of America Press, 1998).
Dreyfus, Michel, 'Des femmes pacifistes dans les années trente', *Matériaux pour l'histoire de notre temps*, 30 (1993), pp. 32–34.
Duclert, Vincent, *L'Affaire Dreyfus* (1994; New ed., Paris: Larousse, 2009).
Duclert, Vincent & Christophe Prochasson (eds), *Dictionnaire critique de la République* (Paris: Flammarion, 2002).
Duffy, Eamon, *Saints and Sinners: A History of the Popes* (1997; New Haven, CT & London: Yale University Press, 2002).
Duquesne, Jacques, *Les Catholiques français sous 1'Occupation* (Paris: Grasset, 1966).
Durand, Jean-Dominique, *L'Europe de la démocratie chrétienne* (Paris: Editions Complexe, 1995).
Durand, Jean-Dominique, 'Pie XI, la paix et la construction d'un ordre international', in Ecole Française de Rome (ed.), *Achille Ratti-Pape Pie XI: Actes du colloque organisé par l'Ecole Française de Rome (15–18 mars 1989)* (Rome: Ecole Française de Rome, 1997), pp. 873–91.
Duriez, Bruno, Etienne Fouilloux, Denis Pelletier & Nathalie Viet-Depaule (eds), *Les catholiques dans la république, 1905–2005* (Paris: Editions de l'Atelier, 2005).
Duroselle, Jean-Baptiste, *France and the Nazi Threat: The Collapse of French Diplomacy 1932–39* (1979; Eng. trans., New York: Enigma, 2004).
Epstein, Simon, *Un paradoxe français: Antiracistes dans la Collaboration, antisémites dans la Résistance* (Paris: Albin Michel, 2008).
Evans, Richard J., *The Coming of the Third Reich* (London: Penguin, 2003).
Faron, Olivier, 'Le deuil des vivants', in Stéphane Audoin-Rouzeau & Jean-Jacques Becker (eds), *Encylopédie de la Grande Guerre, 1914–1918: Histoire et culture* (Paris: Bayard, 2004), pp. 1113–22.
Farrar, Marjorie Milbank, *Principled Pragmatist: The Political Career of Alexandre Millerand* (New York: Berg, 1991).
Farrugia, Peter, 'French Religious Opposition to War, 1919–1939: The Contribution of Henri Roser and Marc Sangnier', *French History*, 6(3) (1992), 279–302.
Farrugia, Peter, 'The Conviction of Things Not Seen: Christian Pacifism in France, 1919–1945', in P. Brock & T. P. Socknat (eds), *Challenge to Mars: Essays on Pacifism from 1918 to 1945* (Toronto: University of Toronto Press, 1999), pp. 101–16.
Feldman, Gerald D., 'The Reparations Debate', *Diplomacy and Statecraft*, 16 (2005), 487–98.

Fink, Carole, *The Genoa Conference: European Diplomacy, 1921–22* (Chapel Hill, NC: University of North Carolina Press, 1984).

Fink, Carole, *Defending the Rights of Others: The Great Powers, the Jews, and International Minority Protection, 1878–1938* (Cambridge: Cambridge University Press, 2004).

Fischer, Conan, *Europe between Democracy and Dictatorship, 1900–1945* (Chichester: Wiley-Blackwell, 2011).

Fischer, Conan, *The Ruhr Crisis, 1923–1924* (Oxford: Oxford University Press, 2003).

Fischer, Conan, 'The Human Price of Reparations', *Diplomacy and Statecraft*, 16(3) (2005), 499–514.

Fleury, Alain, *La Croix et l'Allemagne, 1920–30* (Paris: Cerf, 1986).

Fleury, Antoine & Lubor Jílek (eds), *Le Plan Briand d'Union fédérale européenne: Perspectives nationales et transnationales, avec documents: actes du colloque international tenu à Genève du 19 au 21 septembre 1991* (Bern: Peter Lang, 1998).

Fontana, Jacques, *Les catholiques français pendant la grande guerre* (Paris: Cerf, 1990).

Forth, Christopher, *The Dreyfus Affair and the Crisis of French Manhood* (London & Baltimore: Johns Hopkins University Press, 2003).

Fouilloux, Étienne, *Les chrétiens entre crise et libération, 1937–47* (Paris: Seuil, 1997).

Fouilloux, Étienne, *Une Église en quête de libérté: la pensée catholique française entre modernisme et Vatican II: 1914–1962* (Paris: Desclée de Brouwer, 1998).

Fouilloux, Etienne, 'Première guerre mondiale et changement religieux en France', in Jean-Jacques Becker (ed.), *Histoire culturelle de la Grande Guerre* (Paris: Armand Colin, 2005), pp. 115–24.

Gaillot, Helène & Simone Gaillot, *Marc Sangnier, 1873–1950* (Le Mans: private publication, 1960).

Gehler, Michael & Wolfram Kaiser (eds), *Christian Democracy in Europe since 1945*, Vol. 2 (London: Routledge, 2004).

Gehler, Michael, Wolfram Kaiser & Helmut Wohnout (eds), *Christian Democracy in Twentieth-century Europe* (Vienna: Böhlau, 2001).

Germond, Carine & Henning Türk (eds), *A History of Franco-German Relations in Europe: From 'Hereditary Enemies' to Partners* (Basingstoke: Palgrave Macmillan, 2008).

Geyer, Martin H. & J. Paulmann, *The Mechanics of Internationalism: Culture, Society and Politics from the 1840s to the First World War* (Oxford: Oxford University Press, 2001).

Geyer, Michael, 'The Militarization of Europe, 1919–39', in John R. Gillis (ed.), *The Militarization of the Western World* (New Brunswick, NJ: Rutgers University Press, 1989), pp. 74–79.

Gibson, Ralph, *A Social History of French Catholicism, 1789–1914* (London: Routledge, 1989).

Gildea, Robert, *The Past in French History* (New Haven, CT & London: Yale University Press, 1994).

Gorguet, Ilde, *Les mouvements pacifistes et la réconciliation franco-allemande dans les années vingt (1919–1931)* (Bern: Peter Lang, 1999).

Grange, Daniel J., 'Les catholiques français et la coopération internationale durant le premier après-guerre: le Comité catholique des Amitiés francaises', *Relations Internationales*, 72 (1992), 443–74.

Grayzel, Susan R., *Women's Identities at War: Gender, Motherhood, and Politics in Britain and France during the First World War* (Chapel Hill, NC: University of North Carolina Press, 1999).
Grayzel, Susan R., *Women and the First World War* (London: Pearson, 2002).
Greteau, Jean-Jacques, *Marc Sangnier: Le semeur d'espérances* (Paris: L'Harmattan, 2009).
Grünewald, Guido, 'War Resisters in Weimar Germany', in P. Brock & T. P. Socknat (eds), *Challenge to Mars: Essays on Pacifism from 1918 to 1945* (Toronto: University of Toronto Press, 1999), pp. 68–88.
Guieu, Jean-Michel, *Le Rameau et le glaive: Les militants français pour la Société des Nations* (Paris: Presses de Sciences Po, 2008).
Guieu, Jean-Michel, 'Les Allemands et la Société des Nations (1914-1926)', *Les Cahiers IRICE*, 8 (2011), 61-90.
Guieu, Jean-Michel, 'Le militantisme européen, une approche générationelle (des années 1920 au début des années 1950)', *Histoire@Politique*, 10 (2010), http://histoire-politique.fr, accessed 1 June 2011.
Hadley, Frédérick, 'La paix par la jeunesse', *La Lettre de l'Historial* [Historial de la Grande Guerre, Péronne], 23 (November 2008), 13.
Halls, Wilfrid D., *The Youth of Vichy France* (Oxford: Clarendon, 1981).
Halls, Wilfrid D., *Politics, Society and Christianity in Vichy France* (Oxford: Berg, 1995).
Hamann, Brigitte, *Bertha Von Suttner: A Life for Peace* (New York: Syracuse University Press, 1996).
Hanna, Martha, *The Mobilization of Intellect: French Scholars and Writers during the Great War* (Cambridge, MA: Harvard University Press, 1996).
Hanna, Martha, 'A Republic of Letters: The Epistolary Tradition in France during World War I', *American Historical Review*, 108 (2003), 1338–61.
Harris, Ruth, *The Man on Devil's Island: Alfred Dreyfus and the Affair that divided France* (London: Allen Lane, 2010).
Harris, Ruth, *Lourdes: Body and Spirit in the Secular Age* (London: Penguin, 2000).
Harvey, Elizabeth, *Youth and the Welfare State in Weimar Germany* (Oxford: Clarendon, 1993).
Haupt, Heinz-Gerhard & Jürgen Kocka, 'Comparative History: Methods, Aims, Problems', in Cohen, Deborah & Maura O'Connor (eds), *Comparison and History: Europe in Cross-National Perspective* (London: Routledge, 2004), pp. 23–39.
Histoire@Politique. Politique, culture, société, 10 (2010), http://histoire-politique.fr – 'Jeune Europe, jeunes d'Europe', eds. Ludivine Bantigny & Arnaud Baubérot.
Hellmann, John, *Emmanuel Mounier and the New Catholic Left in France 1930–1950* (Toronto: University of Toronto Press, 1981).
Henig, Ruth, *Versailles and After, 1919–1933* (London: Routledge, 1984).
Herrmann, Ulrich (ed.), *'Mit uns die neue Zeit ...': Der Wandervogel in der deutschen Jugendbewegung* (Weinheim: Juventa, 2006).
Holl, Karl, 'The Peace Movement in German Politics 1890–1933', in Art Cosgrove & J. I .McGuire (eds), *Parliament and Community: Papers read before the Irish Conference of Historians, Dublin 27-30 May 1981* (Belfast: Appletree Press, 1983), pp. 177–89.
Holmes, J. Derek, *The Papacy in the Modern World, 1914–78* (London, 1981).
Horne, John, 'The State and Challenge of Labour in France, 1917–1920', in Chris Wrigley (ed.), *Challenges of Labour: Central and Western Europe, 1917–1920* (London: Routledge, 1993), pp. 239–61.

Horne, John (ed.), *State, Society and Mobilisation in Europe during the First World War* (Cambridge: Cambridge University Press, 1997).
Horne, John, 'Introduction: Mobilizing for "Total War", 1914–1918', in Horne, John (ed.), *State, Society and Mobilisation in Europe during the First World War* (Cambridge: Cambridge University Press, 1997), pp. 1–17.
Horne, John, 'Remobilizing for "total war": France and Britain, 1917–18', in Horne (ed.), *State, Society and Mobilization*, pp. 195–211.
Horne, John, 'Socialism, Peace, and Revolution, 1917–1918', in Hew Strachan (ed.), *The Oxford Illustrated History of the First World War* (Oxford: Oxford University Press, 1998), pp. 227–38.
Horne, John, 'Smobilitazioni culturali dopo la grande guerra, 1919–1939', *Italia contemporanea*, 215 (1999), 331–39.
Horne, John, ' "Introduction" in "Démobilisations culturelles après la Grande Guerre" ', *14–18: Aujourd'hui*, 5 (2002), 45–53.
Horne, John, 'Locarno et la politique de démobilization culturelle: 1925–30', *14–18: Aujourd'hui*, 5 (2002), 78–79.
Horne, John, 'La reconstruction du nord-est de la France après 1918', *Les chemins de la mémoire*, 173 (2007), 7–10.
Horne, John, 'Demobilizing the Mind: France and the Legacy of the Great War, 1919–1939', *French History and Civilization*, Papers from the George Rudé Seminar, 2 (2009), 100–19. At George Rudé Society website: http://www.h-france.net/rude/rudepapers.html/, accessed 10 August 2011.
Horne, John (ed.), *A Companion to World War I* (London: Wiley-Blackwell, 2010).
Horne, John & Alan Kramer, *German Atrocities in 1914: A History of Denial* (New Haven, CT & London: Yale University Press, 2001).
Hucker, Daniel, 'French Public Attitudes towards the Prospect of War in 1938–1939: "Pacifism" or "War Anxiety" ', *French History*, 21 (2007), 431–49.
Hucker, Daniel, *Public Opinion and the End of Appeasement in Britain and France* (Farnham: Ashgate, 2011).
Humbert-Knitel, Geneviève, 'La Jeunesse allemande et le mythe du renouveau de l'Allemagne au début du XXe siècle', *Revue d'Allemagne et des pays de langue allemande*, 39 (2007), 590–608.
Ingram, Norman, 'A la recherche d'une guerre gagnée: The Ligue des Droits de l'Homme and the War Guilt Question (1918-1922)', *French History*, 24 (2010), 218–35.
Ingram, Norman, 'The «Circulaire Chautemps», 1933: The Third Republic Discovers Conscientious Objection', *French Historical Studies*, 17(2) (1991), 387–409.
Ingram, Norman, *The Politics of Dissent: Pacifism in France, 1919–1939* (Oxford: Clarendon, 1991).
Ingram, Norman, 'Pacifisme Ancien Style', *Matériaux pour l'histoire de notre temps*, 30 (1993), pp. 2–5.
Ingram, Norman, 'Defending the Rights of Man: The Ligue des Droits de l'Homme and the Problem of Peace', in Brock, Peter & Thomas P. Socknat (eds), *Challenge to Mars: Essays on Pacifism from 1918 to 1945* (Toronto: University of Toronto Press, 1999), pp. 117–33.
Ingram, Norman, ' "Nous allons vers les monastères" : French Pacifism and the Crisis of the Second World War', in Kenneth Mouré & Martin S. Alexander (eds), *Crisis and Renewal in France: 1918–1962* (New York: Berghahn, 2002), pp. 132–51.

Ingram, Norman, 'Gender and the Politics of Pacifism: Feminist Pacifism and the Case of the French Section of the Women's International League for Peace and Freedom', in Eva Schöch-Quinteros, Anja Schüler, Annika Wilmers & Kerstin R. Wolff (eds), *Politische Netzwerkerinnen: Internationale Zusammenarbeir bei Frauen, 1830–1960* (Berlin: Trafo Verlag, 2007), pp. 267–85.

BerghahnIngram, Norman, 'Les pacifistes et Aristide Briand', in Jacques Bariéty (ed.), *Aristide Briand, la Société des Nations, 1919–1932* (Strasbourg: Presses universitaires de Strasbourg, 2007), pp. 200–13.

Ingram, Norman, 'Selbsmord or Euthanasia? Who Killed the Ligue des Droits de l'Homme?', *French History*, 22 (2008), 337–57.

Ingrao, Christian, 'Étudiants allemands, mémoire de guerre et militarisme nazi: étude de cas', *14–18: Aujourd'hui*, 5 (2002), 55–71.

Iriye, Akira & Pierre-Yves Saunier (eds), *The Palgrave Dictionary of Transnational History* (Basingstoke: Palgrave Macmillan, 2009).

Irvine, William D., 'Women's Rights and the "Rights of Man" ', in Mouré, Kenneth & Martin S. Alexander (eds), *Crisis and Renewal in France: 1918–1962* (New York: Berghahn, 2002), pp. 46–65.

Irvine, William D., *Between Justice and Politics: The Ligue des Droits de l'Homme, 1898–1945* (Stanford: Stanford University Press, 2007).

Irving, R. E. M., *The Christian Democratic Parties of Western Europe* (London: Allen & Urwin, 1979).

Jackson, Julian, *The Politics of Depression in France, 1932–36* (Cambridge: Cambridge University Press, 1985).

Jackson, Julian, *The Popular Front in France: Defending Democracy 1934–38* (Cambridge: Cambridge University Press, 1988).

Jackson, Julian, *France: The Dark Years, 1940–44* (Oxford: Oxford University Press, 2001).

Jackson, Peter, 'France and the Problems of Security and International Disarmament after the First World War', *The Journal of Strategic Studies*, 29 (2006), 247–80.

Jacobson, Jon, 'Locarno, Britain and the Security of Europe', in Gaynor Johnson (ed.), *Locarno Revisited: European Diplomacy, 1920–1929* (London: Routledge, 2004), pp. 11–32.

Jacobson, Jon, *Locarno Diplomacy: Germany and the West, 1925–29* (Princeton, NJ: Princeton University Press, 1972).

Jeannesson, Stanislas, 'Pourquoi la France a-t-elle occupé la Ruhr?', *Vingtième siècle*, 51 (1996), 56–57.

Jeannesson, Stanislas, *Poincaré, la France et la Ruhr 1922–1924: Histoire d'une occupation* (Strasbourg: Presses universitaires de Strasbourg, 1998).

Jeannesson, Stanislas, 'French Policy in the Rhineland', *Diplomacy and Statecraft*, 16 (2005), 475–86.

Jefferson, Carter, 'Worker Education in England and France, 1800–1914', *Comparative Studies in Society and History*, 6 (1964), 345–66.

Johnson, Gaynor (ed.), *Locarno Revisited: European Diplomacy, 1920–1929* (London: Routledge, 2004).

Julliard, Charles, 'Marc Sangnier, l'église et la guerre (1905–1914)', *Bulletin de la société d'histoire moderne* (1975), 74 25–29.

Kaiser, Wolfram, *Christian Democracy and the Origins of European Union* (Cambridge: Cambridge University Press, 2007).

Kaplan, Zvi Jonathan, 'The Uses and Abuses of the Dreyfus Affair in the Church-State Debate', *Historical Reflections*, 35 (2009), 85–94.

Kedward, H. R., *Resistance in Vichy France: A Study of Ideas and Motivation in the Southern Zone, 1940–1942* (Oxford: Oxford University Press, 1978).

Keiger, John F. V., *Raymond Poincaré* (Cambridge: Cambridge University Press, 1997).

Keiger, John F. V., 'Poincaré, Briand and Locarno: Continuity in French Diplomacy in the 1920s', in Johnson, Gaynor (ed.), *Locarno Revisited: European Diplomacy, 1920–1929* (London: Routledge, 2004), pp. 95–107.

Kennedy, Finola, *Frank Duff : A Life Story* (London : Continuum, 2011).

Kesler, Jean-François, 'La Jeune-République de sa naissance au tripartisme, 1912–1947', *Revue d'histoire moderne et contemporaine*, 25 (1978), 61–85.

Kitchen, Martin, *Europe between the Wars* (1988: 2nd ed.: London: Pearson/Longman, 2006).

Kolb, Eberhard, *The Weimar Republic* (1984; Eng. trans., London: Routledge, 1988).

Kriegel, Annie, *Aux origines du communisme français*, Vol. 2 (Paris: Mouton, 1964).

Kriegel, Annie, *La grève des cheminots, 1920* (Paris: Armand Colin, 1988).

Krumeich, Gerd, *Armaments and Politics in France on the Eve of the First World War: The Introduction of Three-Year Conscription, 1913–1914* (Leamington Spa: Berg, 1984).

Kselman, Thomas, 'Catholicism, Christianity and Vichy', *French Historical Studies*, 23 (2000), 513–30.

Kuhlman, Erika, *Reconstructing Patriarchy after the Great War: Women, Gender, and Postwar Reconciliation between Nations* (Basingstoke: Palgrave Macmillan, 2008).

Kuisel, Richard F., *Capitalism and the State in Modern France: Renovation and Economic Management in the Twentieth Century* (Cambridge: Cambridge University Press, 1981).

Lagadec, Yann, 'L'échec d'un parachutage electoral: les mésaventures de Marc Sangnier et du Sillon en Ille-et-Viliane (1901)', *Société Archéologique et Historique d'Ille-et-Vilaine*, 109 (2005), 337–60.

Lamberts, Emiel (ed.), *The Black International/ L'International noire 1870–1878* (Leuven: Leuven University Press, 2002).

Lamberts, Emiel, 'Catholic Congresses as Amplifiers of International Catholic Opinion', in, Viaene, Vincent (ed.), *The Papacy and the New World Order: Vatican Diplomacy, Catholic Opinion and International Politics at the Time of Leo XIII, 1878–1903* (Leuven: KADOC, 2005), pp. 213–24.

Lappenküpper, Ulrich, 'On the Path to a "Hereditary Friendship"?', in Germond, Carine & Henning Türk (eds), *A History of Franco-German Relations in Europe: From 'Hereditary Enemies' to Partners* (Basingstoke: Palgrave Macmillan, 2008) pp. 151–64.

Laqua, Daniel (ed.), *Internationalism Reconfigured: Transnational Ideas and Movements between the World Wars* (London: I.B. Tauris, 2011).

Laqueur, Walter, *Young Germany: A History of the German Youth Movement* (London: Routledge & Kegan Paul, 1962).

Latour, Francis, *La Papauté et les problèmes de la paix pendant la Grande Guerre* (Paris: L'Harmattan, 1996).

Launay, Michel, *La C.F.T.C.: Origines et dévoloppement, 1919–1940* (Paris: Publications de la Sorbonne, 1986).

Lauter, Anna-Monika, *Sicherhiet und Reparationen: Die französische Őffentlichkeit, der Rhein und die Ruhr (1919–1923)* (Essen: Klartext, 2006).

Lefèvre, Denis, *Marc Sangnier: L'aventure du catholicisme social* (Paris: Mame, 2008).

Le Goff, Jacques, 'Reims, City of Coronation', in Pierre Nora (ed.), *Realms of Memory*, Vol. 3, *Symbols* (New York: Columbia University Press, 1998), pp. 193–251.

Le Moigne, Frédéric, *Les évêques français de Verdun à Vatican II: une génération* en mal d'héroïsme (Rennes: Presses universitaires de Rennes, 2005).

Létourneau, Paul, ' "La main au collet" et le révisionisme allemande durant la période Rathenau: l'occasion ratée?', *Revue d'Allemagne et des Pays de langue allemande*, 38(2) (2006), pp. 185–96.

Levillain, Philippe, 'Le Saint-Siège et la première guerre mondiale' in Ecole Française de Rome (ed.), *Les Internationales et le problème de la guerre au XXe siècle: Actes du colloque organisé par l'Ecole Française de Rome, 22–24 novembre 1984* (Rome: Ecole Française de Rome, 1985).

Leymarie, Michel & Jacques Prévotat (eds), *L'Action Françise: culture, société, politique* (Villeneuve d'Ascq: Presses universitaires de Septentrion, 2008).

Library of the Religious Society of Friends in Britain [LSF], *Dictionary of Quaker Biography* (typescript, work in progress) Entry for Anna Ruth Fry (1878–1962).

Lloyd, David William, *Battlefield Tourism: Pilgrimage and the Commemoration of the Great War in Britain, Australia and Canada, 1919–1939* (Oxford: Berg, 1998).

Lönne, Karl-Egon, 'Germany', in Tom Buchanan & Martin Conway (eds), *Political Catholicism in Europe, 1918–1965* (Oxford: Clarendon, 1996), pp. 156–86.

Lorrain, Sophie, *Des pacifistes français et allemands, pionniers de l'entente franco-allemande, 1871–1925* (Paris: L'Harmattan, 1999).

Lyons, Martyn, 'French Soldiers and their Correspondence: Towards a History of Writing Practices in the First World War', *French History*, 17 (2003), 79–95.

MacCulloch, Diarmaid, *A History of Christianity: The First Three Thousand Years* (London: Allen Lane, 2009).

Maclear, J. F., *Church and State in the Modern Age: A Documentary History* (New York: Oxford University Press, 1995).

Macmillan, Margaret, *Peacemakers: The Paris Conference of 1919 and its Attempt to End War* (London: John Murray, 2001).

Madigan, Edward, *Faith under Fire: Anglican Army Chaplains and the Great War* (Basingstoke: Palgrave Macmillan, 2011).

Maitron, Jean (ed.), *Dictionnaire biographique du mouvement ouvrier français*, vol. 22 (Paris: Editions Ouvrières, 1984).

Manela, Erez, *The Wilsonian Moment: Self-Determination and the International Origins of Anticolonial Nationalism* (Oxford: Oxford University Press, 2007).

Marks, Sally, *The Illusion of Peace: International Relations in Europe, 1918–1933* (1976; 2nd ed., Basingstoke: Palgrave Macmillan, 2003).

Marks, Sally, ' "Poincaré-La-Peur": France and the Ruhr Crisis of 1923', in Kenneth Mouré & Martin S. Alexander (eds), *Crisis and Renewal in France: 1918–1962* (New York: Berghahn, 2002), pp. 28–45.

Marrus, Michael & Robert Paxton, *Vichy France and the Jews* (New York: Basic Books, 1981).

'Martial-Justin Verraux', École Supérieure de Guerre website, http://ecolesuperieure-de-guerre.fr/promotions/biographie/422, accessed 25 July 2011.

Martin, Benjamin F., *Albert de Mun: Paladin of the Third Republic* (Chapel Hill, NC: University of North Carolina Press, 1978).
Martin, Benjamin F., *France and the Après-Guerre, 1918–24: Illusions and Disillusionment* (Baton Rouge, LA: Louisiana State University Press, 1999).
Mayeur, Jean-Marie, *L'abbé Lemire. Un prêtre démocrate, 1853–1928* (Paris: Casterman, 1968).
Mayeur, Jean-Marie, *Des partis catholiques à la démocratie chrétienne XIXe-XXe siècle* (Paris: Armand Colin, 1980).
Mayeur, Jean-Marie (ed.), *Histoire du christianisme des origines à nos jours*, Vol. 12, *Guerres mondiales et totalitarismes (1914–1958)* (Paris: Desclée, 1990).
Mayeur, Jean-Marie, 'Les catholiques français et Benoît XV en 1917', in Nadine-Josette Chaline (ed.), *Chrétiens dans la première guerre mondiale: Actes des journées tenues à Amiens et à Péronne les 16 mai et 22 juillet 1992* (Paris: Cerf, 1993), pp. 153–65.
Mayeur, Jean-Marie (ed.), *Le Sillon de Marc Sangnier et la démocratie sociale: Actes du colloque des 18 et 19 mars 2004 Besançon* (Besançon: Presses universitaires de Franche-Comté, 2006).
Mazuy, Rachel, 'Le Rassemblement Universel pour la Paix (1935–1939): une organisation de masse?', *Matériaux pour l'histoire de notre temps* 30, (1993), pp. 40–44.
McDougall, Walter, *France's Rhineland Diplomacy 1914–1924* (Princeton, NJ: Princeton University Press, 1978).
McMillan, James F., *Housewife or Harlot: The Place of Women in French Society 1870–1940* (Brighton: Harvester Press, 1981).
McMillan, James F., 'French Catholics: *Rumeurs Infâmes* and the *Union Sacrée*, 1914–1918', in Frans Coetzee & Marilyn Shevin-Coetzee (eds), *Authority, Identity and the Social History of the Great War* (Oxford & Providence, RI: Berghahn, 1995), pp. 113–32.
McMillan, James F., 'France', in Tom Buchanan & Martin Conway (eds), *Political Catholicism in Europe 1918–65* (Oxford: Clarendon, 1996), pp. 34–68.
Merlio, Gilbert, 'Le pacifisme en Allemagne et en France entre les deux guerres mondiales', *Les Cahiers IRICE*, 8 (2011), 39–59.
Meslin, Michel (ed.), *Marc Sangnier, la guerre, la paix, 1914–39. Actes de la journée d'études du 26 septembre 1997* (Paris: Institut Marc Sangnier, 1999).
Miller, Paul B., *From Revolutionaries to Citizens: Antimilitarism in France, 1870–1914* (Durham, NC: Duke University Press, 2001).
Miquel, Pierre, *Le traité de Versailles et l'opinion publique française* (Paris: Flammarion, 1972).
Misner, Paul, *Social Catholicism in Europe: From the Onset of Industrialization to the First World War* (London: Darton, Longman & Todd, 1991).
Mitterauer, Michael, *A History of Youth* (Oxford: Blackwell, 1992).
Mouré, Kenneth & Martin S. Alexander (eds), *Crisis and Renewal in France: 1918–1962* (New York: Berghahn, 2002).
Müller, Guido, 'France and Germany after the Great War: Business Men, Intellectuals and Artists in Non-Governmental European Networks', in Jessica C. E. Gienow-Hecht & Frank Schumacher (eds), *Culture and International History* (New York: Berghahn, 2003), pp. 97–114.
Mulligan, William, *The Origins of the First World War* (Cambridge: Cambridge University Press, 2010).

Mombert, Monique, 'Notes de lecture: "Mit uns die neue Zeit...", *Revue d'Allemagne et des pays de langue allemande*, 39 (2007), 609–19.

Mosse, George L., *Fallen Soldiers, Reshaping the Memory of the World Wars* (New York: Oxford University Press, 1990).

Neiberg, Michael S., *Dance of the Furies: Europe and the Outbreak of World War I* (Cambridge, MA: The Belknap Press of Harvard University Press, 2011).

Nehring, Holger, 'Peace', in Iriye, Akira & Pierre-Yves Saunier (eds), *The Palgrave Dictionary of Transnational History* (Basingstoke: Palgrave Macmillan, 2009), pp. 803–6.

Nehring, Holger & Helge Pharo, 'Introduction: A Peaceful Europe? Negotiating Peace in the Twentieth Century', *Contemporary European History*, 17 (2008), 277–99.

Néré, Jacques, *The Foreign Policy of France from 1914 to 1948* (1974; Eng. trans., London: Routledge & Kegan Paul, 1975).

Noli, Mathieu, ' "L'Éveil des peuples" ', "le Volontaire" et "les Volontaires de la Paix" ', in Michel Meslin (ed.), *Marc Sangnier la guerre, la paix 1914–39: Actes de la journée d'études du 26 septembre 1997* (Paris: Institut Marc Sangnier, 1999), pp. 83–103.

Nord, Philip, 'Catholic Culture in Interwar France', *French Politics, Culture & Society*, 21 (2003), 1–20.

Offenstadt, Nicolas, 'Le pacifisme extrême à la conquête des masses: la Ligue Internationale des Combattants de la Paix (1931–1939) et la propagande', *Matériaux pour l'histoire de notre temps*, 30, (1993), pp. 35–39.

Oldfield, Sybil, 'Pye, Edith Mary (1876–1965)' in H.C.G. Matthew, Brian Howard Harrison & Lawrence Goldman (eds),*Oxford Dictionary of National Biography* (Oxford: Oxford University Press, 2004), http://www.oxforddnb.com/view/article/37871 (accessed 6 August 2009).

O'Malley, John W., *What Happened at Vatican II* (Cambridge, MA: The Belknap Press of Harvard University Press, 2008).

Overy, Richard, *The Morbid Age: Britain between the Wars* (London: Allen Lane, 2009).

'Oxford-Leuven research project on Religious Internationals in the nineteenth century.' http://www.history.ox.ac.uk/mehrc/research.htm, accessed 25 May 2009.

Panchasi, Roxanne, *Future Tense: The Culture of Anticipation in France between the Wars* (Ithaca, NY: Cornell University Press, 2009).

Passman, Elana, 'Civic Activism and the Pursuit of Cooperation in the Locarno Era', in Carine Germond & Henning Türk (eds), *A History of Franco-German Relations in Europe: From 'Hereditary Enemies' to Partners* (Basingstoke: Palgrave Macmillan, 2008), pp. 101–12.

Passmore, Kevin, 'The Ideological Origins of Fascism before 1914', in R. J. B. Bosworth (ed.), *The Oxford Handbook of Fascism* (Oxford: Oxford University Press, 2010), pp. 11–31.

Pedersen, Susan, 'Back to the League of Nations', *American Historical Review*, 112 (2007), 1091–117.

Pelletier, Denis, *Les catholiques en France depuis 1815* (Paris: La Découverte, 1997).

Pelletier, Denis, 'Les pratiques charitables françaises entre "histoire sociale" et "histoire religieuse": Essai d'historiographie critique', in Isabelle von Bueltzingloewen & Denis Pelletier (eds), *La charité en pratique: Chrétiens français et allemands sur le terrain social: xixe-xxe siècles* (Strasbourg: Presses universitaires de Strasbourg, 1999), pp. 1–217.

Pelletier, Denis, '1905–2005; Un siècle d'engagements catholiques', in Bruno Duriez, Etienne Fouilloux, Denis Pelletier & Nathalie Viet-Depaule (eds), *Les catholiques dans la république, 1905–2005* (Paris: Editions de l'Atelier, 2005), pp. 19–50.

Perrier, Jacques, *L'abbé Stock (1904–48): Heureux les doux* (Paris: Cerf, 1998).

Perry, Matt, *Memory of War in France, 1914–45: César Fauxbras, the Voice of the Lowly* (Basingstoke: Palgrave Macmillan, 2011).

Peukert, Detlev J. K., *The Weimar Republic* (1987; Eng. trans., London: Allen Lane, 1991).

Pezet, Ernest, *Chrétiens au service de la cité. De Léon XIII au Sillon et au MRP, 1891–1965* (Paris: Nouvelles Editions Latines, 1965).

Pierrard, Pierre, *L'Église et les ouvriers en France (1840–1940)* (Paris: Hachette, 1984).

Pierrard, Pierre, M. Launay & R. Trempe (eds), *La JOC: Régards d'historiens* (Paris: Editions Ouvrières, 1984).

Pierrard, Pierre, *Un siècle de l'Église de France, 1900–2000* (Paris: Desclée de Brouwer, 2000).

Piketty, Guillaume, *Pierre Brossolette: un héros de la Résistance* (Paris: O. Jacob, 1998).

Piketty, Guillaume, 'Groupe de la rue de Lille', in François Mascot, Bruno Leroux & Christine Levisse-Touzé (eds), *Dictionnaire historique de la Résistance Intérieure et France Libre* (Paris: Robert Laffont, 2006), pp. 190–1.

Pollard, John F., *Benedict XV: The Unknown Pope and the Pursuit of Peace* (1999; 2nd ed., London: Continuum, 2005).

Pompfret, David, 'The City of Evil and the Great Outdoors: The Modern Health Movement and the Urban Young, 1918–40', *Urban History*, 28 (2001), 405–27.

Portier, Philippe, 'Refaire la république. L'engagement des catholiques français en politique au XXe siècle', in Bruno Duriez, Etienne Fouilloux, Denis Pelletier, Nathalie Viet-Depaule (eds), *Les catholiques dans la république, 1905–2005* (Paris: Editions de l'Atelier, 2005), pp. 239–52.

Prat, Olivier, 'La Paix par la Jeunesse: Le Congrès de Bierville; Août 1926', in Michel Meslin (ed.), *Marc Sangnier, la guerre, la paix (1914–1939): Actes de la journée d'études du 26 septembre 1997* (Paris: Institut Marc Sangnier, 1999), pp. 55–80.

Prat, Olivier, 'Le combat pour la paix de Marc Sangnier, 1919–1939', *Revue des Lettres, Sciences et Arts de la Corrèze*, 103 (2000), 53–68.

Prat, Olivier, 'Marc Sangnier et la paix à la Chambre «Bleu Horizon», 1919–1924', in Claude Carlier & Georges-Henri Soutou (eds), *1918–1925: Comment faire la paix? Actes du colloque international organisé à Versailles les 26 et 27 novembre 1999* (Paris: Economica, 2001), pp. 53–79.

Prat, Olivier, 'Marc Sangnier et l'idée européenne', in Hélène Fréchet & Richard Ayoun (eds), *Penser et construire l'Europe (1919–1992)* (Nantes: Editions du Temps, 2007), pp. 46–62.

Prat, Olivier (ed.), *Alphonse Gratry (1805–1872): Marginal ou précurseur* (Paris: Cerf, 2009).

Prat, Olivier, ' "La Paix par la jeunesse": Marc Sangnier et la réconciliation franco-allemande, 1921–1939', *Histoire@Politique*, 10 (2010), http://histoire-politique.fr, accessed 1 June 2011.

Prévotat, Jacques, *Les catholiques et l'Action Française: Histoire d'une condamnation, 1899–1939* (Paris: Fayard, 2001).

Prochasson, Christophe, 'Les congrès lieux de l'échange intellectuel 1850–1914', *Mil neuf cent: Revue d'histoire intellectuelle*, 7 (1989), 5–8.

Prochasson, Christophe, *Au nom de la patrie: Les intellectuels et la première guerre mondiale* (Paris: La Découverte, 1996).

Proctor, Tammy M., 'Scouts, Guides and the Fashioning of Empire, 1919–39', in Wendy Parkins (ed.), *Fashioning the Body Politic: Dress, Gender, Citizenship* (New York: Berg, 2002), pp. 125–44.

Prost, Antoine, *Les anciens combattants, 1914–1939*, Vol. 3, *Mentalités et idéologies* (Paris: Fondation Nationale des Sciences Politiques, 1977).

Prost, Antoine, 'The Impact of War on French and German Political Culture', *Historical Journal*, 37(1) (1994), 209–17.

Prost, Antoine, 'Verdun', in Pierre Nora (ed.), *Realms of Memory*, Vol. 3, *Symbols* (1984–92; Eng. trans., New York, 1998), pp. 377–401.

Prost, Antoine, 'Youth in France between the Wars', in Antoine Prost (ed.) *Republican Identities in War and Peace: Representations of France in the Nineteenth and Twentieth Centuries* (Oxford & New York: Berg, 2002), pp. 221–34.

Prost, Antoine & Jay M. Winter, *René Cassin et les Droits de l'Homme: Le projet d'une génération* (Paris: Fayard, 2011).

Purseigle, Pierre (ed.), *Warfare and Belligerence: Perspectives in First World War Studies* (Leiden: Brill, 2005).

Reisenberger, Dieter, *Die Katholische Friedensbewegung in der Weimarer Republik* (Dusseldorf: Droste, 1976).

Rémond, René, 'L'évolution du journal "La Croix" et son rôle auprès de l'opinion catholique, 1919–1939', *Bulletin de la Société d'Histoire Moderne*, 57 (1958), 3–10.

Rémond, René, *Les catholiques dans la France des années trente* (Paris: Cana, 1979).

Renoton-Beine, Nathalie, *La Colombe et les tranchées: Les tentatives de paix de Benoît XV pendant la Grande Guerre* (Paris: Cerf, 2004).

Revue d'Allemagne et des Pays de langue allemande, 38, 2 (2006) – 'Révisionisme allemande et puissances occidentales entre 1919 et 1939', eds. Paul Létourneau & Georges-Henri Soutou.

Reynolds, Sian, *France between the Wars: Gender and Politics* (London: Routledge, 1996).

Reytier, Marie-Emmanuelle, 'Les Katholikentage dans l'entre-deux-guerres', *14–18: Aujourd'hui*, 1 (1998), 71–85.

Reytier, Marie-Emmanuelle, 'I cattolici tedeschi e l'Europa all'indomani della Prima Guerra Mondiale: L'esempio dei Katholikentage', in Alfredo Canavero & Jean-Dominique Durand (eds), *Il fattore religioso nell'integrazione europea* (Milan: Unicolpi, 1999), pp. 359–71.

Reytier, Marie-Emmanuelle, 'Des catholiques pacifistes: Die Katholische Friedenswarte (1924–1927) et Der Friedenskämpfer (1928–1933)', in Michel Grunewald, Uwe Puschner, & Hans-Manfred Bock (eds), *Le milieu intellectual catholique en Allemagne, sa presse et ses résaux (1871–1960)* (Berne: Peter Lang, 2006), pp. 255–80.

Robbins, Keith, *The Abolition of War: The Peace Movement in Britain, 1914–1919* (Cardiff: University of Wales Press, 1976).

Rochefort, Florence & Laurence Klejman, *L'Egalité en marche: Le Féminisme sous la Troisième République* (Paris: Fondation Nationale des Sciences Politiques, 1989).

Rogard, Vincent, 'Marc Sangnier et la Séparation', *Revue d'Histoire de l'Église de France*, 91 (2005), 299–307.
Santamaria, Yves, *L'enfant du malheur: Le parti communiste français dans la Lutte pour la paix (1914–1947)* (Paris: Armand Colin, 2002).
Santamaria, Yves, *Le pacifisme: une passion française* (Paris: Armand Colin, 2005).
Sassoon, Donald, *One Hundred Years of Socialism: The West European Left in the Twentieth Century* (New York: New Press, 1996).
Schirmann, Sylvain, 'Franco-German Relations, 1918–45', in Germond, Carine & Henning Türk (eds), *A History of Franco-German Relations in Europe: From 'Hereditary Enemies' to Partners* (Basingstoke: Palgrave Macmillan, 2008), pp. 75–88.
Schloesser, Stephen, *Jazz Age Catholicism: Mystic Modernism in Postwar Paris, 1919–1933* (Buffalo: University of Toronto Press, 2005).
Schuker, Stephen A., *The End of French Predominance in Europe: The Financial Crisis of 1924 and the Adoption of the Dawes Plan* (Chapel Hill, NC: University of North Carolina Press, 1976).
Sharp, Alan, *The Versailles Settlement: Peacemaking after the First World War, 1919–1923* (2nd ed.; Basingstoke: Palgrave Macmillan, 2008).
Sharp, Alan & Conan Fischer, 'The Versailles Settlement: Enforcement, Compliance, Contested Identities', *Diplomacy and Statecraft*, 16 (2005), 419–22.
Sherman, Daniel J., *The Construction of Memory in Interwar France* (Chicago, IL: Chicago University Press, 1999).
Showalter, Dennis ' "Plus jamais" du moins pas comme cela: imaginer la guerre après 1918', *14–18: Aujourd'hui*, 5 (2002), 144–57.
Siegel, Mona L., ' "To the Unknown Mother of the Unknown Soldier": Pacifism, Feminism, and the Politics of Sexual Difference among French *Institutrices* between the Wars', *French Historical Studies*, 22 (1999), 421–51.
Siegel, Mona L., *The Moral Disarmament of France: Education, Pacifism, and Patriotism* (Cambridge: Cambridge University Press, 2004).
Singer, Barnett, 'From Patriots to Pacifists: The French Primary School Teachers, 1880–1940', *Journal of Contemporary History*, 12 (1977), 413–34.
Sirinelli, Jean-François, 'La France de l'entre-deux-guerres: un "trend" pacifiste?', in Maurice Vaisse (ed.), *Le pacifisme en Europe des années 1920 aux années 1950: Actes du colloque tenu à Reims du 3 au 5 décembre 1992 par le Centre ARPEGE* (Brussels: Bruylant, 1993), pp. 43–50.
Smith, Leonard V., 'Narrative and Identity at the Front: Theory and the Poor Bloody Infantry', in Jay Winter, Geoffrey Parker & Mary Habeck (eds), *The Great War and the Twentieth Century* (New Haven, CT & London: Yale University Press, 2000), pp. 132–65.
Smith, Leonard V., Stéphane Audoin-Rouzeau & Annette Becker, *France and the Great War, 1914–18* (Cambridge: Cambridge University Press, 2003).
Smith, Leonard V., 'The "culture de guerre" and French Historiography of the Great War of 1914–1918', *History Compass*, 5 (2007), 1967–79.
Smith, Leonard V., *The Embattled Self: French Soldiers' Testimony of the Great War* (Ithaca, NY & London: Cornell University Press, 2007).
Smith, Paul, *Feminism and the Third Republic: Women's Political and Civil Rights in France* (Oxford: Clarendon, 1996).
Snape, Michael, *God and the British Soldier: Religion and the British Army in the First and Second World Wars* (London: Routledge, 2005).

Sorrel, Christian, 'Le prêtre et le congrès (1870–1940): un rendez-vous manqué?', *Revue d'histoire de l'Église de France*, 93(1) (2007), 71–88.

Soutou, Georges-Henri, *L'or et le sang: les buts de guerre économiques de la Première Guerre mondiale* (Paris: Fayard, 1989).

Soutou, Georges-Henri, 'The French Peacemakers and their Home Front', in Manfred F. Boemke, Gerald D. Feldman & Elisabeth Glaser (eds), *The Treaty of Versailles: A Reassessment after 75 Years* (Cambridge: Cambridge University Press, 1998), pp. 167–88.

Soutou, Georges-Henri, 'L'ordre européen de Versailles à Locarno', in Claude Carlier & Georges-Henri Soutou (eds), *1918–1925: Comment faire la paix? Actes du colloque international organisé à Vincennes les 26 et 27 novembre 1999* (Paris: Economica, 2001), pp. 301–31.

Soutou, Georges-Henri, 'Les Occidentaux et l'Allemagne durant l'entre-deux-guerres', *Revue d'Allemagne et des Pays de langue allemande*, 38 (2006), 165–84.

Soutou, Georges-Henri, '1918: la fin de la Première Guerre mondiale?', *Revue historique des armées*, 251 (2008), 4–17.

Stachura, Peter D., *The German Youth Movement 1900–1945: An Interpretative and Documentary History* (London: Palgrave Macmillan, 1981).

Steiner, Zara S., *The Lights That Failed: European International History, 1919–1933* (Oxford: Oxford University Press, 2005).

Stevenson, David, *French War Aims against Germany, 1914–1919* (Oxford: Oxford University Press, 1992).

Thiers, Eric, 'Droit et culture de guerre 1914–1918: Le Comité d'études et documents sur la guerre', *Mil neuf cents. Revue d'histoire intellectuelle*, 23 (2005), 23–48.

Thorn, William J., Phillip M. Runkel & Susan Mountin, *Dorothy Day and the Catholic Worker movement: centenary essays* (Milwaukee WI: Marquette University Press, 2001).

Ticchi, J. M., *Aux Frontières de la Paix. Bons offices, médiations, arbitrages du Saint-Siège (1878–1922)* (Rome: Ecole Française de Rome, 2002).

Tiersky, Ronald, *French Communism, 1920–72* (London: Columbia University Press, 1974).

Todman, Dan, *The Great War: Myth and Memory* (London: Hambledon Continuum, 2005).

Trachtenburg, Marc, *Reparation in World Politics: France and European Economic Diplomacy 1916–1923* (New York: Columbia University Press, 1980).

Unger, Gérard, *Aristide Briand, le ferme conciliateur* (Paris: Fayard, 2005).

Vaïsse, Maurice, *Sécurité d'abord: La politique française en matière de désarmement. 9 décembre 1930–17 avril 1934* (Paris: Pedone, 1981)

Vaïsse, Maurice (ed.), *Le pacifisme en Europe des années 1920 aux années 1950: Actes du colloque tenu à Reims du 3 au 5 décembre 1992 par le Centre ARPEGE* (Brussels: Bruylant, 1993).

Varley, Karine, *Under the Shadow of Defeat: The War of 1870–71 in French Memory* (Basingstoke: Palgrave Macmillan, 2008).

Vergnon, Gilles, 'L'antifascisme, un trait d'union entre les gauches', in Gilles Morin & Gilles Richard (eds), *Les deux France du Front populaire: chocs et contre-chocs* (Paris: L'Harmattan, 2008), pp. 359–69.

Viaene, Vincent, 'International History, Religious History, Catholic History: Perspectives for Cross-Fertilization (1830–1914)', *European History Quarterly*, 38(4) (2008), 578–607.
Viaene, Vincent (ed.), *The Papacy and the New World Order: Vatican Diplomacy, Catholic Opinion and International Politics at the Time of Leo XIII, 1878–1903* (Leuven: KADOC, 2005).
Viaene, Vincent, 'The Roman Question: Catholic Mobilization and Papal Diplomacy during the Pontficate of Pius IX (1846-1878)' in Emiel Lamberts (ed.), *The Black International/L'International noire 1870–1878* (Leuven: Leuven University Press, 2002) pp. 150–6.
Wallis, Jill, *Valiant for Peace: A History of the Fellowship of Reconciliation, 1914 to 1989* (London: Fellowship of Reconciliation, 1991).
Walsh, Maurice, *The News from Ireland: Foreign Correspondents and the Irish Revolution* (New York: I.B. Tauris, 2008).
Wardhaugh, Jessica, *In Pursuit of the People: Political Culture in France* (Basingstoke: Palgrave Macmillan, 2008).
Wardhaugh, Jessica, 'Un Rire Nouveau: Action Française and the Art of Political Satire', *French History*, 22 (2008), 273–307.
Wardhaugh, Jessica, 'Sacred Unions: Religion and Reconciliation in French Society, 1919–1945', *French Politics, Culture & Society*, 27 (2009), 116–28.
Weber, Eugen, *Action Française: Royalism and Reaction in Twentieth Century France* (Stanford: Stanford University Press, 1962).
Weber, Eugen, *The Nationalist Revival in France, 1905–1914* (Berkeley, CA: University of California Press, 1968).
Weber, Eugen, *The Hollow Years: France in the 1930s* (New York: Norton, 1994).
Weber, Thomas, *Hitler's First War: Adolf Hitler, the Men of the List Regiment, and the First World War* (Oxford: Oxford University Press, 2011).
Webster, Andrew, 'From Versailles to Geneva: The Many Forms of Interwar Disarmament', *The Journal of Strategic Studies*, 29 (2006), 225–46.
Weindling, Paul, ' "For the Love of Christ": Strategies of International Catholic Relief and the Allied Occupation of Germany, 1945–48', *Journal of Contemporary History*, 43 (2008), 477–92.
Whitney, Susan B., *Mobilizing Youth: Communists and Catholics in Interwar France* (Durham, NC & London: Duke University Press, 2009).
Williams, John Alexander, *Turning to Nature in Germany: Hiking, Nudism, and Conservation, 1900–1940* (Stanford: Stanford University Press, 2007).
Winock, Michel, *La trahison de Munich: Emmanuel Mounier et la grande débâcle des intellectuels* (Paris: CNRS, 2008).
Winter, Jay, *Sites of Memory, Sites of Mourning: The Great War in European Cultural History* (Cambridge: Cambridge University Press, 1995).
Winter, Jay, 'Propaganda and the Moblization of Consent', in Hew Strachan (ed.), *The Oxford Illustrated History of the First World War* (1998: 2nd ed., Oxford: Oxford University Press, 2000), pp. 216–26.
Winter, Jay, 'Henri Barbusse and the Birth of the Moral Witness', introduction to *Under Fire*, Henri Barbusse (London: Penguin, 2003), pp. vii–xix.
Winter, Jay, *Remembering War: The Great War between Memory and History in the Twentieth Century* (New Haven, CT & London: Yale University Press, 2006).
Winter, Jay, *Dreams of Peace and Freedom: Utopian Moments in the Twentieth Century* (New Haven, CT & London: Yale University Press, 2006).

Winter, Jay & Antoine Prost, *The Great War in History: Debates and Controversies, 1914 to the Present* (Cambridge: Cambridge University Press, 2005).
Woloch, Isser, 'Left, Right and Centre: The MRP and the Post-War Moment', *French History*, 21 (2007), 85–106.
Wright, Jonathan & Julian Wright, 'One Mind at Locarno? Aristide Briand and Gustav Stresemann', in Steven Casey & Jonathan Wright (eds), *Mental Maps in the Era of Two World Wars* (Basingstoke: Palgrave Macmillan, 2008), pp. 58–76.
Wright, Julian, 'Social Reform, State Reform, and Aristide Briand's Moment of Hope in France, 1909–1910', *French Historical Studies*, 28(1) (2005), 31–67.
Yagil, Limor, *Chrétiens et Juifs sous Vichy, 1940–44: sauvetage et désobéissance civile* (Paris: Cerf, 2005).
Young, Nigel (ed.), *The Oxford International Encyclopedia of Peace*, 4 vols (Oxford: Oxford University Press).
Zeldin, Theodore, *France 1848–1945*, Vol. 1: *Ambition, Love, Politics* (Oxford: Clarendon, 1973); Vol. 2: *Intellect, Taste, and Anxiety* (Oxford: Clarendon, 1977).
Ziegerhofer, Anita, *Botschafter Europas: Richard Nikolaus Coudenhove-Kalergi und die Paneuropa-Bewegung in den zwanziger und dreißiger Jahren* (Vienna: Boehlau, 2004).

Theses and dissertations

Bellon, Christophe, 'Aristide Briand et la naissance d'un centrisme politique, 1905–14', Mémoire pour le DEA, Institut d'Etudes Politiques, Paris, 2002.
Denoix de Saint Marc, Florence, 'Joseph Folliet et les Compagnons de Saint François de 1926 à 1958', Mémoire de Maîtrise, Université de Lyon 2, 1986.
Gaspard, Françoise, 'La Jeune-République, 1924–32', Mémoire de Maîtrise, Université de Paris, 1969.
Guerrier, Claudine, 'La Jeune République de 1912 à 1945', Thèse de doctorat, Université de Paris II, 1979.
Heller-Goldenberg, Lucette, 'Histoire des Auberges de la Jeunesse en France des origines à la Libération, 1929–1945', Thèse de doctorat d'Etat, Université de Nice, 1985.
Marotaux, Étienne, 'L'action pastorale de Mgr. Gibier dans le diocèse de Versailles, 1906–31', Mémoire de Maîtrise, Université de Paris IV-La Sorbonne, 1984.
Noli, Mathieu, ' "L'Eveil des Peuples" ou le combat pour la paix', Mémoire de Maîtrise, Université de Paris X, Nanterre, 1993.
Wierzbicki, Sandrine, 'Germaine Malaterre-Sellier: un destin aux croisés du féminisme et du pacifisme (1889–1967)', Mémoire de Maîtrise, Université de Paris I – Panthéon-Sorbonne, 2001.

Index